Ancient Gospel or Modern Forgery?

Ancient Gospel or Modern Forgery?

The *Secret Gospel of Mark* in Debate

Proceedings from the 2011 York University
Christian Apocrypha Symposium

Edited by
TONY BURKE

Foreword by
PAUL FOSTER

CASCADE *Books* · Eugene, Oregon

ANCIENT GOSPEL OR MODERN FORGERY?
The *Secret Gospel of Mark* in Debate
Proceedings from the 2011 York University Christian Apocrypha Symposium

Copyright © 2013 Wipf and Stock Publishers. All rights reserved. Except for brief quotations in critical publications or reviews, no part of this book may be reproduced in any manner without prior written permission from the publisher. Write: Permissions. Wipf and Stock Publishers, 199 W. 8th Ave., Suite 3, Eugene, OR 97401.

Cascade Books
An Imprint of Wipf and Stock Publishers
199 W. 8th Ave., Suite 3
Eugene, OR 97401

www.wipfandstock.com

ISBN 13: 978-1-62032-186-7

Cataloging-in-Publication data:

Ancient gospel or modern forgery? : the Secret Gospel of Mark in debate : proceedings from the 2011 York University Christian Apocrypha Symposium / edited by Tony Burke ; foreword by Paul Foster.

xxviii + 358 p. ; 23cm—Includes bibliographical references and index.

ISBN 13: 978-1-62032-186-7

1. Secret Gospel according to Mark. 2. Smith, Morton, 1915–1991. 3. Bible. N.T.—Controversial literature. 4. Bible. N.T.—Authorship. I. Burke, Tony. II. Foster, Paul.

BS2860 S42 A51 2012

Manufactured in the USA

Scripture quotations are from the Revised Standard Version Bible, copyright © 1946, 1952 and 1971 by the Division of Christian Education of the National Council of the Churches of Christ in the USA and used by permission.

Greek text and English translation of the *Letter to Theodore* reprinted from Morton Smith, *Clement of Alexandria and a Secret Gospel of Mark* (Cambridge, Mass.: Harvard University Press, 1973). Used with permission.

Quotations from the Papers of Harry Austryn Wolfson, Correspondence ca. 1900–1974 and the Papers of Werner Jaeger, 1934–1961 courtesy of the Harvard University Archives.

Photograph of Morton Smith and documents from the Morton Smith Archive provided by the Archives of The Jewish Theological Seminary Library.

Front cover image of Mar Saba manuscript 65 used by permission of the Westar Institute.

The contributors to this volume dedicate their work to the memory of their colleague and friend Marvin Meyer (1948–2012). Marvin demonstrated in both his personal and professional interactions with scholars that differences of opinion should not divide us as people, that colleagues can disagree without being disagreeable.

Contents

List of Contributors / ix
List of Illustrations and Tables / xi
Foreword—Paul Foster / xiii
Preface—Tony Burke / xxiii
Abbreviations / xxv

1 Introduction—Tony Burke / 1

2 *Secret Mark*: Moving on from Stalemate—Charles W. Hedrick / 30

3 Provenience: A Reply to Charles Hedrick—Bruce Chilton / 67

4 Morton Smith and the *Secret Gospel of Mark*: Exploring the Grounds for Doubt—Craig A. Evans / 75

5 Craig Evans and the *Secret Gospel of Mark*: Exploring the Grounds for Doubt—Scott G. Brown and Allan J. Pantuck / 101

6 Was Morton Smith the Bernie Madoff of the Academy?—Hershel Shanks / 135

7 The Young Streaker in Secret and Canonical Mark—Marvin Meyer / 145

8 Halfway between Sabbatai Tzevi and Aleister Crowley: Morton Smith's "Own Concept of What Jesus 'Must' Have Been" and, Once Again, the Questions of Evidence and Motive—Pierluigi Piovanelli / 157

9 A Question of Ability: What Did He Know and When Did He Know It? Further Excavations from the Morton Smith Archives—Allan J. Pantuck / 184

Contents

10 Clement's Mysteries and Morton Smith's Magic—Peter Jeffery / 212

11 Behind the Seven Veils, I: The Gnostic Life Setting of the Mystic Gospel of Mark—Scott G. Brown / 247

12 The *Secret Gospel of Mark* in Debate: A Scholarly Q and A / 284

Appendix 1
Can the Academy Protect Itself from One of Its Own? The Case of Secret Mark—Stephen C. Carlson / 299

Appendix 2
The Letter to Theodore / 308

Bibliography / 313
Index of Ancient Documents / 337
Index of Modern Authors / 349
Index of Subjects / 355

Contributors

Scott G. Brown is an independent scholar from Toronto, Ontario.

Tony Burke is Associate Professor of Early Christianity at York University in Toronto, Ontario.

Stephen C. Carlson is a Ph.D. candidate at Duke University in Durham, North Carolina.

Bruce Chilton is Bernard Iddings Bell Professor of Religion at Bard College, Annandale-on-Hudson, New York and Rector of the Church of St. John the Evangelist in Barrytown, New York.

Craig A. Evans is Payzant Distinguished Professor of New Testament at Acadia Divinity College of Acadia University in Wolfville, Nova Scotia.

Paul Foster is Lecturer in New Testament Language, Literature, and Theology at the University of Edinburgh.

Charles W. Hedrick is Distinguished Emeritus Professor at Missouri State University, Springfield, Missouri.

Peter Jeffery is Michael P. Grace II Professor of Medieval Studies at the University of Notre Dame, and Scheide Professor of Music History Emeritus at Princeton University.

Allan J. Pantuck is Professor of Urology at the University of California, Los Angeles.

Contributors

Marvin Meyer is Griset Professor of Bible and Christian Studies and Director of the Albert Schweitzer Institute at Chapman University in California.

Pierluigi Piovanelli is Professor of Second Temple Judaism and Early Christianity and Chair of the Department of Classics and Religious Studies at the University of Ottawa, Ottawa, Ontario.

Hershel Shanks is the founder of the Biblical Archeology Society and Editor of *Biblical Archaeology Review*.

Illustrations and Tables

1. Photograph of Morton Smith in Greece circa 1951–1952 (Harvard University Archives) / 197

2. "Manuscript Material from the Monastery of Mar Saba: Discovered, Transcribed, and Translated" by Morton Smith (The Archives of The Jewish Theological Seminary Library) / 205

3. Smith's personal copies of critical texts of Clement's writings published in 1960 with marginal notations to scholarship published in 1959 (Archives of The Jewish Theological Seminary Library) / 207

4. The process of becoming a Christian, in five early sources / 218

5. Four trajectories through the Christian life according to Clement / 221

6. Clement of Alexandria's conception of the path to perfection within the church / 283

Foreword

Paul Foster

THE SECRET GOSPEL OF MARK remains one of the most controversial and contested texts discussed by scholars of the New Testament and early Church history. Passions rage, opinions are entrenched, and discussions become inflamed among otherwise mild-mannered academics whenever the topic is raised. It is therefore, a joy to see a volume on this subject that actually sheds more light than heat. A range of opinions and approaches are brought together in this collaborative and enlightening treatment of *Secret Mark*. The last decade has seen a flurry of activity surrounding the text, with three monographs devoted to it, along with numerous articles, book chapters, and conference papers. These single-authored publications have invariably been hard-hitting. Articulating a vast range of perspectives, they have argued that *Secret Mark* is an authentic later and expanded form of Mark's Gospel, or an earlier form of Mark that was abbreviated to produce canonical Mark; alternatively others have declared it to have been a hoax foisted on the academy by its putative discoverer Morton Smith, or similarly a biblical forgery designed to legitimate imaginary rituals and sexual practices. Amid such strident assertions and counter-claims, one may turn to this collection of essays to find a relative sense of scholarly tranquility, as scholars wrestle robustly, but respectfully with one another's views.

In his opening introductory essay, the volume's editor Tony Burke provides a masterful overview of the circumstances surrounding the discovery of *Secret Mark* and a survey of the history of scholarship dealing with this disputed text. He describes Smith's account of the discovery in 1958 at the monastery of Mar Saba of a previously unknown letter purporting to have been written by Clement of Alexandria to a certain Theodore. The handwritten text of the letter was written on the end-papers of one of the printed books contained in the monastery's library, Isaac Voss's 1646 edition of the epistles of Ignatius. Burke then divides the scholarship on this text into two phases. The first phase commences with the publication of Morton Smith's monograph *Clement of Alexandria and a Secret Gospel of Mark* and his more popular exposition of the text, *The Secret Gospel*, both in 1973. Burke traces this phase through to 2003, culminating with Hedrick and Olympiou's publication of new photographs, along with responses to that publication. He sees a second phase of renewed study and interest in the text commencing in 2005 with Scott Brown's major study, *Mark's Other Gospel: Rethinking Morton Smith's Controversial Discovery*. While not sharing all of Smith's perspectives, Brown saw *Secret Mark* as being an authentic, but later and expanded form of Mark. Thus, more neutrally, he labeled the text not as "Secret Mark," but simply the Longer Gospel of Mark (LGM). Burke notes that in the same year, written as a vibrant counterblast to claims of authenticity, Stephen Carlson published *The Gospel Hoax*. Burke rehearses with great clarity the arguments brought by Carlson against the authenticity of *Secret Mark*. He also notes that the impact of Carlson's book was that "[m]any scholars who equivocated over the letter's authenticity found themselves convinced that it was a modern forgery" (p. 13). Two years later Peter Jeffery weighed-in on the debate with his monograph, *The Secret Gospel of Mark Unveiled*. Like Carlson, he wrote against the genuineness of *Secret Mark*. However, his arguments were of a different character. In particular he sought to highlight possible anachronistic references in relation to the text's understanding of liturgical, ecclesiological, and sexual practices as assumed by *Secret Mark*. As Burke notes, Brown has fought against these two recent voices that oppose both the authenticity of *Secret Mark*, and consequently the position he adopts in his own monograph. Burke helpfully highlights how Brown and others have been chipping away at the forgery hypothesis, dismantling arguments one at a time. Burke brings the discussion to the present with his account of the origins of this volume as the published form of papers presented at the York Christian Apocrypha Symposium on *Secret Mark*, which itself arose from the *Secret Mark* session held at the 2008 SBL meeting. Burke's lasting contribution is the caution he issues to scholars that they should "leap less readily upon any new evidence for or against authenticity and vigorously declare their position has been 'proven' right, despite knowing full well that, in the study of history, ambiguity is the norm and certainty always elusive" (p. 29). This note of caution sets the tone for the more irenic spirit that pervades the book, especially in comparison to much previous writing on *Secret Mark*.

The next chapter, written by Charles Hedrick, takes up his own assessment made at the conclusion of Burke's first phase of research, when he declared *Secret Mark* studies to be in a state of stalemate. Hedrick considers ways to move beyond such a stalemate. The task allotted to him at the symposium, as he describes it, was to make "a case for the authenticity of the *Letter to Theodore* and the *Secret Gospel of Mark*" (p. 30). He makes an observation that resonates with many other papers in this volume, namely that claims of authenticity or otherwise must be determined through careful analysis of the handwriting style exhibited in the text. Unfortunately, since at present the location of the text is unknown, such an aspiration remains unrealizable. Also of great significance is the way in which Hedrick emphasizes the ambiguity of the term "authenticity," especially in relation to a text such as *Secret Mark*. He notes that the transcription of the writing found in the back of the sixteenth-century book is a composite of two texts, and both may be authentic or inauthentic, or perhaps only one is authentic. Thus, there is a greater range of possibilities than simply saying the text is genuine or not.

In the third chapter Bruce Chilton responds by considering a number of parallel cases—in particular a manuscript kept at his own institution Bard College entitled "George Washington's Manuscript Book of Prayers." His warning drawn from this analogous case is that "finding manuscripts so distant from their point of origin provokes caution" (p. 69). He also discusses the case of the alleged ossuary of James, the brother of Jesus, which came to prominence around 2002. From these and other cases, Chilton wishes to extract some helpful observations about a manuscript's, or artifact's provenance. In relation to the *Letter of Clement to Theodore*, Chilton repeats the observation that the text was found in "Isaac Voss's edition of Ignatius of Antioch, a work that played a key role in the discussion of Ignatian pseudepigraphy" (p. 73). Of more significance for Chilton are questions surrounding the process that would have led to the arrival of Voss's volume in the Mar Saba library. Chilton argues that even this preliminary step in determining the provenance of the book in which the text was written has not been established. Consequently, he states, "we are not dealing with evidence, or even with a stalemate about evidence. We are dealing with an unverified claim" (p. 74).

Next Craig Evans mounts incisive arguments concerning the grounds upon which one may doubt the authenticity of *Secret Mark*. Evans acknowledges, however, that "if genuine, Smith's discovery represents a significant contribution to New Testament and Patristic studies" (p. 76). The central argument that Evans mounts is that Morton Smith demonstrates knowledge of the distinctive elements of the Mar Saba discovery prior to finding it. As a parallel he describes the case of a hoax perpetrated by Paul Coleman-Norton, who published an "Amusing *Agraphon*" attributed to Jesus and allegedly discovered in North Africa, but without the manuscript being able to be recovered, or even to be photographed. However, Evans goes on to document recollections of Coleman-Norton telling the amusing story about Jesus saying teeth will be provided to allow the toothless to gnash them, prior to his alleged discovery of the text that contained this story. Similarly, Evans suggests that Smith's "discovery" mirrors the account contained in the earlier 1940 novel *The Mystery of Mar Saba* in which a certain Lord Moreton is involved in investigating the discovery of a leaf of a Greek text planted at the monastery by the Nazis to undermine British morale. He also argues that Smith's interpretation of Mark 4:11, which was suggested in his 1944 doctoral thesis, is validated in the text of *Secret Mark*. For Evans these "coincidences" and others that he notes, are simply too coincidental. Yet, in a conciliatory and even-handed concluding comment, Evans notes that such assessments are provisional: "we should speak cautiously in this matter, not simply out of fairness to the late Morton Smith but also out of professional courtesy for our colleagues who have reached a different conclusion" (p. 100).

The next chapter is a response to Evans's observations, mounted by Scott Brown and Allan Pantuck, two of the most prominent defenders of the authenticity of *Secret Mark*. They disagree that the "Amusing *Agraphon*" forms a meaningful parallel to Smith's discovery of *Secret Mark*. A major part of their response is problematizing Evans's equation between Smith's own interpretation of Mark 4:11, and the way he sees Smith's reading being supported by the citations of *Secret Mark* contained in Clement's letter. In a concluding twist Brown and Pantuck turn Evans's approach against him. They state, "we have applied the same skepticism to Evans's arguments, systematically compared them to the facts, and found these arguments sorely wanting" (p. 134). With this response and Evans's arguments readers have a model of the thrust and parry of hard-fought and yet responsible academic scholarship.

Hershel Shanks's contribution focuses the discussion squarely on the central concern surrounding the text—namely, "whether Morton Smith is guilty of forging the *Secret Gospel of Mark*" (p. 135). Shanks likens the accusations of forgery against Smith to Madoff and his scam involving a Ponzi or pyramid marketing scheme. In some ways, Shanks's treatment is the most rhetorically charged piece in the volume. However, his basic point requires reflection and consideration. He notes that those who support the authenticity of the text are trapped in a never-ending cycle of rebutting the latest argument against *Secret Mark*. Shanks challenges doubters of authenticity to stand back from a clutter of weak and insubstantial arguments and weak cases, and to present the strongest point against the text. He ends with another challenge, "[n]one of Morton Smith's detractors address the matter of his character. To me, Morton's character is the central issue. Does anyone really believe that a man of this sterling character and reputation and scholarly achievement would be a Bernie Madoff to the academy?" (p. 142). Finally, there follows an appendix, in which he summarizes Agamemnon Tselikas's report concerning the handwriting of the *Secret Mark* manuscript. His assessment is that "the letter is the product of a forgery and all the evidences suggest that the forger cannot be other person than Morton Smith or some other person under his orders" (p. 144).

In chapter seven there is a noticeable shift in approach. Marvin Meyer expresses his distaste at the "almost libelous" (p. 147) charges leveled against Morton Smith. He takes the authenticity of *Secret Mark* as a starting point, and then looks at one of the exegetical pay-offs that results from integrating the perspectives of *Secret Mark* into mainstream New Testament studies. His interest is in the young man or *neaniskos* who flees naked in Mark 14:51–52. He argues that consideration of *Secret Mark* with the restoration of passages to canonical Mark explains a subplot that has become truncated in the canonical form of the gospel. That subplot revolves around the life of discipleship as exemplified through tracing the character development the *neaniskos* undergoes. With the two passages from *Secret Mark* restored, Meyer has five scenes from the longer form of Mark with which to trace this character's journey of discipleship. Then at the end of his discussion, Meyer offers a creative reflection on the reading of the longer form of Mark made by a liminal community of believers towards the end of the first century. From this creative reflection, Meyer infers that the point of this figure is that at "the end of the gospel the youth has come back to Jesus in his death; he is joined to Jesus in his death, and he even looks and sounds rather like Jesus" (p. 156). Like other thematically related portrayals in Mark, this figure exemplifies the costly call of discipleship, which links to the death of Jesus.

Next Pierluigi Piovanelli opens his discussion by noting the polarization in the guild of New Testament scholars between those who consider non-canonical texts "as old and valuable as those of their canonical counterparts" and those who view them as "no more than secondary rewritings of New Testament texts" (p. 158). Piovanelli draws attention to two incontrovertible facts that need to be addressed in discussion of authenticity. The first is that the Clement fragment turned up "in the wrong place—this means that it was discovered in a location in which it would be both unnatural and even suspect to find such an amazing document" (p. 160). The second is that in the opinion of certain leading specialists "the *Letter to Theodore* does not fit very well with what we presently know about Clement of Alexandria and the history of the Egyptian church" (p. 161). However, it is noted that, while Carlson suggests Smith perpetrated this hoax to ridicule those who had deprived him of academic tenure, Piovanelli notes this must be balanced against "the absence of any clearly identifiable 'joke' embedded within the *Letter to Theodore*, along with Smith's sincere commitment to true scholarship and, especially, his perseverance in defending the authenticity of his discovery without concessions until the very end" (p. 169). Notwithstanding this observation, Piovanelli is ultimately hesitant about the authenticity of *Secret Mark* since *Secret Mark* is "the wrong document, at the wrong place, discovered by the wrong person, who was, moreover, in need of exactly that kind of new evidence to promote new, unconventional ideas" (p. 182). Instead he advises fellow scholars to devote less time to *Secret Mark*, and instead to focus on Smith's truly innovative work in the areas of the study of the historical Jesus and early Jewish mysticism.

Next, one of the staunch defenders of the authenticity of *Secret Mark*, Allan Pantuck, raises the fundamental question of whether Smith would have had the required ability to carry out the type of hoax that is attributed to him. He examines Smith's ability in Greek, his skills in palaeography, his knowledge of ancient epistolography, and his previous knowledge of Clement of Alexandria. After a close examination of the archives of Smith's papers and correspondence, Pantuck works to explode the myth that Smith was a rare genius with the required skill set to perpetrate the hoax attributed to him. He argues that Smith developed some of the requisite skills to allow him to analyze *Secret Mark* only after the document's discovery. By contrast, prior to the discovery, Pantuck argues that the "evidence suggests that his Greek had not advanced to the point that he could compose a new work of Clement, that he had not acquired the necessary expertise in Clement's thought and style, and that he lacked the palaeographical knowledge and the writing skill needed to produce the Greek script of the manuscript" (p. 211). For these reasons Pantuck maintains that the text is not the product of Smith's own hand.

For Peter Jeffery, *Secret Mark* offers something that other snippets of ancient apocryphal gospel text do not—that is, a literary context. He suggests that part of the confusion surrounding authenticity that has arisen "comes from focusing too exclusively on the gospel and too little on the epistle—from trying, that is, to read what we have of *Secret Mark* without reference to its frame, as if it actually had been discovered on papyrus fragments in a dealer's shop" (p. 212). However, for Jeffery it is that literary frame that establishes the inauthenticity of the entire fragment. One of Jeffery's key arguments is that the literary frame of the epistle is anachronistic at a number of places, and consequently betrays its modern, rather than ancient composition. Moreover, he suggests that the whole discussion requires one to search through Smith's literary corpus for his phraseology, his facility with Greek, compositional patterns, use of double entendres, and for discovering the topics that interested Smith. Jeffery's conclusion is stark, "[t]he simplest and most logical interpretation of all this is that the Mar Saba epistle and its secret gospel must have been written by the same enigmatic figure that composed Morton Smith's publications" (p. 246). In this discussion Jeffery has added further arguments to those in his book *The Secret Gospel of Mark Unveiled* (2007), which suggest the text is a twentieth-century composition.

In many ways, Scott Brown takes up Jeffery's challenge to consider the literary frame of *Secret Mark*—that is, the Clementine letter. Brown looks at mysteries and the mysticism depicted in *Secret Mark*, the *Letter to Theodore*, and in Clement's wider writings. His analysis leads him to the conclusion that, contrary to Jeffery, the longer mystical form of Mark is intelligible in the context of early Alexandrian Christianity, and the comments in the *Letter to Theodore* make sense as a response to such a text. The strength of Brown's discussion is his close reading of texts from Clement's *Stromateis*, which he sees as reflecting outlooks and perspectives closely aligned with those contained in the text discovered at Mar

Saba. Thus, in opposition to Jeffrey's understanding of the literary frame as anachronistic, Brown states "I can see no justification for treating this letter as a work about some other practice, from some other era, written by someone else for reasons that nobody is quite sure about" (p 278–79).

The penultimate chapter is a transcript of a scholarly panel "question and answer" session involving Scott Brown and Marvin Meyer as defenders of authenticity, and Craig Evans and Peter Jeffery who consider the text to be a forgery. What shines through in this discussion is the constructive tone of the discussion, as well as how many views this quartet of scholars actually hold in common. While they do not see eye-to-eye on *Secret Mark*, they all recognize the seminal importance of Smith's work on magic, and they conclude for various reasons that this text should not be forgotten.

The book is rounded out with an appendix containing a paper written by Stephen Carlson that was presented at the 2008 SBL conference in Boston. Without inclusion of "Carlson's voice," the volume would have lacked the perspective of a key player in the recent debate. In this paper Carlson asks the provocative question, "can the academy protect itself from one of its own, even one of its most brilliant members?" (p. 307). Apart from raising a question that is thought-provoking in its own right, something else emerges as fascinating in this study—namely, frequently those who see Smith as a forger tend to cast him, as Carlson does, as an extraordinarily gifted scholar, with multiple specialisms at his disposal. By contrast, those who argue for the authenticity of *Secret Mark*, often suggest either that Smith lacked the background knowledge in Clement, or that he did not possess the range of skills that such a hoax would require. This highlights the fact that, with assessments of the authenticity or otherwise of *Secret Mark*, it appears impossible to divorce such judgments from assessments of Smith's character and scholarly capabilities. Perhaps what Carlson's study throws up clearly is the uncomfortable and inconvenient truth that while most would like to be objective in assessing *Secret Mark* as a text, it appears impossible to separate making intertwined judgments both about *Secret Mark* and its putative discoverer Morton Smith. This, however, is not comfortable territory for the majority of scholars.

In the end what makes this collection of essays so valuable is not that it has achieved a major breakthrough in solving the riddle of *Secret Mark*—for it most certainly has not achieved that—rather, it exemplifies how robust and rigorous scholarship should be carried out. There is a place for strong arguments, and space to disagree with dialogue partners. However, what characterizes this book is the sense of mutual respect, and that despite huge differences of perspective surrounding *Secret Mark*, there is indeed a commonality of purpose as leading scholars bring their perspicacious intellectual skills to again probe the mystery that is *Secret Mark*. This book has the potential to usher in a new phase of collaborative work on this enigmatic text. But, perhaps as the contributors suggest, now it is time to pause, to take stock, to reflect, and above all to actually locate that now-missing manuscript! The riddle of *Secret Mark* is not solved yet, but one could have no better companions in that task than the cast of leading scholars who have contributed to this volume. The guild of New Testament and Patristics scholars are indebted to all of them, and because of their insights are now better placed to appreciate the divergent views that are held in relation to *Secret Mark*.

Preface

THE PAPERS IN THIS volume were presented at the York Christian Apocrypha Symposium on the *Secret Gospel of Mark* on April 29, 2011, at York University in Toronto, Canada. The symposium, convened by York professors Tony Burke and Philip Harland, had one goal: to gather together experts on the text to consider recent developments in its study—including the uncovering of apparent "clues" revealing it to be a hoax and recently-commissioned handwriting analyses—with the hope of reaching some consensus on which arguments advanced for its origins remained viable. Over the course of several months, we solicited involvement from North America's most prominent *Secret Mark* scholars. Not everyone we asked was available or interested in participating, but we ended up with an outstanding panel of experts eager to contribute new work on the text and to discuss the efficacy of the various positions advanced about its origins and its meaning.

This volume aims to capture the experience of the symposium, both for those who attended the event and for those who could not. All of the papers are included, along with a transcription of the evening Question and Answer session with several of the participating scholars. Also incorporated is an earlier paper by Stephen Carlson presented at the 2008 Annual Meeting of the Society of Biblical Literature; due to scheduling conflicts, Stephen was not able to attend the symposium, but suggested we include his paper, which is mentioned by several of the contributors, in the published proceedings. By the symposium's end, the debate over the origins of *Secret Mark* clearly was moving away from the distractions of the weaker arguments for forgery, but, not surprisingly, the participants remained entrenched in their positions. On the effort to reach consensus, Marvin Meyer spoke, hopefully, for everyone when he said, "I'd love to think there is some consensus. I guess the consensus that I feel at this

Preface

point is that we all came to Toronto and had a good time together and enjoyed each other's company and had a rousing debate."

The gathering was made possible with contributions from several funding bodies within the university: the Department of the Humanities, the Office of Research Services, David B. Dewitt at the office of the Associate Vice-President Research, and Barbara Crow, the Assistant Dean of Research for the Faculty of Liberal Arts and Professional Studies. We are grateful also to all those who registered for the symposium, travelling from near and far to listen to the papers and to participate in the discussions that arose.

Additional thanks go to our panelists who contributed their time and expertise to the symposium, but especially Scott Brown, Allan Pantuck, and Peter Jeffery who were involved in planning the event. And to Paul Foster who brings an international voice to the project with his foreword. Special appreciation goes to Laura Cudworth for transcribing the evening Question and Answer session, and to Joe Oryshak for compiling the indices.

The *Secret Mark* symposium was the first in a planned ongoing series of symposia on the Christian Apocrypha to take place semi-annually at York University. The idea began out of a desire to being more attention to the work of North American scholarship on this literature. For information on future symposia in the series, look for announcements on the Apocryphicity blog (http://www.tonyburke.ca/apocryphicity/).

February, 2012
Tony Burke

Abbreviations

ANCIENT

4Q403 *Songs of the Sabbath Sacrifice*

Aphrahat
Dem. *Demonstrations*

Cicero
De Or. *De oratore*

Clement of Alexandria
Ecl. *Eclogae propheticae*
Exc. *Excerpta ex Theodoto*
Paed. *Paedagogus*
Protr. *Protrepticus*
Quis div. *Quis dives salvetur*
Strom. *Stromateis*

Eusebius
Hist. eccl. *Historia ecclesiastica*

Hag. *Hagigah*

Hippolytus
Haer. *Refutatio omnium haeresium*
Trad. Ap. *Traditio apostolica*

Ignatius
Trall. *To the Trallians*

Abbreviations

Irenaeus
Haer.   *Adversus haereses*

Lucian
Hist. Conscr. *Quomodo Historia conscribenda sit*

Origen
Hom. Judic.   *Homiliae in Judices*

Philo
Cher.   *De cherubim*
Contempl.   *De vita contemplativa*
Decal.   *De decalogo*
Ebr.   *De ebrietate*
Her.   *Quis rerum divinarum heres sit*
Mos.   *De vita Mosis*
Opif.   *De opificio mundi*
QE   *Quaestiones et solutions in Exodum*
QG   *Quaestiones et solutions in Genesin*
Spec.   *De specialibus legibus*

Plato
Gorg.   *Gorgias*
Symp.   *Symposium*
Theaet.   *Theaetetus*

Pliny
Ep.   *Epistulae*

Quintilian
Inst.   *Institutio oratoria*

MODERN

AB	Anchor Bible
ABD	*The Anchor Bible Dictionary*. 6 vols. Edited by David Noel Freedman. New York: Doubleday, 1992
ABRL	Anchor Bible Reference Library
AHR	*American Historical Review*
AJP	*American Journal of Philology*

Abbreviations

ANF	*The Ante-Nicene Fathers*. 10 vols. Edited by Alexander Roberts and James Donaldson. Revised by A. Cleveland Coxe. 1885–1887. Reprint, Peabody, MA: Hendrickson, 1994
AUSS	*Andrews University Seminary Studies*
BAR	*Biblical Archaeology Review*
BBR	*Bulletin for Biblical Research*
BETL	Bibliotheca ephemeridum theologicarum lovaniensium
Bib	*Biblica*
BJRL	*Bulletin of the John Rylands Library of Manchester*
CBQ	*Catholic Biblical Quarterly*
CCCPG	Clavis Patrum Graecorum Patres antenicaeni
CCSA	Corpus Christianorum: Series apocryphorum
CCSL	Corpus Christianorum: Series latina
CRINT	Compendia rerum iudaicarum ad Novum Testamentum
ErJb	*Eranos-Jahrbuch*
EsBi	Essais bibliques
ESCJ	Studies in Christianity and Judaism/Études sur le christianisme et le judaïsme
ExpTim	*Expository Times*
FC	Fathers of the Church
GCS	Die griechische christliche Schriftsteller der ersten [drei] Jahrhunderte
GRBS	*Greek, Roman, and Byzantine Studies*
HR	History of Religions
HSCP	*Harvard Studies in Classical Philology*
HTR	*Harvard Theological Review*
HUCA	*Hebrew Union College Annual*
JBL	*Journal of Biblical Literature*
JBLMS	*Journal of Biblical Literature* Monograph Series
JBR	*Journal of Bible and Religion*
JECS	*Journal of Early Christian Studies*
JQR	*Jewish Quarterly Review*
JSHS	*Journal for the Study of the Historical Jesus*
JSJSup	Supplements to *Journal for the Study of Judaism*
JSNT	*Journal for the Study of the New Testament*
JTS	*Journal of Theological Studies*
LCL	Loeb Classical Library
MoBi	Monde de la Bible
NHMS	Nag Hammadi and Manichean Studies

Abbreviations

NovT	*Novum Testamentum*
NovTSup	Novum Testamentum Supplement
NTGF	New Testament in the Greek Fathers
OED	*Oxford English Dictionary*
PAAJR	*Proceedings of the American Academy of Jewish Research*
PGM	Papyri Graecae Magicae
PRSt	*Perspectives in Religious Studies*
QJS	*Quarterly Journal of Speech*
RB	*Revue biblique*
RBL	*Review of Biblical Literature*
REAug	*Revue des études augustiniennes*
RHR	*Revue de l'histoire des religions*
RSPT	*Revue des sciences philosophiques et théologiques*
SAC	Studies in Antiquity and Christianity
SBLDS	Society of Biblical Literature Dissertation Series
SBLEJL	Society of Biblical Literature Early Judaism and Its Literature
SBLSymS	Society of Biblical Literature Symposium Series
SC	Sources chrétiennes
SecCent	*Second Century*
SFSHJ	South Florida Studies in the History of Judaism
SHR	Studies in the History of Religions (supplement to *Numen*)
SJLA	Studies in Judaism in Late Antiquity
SNTSMS	Society for New Testament Studies Monograph Series
SR	*Studies in Religion*
StPatr	Studia patristica
TDOT	*Theological Dictionary of the Old Testament*. 14 vols. Edited by G. Johannes Botterweck and Helmer Ringgren. Translated by Geoffrey W. Bromiley et al. Grand Rapids: Eerdmans, 1974–2004
TS	*Theological Studies*
TU	Texte und Untersuchungen
USQR	*Union Seminary Quarterly Review*
VC	*Vigiliae christianae*
VCSup	Supplements to *Vigiliae Christianae*
WUNT	Wissenschaftliche Untersuchungen zum Neuen Testament

1

Introduction[1]

Tony Burke

THE STORY OF MORTON Smith's discovery of the *Letter to Theodore* with its references to the *Secret Gospel of Mark* has been recounted often and may seem superfluous to repeat here. Yet, the misinformation and obfuscation about Smith's role in the discovery has had such a profound impact on discussion of the text that it requires an objective restatement of the facts. Readers of the papers in this volume may benefit also from a short recounting of the major works on *Secret Mark* published over the past forty years so as to see the transmission of arguments made for and against the text's authenticity and understand the origins of various personal attacks made against Smith by his detractors. *Secret Mark* is not the only text from antiquity to polarize scholars, but it certainly stands out among others for the attention it has attracted, among both scholars and the wider public, as a result of this conflict. In addition, the personalities and biases of the scholars interested in this text, for better or worse, come through in their work. It is useful, therefore, to focus this introduction particularly on the contributions to the study of *Secret Mark* made by the authors of the papers in this volume and on the origins of the arguments they continue to champion.

---

1. My thanks to Scott Brown and Allan Pantuck for reading earlier drafts of this chapter, offering their feedback, and helping to correct factual errors.

Ancient Gospel or Modern Forgery?
MORTON SMITH AND THE DISCOVERY OF SECRET MARK

In 1958, American historian Morton Smith journeyed to the monastery of Mar Saba, located 20 kilometers (12 miles) south-east of Jerusalem in the Judean desert, to catalogue the library in the monastery's great tower.[2] Smith had previously visited Mar Saba when a graduate student in 1942 and remained there for two months. This began a friendly relationship with the Archimandrite allowing for Smith's return. Though much of the library's holdings had been moved to the Patriarchate library in Jerusalem in the late nineteenth century, Smith found there a number of printed books and a handful of manuscripts.[3] Smith noted that the pages of printed books often contained additional writing in Greek, which demonstrated how scarce paper was in recent centuries of the monastery's history. The end-papers of one of these printed books, a 1646 edition of Isaac Voss's epistles of Ignatius,[4] particularly attracted Smith's attention. In an apparent eighteenth-century hand there is a text that begins: "From the letters of the most holy Clement, the author of the *Stromateis*; to Theodore." Smith had chanced upon a previously unknown letter by Clement of Alexandria, a well-known early Christian writer whose other works were written between 175 and 215 CE That alone would be a major discovery, but the writer of this *Letter to Theodore* mentions also the existence of a longer version of Mark current in his time. The complete letter reads as follows:[5]

> From the letters of the most holy Clement, the author of the *Stromateis*. To Theodore.
>
> You did well in silencing the unspeakable teachings of the Carpocratians. For these are the "wandering stars" referred to in the prophecy, who wander from the narrow road of the commandments into a boundless abyss of the carnal and bodily sins. For, priding themselves in knowledge, as they say, "of the deep things of Satan," they do not know that they are casting themselves away into "the nether world of the darkness" of falsity, and, boasting that they are free, they have become slaves

---

2. Read Smith's account of his visits in *The Secret Gospel*, 1–9.

3. For a description of the seventy-five manuscripts Smith catalogued see Smith, "Monasteries and Their Manuscripts"; and Smith "Ἑλληνικὰ χειρόγραφα ἐν τῇ Μονῇ τοῦ ἁγίου Σάββα" ("Greek Manuscripts in the Monastery of St. Saba").

4. Voss, *Epistulae genuinae S. Ignatii Martyris*.

5. The text is taken from Smith, *Clement of Alexandria and a Secret Gospel of Mark*, 446–47; see also Smith, *Secret Gospel*, 14–17. For a Greek and English synopsis of the text see Appendix II.

of servile desires. Such men are to be opposed in all ways and altogether. For, even if they should say something true, one who loves the truth should not, even so, agree with them. For not all true things are the truth, nor should that truth which merely seems true according to human opinions be preferred to the true truth, that according to the faith.

Now of the things they keep saying about the divinely inspired Gospel according to Mark, some are altogether falsifications, and others, even if they do contain some true elements, nevertheless are not reported truly. For the true things being mixed with inventions, are falsified, so that, as the saying goes, even the salt loses its savor.

As for Mark, then, during Peter's stay in Rome he wrote an account of the Lord's doings, not, however, declaring all of them, nor yet hinting at the secret ones, but selecting what he thought most useful for increasing the faith of those who were being instructed. But when Peter died a martyr, Mark came over to Alexandria, bringing both his own notes and those of Peter, from which he transferred to his former book the things suitable to whatever makes for progress toward knowledge. Thus he composed a more spiritual Gospel for the use of those who were being perfected. Nevertheless, he yet did not divulge the things not to be uttered, nor did he write down the hierophantic teaching of the Lord, but to the stories already written he added yet others and, moreover, brought in certain sayings of which he knew the interpretation would, as a mystagogue, lead the hearers into the innermost sanctuary of that truth hidden by seven veils. Thus, in sum, he prepared matters, neither grudgingly nor incautiously, in my opinion, and, dying, he left his composition to the church in Alexandria, where it even yet is most carefully guarded, being read only to those who are being initiated into the great mysteries.

But since the foul demons are always devising destruction for the race of men, Carpocrates, instructed by them and using deceitful arts, so enslaved a certain presbyter of the church in Alexandria that he got from him a copy of the secret Gospel, which he both interpreted according to his blasphemous and carnal doctrine and, moreover, polluted, mixing with the spotless and holy words utterly shameless lies. From this mixture is drawn off the teaching of the Carpocratians.

To them, therefore, as I said above, one must never give way; nor, when they put forward their falsifications, should one concede that the secret Gospel is by Mark, but should even deny it on oath. For, "Not all true things are to be said to all men." For this reason the Wisdom of God, through Solomon, advises, "Answer the fool from his folly," teaching that the light of the truth should be hidden from those who are mentally blind. Again it says, "From him who has not shall be taken away," and, "Let the fool walk in darkness." But we are "children of light," having been illuminated by "the dayspring" of the spirit of the Lord "from on high," and "Where the Spirit of the Lord is," it says, "there is liberty," for "All things are pure to the pure."

To you, therefore, I shall not hesitate to answer the questions you have asked, refuting the falsifications by the very words of the Gospel. For example, after, "And they were in the road going up to Jerusalem," and what follows, until "After three days he shall arise," the secret Gospel brings the following material word for word:

"And they come into Bethany. And a certain woman whose brother had died was there. And, coming, she prostrated herself before Jesus and says to him, 'Son of David, have mercy on me.' But the disciples rebuked her. And Jesus, being angered, went off with her into the garden where the tomb was, and straightway a great cry was heard from the tomb. And going near Jesus rolled away the stone from the door of the tomb. And straightway, going in where the youth was, he stretched forth his hand and raised him, seizing his hand. But the youth, looking upon him, loved him and began to beseech him that he might be with him. And going out of the tomb they came into the house of the youth, for he was rich. And after six days Jesus told him what to do and in the evening the youth comes to him, wearing a linen cloth over his naked body. And he remained with him that night, for Jesus taught him the mystery of the kingdom of God. And thence, arising, he returned to the other side of the Jordan."

After these words follows the text, "And James and John come to him," and all that section. But "naked man with naked man," and the other things about which you wrote, are not found.

And after the words, "And he comes into Jericho," the secret Gospel adds only,

"And the sister of the youth whom Jesus loved and his mother and Salome were there, and Jesus did not receive them." But the many other things about which you wrote both seem to be and are falsifications.

Now the true explanation and that which accords with the true philosophy . . .

Though surprised at his find, Smith continued with his work, photographing the manuscript, and adding a reference number on the front page ("Smith 65"). The manuscript then was left in the monastery library where Smith found it. Upon his return to America, Smith began the work of deciphering and translating the text and puzzling over its meaning. In 1960 he made a formal announcement of the discovery at the Annual Meeting of the Society of Biblical Literature.[6] Thereafter he continued to consult paleographers and scholars of the New Testament, patristics, and Judaism before finally publishing his findings in 1973 in both a detailed commentary (*Clement of Alexandria*) and a short, non-scholarly account of the discovery (*The Secret Gospel*).

Smith's find achieved instant notoriety, principally because it was intertwined with his own particular interpretation of the text.[7] He believed the letter to be an authentic composition by Clement and cited a dozen scholars who agreed with his assessment. The "secret gospel" cited in the letter was a revision of Mark that drew upon a lost source common to canonical Mark and John, thus explaining the parallel to John's raising of Lazarus (11:1–44) and why *Secret Mark*'s version of the tale seemed to be more primitive than the one in John. The story itself Smith interpreted as an indication of secret, mystical practices in the Jesus movement by which Jesus, in the manner of a magician, initiated his followers into the kingdom of God; these included a ritual that united the initiate with the spirit of Jesus through a preparatory baptism and then an ascent into the heavens. In passing, Smith speculated also that the spiritual union with Jesus may have included physical union.[8]

---

6. An account of Smith's presentation appeared the next morning on the front page of the *New York Times*: Knox, "A New Gospel Ascribed to Mark." Pierson Parker's reservations that the gospel was not written by Mark appeared in a second article the following day: Knox, "Expert Disputes 'Secret Gospel.'"

7. For summaries of the early scholarship on *Secret Mark* (up to 2005), see Brown, *Mark's Other Gospel*, 23–74 (to which this overview is greatly indebted); Eyer, "The Strange Case of the Secret Gospel according to Mark"; Foster, "Secret Mark: Its Discovery and the State of Research" (and for scholarship up to 2008, Foster, "*Secret Mark*"; Hedrick, "The Secret Gospel of Mark," 136–38; Piovanelli, "*L'Évangile Secret de Marc*," 52–72; Schenke, "Mystery of the Gospel of Mark," 69–74; and Smith, "Clement of Alexandria and Secret Mark."

8. For this last element in particular see the brief mention in Smith, *Secret Gospel*, 114.

Ancient Gospel or Modern Forgery?

THE FIRST PHASE OF SCHOLARSHIP ON SECRET MARK: 1973–2003

Initially, Smith's peers trusted in his integrity and the authenticity of the *Letter to Theodore* was not in doubt. Early reactions focused on *Secret Mark*, declaring it a typical second-century apocryphal gospel with its attendant expansion and combination of canonical traditions. The first scholar to question publicly the origins of the letter was Quentin Quesnell. In a 1975 article for *Catholic Biblical Quarterly*,[9] Quesnell declared that the text bore the characteristics of a hoax and therefore must be authenticated, and that this can be done only by personally examining the manuscript. Quesnell considered Smith's photographs, which are included in his commentary, inadequate for the study of the text as they were mediocre in quality and had been cropped by the publisher for publication. Quesnell placed the onus on Smith to produce the manuscript for forensic examination. Smith's failure to do so looked suspicious to many and led to speculation that there was no manuscript at all. Quesnell also remarked that the *Letter to Theodore* could have been created in recent times with the assistance of studies of Clement's style such as the Clement index published by Otto Stählin in 1936.[10] Though Quesnell made no explicit indictment, readers of his article saw in it an accusation that Smith himself forged the text. So, too, did Smith, who, in his reply in the following year's volume of *CBQ*, objected to the veiled accusation.[11] To Quesnell's dissenting voice was added that of Charles E. Murgia, who participated in an early colloquium devoted to the text at Berkeley.[12] Murgia characterized the letter as a carefully-constructed "seal of authenticity" for the secret gospel—that is, it is written to preemptively answer the readers' question of why they have never heard of this text before—and thought it suspicious that the manuscript lacks the serious scribal errors one would expect of a text after sixteen centuries of transmission. Smith reportedly gave some thought to Murgia's "seal of authenticity" argument but later dismissed it because it was based on a misreading of the text.[13]

9. Quesnell, "Mar Saba Clementine."

10. Stählin, ed., *Clemens Alexandrinus*, vol. 4, register 1.

11. Smith, "On the Authenticity." A response from Quesnell followed: "Reply to Morton Smith."

12. Murgia, "Secret Mark."

13. See the discussion in Brown, *Mark's Other Gospel*, 29–30.

By far the loudest and most prolonged argument for forgery was put forward by Smith's former student Jacob Neusner. Though at first Neusner wrote favorably about Smith and his work on *Secret Mark* (even contributing a laudatory dust jacket testimonial to *The Secret Gospel*), his relationship with Smith suffered in the '70s and '80s, culminating in Smith's public denunciation of Neusner for academic incompetence at the 1984 Annual Meeting of the AAR/SBL. The event has been recounted several times, even by Neusner himself,[14] but one of the most memorable was by Hershel Shanks who wrote an overview of the meeting for *Biblical Archaeological Review*.[15] This report led to threat of a lawsuit from Neusner and a letter to the editor from Smith. After the 1984 meeting, Neusner increasingly criticized Smith's work in print. The invective intensified and turned more personal after Smith's death in 1991, beginning with a lengthy 1993 critique of Smith's dissertation.[16] Here Neusner calls the *Letter to Theodore* "the forgery of the century" and Smith "a charlatan and a fraud." Where Quesnell showed some restraint, Neusner did not hesitate to name Smith as the forger:

> Smith's presentation of the evidence for his homosexual magician, a Clement fragment he supposedly turned up in a library in Sinai in 1958, ranks as one of the most slovenly presentations of an allegedly important document in recent memory; and, to understate matters, it left open the very plausible possibility of forgery. Smith himself was an expert on such matters, having devoted scholarly essays to great forgeries in antiquity.[17]

Donald Harman Akenson, a devotee of Neusner, later echoed his mentor's opinions on Smith and the text,[18] though this time with great emphasis placed on the seeming homoeroticism of the *Secret Mark* excerpts: "what we have here is a nice ironic gay joke at the expense of all the self-important scholars who not only miss the irony, but believe this alleged piece of gospel comes to us in the first-known letter of the great Clement of Alexandria."[19] Morton Smith is identified as "the most likely prankster."[20]

---

14. See ibid., 44–45.
15. Shanks, "Annual Meetings."
16. Neusner, *Are There Really Tannaitic Parallels to the Gospels?*
17. Ibid., 28; for more details see Brown, *Mark's Other Gospel*, 39–40.
18. First in Akenson, *Surpassing Wonder*, 595–97; and expanded in Akenson, *Saint Saul*, 84–90.
19. Akenson, *Surpassing Wonder*, 597 (and similarly Akenson, *Saint Saul*, 88).
20. Akenson, *Saint Saul*, 89.

Ancient Gospel or Modern Forgery?

Around this time also Craig Evans joined the debate on the text. In a 1994 response to one of Neusner's attacks, Evans defended Smith by stating that it is "hard to believe that anyone would devote years of painstaking labor to the production of a 450-page technical book that studies a writing that the author himself faked."[21] As the paper in this volume shows, Evans has since changed his views on Smith's part in the origins of *Secret Mark*.

Smith's detractors grew adept at hurling insults and making (or repeating) insinuations but few provided real evidence for forgery. The closest any scholars came to doing so were in arguments presented by Andrew Criddle, Ernest Best, and Philip Jenkins. In 1995 Criddle performed a statistical analysis of the *Letter to Theodore* purporting to show the letter "contains too high a ratio of Clementine to non-Clementine traits to be authentic and should be regarded as a deliberate imitation of Clement's style."[22] Presumably this feat is possible only for someone with the modern tools mentioned by Quesnell. Best provided a similar argument, but this time examining *Secret Mark*'s correspondences to the style of the Gospel of Mark. He concluded that the longer excerpt in the *Letter to Theodore* is "too much like Mark" to be Mark—that is, *Secret Mark* contains a suspiciously high proportion of Markan phrases.[23] Jenkins's contribution, in his 2001 study *Hidden Gospels: How the Search for Jesus Lost Its Way*,[24] is an insinuation of parallels between Smith's discovery of the *Letter to Theodore* and the discovery of a similarly controversial text at Mar Saba in James Hogg Hunter's 1940 novel *The Mystery of Mar Saba*. One of Hunter's characters also finds a controversial non-canonical text at Mar Saba. Though Jenkins did not explicitly state that Smith was inspired by the novel to forge the text, Robert M. Price was far less hesitant to make the charge.[25] He saw also something suspicious in Smith writing his name on the manuscript. "If Smith had forged the text," he wrote, this and other items "would make additional sense . . . Was he signing his own work?"[26]

Regardless of all of these concerns, the majority of Clement scholars at first considered the text to be genuine[27] and the scholars who worked

---

21. Evans, "The Need for the 'Historical Jesus,'" 129, cited in Brown, *Mark's Other Gospel*, 41.

22. Criddle, "On the Mar Saba Letter," 216. See also the follow-up discussion, Criddle, "Secret Mark–Further Comments."

23. Best, "Uncanonical Mark."

24. Jenkins, *Hidden Gospels*, 102.

25. Price, "Second Thoughts on the Secret Gospel," 131.

26. Ibid.

27. See Brown, *Mark's Other Gospel*, 59, with further discussion 59–71.

closely on *Secret Mark* were confident enough in its authenticity to integrate it into their reconstructions of the development of the canonical Gospel of Mark. The best known and most controversial of these reconstructions was advanced by Helmut Koester.[28] He argued that Matthew and Luke used an early, pre-canonical version of Mark to craft their gospels; this "Proto-Mark" was then expanded with several changes and additions including the raising of the young man from *Secret Mark* and its sequel, the naked flight of the mysterious young man at Jesus' arrest in Mark 14:51–52. Canonical Mark is considered to be an abridgement of this longer text, while Carpocratian Mark is an expansion and interpretation. Hans-Martin Schenke wrote in support of Koester's theory, but with some modifications, so that canonical Mark is placed last in the chain of development as a purified abridgement of Carpocratian Mark.[29] John Dominic Crossan also saw canonical Mark as a deliberate revision of *Secret Mark*. Concerned about Carpocratian usage of the original, longer Mark, a later editor in the same "school" dismembered the raising and instruction narrative of the text, scattering its pieces throughout the text of Mark (e.g., Mark 14:51–52) so that this troublesome incident would appear to be an inauthentic pastiche composed from the scattered phrases; canonical Mark was the resulting text.[30] Each of these views is summarized in Marvin Meyer's first of several articles on the text in 1990.[31] Like his predecessors, Meyer assumed the authenticity of *Secret Mark* and performed a study of the use of the young man (*neaniskos*) in the text as a model of discipleship. The support lent to the text by these four scholars helped to cement its place among the material affirmed by the Jesus Seminar to be essential for the study of the Historical Jesus, thus helping to bring knowledge of *Secret Mark* to the wider reading public.[32]

This first phase of scholarship on *Secret Mark* concludes with Charles Hedrick's 2003 survey article expressing frustration over the "stalemate" in the academy over the authenticity of the text. Despite the efforts of Koester and his admirers, there remained a reluctance among the majority of New Testament scholars to include *Secret Mark* in their data for examining

---

28. Koester, "History and Development of Mark's Gospel"; Koester, *Ancient Christian Gospels*, 293–303.

29. Schenke, "Mystery of the Gospel of Mark," particularly 76.

30. Crossan, *Four Other Gospels*, 91–124.

31. Meyer, "Youth in the *Secret Gospel of Mark*." This and three other articles are revised and updated in Meyer, *Secret Gospels*.

32. Eyer, "Strange Case," 118. For a spirited response to this development, see Akenson, *Saint Saul*, 86.

early Christianity. "Debate has been sidelined," he wrote, "in favor of more spectacular issues—a missing manuscript, Smith's passing suggestion of homosexual encounters, and the visceral defense of standard views of Christian origins."[33] Hedrick provided a summary of Smith's handling of the manuscript in an attempt to dispel some of the misconceptions about its discovery (e.g., Smith did not "add" the pages containing the *Letter to Theodore* to the copy of Voss's book). In this summary, Hedrick draws upon developments on the status of the manuscript reported in an article written a few years earlier (with Nikolaos Olympiou) for *The Fourth R*.[34] The article reveals that, before 2000 a number of scholars had made efforts to see the Mar Saba manuscript. Thomas Talley tried but failed to see it in 1980, but its existence was verified by Archimandrite Meliton of the Jerusalem Greek Patriarchate, who told Talley that he had transferred the Voss book to the Patriarchate Library, and by the Patriarchate librarian, Father Kallistos Dourvas, who told him that the two pages featuring the *Letter to Theodore* had been removed from the book in 1977 and were being repaired.[35] However, it has been revealed recently that Quentin Quesnell saw the book in 1983 along with the pages, now encased in plastic; he even participated in having the pages photographed.[36] Others subsequently made efforts to see the manuscript at the monastery or at the Patriarchate Library, including Hedrick, Olympiou, James H. Charlesworth, James Edwards, Shaye Cohen, and John Dart, but they succeeded only in seeing the book and not the *Letter to Theodore* pages.[37] Then, in 2000, Hedrick and Olympiou contacted Kallistos, now retired, about the manuscript and were informed that the librarian no longer knew the whereabouts of the letter but had made color photographs of the pages, which Hedrick published in the *Fourth R* article.[38] Also, in a companion piece to Hedrick's "Stalemate" article, Guy Stroumsa told his own story of journeying to Mar Saba in 1976 with David Flusser, Shlomo Pines, and Archimandrite

33. Hedrick, "Stalemate," 139.

34. Hedrick and Olympiou, "Secret Mark."

35. Talley, "Liturgical Time in the Ancient Church," 45; noted in Hedrick and Olympiou, "New Photographs," 7 and by Smith in "Clement of Alexandria," 458–59.

36. Adela Yarbro Collins (*Mark*, 491) reports that in the early 1980s Quesnell was allowed to see the manuscript and obtained permission to have it photographed. Timo Panaanen interviewed Quesnell in 2009 about this event, but the interview yielded little elaboration. Read his account at "A Short Interview with Quentin Quesnell."

37. See the summary in Brown, *Mark's Other Gospel*, 25.

38. Hedrick and Olympiou, "Secret Mark," 7–9 (the account of the discussion with Kallistos), 11–15 (the manuscript photographs).

Meliton.[39] There they found the Voss book, with the *Letter to Theodore* pages intact, in the tower library where Smith had left it. The group decided at that time to take the manuscript to the Greek Patriarchate for safekeeping. Stroumsa included in his article some of the lengthy correspondence between Smith and Gershom Scholem documenting Smith's efforts to understand and contextualize the text. Today, the location of the *Letter to Theodore* manuscript remains a mystery, but thanks to Kallistos, Hedrick, Olympiou, Talley, and Stroumsa, it can no longer be argued that the manuscript does not exist, nor that Smith was somehow restricting access to it. If anyone was guilty of doing so it was the Greek Patriarchate who, Olympiou suggested, may be withholding it because of concerns over Smith's homoerotic interpretation of the text.[40]

THE SECOND PHASE OF SCHOLARSHIP ON SECRET MARK: 2005 TO THE PRESENT

The "stalemate" Hedrick observed in 2003 soon began to show movement due to the dynamic discussion prompted by three books on *Secret Mark* arguing both for and against the text's authenticity. The first of these was Scott Brown's *Mark's Other Gospel: Rethinking Morton Smith's Controversial Discovery*, a revision of his 1999 University of Toronto dissertation, published in 2005. *Mark's Other Gospel* was the first monograph entirely devoted to *Secret Mark* to appear since Smith's two 1973 volumes. It confronted many of the criticisms and indictments of Smith's work, often with a passion that would do Smith proud. Arguments against the authenticity of the text Brown called "the folklore of forgery";[41] the gospel he characterized as "a ten-ton magnet for the bizarre and controversial."[42] Brown attacked the early critics for not presenting proof for their assertions of forgery, questioned the methodology of Criddle's statistical analysis, and claimed Price misrepresented the parallels with Hunter's novel.[43] Brown's own arguments about the text were aimed at divorcing the meaning of the gospel from Smith's own interpretation of it. "He was a brilliant and erudite scholar," Brown wrote, "but he did not comprehend the *Letter to Theodore*

---

39. Stroumsa, "Comments on Charles Hedrick's Article."
40. Hedrick and Olympiou, "Secret Mark," 8.
41. Brown, *Mark's Other Gospel*, 12.
42. Ibid, 57.
43. Ibid., 54–59.

well enough to have composed it."[44] Eliminating from consideration the notion that the letter is a witness to Alexandrian baptismal rituals, Brown associated it instead with "the progressive disclosure of secret theological truths through directed scriptural exegesis."[45] As for the origins of *Secret Mark*, he identified several previously-unexplored Markan literary traits in the text—intercalation, framing stories, and verbal echoes—and concluded that the author of the gospel wrote so much like Mark that he could very well be Mark himself, who revisited the text to create a longer version specifically for the Alexandrian church. *Mark's Other Gospel* was the most comprehensive study of *Secret Mark* in the thirty years since the gospel's first publication. It presented a forceful challenge to all previous statements and arguments made against the letter's authenticity. However, to some extent it preached to the converted, appealing as it did to experts in the text who refused to accuse Smith of wrongdoing. In wider scholarly circles Hedrick's stalemate remained and in popular circles the arguments for forgery remained attractive, even if only because many felt the text's contents were so *un*attractive. The only thing those who disliked this text needed was validation for what they already held to be true.

That validation came in the same year with the publication of Stephen Carlson's *The Gospel Hoax*.[46] In this brief, accessible, and inexpensive book, Carlson, a former patent attorney, sought to break the stalemate on the authenticity of the text by tackling the problem with his legal expertise. He concluded that Smith had "the means, motive, and opportunity" to create the text,[47] and did so as a hoax designed to test the academy's abilities to detect forgeries or perhaps to prove himself at a delicate point in his career.[48] As proof of this hoax, Carlson cited two "concealed jokes" Smith left in the *Letter to Theodore* as hints to his authorship. The first is a reference to free-flowing salt, which Carlson claimed is a modern invention first made available by the Morton Salt Company in 1910.[49] The second is a photograph of another Mar Saba manuscript (no. 22), which Smith reproduced in his non-scholarly book to illustrate the monks' practice of writing on blank pages in printed books. According to Carl-

44. Ibid., 74.

45. Ibid., 218.

46. Carlson, *Gospel Hoax*. For a lengthy response to Carlson's arguments and a handy summary of scholarship after Carlson see Edward Reaugh Smith, *Temple Sleep of the Rich Young Ruler*.

47. Carlson, *Gospel Hoax*, 74.

48. Ibid., 78–80.

49. Ibid., 59–62.

son, the handwriting of one manuscript in the photograph is identical to that of the *Letter to Theodore*, but in Smith's published catalogue of this library's manuscripts, he assigned this handwriting to the twentieth century and attributed it to "M. Madiotes," a name which, Carlson argued, is fictional but etymologically related to both "baldy" and "swindler" (Smith was bald).[50] Carlson also noted the connections to Hunter's novel, cited Criddle's statistical analysis, and called attention to similarities with two other biblical hoaxes: Christoph Matthäus Pfaff's Irenaeus fragments and Paul R. Coleman-Norton's "amusing *agraphon*."[51] As in Coleman-Norton's case, Smith's work shows prior awareness of ideas present in his discovery, and the *Letter to Theodore* contains anachronisms—specifically, in its modern treatment of homoeroticism (such as the phrase "and he spent that night with him," Carlson's translation of καὶ ἔμεινε σὺν αὐτῷ τὴν νύκτα ἐκείνην, III.8–9). Most compelling for many readers, however, was Carlson's discussion of several indications of forgery in the handwriting of the manuscript, including forger's tremor, unnatural pen lifts, inconsistency of letter forms, and retouching of letters—all indicative of "drawn imitation of an eighteenth-century hand."[52]

Reaction to Carlson's book was dramatic. Many scholars who equivocated over the letter's authenticity found themselves convinced that it was a modern forgery; some former supporters now changed their position, such as Craig Evans, who declared that Carlson had proven Smith had created the text.[53] Other prominent scholars wrote in support of the book, including Larry Hurtado, who contributed a favorable introduction to Carlson's book, and Bruce Chilton, whose lengthy op-ed piece for the *New York Sun* asserts that, due to Carlson's arguments, "Smith's contention that the text was copied during the 18th century has lost any basis."[54] Further, Chilton's review for the *Review of Rabbinic Judaism*, though casting doubt on some aspects of Carlson's indictment, nevertheless states: "Although in my view he does not quite prove that Smith was a forger, he does demonstrate—within the limits to certainty that incomplete evidence involves—that 'Secret Mark' is someone's forgery, and that Smith is the likely culprit."[55] Also entering the discussion at this time is Pierluigi

50. Ibid., 43–44.
51. Ibid., 16–20.
52. Ibid., 31
53. See, for example, Evans, "The Apocryphal Jesus," 167–71.
54. Chilton, "Unmasking a False Gospel."
55. Chilton, Review of *Gospel Hoax*, 123.

Ancient Gospel or Modern Forgery?

Piovanelli, who in 2007 presented the first installment of an overview of scholarship on the text covering the years 1958 to 2003.[56] *The Gospel Hoax* marked another turning point in *Secret Mark* scholarship in that much subsequent discussion of the text has appeared online in blogs and other forums rather than in monographs or scholarly journals.[57] No other study of an apocryphal Christian text has benefitted so much from this interplay of scholarship and electronic media.

Further arguments for forgery were advanced in Peter Jeffery's 2007 monograph *The Secret Gospel of Mark Unveiled*.[58] Like Carlson, Jeffery, a musicologist then teaching at Princeton, is an outsider to biblical studies. His book approached the *Letter to Theodore* from two angles: its ecclesiology (i.e., its presentation of baptism) and its sexology (i.e., its portrayal of a homosexual Jesus). Jeffery found that in both areas the letter reflected practices and theories of the twentieth century, not the second. On the letter's baptismal imagery, Jeffery claimed that Smith was influenced by modern Anglican theories about early Christian Paschal Vigil rituals.[59] And the homosexual relationship described in the text flouts the Hellenistic conventions of homosexuality—Jesus and the young man are presented as social equals, whereas Hellenistic same-sex relationships are between a teacher and student.[60] Furthermore, Jeffery, like Akenson before him, sees *Secret Mark* as a "gay joke" created by Smith as "arguably the most grandiose and reticulated 'Fuck You' ever perpetrated in the long and vituperative history of scholarship."[61] This gay joke is evident in a series of double entendres: the sister of the young man "coming" to Jesus, the tomb as closet, Jesus seizing the young man's "hand," and Jesus rejecting the women.[62] Jeffery also heavily criticized Smith with a venom rivaling

---

56. Piovanelli, "*L'Évangile secret de Marc.*" The third and fourth parts of the overview were presented at a 2006 gathering of the AELAC (l'Association pour l'étude de la littérature apocryphe chrétienne).

57. Mention should be made here particularly of two sites: Timo S. Paananen's *Salainen evankelista* (http://salainenevankelista.blogspot.com/), which has been a hub for several discussions on the text and contains a summary of Paananen's Master's thesis: "A Conspiracy of the Secret Evangelist: Recent Debate concerning Clement of Alexandria's Letter to Theodore" and Wieland Wilker's *Secret Gospel of Mark Homepage* (http://www-user.uni-bremen.de/~wie/Secret/secmark_home.html), which keeps track of new developments on the text.

58. Jeffery, *Secret Gospel of Mark Unveiled*.

59. Ibid., 60–70.

60. Ibid., 185–212.

61. Ibid., 242.

62. Ibid., 92–99.

that of Jacob Neusner. Smith is disparaged in the book both for his public scholarship (his *Clement of Alexandria* book is described as "hundreds of slovenly pages filled with ignorance, foolishness, and angry jokes about the meaning of early Christian baptism")[63] and for his private life (Jeffery's acknowledgements page finishes with: "And I pray for the late Morton Smith—may God rest his anguished soul").[64] Jeffery's arguments have not gone unchallenged. Scott Brown contributed a lengthy "review essay" for the online *Review of Biblical Literature* stating, among many other things, that Jeffery's discussion of *Secret Mark*'s apparent homoeroticism "consists of private associative reasoning presented as if it were exegesis" and that, "like most interpreters, Jeffery has confused Morton Smith's misinterpretation of the letter with the letter itself."[65] Jeffery countered with a response on his own web page.[66]

Brown has also been the principle critic of Carlson's *The Gospel Hoax*. Before 2008 Brown contributed three journal articles challenging aspects of Carlson's case,[67] including the basis for the "gay gospel" hypothesis and the hoax hypothesis as Smith's motives for forging the text, and the often-cited Morton Salt Company clue,[68] which was confronted also in a 2005 paper by Kyle Smith illustrating that the letter's references to salt are not anachronistic.[69] While Carlson quickly responded to Kyle Smith's challenge,[70] he was shy to respond to Brown's criticisms until the two shared a podium at a session dedicated to *Secret Mark* at the 2008 Annual Meeting of the Society of Biblical Literature. Carlson's presentation, "Can the Academy Protect Itself from One of Its Own? The Case of Secret Mark" (included as an appendix to this volume) primarily restated arguments from *The Gospel Hoax*. Brown's contribution to the session, "Fifty Years of Befuddlement: Ten Enduring Misconceptions about the 'Secret' Gospel of Mark," focused on previous scholars' interpretations of the "great mysteries" as baptism. In the ensuing discussion, Brown asked Carlson to respond to his published articles, frustrated that there had yet to be a

---

63. Ibid., 251.
64. Ibid., ix.
65. Brown, Review of *The Secret Gospel of Mark Unveiled*.
66. Jeffery, "The Secret Gospel of Mark Unveiled."
67. Brown, "Reply to Stephen Carlson"; Brown, "Factualizing the Folklore"; and Brown, "Question of Motive."
68. Brown, "Factualizing the Folklore," 306–11.
69. Kyle Smith, "'Mixed with Inventions.'"
70. Carlson responded to Smith's paper in a post on his own blog; "Kyle Smith's Critique of Gospel Hoax."

proper debate between proponents of the two sides in the conflict over authenticity. Carlson said such a response will come at the appropriate time. Brown asked, "When?" Carlson shrugged his shoulders. Brown asked, "After your PhD thesis?" Another shrug. Brown then added, "I won't hold my breath." Also participating in the session was Allan Pantuck, whose presentation "Can Morton Smith's Archival Writings and Correspondence Shine Any Light on the Authenticity of Secret Mark?" questioned Carlson's theory of motive, and Charles Hedrick, who spoke in support of Brown and Pantuck. Siding with Carlson were Birger Pearson and Bart Ehrman.[71] Audience member Helmut Koester also joined in the discussion. I too was present at the session and was struck by how poorly the principle voices in the debate were communicating with each other, particularly in regards to how Brown's writen responses to Carlson had so far been ignored (for example, Ehrman touted the Morton Salt Company clue as proof for forgery without acknowledgment of either Brown's or Kyle Smith's challenges to the argument). My desire to break this impasse led to the creation of the *Secret Mark* symposium a few years later.

In the meantime, several articles have appeared further chipping away at the forgery hypothesis. Refuting Charles Murgia's "seal of authenticity" argument, Jeff Jay demonstrated that the *Letter to Theodore* coheres in form, content, and function with a newly-identified genre of literature from antiquity designed to combat the unauthorized use of writings not intended for publication.[72] Another article by Brown similarly responded to some aspects of Murgia's position that were adopted by Carlson, claiming that the letter is consistent with how Clement, in his acknowledged writings, responded to concerns analogous to the situation described by Theodore.[73] Brown also joined Pantuck for two articles. Aided by documents from the Morton Smith Papers at the Archives of the Jewish Theological Seminary, Pantuck and Brown demonstrated, contrary to Carlson's "bald swindler" argument, that the script of the top hand of Smith's manuscript 22 is not the hand that Smith attributed to a twentieth-century individual but an eighteenth-century hand that is unrelated to both the *Letter to Theodore* and the individual named Madiotes; the signature of the "swindler" Madiotes is written in a different hand and may actually read Modestos, a

---

71. Pearson's presentation was published as "The Secret Gospel of Mark," article 6, 1–14. Ehrman initially became involved in the debate on *Secret Mark* with a brief response to Hedrick's 2003 article, "Response to Charles Hedrick's Stalemate."

72. Jay, "New Look at the Epistolary Framework."

73. Brown, "The *Letter to Theodore*."

common name at Mar Saba.[74] The second article is an online essay that casts doubt on Carlson's analysis of the handwriting of the *Letter to Theodore*. It demonstrates that Carlson misrepresented the support of professional document examiner Julie C. Edison in his argument that the manuscript is a forgery.[75] Another scholar working online, Roger Viklund, contributed a series of articles, the most compelling of which was an article demonstrating that Carlson's list of indications of forgery in the manuscript (forger's tremor, unnatural pen lifts, and retouching) are observable only in the low-quality black-and-white photographs published in half-tone by Smith and not in the higher-quality color photographs.[76] And those interested in the letters exchanged between Smith and Gershom Scholem mentioned in Guy Stroumsa's 2003 article, can now read the correspondence in the 2008 collection edited by Stroumsa.[77] *Secret Mark* is discussed in some length in Stroumsa's introduction to the volume, as Smith often consulted Scholem on the text.[78] The length and depth of this discussion led Stroumsa to conclude, "the correspondence should provide sufficient evidence of his intellectual honesty to anyone armed with common sense and lacking malice."[79] Only one additional author has written recently in defense of the forgery hypothesis. With his lengthy 2010 article, "Beyond Suspicion: On the Authorship of the Mar Saba Letter and the Secret Gospel of Mark,"[80] Francis Watson aimed to prove "beyond a reasonable doubt" that Smith forged the letter, but actually Watson contributed little new to the debate aside from a more-sustained argument for Smith's knowledge and use of Hunter's novel,[81] and an expansion of the Morton Salt Company clue to include two Greek puns on Smith's name (παραχαράσσω in I.14, which can be translated as "to forge" and is etymologically related to the English

---

74. Pantuck and Brown, "Morton Smith as M. Madiotes"; cf. Brown, "Factualizing the Folklore," 293–306.

75. Brown and Pantuck, "Stephen Carlson's Questionable Questioned Document Examination." Carlson responded to the article, though on a different blog: Philip Harland's Religions of the Ancient Mediterranean (http://www.philipharland.com/Blog/). The response is reproduced in the comments on the original article.

76. Viklund, "Tremors, or Just an Optical Illusion?" The site features three additional articles by Viklund on *Secret Mark*.

77. Stroumsa, ed., *Morton Smith and Gershom Scholem, Correspondence 1945–1982*.

78. Ibid., xii–xxii.

79. Ibid., xv.

80. Watson, "Beyond Suspicion."

81. Ibid., 161–70.

name Smith; and μωρανθῆναι in I.15, which Watson sees as a hint to the name Morton and can be translated as "to be made foolish").[82]

Interest in *Secret Mark* was stimulated further at this time, both in scholarly and non-scholarly circles, by a special feature on the text in *Biblical Archaeology Review*. Charles Hedrick provided an introduction for the feature,[83] Helmut Koester made a case for the text's authenticity,[84] and Hershel Shanks[85] was forced to craft an argument for forgery when three pro-forgery scholars (Carlson, Pearson, and Ehrman) declined to participate. A second contribution by Shanks, "Restoring a Dead Scholar's Reputation,"[86] came out in support of Smith and revealed to readers that the magazine had commissioned two handwriting experts to authenticate the text: Greek paleographer Agamemnon Tselikas and Venetia Anastasopoulou, a certified expert in handwriting analysis and forensic sciences in Athens.[87] The first of the experts' reports, by Anastasopoulou, appeared on a web page hosted by *BAR* dedicated to continuing the discussion on *Secret Mark*;[88] the magazine provided a summary of the report shortly after.[89] Anastasopoulou concluded that Smith's Greek handwriting did not match that of the *Letter to Theodore*, which was written by a native Greek-speaker, writing quickly and unconsciously.[90] The *BAR* site included a response to the report from Peter Jeffery[91] and a second came later from Scott Brown.[92] Both agreed that the report demonstrated that Smith could not have created the handwriting in the manuscript himself, though to Jeffery this suggests that Smith might have worked with an accomplice. While readers waited for the outcome of the second expert's analysis, *BAR* posted

---

82. Ibid., 152–55.
83. Hedrick, "An Amazing Discovery."
84. Koester, "Was Morton Smith a Great Thespian and I a Complete Fool?"
85. Shanks, "Morton Smith—Forger."
86. Shanks, "Restoring a Dead Scholar's Reputation."
87. Ibid., 61.
88. Online: http://www.bib-arch.org/scholars-study/secret-mark.asp.
89. Anastasopoulou, "Experts Report Handwriting Examination," and published in summary in the magazine as Shanks, "Handwriting Experts Weigh in on 'Secret Mark.'"
90. Anastasopoulou, "Experts Report Handwriting Examination," 9.
91. Jeffery, "Response to Handwriting Analysis." Anastasopoulou later contributed a second piece responding to Jeffery's questions about signs of forgery (forger's tremor, etc.): "Can a Document in Itself Reveal a Forgery?" Jeffery countered with "Additional Response to Handwriting Analysis."
92. Brown, "My Thoughts on the Reports by Venetia Anastasopoulou."

several follow-up articles to its initial special feature, including Pantuck's response to Francis Watson, in which Pantuck counters Watson's discussion of Hunter's book with several innocent examples of life imitating art, including Morgan Robertson's 1898 novel *Futility, or the Wreck of the Titan* and its eerie similarities to the destruction of the Titanic in 1912.[93] Watson countered soon after with his own response, again hosted on the *BAR* site.[94] Tselikas's report finally appeared in May 2011, just days after the *Secret Mark* symposium.[95] In it he proposed that Smith could have forged his discovery using four eighteenth-century manuscripts that Smith had previously catalogued from Cephalonia as models of handwriting. Pantuck responded to this hypothesis, pointing out evidence that Smith did not photograph the Cephalonia manuscripts and could not therefore have used them as models; he challenged also the degree of correspondence between these manuscripts and the *Letter to Theodore*, and questioned Tselikas's reasoning for selecting these manuscripts for comparison.[96] Unfortunately, Tselikas refused to engage Pantuck's arguments.[97] A summary of Tselikas's lengthy report was made available by Hershel Shanks at the *Secret Mark* symposium allowing participants a look at his findings and providing the first opportunity for public discussion of this recent development in the study of the text.

THE YORK CHRISTIAN APOCRYPHA SYMPOSIUM

As mentioned earlier, the origins of the York Christian Apocrypha Symposium on *Secret Mark* grew out of the *Secret Mark* session at the 2008 SBL Annual Meeting. The participants on the panel and audience members seemed unable to communicate well enough with one another to advance discussion on the text. Though progress had already been made on dispelling some of the weaker arguments for forgery, these arguments continued to be advanced as proof positive of fraud. A better forum for discussion

---

93. Pantuck, "Solving the *Mysterion* of Morton Smith." A point-by-point response to Watson was published also by Michael T. Zeddies on the Synoptic Solutions blog, which starts with "A Critique of Watson".
94. Watson, "Beyond Reasonable Doubt."
95. Tselikas, "Agamemnon Tselikas' Handwriting Analysis Report."
96. Pantuck, "Response to Agamemnon Tselikas."
97. *Biblical Archaeology Review* published a letter from Tselikas in which he stated his refusal to respond to what he called "personal criticism": Tselikas, "Response to Allan J. Pantuck."

was needed. My impressions of the session posted on my blog Apocryphicity[98] led to early conversations with Pantuck, Brown, and Jeffery on planning a new gathering at which the principle scholars of the text could debate the elements of the forgery hypothesis and perhaps arrive at some consensus on which aspects of this hypothesis, if any, remained viable. The symposium, the first in a planned series, was intentionally focused on North American Christian Apocrypha scholarship; so, all those who were invited to present papers were residents of Canada or the United States. As it happens, the bulk of the debate over *Secret Mark* has taken place among North American scholars. It was important to all of us that the symposium featured a balance of perspectives, with an equal number of scholars arguing for and against authenticity. Though several prominent supporters of the forgery hypothesis declined our invitations, we succeeded at securing the participation of many of the major writers on the text.

The symposium was divided into two sessions. The first focused specifically on the arguments that have been advanced for and against authenticity and the second continued the conversation with new avenues of investigation. Charles Hedrick began the day with a defense of authenticity. His paper spotlights the scholarship and developments on the text since his "Stalemate" paper of 2003, including the recent handwriting analyses, which are augmented with notes from an interview with Agamemnon Tselikas from September 2010. Several of the statements made by Tselikas about the text are addressed in the paper, most notably the likelihood of finding an ancient text in a single, late manuscript, and Tselikas's claim that Smith, lacking the ability to write in an eighteenth-century Greek hand, must have had an accomplice in his crime of forgery. But the bulk of the paper focuses on *Secret Mark*'s relationship to canonical Mark, with a rebuttal to Best's argument that the longer *Secret Mark* excerpt in the *Letter to Theodore* is "too much like Mark" to be by Mark, and a proposal to situate expansions of Mark (including both *Secret Mark* and the longer endings of canonical Mark) in the exercise of imitation practiced in Greco-Roman schools. The *Secret Mark* expansions, however, are far better imitations of Mark's style than the longer endings, so much that Hedrick suggests that the writer behind *Secret Mark* was none other than the author of Mark, just as Clement says.

Bruce Chilton's response to Hedrick does not engage with any of Hedrick's detailed arguments; instead, it focuses on the problem of working with unprovenanced documents and artifacts. Chilton details several

---

98. Burke, "Secret Mark at the 2008 SBL Meeting."

examples of such material with which he has been personally involved, cautioning for each that a text of uncertain origins is best to be avoided. As for *Secret Mark*, Chilton considers Smith's account of its discovery "an unverified claim" (p. 74) unless or until the manuscript's ink has been tested and questions about the Voss volume are satisfactorily answered.

The arguments against authenticity were presented by Craig Evans, who once believed the manuscript to be genuine, but now is quite outspoken about the text being a creation of Morton Smith. His paper details the case of Paul Coleman-Norton's "amusing *agraphon*," which was declared a hoax on the basis of Coleman-Norton's knowledge of the saying of Jesus before he "discovered" it in a North African mosque. Evans applies the same principle to the *Letter to Theodore*, attempting to show that elements of the text appear in Smith's work prior to his public announcement of the letter's discovery in 1960. He also mentions several "curious features" about the find noted by previous supporters of the forgery hypothesis, including contradictions in thought between the letter and Clement's authenticated writings, and the familiar problems with the Voss volume (it is distinct among other books in the monastery, it is not listed in the monastery's 1910 catalogue, Smith never returned to examine the book, and the letter is found on the page opposite to a discussion of interpolated texts); particular emphasis is placed on the parallels between Smith's account of his find and Hunter's novel *The Mystery of Mar Saba*. As for the handwriting analyses, Evans says we now have conflicting expert opinion, with Carlson and Tselikas arguing Smith created the manuscript and Anastasopoulou arguing he could not. Evans recalls the example of the Hitler diaries, which handwriting experts had authenticated but were later established to be forgeries. Handwriting analysis, therefore, is not sufficient for establishing a text's authorship.

The original response to Evans was presented at the symposium by Allan Pantuck. In the more-detailed paper included here, Pantuck is joined by his frequent collaborator Scott Brown. The two work systematically through the arguments advanced by Evans, endeavoring to demonstrate that Evans has overstated his case that Smith's early work reveals knowledge of the text (or themes uniquely combined in the text) prior to its discovery. Along the way they deal with several components of the "folklore of forgery"—e.g., that Smith did not appeal to *Secret Mark* in his book *Jesus the Magician* (he did) and that, because the Voss volume was not published in Venice nor written in Greek, it is unique among the books found at Mar Saba (it is not)—and declare that some of the parallels that Evans adduces with Hunter's novel are "not real" (p. 104). Finally, they conclude from the handwriting analyses that "only one properly qualified expert in questioned document examination has thus far studied suitable images of Mar Saba 65" and "this expert's observations indicate that the manuscript most likely contains someone's natural handwriting, which in turn implies that it is from the eighteenth century" (p. 125).

The morning session finished with a paper from Hershel Shanks, editor of *Biblical Archaeology Review*. Shanks was asked to comment specifically on *BAR*'s involvement with authenticating the text, which he did mention, but his presentation was more a spirited defense of Smith's character. His paper, which captures the passion with which Shanks made his case, emphasizes that it is not possible to prove 100 percent that a text is authentic; there will always be one more test that "may theoretically prove the document a forgery" (p. 139). A better method of proving the text genuine, Shanks says, is to consider human nature. "Is there any hint that Morton Smith was of a character that would allow him to do this horrendous thing?" he asks. "I think not" (p. 140). For support he cites the opinions of Helmut Koester, Gershom Scholem, and Jeffrey Tigay. The discussion of Smith's character continued after Shanks's presentation. Shanks called the increasingly complicated forgery theory—that Smith bought a copy of the Voss book and had a native Greek writer copy a text Smith had invented into its endpapers—"outlandish" and asked if any scholar with the credentials of someone like Smith had ever been discovered as having done such a thing. Evans responded, once again citing Coleman-Norton, that forgeries have been made and to rule them out with "I can't think anyone would do that" is naïve. The panel had difficulty recalling the kind of example Shanks requested, but Chilton mentioned the case of the Greek manuscripts created by a sixteenth-century scholar to provide Greek evidence for the Johannine Comma, the only explicit declaration in the New Testament of the doctrine of the Trinity. Regarding the likelihood of Smith creating the *Letter to Theodore*, both Evans and Chilton stated that there are scholars still living who knew Smith and think he was capable of doing such a thing.

The afternoon session began with Marvin Meyer's short paper, "The Young Streaker in Secret and Canonical Mark." The paper builds on Meyer's previous efforts to understand the role of the *neaniskos* in the longer version of Mark, a text which he is convinced is authentic and even predates canonical Mark. He begins the paper echoing Shanks's concerns about accusations of forgery—charges which, to him, "seem almost libelous" (p.

147). Then he turns to examining other fleeing, sometimes naked, youths in ancient literature, who are found often in scenes of initiation and discipleship. These parallels help us to understand the presentation of the *neaniskos* in longer Mark: he functions as a model disciple, one who has died and been raised, has feared and fled, but at the end of the gospel he remains the only disciple proclaiming Christ risen.

Meyer's literary study of *Secret Mark* was followed by two presentations studying the man behind the text, Morton Smith. Piovanelli drew heavily on the recently published Smith-Scholem correspondence to demonstrate that Smith had a prior interest in the "main fields of research, topics, and methods" reflected in the *Letter to Theodore* (p. 164). In his paper, Piovanelli shows that Smith wrote to Scholem about the intersection between Smith's views on Jesus and Scholem's characterization of the seventeenth-century antinomian messiah Sabbatai Tzevi, and about an interest in the British occultist Aleister Crowley. Smith combined these interests to construct the magical and libertine Jesus observable in *Jesus the Magician*, but, Piovanelli argues, for Smith to make a "stronger proposal about the historical Jesus as a miracle worker/magician, he was in need of more consistent proof" (p. 181), proof he manufactured in the form of the *Letter to Theodore* in 1958. Piovanelli thus characterizes the letter as a "learned forgery," which, though "inexcusable," helped pave the way for a new wave of scholarship emphasizing the Jewishness of Jesus (pp. 181–83). Pantuck also uses Smith's correspondence in his efforts to dispel the myth that Smith had the abilities needed to create the *Letter to Theodore*. The correspondence, with Scholem and other scholars, indicates that Smith struggled with Greek; indeed, as Pantuck notes, on two occasions he "declined the opportunity to have composed in Greek when it would have been expected and appropriate" (p. 195). Smith also lacked the necessary skills in paleography and ancient epistolography, and was not sufficiently knowledgeable about the works of Clement of Alexandria. Pantuck then appeals to archive material from the Jewish Theological Seminary and Union Theological Seminary to demonstrate that Smith had no knowledge of the Voss edition before 1958 and that, from 1958 to 1963, Smith worked gradually to translate, understand, and interpret the letter, work that would be unnecessary if he had created it himself.

The final two presentations focused on the *Letter to Theodore*'s relationship to undisputed works of Clement of Alexandria. Peter Jeffery's paper constructs from Clement's writings a multi-stage scheme of Christian initiation. This he compares with the letter to determine what kind of initiation or ritual it is describing and if it is consistent with the mystery cult vocabulary used by Clement. Among the disagreements he finds between the letter and Clement's undisputed writings are the appeal to written rather than oral hidden truths and a special initiation ceremony for those being perfected separating them from the merely baptized. Thus, Jeffery characterizes the letter as a collection of ritual terms from Clement "indiscriminately mashed together" (p. 230). The same method, he says, is observable in Smith's academic works. During his presentation, Jeffery encouraged the graduate students in the room to observe for themselves Smith's "'scattered indications' technique of reassembling words and phrases from ancient writings" (p. 246) by taking what he called the Jeffery Challenge: "Go to the library, check out [Smith's *Clement of Alexandria*], take any random page, and check his sources. Frequently the source does not support what Smith is saying, it is distorted, taken out of context. If you can do that for ten hours and not figure out that you are being conned, then I will write you a glowing letter of recommendation on Princeton stationery to the business school of your choice." Because Smith's writing is "extremely deceptive, distorted, untrustworthy," Jeffery said, "[Smith] is not a man whose announcement of a discovery is entitled to the benefit of the doubt." And to those scholars, such as Hedrick, Meyer, and Brown, who question how Smith could have forged a document he did not understand, Jeffery declared, "Morton Smith misinterpreted everything and he did it on purpose! All you're saying is that he didn't interpret this text the way you do."

Scott Brown, the author of the final paper from the symposium, has long held that "most scholars who have studied [*Secret Mark*] have fundamentally misconstrued what the letter is talking about" (p. 248). Arguing specifically against Jeffery's view that the *Letter to Theodore* is revealed as a forgery because it misrepresents baptism in the Alexandrian church, Brown places the life setting of *Secret Mark*, with its traditions that would "lead the hearers into the innermost sanctuary of the seven-fold veiled truth" (I.25–26), not among the merely baptized neophytes but among "those who were being perfected" (I.22)—that is, would-be gnostics. Brown comes to this conclusion after extensive investigation into Clement's writings, which he confesses are not easy to work with: "It can take years to make sense of the most esoteric aspects of the *Stromateis*," he writes, "and you are never sure you have properly figured something out" (p. 255). Nevertheless, he believes he has understood the purpose of *Secret Mark* correctly, as an expanded version of Mark to be read and expounded allegorically to aid in transmitting unwritten gnostic tradition to advanced students.

The symposium concluded with a question-and-answer session with Brown, Evans, Jeffery, and Meyer chaired by Philip Harland. A partial transcript of the event is included in this volume. Then follows one final paper: Stephen Carlson's presentation from the 2008 Annual Meeting of the SBL. Carlson was unable to attend the symposium but he did want to contribute, and since his is one of the major voices on this text in the last decade, I agreed to publish the paper, particularly since it is mentioned by several of the other authors. The paper is Carlson's only published response to critics of *The Gospel Hoax*, but it has been criticized in turn as being little more than a restatement of his earlier arguments. New, however, is the appeal to the Smith-Scholem correspondence (published subsequent to Carlson's book) to bolster his argument that Smith had worked on Clement prior to his "discovery" of the text in 1958. Only one of the responses to Carlson's book is addressed in the paper (Carlson says it is due to lack of space, but there were no restrictions placed on the size of the paper, which is relatively brief; the space limitation is due to the time allowed for the original presentation): Brown's refutation of Carlson's claim that the first *Secret Mark* excerpt "easily conjures up to the twentieth-century reader the image that Jesus was arrested for soliciting a homoerotic encounter in a public garden."[99] Brown had commented, "Among the hundreds of twentieth-century discussions of 'secret' Mark that exist in print and on the internet, I have yet to come across the observation that LGM 1 implies that 'Jesus was arrested for soliciting a homoerotic encounter in a public garden.'"[100] Carlson counters with two examples, one of which was from Smith himself (pp. 305–6). The paper concludes with an exoneration of early scholars who did not recognize the text as a forgery (or "hoax," as Carlson prefers), for such recognition is made easier the greater the distance from a text's composition, when the concerns of its time come more sharply into focus.

REACHING CONSENSUS AND MOVING FORWARD

The goal of the symposium on *Secret Mark*, as mentioned earlier, was to gather the principal North American scholars of the text and, through discussion, determine what arguments regarding the authenticity of the

---

99. Carlson, *Gospel Hoax*, 70.
100. Brown, "Factualizing the Folklore," 320.

text remain viable. Several bloggers in attendance at the symposium commented after that none of the scholars present changed their positions on the text.[101] But a "conversion experience" is not what was expected, and though there was no formal discussion separating strong from weak arguments, it was clear by the end of the event, and from reading the papers collected here, that even those arguing for forgery have abandoned, or at least carefully avoided, certain claims that once seemed persuasive. Where, then, does the debate on the authenticity of *Secret Mark* now stand? And where does it go from here?

The recent release of the *BAR* reports has changed the direction of the discussion of the *Letter to Theodore* manuscript. Previously the only person to submit the manuscript photos to handwriting analysis was Stephen Carlson. And many readers and reviewers of *The Gospel Hoax* found his discussion of forger's tremor, unnatural pen lifts, etc. in the manuscript compelling evidence for forgery. It seemed that the case for forgery finally had the support of empirical data and expert analysis. Alas, Carlson's evidence is problematic on several grounds: it was based on examination of inadequate half-tone photographs, its endorsement by a professional document examiner was misrepresented, and the "clue" to the text's authorship in the signature of "M. Madiotes" in manuscript 22 appears to be baseless. If there is any agreement among the scholars of the symposium it is that these arguments are no longer useful, for aside from a brief mention in Evans's paper, Carlson's analysis was all but ignored even by supporters of forgery. Whatever Carlson's expertise as a lawyer and budding biblical scholar, he is no expert in handwriting analysis. Those who are and have applied their skills to the manuscript images agree that the manuscript was written by a native Greek writer in a difficult-to-duplicate eighteenth-century hand. And the scribe was not Morton Smith. This means that either Smith had nothing to do with the manuscript's creation, and therefore it is authentic, or that he had someone create it for him. If the latter, the forgery hypothesis becomes a conspiracy theory with its own metaphorical second shooter on the grassy knoll. Allan Pantuck's paper even places in doubt that Smith had the necessary capability in Greek to compose a draft of the letter that his accomplice could transfer to Voss's book. This may come as a shock to proponents of the forgery hypothesis who have

---

101. The various early responses to the symposium are collected at Timo S. Paananen, "Toronto Conference in Review—A Summary." Paananen also comments here on the "Jeffery Challenge," and takes issue with Jeffery's off-hand comments about Smith's scholarly abilities. Jeffery responded to Paananen's concerns in the comments to the post.

perhaps overestimated Smith's brilliance. Hopefully we have heard the last also of the false assertions that used to plague commentary on *Secret Mark*: that there is no manuscript, that Smith destroyed it, and that there is something suspicious about his handling of it. Smith appears to have done what is expected of anyone in his position: he found an interesting manuscript, photographed it, cataloged it (adding his own reference number to the front page), left it where he found it, and returned home to publish his findings.

Could Smith and his accomplice have written the text into the Voss volume and planted it in the Mar Saba library? This seems increasingly unlikely. The support for this contention is that the Voss book is unique in the library—in Carlson's words, it "sticks out like a sore thumb."[102] But, as Brown and Pantuck show in their paper, Voss's *Epistulae genuinae S. Ignatii Martyris* is not the monastery's only book in Latin, and not the only book that was published in a place other than Venice. Nevertheless, several details about the book remain puzzling. Why was it not included in the 1910 list of the library's holdings? Why was the letter copied into this particular book? And what happened to the manuscript from which it was presumably copied? Likely the answers to these questions are more mundane than supporters of forgery would hope and are due simply to accidents of history. Still, some commentators have seen something suspicious about finding an authentic ancient text in a single, late manuscript. As it happens, many apocryphal texts were first encountered in and published from a single late manuscript. The *Infancy Gospel of Thomas*, for example, first appeared in scholarship in a 1675 catalogue of Viennese manuscripts by Peter Lambeck.[103] Lambeck excerpted several lines of the text from a fifteenth-century Greek manuscript, which, funny enough, is now missing. A second manuscript was published twenty years later, but no one, it seems, in the intervening years doubted the existence of the text or accused Lambeck of forgery. A similar situation occurs for the *Infancy Gospel of James*, the early publishing history of which is shrouded in mystery. It first appeared in Guillaume Postel's 1552 Latin translation of an unnamed but late Greek manuscript, and then in a Greek edition from another unnamed manuscript by Michael Neander in 1564.[104] Of course, knowledge of manuscripts of *Infancy James* grew rapidly thereafter. Maybe

102. Carlson, *Gospel Hoax*, 38.

103. Lambeck, *Commentariorum de augusta bibliotheca caesarea vindobonensi*, 7:270–73. The manuscript is Vienna, *Phil. gr. 162 (144)*. For more details see Burke, *De infantia Iesu euangelium Thomae graece*, 129–31.

104. See the summary in Hock, *Infancy Gospels of James and Thomas*, 28.

that is the only way to settle the debate over *Secret Mark* once and for all: finding more copies, either of the *Letter to Theodore* or the longer version of Mark that it describes.

But the forgery hypothesis relies also on motive, and perhaps there would be no question of the antiquity of the *Letter of Theodore* were it not for the folklore surrounding the man who discovered it and the controversial contents of some of his scholarship. Was Smith testing the academy's ability to spot a forgery? Was he trying to advance his career by associating himself with a major discovery? Or was he enacting vengeance against his adversaries, or bolstering theories he had in development, or telling a "gay joke" at the expense of his self-important colleagues. Any of these motives are possible, but many of them lack adequate support. Smith's papers and correspondence suggest he was not particularly angry or vengeful during the low points in his career; and his books on the *Letter to Theodore* were published when his career was on the upswing. Smith's prior interest in themes present in the letter—whether of a libertine Jewish Jesus (Piovanelli) or a "troubling" combination of Clement of Alexandria, the Gospel of Mark, secrecy, etc. (Evans)—can be traced in his published work and his correspondence, but are these enough to warrant an accusation of forgery? After all, it is not uncommon for biblical scholars to discuss these topics in their works—more so for a scholar as prolific as Smith and having such a wide array of interests. That Smith's story of the discovery of the letter is based on Hunter's Mar Saba novel makes for a sensational claim that, at first thought, is quite damning; but Pantuck has effectively countered this argument with his examples of life imitating fiction and Brown and Pantuck together demonstrate in their response to Evans that the parallels between Smith and Hunter have been overstated. The playful-hoax hypothesis seems also to be losing steam, as no reference was made at the symposium either to Carlson's Morton Salt Company clue or to Francis Watson's similar examples of puns written into the text. As far as the *Letter to Theodore* as a gay joke, this theory relies primarily on the persuasiveness of Peter Jeffery's list of double entendres. Carlson and Evans also see the relationship between Jesus and the rich young man as a sexual one. The letter's Carpocratians would agree, and even Smith was open to the possibility that the letter hinted at a ritual of physical union that may have been practiced in the Jesus movement; but many scholars, including Brown, Hedrick, and Meyer, continue to argue that the homoeroticism of *Secret Mark* is in the eye of the beholder.

Overshadowing all of these arguments for motive is the evidence from Smith's papers and correspondence, as well as anecdotes from the scholars who knew him, that Smith spent a considerable span of time working on the *Letter to Theodore*, continually revising his theory of the letter's origins, his interpretation of its contents, and even its transcription (i.e., conjectural emendations) and translation. If Smith forged the letter, then he also falsified documents (his research notes) to support his discovery; yet, some of these documents, according to Smith's instructions, were supposed to be destroyed after his death. Why would Smith create this material if no one was meant to see it? To use the legal terminology that has become endemic to the debate on *Secret Mark*, it is becoming increasingly questionable that Smith had either the means or the opportunity to commit the crime of forgery, and no one would prosecute a crime based purely on motive; indeed, in this case, there is no evidence that a crime has been committed at all.

As for the future of *Secret Mark*, Piovanelli says he instructs his students not to use the text and wishes in future that specialists will meet less frequently to discuss it. Chilton, too, warns against appealing to unprovenanced texts and artifacts, and Evans would prefer to spend his time working on material with established antiquity. But no matter what one thinks about *Secret Mark*'s origins, ignoring the text means missing opportunities to consider what it might tell us about a number of important topics and figures in the study of early Christianity, including the development of Mark's gospel, the relationship between Mark and John, solutions to the Synoptic Problem, Christian use of mystery religion terminology, the Carpocratians, Gnosticism, Clement of Alexandria, and others. Even as a possible medieval or modern forgery, the text contributes to the study of post-antique Christian Apocrypha, a body of literature that has received very little attention. At the very least, it is hoped in future that scholars will leap less readily upon any new evidence for or against authenticity and vigorously declare their position has been "proven" right, despite knowing full well that, in the study of history, ambiguity is the norm and certainty always elusive.

2

Secret Mark
Moving on from Stalemate[1]

Charles W. Hedrick

I HAVE BEEN GIVEN the impossible task of making a case for the authenticity of the *Letter to Theodore* and the *Secret Gospel of Mark*. It is an impossible task because the only way to sort out history from realistic fiction is this way: history references events that have actually occurred in common time and space; realistic fiction, on the other hand, however realistic, references imaginary events in the present or past.[2] Establishment of authenticity will require certainty, but all historical reconstructions are necessarily speculative and based on competing probabilities. Here is an example: in the four canonical gospels, which members of the guild regard as at least partially historical, there are four different "plans" for the public career of Jesus. What positive criterion of authenticity would enable us, as a guild, to affirm one plan as unambiguously historical over against the other three? And the other three must then be judged a-historical. In a way it is a "trick" question, since all of the plans appear to be fictional—the unique construct of each author. Assuming, however, that one *might* be

---

1. My thanks go to Robert J. Miller, Scott G. Brown, and Alan J. Pantuck for their helpful comments on this paper.

2. See Konstan, "The Invention of Fiction," 5; and Hedrick, "Survivors of the Crucifixion," 179.

authentic, how exactly would one identify the "real thing" from the counterfeit? What is that positive criterion of authenticity?

A similar situation exists with the *Letter to Theodore*, and barring some kind of corroborating evidence, on which all can agree, the *Letter to Theodore* and the excerpts from *Secret Mark* will undoubtedly remain debatable as historical data. What is absolutely clear in my judgment, however, is that the evidential bar modern forgery theorists have set themselves for proving the *Letter to Theodore* to be a Morton Smith fiction is much too low to overcome an unmistakable aura of historicity that surrounds the letter. The excerpts of *Secret Mark* simply fit too well the circumstances they purport to describe.

Further, the term "authentic," if I may put it this way, is clearly ambiguous, since both "texts" may be inauthentic in the sense that they are ancient forgeries and yet at the same time both may be authentic in the sense that they are ancient texts originating in the early Christian period. We have made little progress in locating a historical matrix for the *Letter to Theodore*, since scholarship lost its way and became preoccupied with proving a case of modern forgery against Morton Smith. My goal in this paper, therefore, is to suggest a general plausible scenario for their antiquity.

THE STATUS QUO: STALEMATE[3]

Here is the current situation with respect to *Secret Mark*.[4] It has been argued—but not, in my judgment, convincingly—that both Clement's fragmentary *Letter to Theodore* and the excerpts from the secret gospel included in the letter are modern forgeries.[5] The most complete case for a forgery (Carlson's more gentle word is "hoax") was made in 2005 by Stephen C. Carlson, who named the discoverer of the letter, Morton Smith, as the forger.[6] A second book by Peter Jeffery, among other things more narrowly focused than that of Carlson, interpreted the longer excerpt of *Secret Mark* as a baptismal liturgy and focused on both Smith's purported

---

3. See Hedrick, "The Secret Gospel of Mark," and the responses to the article in the same issue by Stroumsa ("Comments on Charles Hedrick's Article: A Testimony") and Ehrman ("Response to Charles Hedrick's Stalemate").

4. This text has also been called a Mystic Gospel of Mark and a Longer Gospel of Mark, but could just as easily be titled a Spiritual Gospel of Mark.

5. First alleged by Quesnell, "Mar Saba Clementine."

6. Carlson, *Gospel Hoax*.

character and the longer excerpt of the secret gospel as homoerotic.[7] As Jeffery puts it: "the purported letter of Clement is dependent on Oscar Wilde's *Salomé,* and embodies a critique of Christian heterosexual morality that was widely appreciated by early twentieth-century literary homosexuals . . ."[8] Since these books appeared, those who think the secret gospel is a modern forgery have generally focused on the purported personal character of Morton Smith in order to discredit the antiquity of both the fragmentary *Letter to Theodore* and the excerpts of *Secret Mark.*[9]

Carlson's rationale and arguments have been thoroughly critiqued and convincing arguments have been made in refutation in the years since his book appeared.[10] Carlson has never replied in any detail to these criticisms of his position—not even when given the opportunity in a paper on *Secret Mark* in 2008 at the Society of Biblical Literature annual meeting in Boston.[11] His paper on that occasion was largely a restatement of material from his book, and did not address the intervening scholarly discussion.[12] Essentially, Carlson's arguments rely on a preponderance of what I have called "less-than circumstantial evidence" to make a case for a modern forgery. He has never presented any solid affirmative evidence actually connecting Smith to a forgery, or demonstrated that the document is a forgery.[13] What I mean by "solid affirmative evidence" connecting Smith to a forgery is this: the data he offered as proof cannot be directly tied to Smith. They are only related to Smith by means of Carlson's imagination and his nuanced explanation of data. Only two of Carlson's imagined "clues" can even be construed as specifically relating to Smith.[14] They

---

7. Jeffery, *Secret Gospel of Mark Unveiled.*

8. Jeffery, "Response to Handwriting Analysis."

9. As Jeffery does in the second half of his book, *Secret Gospel of Mark Unveiled.* Reviewed by Brown in *RBL.*

10. Brown, "Reply to Stephen Carlson"; Brown, "The Question of Motive"; Brown, "Factualizing the Folklore"; Brown, "The *Letter to Theodore*"; Pantuck and Brown, "Morton Smith as M. Madiotes."

11. Jeffery, on the other hand, has replied to Brown: "Secret Gospel of Mark Unveiled." He has a lengthy collection of online material about the discussion.

12. Carlson, "Can the Academy Protect Itself," found in the appendix to this volume.

13. See Hedrick, "Evaluating Morton Smith." A more recent attempt to nail Smith to a forgery (not hoax) with circumstantial evidence is Watson, "Beyond Suspicion."

14. Hedrick, "Evaluating Morton Smith," 293; Carlson, *Gospel Hoax,* 58–63. These two "proofs," according to Carlson, are that Smith alluded to himself as "baldy" in his imaginative explanation of the name Madiotes and that Clement's quote of Matt 5:13 presupposes modern salt technology invented by the Morton Salt Company. On this

are not actually "clues," however, unless one assumes *a priori* that Smith forged the text. What I mean is this: the prior assumption leads to seeing the datum as a "clue." However, to Carlson's credit, he recognized that for his circumstantial arguments to have any chance of succeeding he had to discredit the *Letter to Theodore* as an *ancient text*—hence his argument that the handwriting of the fragment revealed the text to be a modern forgery done by Smith himself.

Trying to discredit an ancient text by how one interprets it seems to me a weak argument at best, since it goes to what the interpreter *thinks about the text* rather than to actual *data derived from the text*. Specifically, I am referring to the issue of homosexuality evoked by Carlson's imagination that the statement "spend the night with" means "have sex with" and Jeffery's reading of the excerpts from *Secret Mark* as homoerotic. In actuality the author of the letter rejects such readings. If "spend the night with" is a modern euphemism meaning "to have sex with," what then are we to think of Luke 24:29—that Jesus has just been propositioned for sex? The language used in *Secret Mark* III.9 (ἔμεινε σὺν αὐτῷ τὴν νύκτα) is virtually the same as Luke 24:29 (μεῖνον μεθ' ἡμῶν, ὅτι πρὸς ἑσπέραν ἐστὶν καὶ κέκλικεν ἤδη ἡ ἡμέρα).[15] At some point analysis must return to the text itself.

Where everyone does agree, however, is that the handwriting *style* of the document associates it with the eighteenth century.[16] The eighteenth-century *style* of the handwriting in which the *Letter to Theodore* is inscribed was not challenged by Carlson; rather, he argued that Smith *imitated* an eighteenth-century Greek hand, and betrayed his forgery in the way he wrote certain Greek letters.[17] Subsequently, however, the document was subjected to the critical analysis of a professional Greek questioned

---

latter see a refutation of Carlson in a paper by Kyle Smith, "'Mixed with Inventions.'" And Carlson's response: "Kyle Smith's Critique of Gospel Hoax."

15. See Carlson, *Gospel Hoax*, 66–67. The really odd thing about Carlson's observation is that "spend the night with" are Carlson's own words. Smith had translated the passage "he remained with him that night": Smith, *Clement of Alexandria and a Secret Gospel of Mark*, 447. Carlson objects that Smith translated it as he did because he knew that the expression if "properly" translated would be "too sexually charged." Actually Smith's translation is perfectly acceptable, as Luke 24:29 shows! Carlson's imagination provides the "sexual charge."

16. Smith summarizes how the manuscript was dated: *Clement of Alexandria*, 1–4.

17. Carlson, *Gospel Hoax*, 25–47. Brown responded to Carlson's evidence that the handwriting was forged in "Factualizing the Folklore."

document examiner, Venetia Anastasopoulou,[18] who concluded that the handwriting of the *Letter to Theodore*,

> indicates a hand used to [i.e., accustomed to] writing in this manner. The letters are written unconsciously. (p. 9)
> Conclusion: The whole writing shows freedom, spontaneity and artistic flair. It also shows a skillful penmanship of a well educated and trained writer who uses the language effectively in expressing his thoughts. (p. 13)
> It is my professional opinion that the writers of the questioned document of "Secret Mark" on the document listed as Q1, Q2 an[d] Morton Smith's handwriting on the documents listed as K1–K27, are most probably not the same." (p. 38)

Another Greek scholar, Agamemnon Tselikas,[19] has recently registered his opinions[20] about the scribal hand of the *Letter to Theodore*. Professor Tselikas is the Director of the Centre for History and Paleography of the National Bank of Greece Cultural Foundation. He describes the *Letter to Theodore* as fitting,

> the handwriting of the last years of the seventeenth century and the first years of the eighteenth century. The scribe who wrote the letter wrote in the style of the late seventeenth century and early eighteenth century, but when you observe the *ductus* of the letters, many letters are not written in the usual direction of the *ductus* of letters made by Greek copyists who were trained to write in this period. It is impossible that some of the letters

---

18. For the entire report see Anastasopoulou, "Experts Report Handwriting Examination," and summarized in the magazine as Shanks, "Handwriting Experts Weigh In on 'Secret Mark.'" Here are two subsequent evaluations of the report from two different perspectives: Brown, "My Thoughts on the Reports by Venetia Anastasopoulou," and Jeffery, "Response to Handwriting Analysis," and the follow-up: Jeffery, "Additional Response to Handwriting Analysis."

19. For information on Tselikas see The Antikythera Mechanism Research Project. Online: http://www.antikythera-mechanism.gr/project/team/academic/agamemnon-tselikas.

20. On 30 September 2010 for 2.5 hours at his office at P. Skouse 3 in Athens, Greece, Agamemnon Tselikas was interviewed on the *Letter to Theodore* by Charles W. Hedrick; see the appendix to this paper. Subsequently he published a report for the *BAR* web site: "Agamemnon Tselikas' Handwriting Analysis Report." The report constitutes the following: A. Transcription of the Text; B. Grammatical and Syntatic Comments; C. Palaeographic Observations; D. Textological Observations; E. The Presence of Morton Smith in the Patriarchate of Jerusalem and Greece; F. Conclusion; G. Annex, all preceded by a Summary. My interview with him, while containing some new information, is generally consistent with his report to *BAR*.

in the *Letter to Theodore* were written by a Greek hand of the period. For example the tau is not written with ligatures.[21]

In addition, Tselikas says that the *Letter to Theodore* does not fit well the style of correspondence written in the eighteenth century, for "the style of the letter is mixed."[22] But as Jeff Jay pointed out: "The letter to Theodore is plausible in light of letter writing in the late second or third century and has tight generic coherence in form, content, and function."[23] Hence Tselikas's observation that the epistolary conventions of the *Letter to Theodore* do not fit eighteenth-century conventions is what one would expect if the text were copied from a second- or third-century document. In short, in this case Tselikas's observation against the antiquity of the text becomes an argument in favor of its antiquity.

Unfortunately, Professor Tselikas has not yet produced a detailed critical argument to substantiate his opinions about the text. Mr. Hershel Shanks, editor of the *Biblical Archaeology Review*, invited Professor Tselikas to provide such a study to be published in *BAR* (as reported in the May/June issue of 2010).[24] In response to the invitation he produced a

---

21. See appendix to this paper, #13. However, in material sent to Hershel Shanks he says the following in the "Palaeographic Observations" of his report to the *BAR* web site: The first impression is "that the scribe is experienced, and keeps constant *ductus* in the design of the letters." But Tselikas "observes some completely foreign or strange and irregular forms that do not belong to the generally traditional way and rule of Greek writing." A judgment on the validity of this remark must wait for him to provide examples of the practice of "Greek copyists who were trained to write in this period." Only in that way can he show that the variations in paleography, which he notes in the *Letter to Theodore*, are actually anomalous for the period. Particularly of interest in this regard are the "three or four manuscripts in the monastery [of Thematon] at Kefalonia," which Tselikas claims "are all written in the last years of the seventeenth century and the early years of the eighteenth century. Tselikas claims that "these manuscripts have many similarities to the *Letter to Theodore*" (appendix to this paper, #26). The manuscripts, noted by Tselikas at Thematon as similar to the *Letter to Theodore*, are likely manuscripts 3, 4, 5, 6 as listed in Smith's catalogue of manuscripts at the Monastery of Thematon in his article "Σύμμεικτα." At the time that Smith visited (1951–1952) he found several manuscripts in the monastery. Of the photographs of these manuscripts made by the Historical and Paleographical Institute of the Greek Bank, Tselikas noted only "three complete handwritten manuscripts and one leaf from another" and "a few leaves in bad condition" (see Tselikas, "Τὰ χειρόγραφα τῆς Μονῆς τῶν Θεμάτων στὴν Κεφαλονιά," [with four photographs]). Note that Smith listed manuscripts 3, 4, 5, and 6 as all from the same hand while Tselikas listed manuscript 4 as being from a different hand.

22. See appendix to this paper, #12.

23. Jay, "A New Look at the Epistolary Framework," 596.

24. See Shanks, "First Person."

series of critical observations, raw data, and a summary of his views on the text.[25]

Professor Tselikas explained to me on September 30, 2010 that "The [Greek Orthodox] Patriarchate has no interest in this issue [i.e., the *Secret Mark* affair],"[26] and I sensed at the time of the interview that for that reason it was not a major concern of Professor Tselikas as well. Of course, he has considerable research interests and the "*Secret Mark* affair" does not appear to be among them.

Professor Tselikas described the *Letter to Theodore* to me as a modern forgery, made by someone after the end of the seventeenth century.[27] The hand must have belonged to a Greek copyist, however, since Tselikas says that Greek written by a non-Greek is "easy to spot" by a Greek paleographer.[28] But that has not really been true of the *Letter to Theodore*, and the eighteenth-century dating of the hand has persisted in the literature in spite of theories that it is a forgery. Nevertheless, for Tselikas "it is 90% certain that Smith forged the document outside the monastery."[29] This last comment stands in tension with his theory that the hand of a non-Greek writing in Greek is easily identified. The tension in the statements of Tselikas and particularly the report of Anastasopoulou suggests that it was a native Greek writer who copied the document sometime after the end of the late seventeenth century. Tselikas even suggested to me that Smith must have had someone with him when he visited the monasteries, since "Byzantine script is very difficult to read," and "the 'more' modern hands [i.e., *after the Byzantine period*] are even more difficult to read—not even the experts can read them."[30] Hence, what his remarks to me suggest is that, even if Smith were the "mastermind" behind the forgery, someone else would have had to provide the technical skills to pull it off, which seems to be the position Tselikas holds.[31]

---

25. These observations are published on the *BAR* web site; see n. 20 above for the citation.

26. See appendix to this paper, #2.

27. See ibid., #15–16. See also his Textological Observations.

28. See ibid., #14.

29. See ibid., #28. See also his posted "Conclusion," and his "Textological Observations" (website address listed in n. 20 above). Nevertheless, he admits that "A comparison of the handwriting of the Greek letters of Morton Smith with the handwriting of Clement's letter cannot give significant [i.e., definitive] evidence that Morton Smith is the scribe . . ."

30. See appendix to this paper, #30.

31. See the concluding remarks to his "Summary" (Tselikas, "Handwriting

It seems to me that in the absence of a formal critical argument by Tselikas that lays out the comparative handwriting evidence by which he judges that the *Letter to Theodore* "contains completely foreign or strange and irregular forms" that do not follow traditional forms and rules of writing Greek,[32] we have no option but to begin with the evidence on the table. That evidence points to the late seventeenth and early eighteenth centuries as a date for the inscription of the *Letter to Theodore*. Efforts to prove that the *Letter to Theodore* was forged by Morton Smith have not been successful, and as Tselikas himself said to me: "it is, of course, possible that [the *Letter to Theodore*] is a new discovery, since new discoveries are made all the time. We know this happens as the *Gospel of Judas* shows . . ."[33]

The standard of proof for convicting a distinguished colleague of forgery should be higher than what has been offered by the modern forgery theorists. It must be beyond a reasonable doubt, which is not the case with the suggestive "clues" that have been offered thus far. Point by point the suggestive "clues" and arguments have been countered. With the failure of the Morton-Smith-forgery-theorists to meet a higher burden of proof, we have no choice except to move on to consider other options. The dating of an ancient document should not hinge on disputed interpretations of the text or "subjective clues," but on hard data derived from a physical examination of the text, historical allusions in the text, and the text's general suitability to a particular historical context.[34]

It may be helpful to compare the kind of evidence offered to prove that the *Letter to Theodore* is a modern forgery with the circumstances of the most famous forgery of late antiquity: the *Donation of Constantine*. The *Donation of Constantine* presents itself as an early fourth century

---

Analysis Report").

32. Ibid., under "Palaeographic Observations." But the most these features in themselves suggest is that the scribe was both unskilled and not formally trained.

33. See appendix to this paper, #10.

34. This is the approach taken by Goodspeed in a little book on unmasking forgeries: *Strange New Gospels*. Goodspeed focused principally on the text itself and addressed the forgers as a subsidiary issue. Here is his list of priorities: 1. A scholar needs the ancient document, or a photograph, or a copy made by a reputable scholar (pp. 3–4). 2. Lacking the material in point one, the scholar needs to know exactly where the document is located (pp. 3–4). 3. Next the scholar needs to survey the literature of antiquity for mention of the manuscript (p. 6). 4. "And finally the work itself must be studied in the light of our best knowledge of the thought and times to which it claims to belong" (p. 6). The issue of the forger is secondary to the information that the document reveals about itself. And these points form the procedure by which he addresses the forgeries in his book.

document, but all the manuscript evidence is considerably later—eighth and ninth centuries.[35] In the *Donation of Constantine*, among other things, the Roman Emperor Constantine the Great is made to give a large part of the Roman Empire to Sylvester, Bishop of Rome.[36] From the ninth century to the fifteenth century the document was "almost universally accepted as genuine."[37] In 1440 Lorenzo Valla, described in part as a forerunner of the modern historical critical method,[38] wrote a treatise proving that the *Donation of Constantine* was a forgery.[39] Today, largely due to the evidence offered by Lorenzo Valla, the forgery of the *Donation of Constantine* is dated to the eighth century.[40] Valla's oration is roughly divided into two parts: "In the first, Constantine's alleged donation of a large part of the imperial domains to Pope Sylvester is rejected on grounds of its psychological implausibility. Here we have a series of purely fictitious dialogues between Constantine and his children, and Constantine and the Pope. In the second, the *constitutum Costantini*, the document on which the alleged donation is based, is rejected as a forgery."[41]

Valla's detailed discussion lists unimpeachable evidence for the forgery: historical anachronisms, inconsistencies, and misunderstandings, which would not have been possible had the document been written in the fourth century.[42] But in the case of the *Letter to Theodore* we are only offered imaginative "clues" to support a forgery. Valla, on the other hand, has offered unambiguous and concrete historical data demonstrating that the *Donation of Constantine* is a much later forgery.[43]

---

35. Coleman, *Treatise of Lorenzo Valla on the Donation of Constantine*, 6.

36. Ibid., 1–2.

37. Ibid., 2; see also Coleman, *Constantine the Great and Christianity*, 169–72.

38. Ginzburg, *History, Rhetoric, and Proof*, 57.

39. Ibid., 54; Coleman, *Donation of Constantine*, 3.

40. Coleman, *Donation of Constantine*, 1; Coleman, *Constantine the Great*, 184–202; Ginzburg, *History, Rhetoric, and Proof*, 54.

41. Ginzburg, *History, Rhetoric, and Proof*, 56.

42. Ibid.

43. For anachronisms (things out of place in history), see Coleman, *Donation of Constantine*, 85–89, 95, 133; for historical inconsistencies, see ibid., 67–71; for misunderstandings of the data of the past, see ibid., 97, 105–7, 113, 125.

MOVING ON

Out of the Shadows of History

The unexpected appearance of a seventeenth-/eighteenth-century exemplar of a text that presents itself as a second-/third-century text is only a problem for forgery theorists. Among other things, they wonder why this particular text should emerge only now and presenting such startling new information? On the other hand, with regard to a modern forgery others reason: why would anyone choose such a difficult hand to imitate, when another style would have been simpler to produce with less chance of error. The truth is, it is not unusual for the works of early authors to appear in manuscripts of a very late date and in a considerably different script from the original author's time period. For example, Thucydides' (460–400 BCE) *History of the Peloponnesian War*, except for a few fragments from Oxyrhynchus, only survives in manuscripts of the tenth to fifteenth centuries CE;[44] and books 1–5 of Polybius's (ca. 205–120 BCE) *Histories* exist only in an eleventh-century manuscript (only fragments and quotations cited in other authors exist for the remaining thirty-five books).[45] A large gap of time between the ancient author and the surviving manuscripts of his works seems to be the general rule, rather than the exception. The reason, of course, is that the intellectual achievements of the ancient past represented in the Greek and Latin classics were largely eclipsed in the medieval period following the fall of the Roman Empire.

With the Renaissance, however, came a renewed interest in the ancient culture and learning of Greece and Rome. It was an age of discovery and one exciting aspect of that age was the recovery of both lost and previously unknown manuscripts.[46]

> Until the end of the [nineteenth] century our knowledge of ancient texts depended almost entirely on copies made during the Middle Ages whereas manuscripts dating back to the later centuries [i.e., earlier] of the ancient world formed only a tiny proportion of the total number known. From the Renaissance onwards such discoveries as were made of new texts, or more commonly, better manuscripts of texts already known, usually consisted in the unearthing of neglected medieval manuscripts.[47]

---

44. Hall, *A Companion to Classical Texts*, 279–80.
45. Ibid., 263–64.
46. See in particular Burchardt, *Civilization of the Renaissance in Italy*, 1:196–206.
47. Reynolds and Wilson, *Scribes and Scholars*, 177.

Ancient Gospel or Modern Forgery?

During the Renaissance, the name most readily associated with the discovery of ancient manuscripts was Poggio Bracciolini.[48]

> The first half of the fifteenth century was the period when most of the forgotten texts were discovered. The letters of Cicero and the younger Pliny, the histories of Tacitus, and the poems of Propertius and Tibullus had already come to light during the fourteenth century. But during the next century Poggio Bracciolini (1380–1459) alone discovered between 1415–1417 a very considerable number of Cicero's orations, the epic of Valerius Flaccus, the poem of Lucretius, the *Silvae* of Statius, and Asconius on Cicero's orations, as well as a complete Quintilian, while later he found Petronius' *Coena Trimalchionis* in England and Frontinus' book on the aqueducts of Rome at Monte Cassino.[49]

Two travelers who made extensive trips to Greece in the fifteenth century were Cristoforo Buondelmonti and Ciriaco d'Ancona; while they were primarily interested in other aspects of Greek antiquity, they both searched for Greek manuscripts.[50] And they were not the only ones who dug in the libraries of the East for manuscripts.[51] With a renewed interest in manuscripts, viewed as repositories of the learning of the ancients, which was current during the early Renaissance period, it should be no surprise that discoveries of new manuscripts were made.

The shortage and expense of writing paper in the monasteries led to the use of blank end pages of books for copying new manuscripts that emerged, and to the reuse of old manuscripts in bindings, which was a common practice throughout the ancient world. At Mar Saba, for example, one printed book has as its end papers a fifteenth-century

---

48. See in particular Sandys, *History of Classical Scholarship*, 2:25–34.

49. Weiss, "The New Learning," 119–44. The list appears on 136. See also Reynolds and Wilson, *Scribes and Scholars*, 120–24.

50. Weiss, *The Renaissance Discovery of Classical Antiquity*, 135-42. Buondelmonti spent six years traveling through the islands of the Aegean: Legrand, *Description des îles de l'Archipel par Christophe Buondelmonti*. Buondelmonti's charge was a description of the islands and their cultural and political history (157), so he was not specifically searching for manuscripts. For example, he visited Mt. Athos and, while he gives a description of the rule and the order followed by the monks, he does not even mention the library (249–51). He may not have had access, since in his visit to Constantinople he describes them as hostile "to the Latins." But he did note visits to churches and monasteries throughout the islands.

51. For a survey of the early activity in the East see Sandys, *History of Classical Scholarship*, 3:376–79; 2:36–37.

annotated manuscript of Sophicles' *Ajax*. Another printed book had for end papers pages from a late medieval Georgian manuscript of the life of St. Onophrius.[52]

In this section of the paper I have only aimed at suggesting a plausible scenario for the sudden emergence of the *Letter to Theodore* by recalling the hopefully well-known circumstances of the Renaissance. The particulars of the odyssey of the *Letter to Theodore* that brought it out of the shadows in the seventeenth/eighteenth century, however, are still hidden and likely will never be recovered. But similar mysteries also surround two previously unknown gospel texts that suddenly emerged from the shadows of history in the twentieth century. The *Egerton Gospel* (Papyrus Egerton 2), apparently named for the donor who provided the money for the purchase, was bought from an antiquities dealer in Egypt in 1934. Nothing more is known of its provenance, or who the dealer was from whom it was purchased, or the name of the purchaser.[53] Its odyssey from an unknown date of composition to inscription ca. 150 CE is mysterious, as are its circumstances until purchased in 1934. The second, the *Gospel of the Savior* (Papyrus Berolinensis 22220), was stumbled upon in 1995 in the holdings of a museum and traced back to a Dutch antiquities dealer, Karl J. Möger, from whom the museum purchased the fragments in 1967, but nothing more is known of its odyssey from the late second century (its supposed date of composition in Greek) to its supposed date of inscription in Coptic around the fifth/sixth century CE to its acquisition by a German museum in 1967.[54]

Of course, these two gospel manuscripts date generally within the early Christian period. Here are two other non-canonical texts whose dates of composition are thought to be within the early Christian period

---

52. Smith, "Monasteries and Their Manuscripts," 173–75. I have been unable to locate a study that examines instances of fragments of ancient manuscripts written on flyleaves and other blank parchment, papyrus, or paper in books or ancient codices, but it is not an uncommon occurrence. Recently in a complete parchment manuscript of the New Testament (GA 2554) "dated to the year 1434 (shelf number 3, previously INV 691)" was discovered the text of Luke 10:31—13:29. "Between the end of Revelation and the back cover are two parchment leaves" on which the excerpt from Luke was written. "It is not clear why these two leaves were inserted into the codex other than as flyleaves for the end of the manuscript." The manuscript is located in the National Museum of Art in Romania. Report by Hargis, "New Fragmentary Lectionary in Bucharest."

53. Bell and Skeat, *Fragments of an Unknown Gospel*, 7; Mayeda, *Das Leben-Jesu-Fragment*, 12–13.

54. Hedrick and Mirecki, *The Gospel of the Savior*, 2–4, 13–16.

but whose principal manuscript witnesses are quite late. The principal textual witnesses for the *Infancy Gospel of Thomas* used today are Greek texts of the fourteenth/fifteenth centuries (although there is an eleventh-century Greek manuscript).[55] The scribal hands of these manuscripts are not unlike what one finds in the *Letter to Theodore*.[56] The *Gospel of Peter*, believed to have been composed in the late second century, was found during an excavation in Akhmim in Egypt in 1886–1887 and is preserved only in a manuscript "written at some point between the late sixth century and the beginning of the ninth."[57]

The circumstances of the *Letter to Theodore* are not unlike those of these relatively late gospel manuscripts that today have been fully accepted into the database of ancient witnesses to early Christian history. The *Letter to Theodore* was discovered in 1958 in a Greek Monastery in Israel traditionally dated to the fifth century. It emerged from the shadows of history in a seventeenth/eighteenth-century exemplar, although its supposed date of composition is second/third century. Nothing more of the odyssey of this particular text that can command the agreement of a majority of scholars is known. The truth is, if people want to consider the *Letter to Theodore* as a forgery, it could have been invented at any point between the second/third century, the time at which the text presents itself as being composed, and the seventeenth/eighteenth century, when it was copied into the 1646 edition of the letters of Ignatius of Antioch. And similar caveats might be given for both the *Egerton Gospel*, the *Gospel of the Savior*, the *Infancy Gospel of Thomas*, and the *Gospel of Peter*.

The Purported a quo of the Text

The place to begin evaluating the antiquity of a text is with the manuscript itself. In this case, however, all that exists are photographs of the manuscript. Officials of the Greek Orthodox Patriarchate in Jerusalem must bear the responsibility for having misplaced or destroyed the text,

---

55. For a description of this manuscript see Burke, *De infantia Iesu euangelium Thomae graece*, 127–28; the remaining Greek manuscripts are discussed ibid., 129–44.

56. For a readily-accessible image of one of these manuscripts (Codex Atheniensis 355 folio 64r of the fifteenth century) see Hock, *The Infancy Gospels of James and Thomas*, 102–3.

57. Foster, *The Gospel of Peter*, 3. According to J. K. Elliott, a third-century fragment believed by some to be of the *Gospel of Peter* found in the Fayum (P. Vindobonensis G 2325), shows "considerable variation" when compared to the principal manuscript: Elliott, *The Apocryphal New Testament*, 150.

or for having allowed the text to be stolen while it was in their possession, sometime after the spring of 1976.[58] And the Archimandrite Meliton, a representative of the Greek Orthodox Patriarchate, must bear the responsibility for refusing to allow the ink to be tested in the spring of 1976.[59]

I must confess that I do not understand the silence of the Greek Orthodox Patriarchate in this matter. Had a priceless antique manuscript in any other major library of the world gone missing and the ancient volume in which it was written damaged, at the very least there would have been a subsequent investigation and an official report made that could be released to interested members of the public. But in this case, there is only silence. The unofficial murmurings reportedly coming out of the Patriarchate Library is that the Patriarchate has no interest in this matter—and the Patriarchate continues to maintain its silence.[60] Hence, until the Patriarchate investigates the matter, or the manuscript simply "turns up," the best we can do is work with the photographs and the contents of the text.

The photographs show it to be a seventeenth-/eighteenth-century exemplar and the contents suggest that it originated sometime at the end of the second century or the beginning of the third.[61] As an early Christian forgery, however, it could have originated somewhat later.

Are the *Letter to Theodore* and the excerpts purportedly from a Gospel of Mark, which is longer than our canonical Mark, to be considered "authentic"? Or to put the matter somewhat differently: if the *Letter to Theodore* is not a modern forgery, how should we regard the text? It is not an easy question to answer. The word "authentic" can mean several things in this case. It is possible to consider the text a deliberately contrived forgery in all particulars and yet at the same time to consider it an "authentic" second-/third-century text. The fact that it is an ancient forgery does not

---

58. Stroumsa, "A Testimony," 147–48. The book was taken to the library of the Patriarchate by Archimandrite Meliton. The librarian at the time, Kallistos Dourvas, took photographs of it after having removed it from Voss's 1646 *Letters of Ignatius*, and it has since that time been misplaced, stolen, or destroyed: Hedrick and Olympiou, "Secret Mark," 8–9.

59. Stroumsa, "A Testimony," 148.

60. Reported orally to Charles Hedrick by Agamemnon Tselikas as a statement of the current librarian Aristarchos: "the Patriarchate has no interest in this issue." See appendix to this paper, #1.

61. This date is suggested because it purports to be written by Clement of Alexandria, and mentions the Carpocratians, a Christian-Gnostic group, who were described by the second-/third-century writers Clement (*Strom.* III.2) and Irenaeus (*Haer.* 1.25.1–6).

ruin its value as a witness to early Christian history, as, for example, the Pastoral Letters demonstrate. On the other hand, the *Letter to Theodore* actually may have originated with the second-/third-century human being we know as Clement of Alexandria, but the excerpts of *Secret Mark* described in the letter are nevertheless forgeries—in the sense that they were never part of Mark's first edition and were written by someone other than the author of the first edition of Mark.[62] A similar situation exists with the longer endings to canonical Mark.[63] These multiple endings in some ancient manuscripts are regarded as forged endings to the Gospel of Mark and yet nevertheless they are treated as authentic period manuscripts. It is also possible that the *Letter to Theodore* was an ancient forgery of the late third century made for the purpose of validating a longer Gospel of Mark (which contained the *Secret Mark* excerpts) that actually existed in a manuscript of the third century, though now no longer extant. In the sense that the excerpts were a part of a longer Gospel of Mark, which existed in the third century, they are "authentic," even if they never were part of original or canonical Mark (if these two are judged to be different). And it is always possible that Clement's letter is actually by Clement and is completely accurate, and that Mark did, in fact, later expand the original gospel, as Clement claimed in the letter. All of these are certainly possible.

I doubt, however, that these issues will ever be resolved completely, and neither will some of the other idle questions that scholars raise about the text. For example, both Charles E. Murgia[64] and Agamemnon Tselikas[65] raise this question: why does the text suddenly break off when there is still room at the bottom of the page for more text to be included? Murgia concludes that the gap is a sign of forgery. Tselikas, however, concludes that the gap indicates the remainder of the page was missing in the prototype, but adds that (if the text were genuine) the copyist would have added a note indicating that the model was incomplete. The truth is that all of this is speculative reasoning, and there could have been any number of reasons why the text ended as it did. But without more information it is an idle question whose answer will remain conjectural until new information turns up.

---

62. Of course, if the situation is as the *Letter to Theodore* says, that the original author of the gospel added new material to his original composition, one would have to think of it as a new edition of Mark rather than a forgery.

63. Metzger, *Textual Commentary*, 102–7.

64. In the discussion section of Fuller, *Longer Mark*, 58.

65. See appendix to this paper, #11; Tselikas, "Handwriting Analysis Report," under "Textological Observations," #7.

It is impractical to address all these possibilities in a single paper. But before scholars became distracted with making Morton Smith responsible for forging the letter before he "found" it, attention was rightly directed toward the manuscript itself. I am now turning back the clock to consider one of what I consider the more serious challenges to the "authenticity" of the *Letter to Theodore* and to *Secret Mark*. Both the *Letter to Theodore* and the excerpts from *Secret Mark* have been described as being too much like Clement to be Clement[66] and too much like Mark to be Mark.[67] My discussion from this point will focus only on Mark and the excerpts from *Secret Mark* included in the fragmentary *Letter to Theodore*.

"Too much like Mark to be Mark"?

The idea that the text of the Gospel of Mark was unstable is not new. Text critics have known that gospel texts were unstable from the very beginning of attempts to establish a critical text of Mark. The most graphic instance of this instability in Mark is supplied by the multiple longer endings of Mark,[68] but there are other instances of expansion in Mark as well.[69] In fact, the instability of gospel texts seems to be the rule rather than the exception. The floating story of the woman caught in adultery in John 7:53—8:11 clearly puts fair-minded readers on notice as to how unstable gospel texts were.[70] Hence, that a previously unknown pericope attributed to Mark suddenly emerges from the shadows of history should not be a surprise to anyone familiar with the textual variations in the ancient gospel manuscript tradition. Expanded or abbreviated manuscripts of a given gospel text in circulation in antiquity seem best regarded as new versions of the text—in the sense that expansion and abbreviation make the text a "new version" of the old. And we need always to remember that we do not possess the originals of any of these texts.

Whether the author of these two excerpts from a longer Gospel of Mark quoted in the *Letter to Theodore* was a forger or not, s/he was clearly familiar with Markan stylistic features reflected in the text of "canonical"

---

66. Criddle, "On the Mar Saba Letter"; Carlson, *Gospel Hoax*, 51–53.
67. Ernest Best, *Disciples and Discipleship*, 199–205.
68. Metzger, *Textual Commentary*, 102–7.
69. Ibid., 62–107. See in particular Koester, "History and Development of Mark's Gospel."
70. On the instability of John, see Koester, *Ancient Christian Gospels*, 244–50; and Metzger, *Textual Commentary*, 167–221.

Ancient Gospel or Modern Forgery?

Mark—which, it should not be forgotten, is a modern scholarly reconstruction of a presumed "original Mark." Drawing on the analysis of the characteristic features of Markan style as described by E. J. Pryke,[71] Ernest Best argues that the longer excerpt in the *Letter to Theodore* is "too much like Mark" to be Mark:[72] "We might describe it as a mosaic of Markan phrases. It looks as if its author thumbed through Mark until he found the phrase he wanted, if necessary modified it, and then made it part of his text. Inadvertently he produced 'an overkill.' It is impossible to determine when or by whom this was done."[73]

Of the fourteen characteristic Markan syntactical features listed by Pryke in his statistical summary,[74] Best finds seven instances of Markan style (five instances used once and two instances used more than once) in the longer of the two excerpts from *Secret Mark* (II.23—III.11).[75] He does not address the shorter excerpt (III.14-16). The Markan stylistic features he finds are: use of the impersonal (II.23); use of a redundant participle (II.24; III.1 and 10); use of "and immediately" (II.26—III.1) and "immediately" (III.2); use of ἄρχομαι + infinitive (III.5); use of a γάρ explanatory phrase (III.6); use of the genitive absolute (III.7); use of a parenthetical clause (III.9-10). Hence Best finds ten characteristic features of Markan style appearing in a pericope of twelve periods in the Greek text. Best's number of stylistic features should be reduced in number by one, however, since the verb ἔρχονται (II.23), which Best describes as an impersonal, has Jesus and the twelve as its antecedent in Mark 10:32 (this pericope is, after all, described as an excerpt from the Markan text where it has a presumptive literary setting and in this case antecedent). Only by assuming *a priori* that the excerpt is not really an excerpt from the Markan text is it possible to regard II.23 as a use of the impersonal. Hence in this excerpt from *Secret Mark* there are nine features of Markan style in a pericope of twelve Greek periods, and they appear within the body of the pericope rather than being clustered at the seams of the narrative unit, where, as Best argues, we are accustomed to find Markan "redactional features."

---

71. Pryke, *Redactional Style in the Marcan Gospel*. Pryke attempted to sort out the hand of a redactor who edited traditional material, or in Pryke's word "sources."

72. Best, *Disciples and Discipleship*, 204. See the review of Best's method by Brown, *Mark's Other Gospel*, 109-10.

73. Best, ibid., 205.

74. Pryke, *Redactional Style*, v and 135 (but compare p. 27 where Pryke claims that "some eighteen linguistic features of 'Marcan usage' have been examined..."

75. Best, *Disciples and Discipleship*, 200.

To test his argument that the number of instances of Markan stylistic features is "overkill" and "too much like Mark" to be Mark, I picked at random from canonical Mark a pericope for comparison also having twelve Greek periods (Mark 5:35–43); the selection also has a similar number of words (for *Secret Mark* 157 words;[76] for Mark 5:35–43 there are 151 words).[77] I checked canonical Mark 5:35–43 for the typical Markan stylistic features listed in Pryke, as Best also had done.[78] What I discovered in Mark 5:35–43 was surprising. I found appearing within the body of the pericope, rather than clustered at the seams, ten instances of Markan style (two of these stylistic features were each used twice). Instances of Markan stylistic features in Mark 5:35–43 are: use of the genitive absolute (35a [Pryke 62]); the use of λέγω ὅτι (35a [Pryke 73]); use of the impersonal (35a and 38 [Pryke 107, 112]);[79] use of the periphrastic (41 [Pryke 103, 59, 61]; use of a parenthetical clause (41b [Pryke 34]; use of εὐθύς and καὶ εὐθύς (42 (*bis*) [Pryke 87, 89]); use of γάρ explanatory (42 [Pryke 126]); use of the πολλά accusative (43 [Pryke 70 but 5:43 is omitted by Pryke]).[80] Here is a reproduction of the text with the Markan stylistic features underlined:

---

76. According to Best's count (ibid., 203).

77. I tried to get a section of about equal length and began by checking the instances of εὐθύς to find a similar pericope.

78. See Pryke, *Redactional Style*, in the pages listed below for the parallels.

79. Verse 38: the use of ἔρχονται here is similar to Best's description of an impersonal in *Secret Mark* II.23. Pryke, however, identifies v. 38 as a use of the impersonal (*Redactional Style*, 107, 112).

80. Oddly, Pryke does not include the use of the historic present, which by anyone's reckoning is a distinctive feature of Markan style. He explains: "As for the historic present, well-known as a particular illustration of Markan usage, the figures (64R[edactor], 87S[ource], approximate ratio 2S[ource] to 1R[edactor]) are inconclusive for our study, and might be held to argue the homogeneity of the style of the Gospel" (*Redactional Style*, 27). In other words, it challenges his theory.

35 While he was still speaking, there came from the ruler's house some saying that, "Your daughter is dead. Why trouble the Teacher any further?"	35 Ἔτι αὐτοῦ λαλοῦντος ἔρχονται ἀπὸ τοῦ ἀρχισυναγώγου λέγοντες ὅτι Ἡ θυγάτηρ σου ἀπέθανεν· τί ἔτι σκύλλεις τὸν διδάσκαλον;
36 But ignoring what they said, Jesus said to the ruler of the synagogue, "Do not fear, only believe."	36 ὁ δὲ Ἰησοῦς παρακούσας τὸν λόγον λαλούμενον λέγει τῷ ἀρχισυναγώγῳ· Μὴ φοβοῦ, μόνον πίστευε.
37 And he allowed no one to follow him except Peter and James and John the brother of James.	37 καὶ οὐκ ἀφῆκεν οὐδένα μετ' αὐτοῦ συνακολουθῆσαι εἰ μὴ τὸν Πέτρον καὶ Ἰάκωβον καὶ Ἰωάννην τὸν ἀδελφὸν Ἰακώβου.
38 When they came to the house of the ruler of the synagogue, he saw a tumult, and people weeping and wailing loudly.	38 καὶ ἔρχονται εἰς τὸν οἶκον τοῦ ἀρχισυναγώγου, καὶ θεωρεῖ θόρυβον καὶ κλαίοντας καὶ ἀλαλάζοντας πολλά,
39 And when he had entered, he said to them, "Why do you make a tumult and weep? The child is not dead but sleeping."	39 καὶ εἰσελθὼν λέγει αὐτοῖς· Τί θορυβεῖσθε καὶ κλαίετε; τὸ παιδίον οὐκ ἀπέθανεν ἀλλὰ καθεύδει.
40 And they laughed at him. But he put them all outside, and took the child's father and mother and those who were with him, and went in where the child was.	40 καὶ κατεγέλων αὐτοῦ. αὐτὸς δὲ ἐκβαλὼν πάντας παραλαμβάνει τὸν πατέρα τοῦ παιδίου καὶ τὴν μητέρα καὶ τοὺς μετ' αὐτοῦ, καὶ εἰσπορεύεται ὅπου ἦν τὸ παιδίον·
41 Taking her by the hand he said to her, "Tal'itha cu'mi"; which means, "Little girl, I say to you, arise."	41 καὶ κρατήσας τῆς χειρὸς τοῦ παιδίου λέγει αὐτῇ· Ταλιθα κουμ, ὅ ἐστιν μεθερμηνευόμενον· Τὸ κοράσιον, σοὶ λέγω, ἔγειρε.
42 And immediately the girl got up and walked (for she was twelve years of age), and they were immediately overcome with amazement.	42 καὶ εὐθὺς ἀνέστη τὸ κοράσιον καὶ περιεπάτει, ἦν γὰρ ἐτῶν δώδεκα. καὶ ἐξέστησαν εὐθὺς ἐκστάσει μεγάλῃ.
43 And he strictly charged them that no one should know this, and told them to give her something to eat. (RSV)	43 καὶ διεστείλατο αὐτοῖς πολλὰ ἵνα μηδεὶς γνοῖ τοῦτο, καὶ εἶπεν δοθῆναι αὐτῇ φαγεῖν. (SBLGNT)

In the use of characteristic Marcan stylistic features identified by Pryke, no noticeable difference exists between the longer excerpt from *Secret Mark* in the *Letter to Theodore* and Mark 5:35–43. If we accept Best's argument that stylistically the longer excerpt from *Secret Mark* is too much like Mark to be Mark, then that must be true of Mark 5:35–43 as well.

In a second phase of his argument Best examined phrases (rather than single words and Greek language constructions) in the longer excerpt from *Secret Mark* and assigned them numerical values (one, two, or three) on the basis of their verbal agreement with similar phrases elsewhere in

Mark.[81] He then applied the same criterion to three other passages in Mark and found these three passages in canonical Mark were significantly lower in their use of Markan phraseology. *Secret Mark*, however, was significantly higher in its reproduction of Markan phraseology.

Scott Brown found three weaknesses to Best's method of comparing verbal similarity: (1) It involves undue subjectivity in determining vague parallels and significant words, and in the dividing up of the lengthy phrases; (2) it does not take into consideration the two sentences of the shorter excerpt of *Secret Mark* that had little in the way of repeated phrases; (3) Best's selections chosen from canonical Mark for comparison were too few and too short to be statistically significant.[82] Brown aimed at correcting these deficiencies in method and made his own survey of the phrases. He found that *Secret Mark* 1a (II.23—III.6) had a lower number of verbal repetitions than 1b (III.6–11), and 2 (III.14–16), the shorter excerpt, had a considerably lower percentage of verbal repetitions than did the longer excerpt. Further, canonical Mark 4:1–2 (forty words), what Best would regard as Mark's editorial connection for the following pericope in the canonical gospel, had a verbal repetition of 76.5 percent, whereas the longer excerpt from *Secret Mark* by Best's reckoning had only 58 percent.[83] Brown reasonably concludes: "So the criterion scholars use to isolate Mark's handiwork in the canonical gospel—high concentration of Markan traits—is the same criterion used to isolate an imitator's handiwork in the non-canonical gospel,"[84] something similar to what I suggested above for the stylistic features in Mark 5:35–43. Brown's observation clearly calls Best's method into question, since the decision to interpret the same phenomena as evidence of *imitation* in one text but as evidence of *originality* in another can only have been made *a priori*.

To evaluate the weight of Best's verbal repetitions argument, I sampled the first seven phrases that Best noted in the excerpt from *Secret Mark*, and found them to be common Greek constructions. His first: καὶ ἔρχονται εἰς βηθανίαν uses the historic present, which is typical of Mark (the phrase appears nine times in Mark mostly with variations from the phrase in *Secret Mark*), but the construction appears regularly (of course the object of the preposition changes) with a change in tense or the use of a participle in Matthew, Luke, and John. Best gives the expression a numerical value

---

81. Best, *Disciples and Discipleship*, 201–3.
82. Brown, *Mark's Other Gospel*, 106.
83. Ibid., 108.
84. Ibid., 110.

Ancient Gospel or Modern Forgery?

of two (because there is some minor variation in the expression such as change of person, number, tense mood, gender, etc.). The only time that this phrase appears in canonical Mark exactly as it appears in *Secret Mark* is at Mark 8:22. The only thing about this phrase that is typical of canonical Mark, however, is its use of the historic present. Hence the writer of *Secret Mark* (except for the use of the historic present, perhaps) would likely have been led to the phrase by the force of the Greek language—that is just the way one says it in Koine. At least on the basis of the parallels in Matthew, Luke, and John that judgment cannot be ruled out.

The second phrase that Best notes in *Secret Mark* is: ἦν ἐκεῖ μία γυνή, which Best also values at two because the object will vary with the expression. It appears with variations only in canonical Mark 3:1 and 5:11. But again this phrase is typical Koine (cf. Matt 2:1; 27:61; Luke 6:6; 8:32; John 3:23; 4:6; 5:5; 6:22).

The third phrase (προσεκύνησεν τὸν Ἰησοῦν), appearing at Mark 5:6 and 15:19 receives a two from Best because it does not use the name of Jesus but a pronoun as object. Interestingly, the phrase appears also with variations ten times in Matthew, and once each in Luke and John.

The fourth phrase (καὶ λέγει αὐτῷ) he assigns the value of one because of its frequency. Again what is significant about the phrase with respect to canonical Mark is the historic present, a generally-recognized preferred construction of Mark. The phrase itself (using the present), however, does not need to be found "somewhere in Mark" and copied. It is common in Matthew and John (but not in Luke) and appears to be common Koine.

The fifth phrase (υἱὲ Δαβὶδ ἐλέησόν με), according to the theory of Markan Priority, is borrowed from Mark (10:47–48) by both Matthew (9:27; 20:30–31) and Luke (18:38–39). "Son of David" as a title, however, is used several times in Matthew (1:1; 12:23; 21:9, 15), and a variation of *Secret Mark's* fifth phrase appears in Matt 15:22 (compare Luke 16:24 and 17:13 for the plea "save me"). My point is that the expression need not be copied by *Secret Mark* from Mark 10:47–48. Only by first thinking of the excerpt from *Secret Mark* as a forgery or imitation and completely disallowing an author's compositional freedom can one think of it as "copying."

The sixth phrase (οἱ δὲ μαθηταὶ ἐπετίμησαν αὐτῇ) in *Secret Mark* is not exactly paralleled by Mark 10:13 (or Matt 19:13; Luke 18:15), for in canonical Mark the disciples rebuke them (αὐτοῖς). Hence, at most the parallel should have been valued at two rather than the three given it by Best.

The seventh phrase (ἀπῆλθεν μετ' αὐτῆς) is not particularly distinctive or unusual. And prompts the question: why must the phrase have been searched out through canonical Mark, rather than simply having been freely composed?

In short, for Best's statistical argument to be completely convincing one must first *a priori* assume that the longer excerpt of *Secret Mark* is a forgery cobbled together from phrases (many undistinguished) that are painstakingly ferreted out in canonical Mark. And one must (as Best does) exclude the possibility that such expressions may have been freely composed by the "author" of *Secret Mark* (either by deliberate preference, or unconsciously)—because the story-line of the narrative demanded them to be said that way, the rules of Greek grammar permitted them, and/or they belonged to the author's stylistic repertoire.

In the case of the *Donation of Constantine*, described above, the most convincing aspects of Valla's argument relied on the recognition of discrepancies and inconsistencies in the document that did not fit the time frame in which it presented itself as originating. Such observations have become the traditional way for challenging the dating of a document—and also for identifying forgeries.[85] The issue of forgery arises because the text has presented itself as something quite clearly it cannot be. The logic of the method is virtually irrefutable. In the case of the *Letter to Theodore*, however, the appeal to prove forgery is to excessive consistency,[86] which is a methodological reversal of how we usually argue in the guild, as I suggested in the case of Mark 5:35–43 above. Consistency of style, vocabulary, and syntax are regarded as the signature of a given writer. Interpolations into a text, on the other hand, are usually identified by variations from a given writer's distinctive literary signature.

---

85. It was even used in antiquity, as noted by Anthony Grafton, *Forgers and Critics*, 19–20. Galen happened to be in the area of Rome having the largest concentration of book sellers and overheard an argument over a certain book which bore the title *Galen the Doctor*. The debate concerned whether Galen had written the book or someone else had done so using Galen's name. Someone had purchased the book under the impression that Galen was the author. "On reading the first two lines he immediately tore up the inscription, saying simply, 'This is not Galen's language—the title is false.' Now, the man in question had been schooled in the fundamental early education which Greek children always used to be given by teachers of grammar and rhetoric" (Galen, *Selected Works*, 3; for the text see *Galaudi Galeni Pergameni*, 91). Grafton gives another example of sorting out a forgery attributed to Hippocrates; it must surely be a forgery because it contains certain technical terms not used by Hippocrates and other ancient doctors: "Those words, Galen concludes, must come from recent doctors who did not know the ancient style" (*Forgers and Critics*, 20).

86. My thanks to Charles W. Hedrick Jr. for pointing out this way of stating the distinction.

Ancient Gospel or Modern Forgery?
An Early Social Context for an Imitation of Mark[87]

At the very least the longer excerpt from *Secret Mark* comprises a completely new event not found in the canonical gospel, but is nevertheless written in canonical Mark's characteristic style and utilizes certain phrases that can be found with variations elsewhere in canonical Mark, as well as in other texts. The incident is also connected to certain other events in the narrative of canonical Mark.[88] So the author, whoever it may have been, is clearly thoroughly informed on Mark, including Markan style, plot, and phraseology.

The longer segment of *Secret Mark* in the *Letter to Theodore* is the sort of narrative that might have been produced by someone trained in a Greco-Roman school,[89] where great use was made of imitation (μίμησις; *imitatio*) for learning. Students were taught to imitate the literary classics in order to improve their own speaking and writing skills.[90] The written models they were given to imitate were authors whose works were the clearest in style and the most intelligible. Students were encouraged to imitate the "chief excellencies"[91] of these writers and speakers.

In book four of the first-century *Rhetorica ad Herennium* the anonymous author provides the "oldest systematic treatment of style in Latin, indeed the oldest extant inquiry into the subject since Aristotle."[92] He notes that all the faculties necessary for becoming a successful public speaker can be acquired "by three means: Theory, Imitation, and Practice. By theory is meant a set of rules that provide a definite method and system of speaking. Imitation stimulates us to attain in accordance with a studied method, the effectiveness of certain models in speaking. Practice

---

87. For this description I have drawn from Clark, *Rhetoric in Greco-Roman Education*; see his chapter on "Imitation," 144–76. For a shorter version see Clark, "Imitation: Theory and Practice in Roman Rhetoric." See also McKeon, "Literary Criticism and the Concept of Imitation in Antiquity," particularly 26–29.

88. See Meyer, "The Youth in Secret Mark and the Beloved Disciple in John," 97–98; and for the fuller treatment of his thesis, see Meyer, "The Youth in the *Secret Gospel of Mark*," 138–49.

89. For a brief overview of the Greco-Roman system of education, see Hock, "Writing in the Greco-Roman World."

90. For example, Lucian, *Hist. Conscr.*, says: "the best writer of history comes equipped with these two supreme qualities: political understanding and power of expression; . . . power of expression may come through a deal of practice, continued toil and emulation (ζῆλος) of the ancients." See Clark, "Imitation," 12–15.

91. Ibid., 18–19.

92. Cicero, *Ad C. Herennium*, xx.

is assiduous exercise and experience in speaking" (I.ii.3). One of those faculties that can be acquired through these studied methods is Style, which "is the adaptation of suitable words and sentences to the matter devised" (I.ii.3). In the classroom, the teacher will call on a student to read, and then interject as appropriate to point out aspects of the style of the model to be imitated:

> He will emphasize the appropriateness, elegance or sublimity of particular words, will indicate where the amplification of the theme is deserving of praise and where there is virtue in a diminuendo; and will call attention to the brilliant metaphors, figures of speech and passages combining smoothness and polish with a general impression of manly vigor. (Quintilian, *Inst.*, II.v.9)[93]

And in the case of faulty models, he will "point out how many expressions in them are inappropriate, obscure, high-flown, groveling, mean, extravagant or effeminate . . ." (Quintilian, *Inst.*, II.v.10).

Exercises in the schools used the following methods: learning by heart, paraphrase, and translation.[94] Learning the model by heart imprinted the model on the mind, familiarized the students with the style of the author, and gave them a resource for reproducing the striking phrases of the model:[95]

> For it is a better exercise for the memory to learn the words of others than it is to learn one's own, and those who have practiced this far harder task will find no difficulty in committing to memory their own compositions with which they are already familiar. Further they will form an intimate acquaintance with the best writings, will carry their models with them and unconsciously reproduce the style of the speech which has been impressed upon the memory. They will have a plentiful and choice vocabulary and a command of artistic structure and a supply of figures which will not have to be hunted for, but will offer themselves spontaneously from the treasure-house, if I may so call it, in which they are stored. In addition they will be in the agreeable position of being able to quote the happy sayings of

---

93. Quintilian, *The Institutio Oratoria of Quintilian.*

94. Clark, "Imitation," 18–20.

95. See Clark, *Rhetoric*, 177–212, on the elementary exercises (*progymnasmata*) in the schools.

the various authors, a power which they will find most useful in the courts. (Quintilian, *Inst.*, II.vii.2-4)[96]

The second exercise, translation (in the case of Roman education: from Greek to Latin) gave the student practice in becoming familiar with the judicious use of words:

> By following this practice I gained the advantage, that while I rendered into Latin what I had read in Greek, I not only used the best words, and yet such as were of common occurrence, but also formed some new words by imitation, which would be new to our countrymen, taking care, however, that they were appropriate. (Cicero, *De or.*, I.xxxiv.155)[97]

Paraphrase, the third exercise, required the student to memorize parts of the model and then expound on the same subject, only using different words. Cicero in later life abandoned the practice, since, he thought, it was not productive. He opted instead to translate the Greek model freely rather than paraphrasing (*De or.*, I.xxxiv.154-55). But Quintilian thought the practice was very beneficial for students, particularly for paraphrasing Latin poets into prose:

> For the lofty inspiration of verse serves to elevate the orator's style and the bold license of poetic language does not preclude our attempting to render the same words in the language natural to prose. Nay, we may add the vigor of oratory to the thoughts expressed by the poet, make good his omissions, and prune his diffuseness. But I would not have paraphrase restrict itself to the bare interpretation of the original: its duty is to rather rival and vie with the original in the expression of the same thoughts ... For it is always possible that we may discover expressions which are an improvement on those which have already been used ... Further, the exercise is valuable in virtue of its difficulty; and again there is no better way of acquiring a thorough understanding of the greatest authors. For, instead of running a careless eye over their writings, we handle each separate phrase and are forced to give it close examination and we come to realize the greatness of their excellence from the very fact that we cannot imitate them. (*Inst.*, X.v.4-8)

---

96. Clark's translation ("Imitation," 19) is different at places. For example: "They will have at command, moreover, an abundance of the best words, phrases, and figures ..."

97. Clark's translation, "Imitation," 19.

Pliny, in fact, suggests that when you have an author sufficiently in mind, you should become his rival "and write something on the same topic; then compare your performance and his, and minutely examine in what points either you or he most happily succeeded... You may sometimes venture to pick out and try to emulate the most shining passage of an author" (*Ep.* VII.ix).[98]

In the earliest extant handbook of elementary exercises (ca. 100 CE) Aelius Theon said that the *progymnasmata* were "absolutely necessary, not only for those who intend to be orators but also if someone wants to be a poet or prosewriter, or if he wants to acquire facility with some other form of writing. For these exercises are, so to speak, the foundation stones for every form of writing."[99] Here is a statement by the grammarian Dionysius Thrax (ca. 100 BCE) on what and how grammarians taught in Greco-Roman antiquity:

> *Grammatiké* [grammar in the broad sense of a grammarian's expertise] is an *empeiria* ("acquired expertise") of the general usage of poets and prose writers. It has six parts: first, accurate reading with due regard for the prosody; second, explanation of the literary devises contained; third, the provision of notes on phraseology and subject matter; fourth, the discovery of etymology; fifth, the working out of analogical regularities; sixth, the critical study of literature, which is the finest part of the "*techné*" ("art").[100]

Students coming out of such a system of education are thought to be "writers who could compose in a number of genres, who knew the appropriate style for each and could enhance their style by imitating the great prose writers..."[101]

> In the school of the grammarian, a student had learned to scrutinize the text of an author, isolating its most minute characteristics, often to the point of distorting its overall message and beauty. On the whole, however, a text and its authority were accepted without discussion and were incorporated into an immutable patrimony of knowledge through reading and memorization. Imitation of literary models was at the core of

---

98. Pliny, *Letters*, cited in Clark, "Imitation," 21.

99. From Butts, "Progymnasmata of Theon," 155–56.

100. As quoted in Cribiore, *Gymnastics of the Mind*, 185; see her discussion of how "grammar" was taught, 185–219.

101. Hock, "Writing in the Greco-Roman World," 3.

> a program in rhetoric: through close reading of the texts, it became possible to assimilate vocabulary, style, and organization of the elements of discourse.[102]

As an aside, it is worth noting that one may infer the same rigorous program of study was required by those who used the Bodmer Papyri, where the Greek classics were studied along with Christian religious texts. The setting for the Bodmer manuscripts is described either as a Christian school located at Panopolis (Akhmim)[103] or as a scriptorium located further south at the site of the Pachomian monastery at Pbau in the Panopolite Nome.[104] The texts in the collection range from the second century CE to the fourth/fifth century.[105]

How successful the students were in assimilating the skills of their models is a fair question. In large part the degree of success depended on the abilities of the teacher and the individual students. While it is dangerous to generalize on this question, it appears that sometimes the students achieved a high degree of ability in imitation of their models. Here is one case in point from the School of Libanius in fourth-century CE Antioch. Libanius was a teacher of rhetoric and achieved a wide reputation in letters in the ancient Greek world.[106] Raffaella Cribiore describes the success of teachers in inculcating the best features of the model in this way:

> A student's imitation, which resulted in works that echoed those of his teacher, was the most conclusive proof of his attendance [at the school]. Teachers "begot" their students, who fulfilled their hopes by "begetting" in turn work that reflected their teachers.' If a student's work was better received than his own, a teacher's identification with his "son" sweetened the defeat ... The stylistic similarities in the works of sophists and their students were sometimes so compelling that an audience had trouble attributing them, as letter 125 [i.e., of the Libanius collection] shows. When Libanius presented to different audiences a speech of his former student Leontius, their reaction (did the

---

102. Cribiore, *Gymnastics of the Mind*, 225.

103. Ibid., 200. Cribiore thinks that it is a Christian school because of the discovery of an elementary rhetorical exercise, an "exercise of impersonation," in the *Codex of Visions* (P. Bod. XXIX–XXXVIII). On the exercise of impersonation see ibid., 228–29.

104. See Pietersma, "Bodmer Papyri."

105. Ibid., 766.

106. Browning, "Libanius," 853.

student appropriate a speech of his teacher?) brought him such delight that he ended up considering it his.[107]

Here are excerpts from Libanius' letter to his student Leontius (letter 125 in the quotation above, as translated by Cribiore). Libanius is commenting on a letter just received from Leontius:

> [S]ome people came bringing us a beautiful oration of yours, or, if you wish of mine. This is in fact, as I hear, what people said in the lecture room where you are, and quite rightly so: it is so similar to those that I composed . . . When I thought there was a good opportunity, I brought this oration to another lecture room, right here, and it was exactly as before: people made the same loud remarks and were equally stirred. Someone even shared the same suspicions that arose among you, that is, that Leontius appropriated what was mine, and that the speech was made here, but delivered there. There is much, in fact, that can deceive. Pleased with you and myself, I was also pleased with the students who took the papyrus and claimed the oration their property: they wished to get it and own it, and do own it after getting it.[108]

What I am arguing by this all too brief (and perhaps redundant for most readers[109]) overview of literary imitation as a learning tool in Greco-Roman schools is that students were trained in precisely those literary sensitivities and technical skills that would be necessary in order to produce the expansions to original Mark found in the *Letter to Theodore*. It does not appear, from a glance at the secondary literature, that this social context has been seriously considered as the matrix out of which the longer addition to the Gospel of Mark may have come—even though "imitation" was suggested as a reason for the similarity between *Secret Mark* and original Mark by Smith[110] and Brown.[111]

---

107. Cribiore, *School of Libanius*, 142. My thanks to Charles W. Hedrick Jr. for pointing out this passage to me.

108. Cited in ibid., 289–90.

109. In the sense that it is common knowledge for the classicist.

110. Smith, *Clement of Alexandria*, 144.

111. Brown, *Mark's Other Gospel*, 225–27.

Ancient Gospel or Modern Forgery?

CONCLUSION

I have long been inclined to regard the excerpts from *Secret Mark* quoted in the *Letter to Theodore* in the same way I have regarded the traditional longer endings to the canonical gospel—they are expansions of Mark by later editors.[112] The manuscript evidence for the traditional longer ending is the late fourth century,[113] but scholars tend to regard its composition as early as the first half of the second century.[114] If Mark's gospel originally ended at 16:8, as conventional wisdom thinks,[115] then some manuscripts of Mark have simply been expanded to correct what must have been seen as an unfortunate and ineffective way of ending the gospel.

In a similar way, for whatever reason,[116] on the basis of a close reading of the text of canonical Mark, some enterprising ancient (with skills developed in a Greco-Roman school), created *Secret Mark* after noting the logical gap between canonical Mark 10:46a and 10:46b, where nothing happens between Jesus entering Jericho and leaving Jericho, and the disconnect in the itinerary of Jesus—in 10:1 he goes over the Jordan River (to the east bank) and in 10:32 he on the way going to Jerusalem, but in 10:46a he is suddenly in Jericho back on the west side of the Jordan with no mention made of him crossing back over from the east bank to the west bank. Our hypothetical close reader solves this particular problem by adding the incident in *Secret Mark* 1 between canonical Mark 10:34 and 10:35. In *Secret Mark* 1 Jesus comes to Bethany beyond the Jordan; then, at the conclusion of the incident Jesus returns to the west bank of the Jordan and comes to Jericho. Finally, our hypothetical close reader exploits the logical gap between Mark 10:46a and 10:46b by adding the incident in *Secret Mark* 2.[117]

---

112. The Cameron-Koester theory is that canonical Mark is actually a "purified" version of *Secret Mark* from which elements of the arcane teaching have been removed: Cameron, ed., *The Other Gospels*, 69; Koester, "History and Development of Mark's Gospel," 57.

113. Metzger, *Textual Commentary*, 103–4.

114. Lane, *The Gospel according to Mark*, 605.

115. For a different view see Farmer, *The Last Twelve Verses of Mark*.

116. Emendations to texts, though perhaps the redactor may not think of it in that way, is forgery, since they falsely attribute to a writer something that is not his/her composition. There are many reasons why texts may be forged in antiquity, and attempts to assign reasons for them is less than an exact science; see Metzger, "Literary Forgeries and Canonical Pseudepigrapha."

117. On *Secret Mark*'s resolution of these two gaps, see Brown, "Bethany beyond the Jordan."

This explanation, based on the extensive use of imitation in Greco-Roman schools, is at least as plausible as Morton Smith forging the *Letter to Theodore*—and I would say, because of the failure to prove that the text is a modern forgery, even more so. What gives me pause in completely embracing this solution, however, is the following: The examples I have cited for early emendations to the conclusion of canonical Mark (i.e., the longer endings) are clearly less than informed about Markan style, vocabulary, phraseology, and subject matter,[118] and that obvious datum raises another equally plausible solution: Mark later emended his own text—just as Clement said!

One of the concerns that the historian has about newly discovered texts is this: is there confirmation that the text was known in antiquity? (see Goodenough's comments at n. 34 above). A longer Gospel of Mark is not mentioned, so far as I know, elsewhere in antiquity, but there is an interesting overlap between canonical Mark, *Secret Mark* 1, and the Carpocrations. The overlap lies in the *situation* depicted in *Secret Mark* 1, where Jesus is described as meeting, presumably privately, with the young man who was raised from the dead, and instructing him in the mystery of the kingdom of God (III.6–10). This private teaching context is similar to Mark 4:34 (see also Mark 10:10; 13:3; 14:17), where Jesus taught his disciples privately. It is also found in a description of Irenaeus (*Haer.* 25.5) about how the Carpocratians portrayed Jesus instructing his followers. He taught them privately: "And in their writings it is so written and they explain like this: that Jesus, speaking in a mystery, spoke privately with his disciples and apostles and charged them to pass these things on to those who are worthy and to those who are persuaded."[119] Apparently "these things" that are to be passed on, according to Irenaeus, are the Carpocratian teachings and practices that Irenaeus described earlier (*Haer.* 25.1–4).

At this point, it seems to me that two equally plausible options exist for explaining the previously unknown pericopae cited in Clement's letter: Clement's quotations are either excellent second-/third-century additions to the Gospel of Mark made by an ancient editor fully knowledgeable about Mark's narrative, language, syntax, and style, or they are first-century additions to the gospel in "Mark's" own hand—they fit the gospel just that well.

118. Lane, *Mark*, 604; Taylor, *The Gospel according to St. Mark*, 610–14.

119. Völker, ed., *Quellen zur Geschichte der Christlichen Gnosis*, 38. The Greek text reads: ἐν δὲ τοῖς συγγράμμασιν αὐτῶν οὕτως ἀναγέγραπται καὶ αὐτοὶ οὕτως ἐξηγοῦνται, τὸν Ἰησοῦν λέγοντες ἐν μυστηρίῳ τοῖς μαθηταῖς αὐτοῦ καὶ ἀποστόλοις κατ' ἰδίαν λελαληκέναι καὶ αὐτοὺς ἀξιῶσαι, τοῖς ἀξίοις καὶ τοῖς πειθομένοις ταῦτα παραδιδόναι.

Ancient Gospel or Modern Forgery?

APPENDIX: INTERVIEW WITH AGAMEMNON TSELIKAS

This interview with Agamemnon Tselikas took place at his office on P. Skouse 3 in Athens, Greece on Thursday 30 September 2010. The subject of the interview was the *Letter to Theodore* containing excerpts from a *Secret/Mystic Gospel of Mark*. Professor Tselikas is Director of the Centre for History and Paleography of the National Bank of Greece Cultural Foundation. He is also a member of the Advisory Panel for St. Catherine's Monastery through Legatus. The data in the interview has not been approved by Professor Tselikas. The material in brackets constitutes my interpretation and understanding of Professor Tselikas's comments. I visited with Professor Tselikas for 2.5 hours (10:00 am–12:30 pm). He basically "talked" and here and there I interrupted with a question. My notes were taken as lecture notes on a yellow pad. The notes were then transcribed partly in the afternoon of the same day and partly the following morning.

Per Tselikas:

1. Aristarchos is the current librarian of the Greek Orthodox Patriarchate in Jerusalem. Kallistos Dourvas, who was the former librarian of the Patriarchate library, is no longer Parish Priest at the Church of *Eisodia tes Theotokou*, located in the Plateia Karaiskaki in Ano Glyfada near Athens but has been transferred to somewhere in Macedonia.

2. According to Aristarchos, the Patriarchate has no interest in this issue [*i.e., in finding the missing folios of the Letter to Theodore*]. They [the Patriarchate] are only interested (in such things as) Gospels and the Fathers of the Church (patristic literature). But should the missing folios be found that would be fine with the Patriarchate [*in other words, what I understand is that the Patriarchate has no interest one way or the other in the Letter to Theodore*]. When Professor Tselikas was at the library during its recent renovation he went through the holdings of the library but did not find the folios [*although he was looking for them*]. Professor Tselikas feels himself to have the confidence of the Patriarchate in the work that he is doing in the library. He has made numerous friends among the staff and feels himself to be a member of the Patriarchate family. He reports that the Patriarchate

is very open to the search for the folios. [*But finding them is not a concern of the Patriarchate*].

3. Professor Tselikas checked [*Smith's publication*] to see what kind of manuscripts Smith had been cataloguing [*he referred me to the article by Smith "Notes on Collections of Manuscripts in Greece"; he pulled the volume off the shelf and photocopied a copy for me; in the article Smith records the manuscripts in which he was interested in monasteries at Cephalonia, Dimitsane, Skiathos*, Ἱερὰ Μονὴ τοῦ Εὐαγγελισμοῦ , *the Library of the Rev. George Rigas*, Ἐκκλησία τῶν τριῶν ἱεραρχῶν, *Yannina; Tselikas himself has visited these monasteries*]. Tselikas added that Smith has visited many monasteries and checked their libraries.

4. [*Shortly before Smith made these visits to the monasteries in 1951– 1952, Greece had been involved in a civil war (1946–1949). The war was fought between the Greek governmental army, backed by the United Kingdom and the United States, against the Democratic Army of Greece, the military branch of the Greek Communist Party backed by Bulgaria, Yugoslavia, and Albania*]. There were many secret agents from England[, the United States,] and other countries working throughout Greece [*around this time*]. Tselikas asks, was Smith involved in this [*secret agent*] activity as well [*while on his visits to monasteries and libraries in Greece*]? Tselikas himself was in Kefalonia in 1948 to make a list of monastic manuscripts.

5. Tselikas says that Aristarchos (the current librarian of the Greek Patriarchate) reported to him that Smith just wanted to "represent himself" and was not really interested in doing scientific work. When Smith was in the monastery [*I understood that it was the library at Mar Saba*], he did not make a good impression on the monks. For the monks at Hagios Sabbas [*Mar Saba*] this whole business involving the *Letter to Theodore* is closed. Because Smith created a flap [*with his publications*] the Patriarchate found it necessary to [*alas, I have nothing in my notes at this point and no memory of what he said, but it was probably to have the folios of the Letter to Theodore brought to the Patriarchate*].

6. When Tselikas searched the Patriarchate he searched the materials one by one [*but did not find the folios*].

7. From the perspective of philology, the *Letter to Theodore* has problems with it. His impression of the letter from his own reading of the Gospels was that someone had taken material from the Gospels [*here*

and there] and made a new text [*implying that this is what we have in the Letter to Theodore*] but he did not verify this impression [*by making a detailed analysis*].

8. He is confident that the folios actually existed at one time in the Voss book by comparing the quality of its paper [*from photos, I assume*] with other manuscripts.

9. If the *Letter to Theodore* was a copy of an eighteenth-century original there should have been a copy of the original [*from which it was copied*] in a monastery someplace [*since copyists only work from an original*]. He thinks that the contents of the monasteries and libraries are well documented for the eighteenth-century.

10. [*From memory and not in my first set of notes:*] He adds that it is, of course, possible that it is a new discovery since new discoveries are made all the time. We (i.e., people in his field) know this happens—as the *Gospel of Judas* shows, for example; Judas is a case in point.

11. But if a copyist did make this copy (of the *Letter to Theodore*), why did he stop writing when he did? There is still a half of page left to occupy more text [*which one would presume, was in the original being copied*].

12. [*Another problem is*] the style of the letter. It does not accord with the style of letters written in the eighteenth century. [*I asked what was wrong with the style of the letter; he answered*] the style of the letter is mixed.

13. Paleographically there are problems with the letter. The original folios must have had very small lines and hence very small letters. Nevertheless, the letter does fit with the handwriting of the last years of the seventeenth century and the first years of the eighteenth century. The scribe who wrote the letter wrote in the style of the late seventeenth century and early eighteenth century, but when you observe the *ductus* of the letters many letters are not written in the usual direction of the *ductus* of the letters made by Greek copyists who were trained to write in this period. It is impossible that some of the letters in the *Letter to Theodore* were written by a Greek hand of the period. For example, the tau is not written with ligatures.

14. This raises the question: is the copyist a Greek or not a Greek? It is very clear when a Greek copyist writes Greek. It is easy to recognize. Even the examples of Smith's Greek are clearly not written by a

Greek—and he adds [*speaking directly to me*] even your handwriting is easy to spot as not having been written by a Greek.

15. [*So he asks rhetorically*] who could imitate this style of handwriting? What can you imagine to answer this question? [*Nothing presents itself as a reasonable answer—so he concludes*] someone forged the letter in the modern period. Tselikas is convinced that it is a modern forgery. So who made the forgery, he asks?

16. Was it made in a monastery or outside a monastery? The forgery must have been made by someone after the end of the seventeenth century. In the last years of the seventeenth century Dosithios [*or Chrisanthos?*] rebuilt the monastery [of Mar Saba]. There were only a few monks at Mar Saba during this period and only a few involved in copying books. They would only have been interested in producing liturgical [*and Bible?*] texts for use in the churches. [*Because of this*] it is impossible for a monk in the monastery at this time to have written the folios of the *Letter to Theodore*.

17. Had there been an original manuscript at the monastery [*which, for some reason, we don't have*] from which a copyist made the folios of the *Letter to Theodore*, that monk must have copied other manuscripts as well, but Tselikas found no other similar hands at Mar Saba or at the Patriarchate to match the handwriting of the *Letter to Theodore*. He found nothing like the Theodore hand, although there were other hands that produced multiple manuscripts.

18. In the library at Mar Saba he found a known edition of the works of Clement (French, he thinks, in an edition of 1600, or so). This volume, however, did not have a copy of the *Letter to Theodore* and he asks, why did the scribe not copy the *Letter to Theodore* in this collection of the writings of Clement, but instead copied it into a collection of the writings of Ignatius? One answer may be that the paper of the Clement volume was not good enough. With the passing of time the pages of the Clement volume became brown and the paper was too thin to accept the writing. The Clement volume was a larger volume [*i.e., I gather bigger than the Voss volume; I am not sure what his point was with the size of the volume*].

19. In Tselikas's research in locating old catalogues of monastery libraries, he consulted the three catalogues of Mar Saba [*he showed me images of the covers of the catalogues of Mar Saba*]. The catalogues of Mar Saba contained an entry for the Clement volume, but not for the

Ignatius volume of Voss. There is no mention of the Voss volume in any of the three catalogues. The three catalogues of Mar Saba list the acquisitions before around 1925.

20. Perhaps one could say that the reason that the volume is not in a catalogue is because the Voss book was missing its front matter on which would have been placed the monastery stamp of possession [*i.e., indicating its acquisition by the monastery*]. [*I think he is implying that they would not have known how to list the Voss volume, since it is lacking its title page*].

21. Now [*with this background*] it is easy to see that the Voss book came into the library after 1925 [*i.e., after the catalogues were no longer being kept by the staff was my understanding*].

22. Now, he asks, who could import a book into the library? The answer is, of course, uncertain: one cannot say whether it was Morton Smith or someone else who put the volume there.

23. It was not easy for Smith [*to gain access*] and to stay at the monasteries he visited throughout Greece. [*Many of them are physically difficult to access because of their remote position*]. Kefalonia, for example, had only a small difficult-to-find trail leading to the monastery.

24. The visits of Smith [*the earliest I think in 1941*] took place during the English administration of the area even before the state of Israel [*1948*] was created. One can ask if the young Morton Smith [*I think he was about 33 years at this time*] was so curious about the ascetic lifestyle of the monk? He adds, someone must check his motivation for making this circle of monasteries and libraries. All travelers must have the permission of British and the federal government [*Greek or U.S.?*]. It would have been easy for him to have passed along information about the Middle East because afterward was the war between Israel and the British [*I think he means the Arab-Israeli conflict in 1947–1948 culminating in the establishment of the Jewish State*].

25. Tselikas has on his computer copies of two letters, which he showed me, of Smith requesting permission to organize a committee to raise money to assist in creating a museum at the Patriarchate. He also has a copy of a letter from Patriarch Demitri (?) granting permission. Tselikas thinks that something else must be hidden in his behavior— he is not only interested in a museum. Did it have something to do

with his agency for the British? Patriarch Timotheus (?) was educated in England. [*I am not sure where he was going with this.*]

26. There are three or four manuscripts in Kefalonia whose Greek handwriting is similar to the *Letter to Theodore*. These manuscripts are all written in the last years of the seventeenth century and the early years of the eighteenth century. These manuscripts have many similarities to the *Letter to Theodore*. In one of these manuscripts there is a short note on how ink was made in the seventeenth and eighteenth centuries. Smith must have read this note, and could have even made a copy of it. [*Tselikas is implying, I think, that even if we found the folios of the Theodore letter, testing the ink would prove nothing about the age of the Letter to Theodore. This manuscript can be identified: It is Smith's listing #5 in the monastery at Kefalonia. So Smith saw the note for certain.*]

27. Tselikas thinks that the note about the making of ink is very important. [*The note about the making of ink can be found in Tselikas,* "χειρόγραφα," 187].

28. At this point I asked him who did he think forged the manuscript since he had made it pretty clear that he believed it to have been forged. He replied that it was at least 90% certain that Smith forged the document outside the monastery but did not know when the [*Voss volume containing the*] *Letter to Theodore* came into the monastery. Tselikas does not think that the *Letter to Theodore* is a new patristic text.

29. Simonides is the name of a modern forger who sold forgeries to the Library of France and the French were duped by them and bought the manuscripts. [*I gather he told me this to reassure me that forgeries are a common feature of the antiquities trade.*]

30. Smith must have had someone else with him when he visited these monasteries. Byzantine script is very difficult to read. And there are families of various hands. The more "modern" hands in the monasteries [*after the Byzantine period*] are even more difficult to read—not even the experts can read them.

31. Tselikas was at Skiathos in 1982 and reported that travel there [*many years after Smith's visit*] was very difficult. There was no electricity and it was hard even to see the manuscripts [*in order to read them*]. And Smith was there even earlier.

Ancient Gospel or Modern Forgery?

32. The Greek civil war was with the communists in 1947–1948 [but see my dates in #5 above]. [*After the war*], Tselikas says, the Bishop of Skiathos was exiled to Skiathos because he had sided with the communists. So why did Smith go to Skiathos rather than to one of the better-known monasteries? [*I assume that this point is to link Smith with more "cloak and dagger" type activities, but he did not make it clear.*]

3

Provenience
Reply to Charles Hedrick

Bruce Chilton

ANCIENT DOCUMENTS AND ARTIFACTS are not rarities. There are, for example, more than 5,000 pre-medieval manuscripts of the Greek New Testament in its original language. Each of them needs to be evaluated before it can be assessed for its readings, especially readings that introduce new material. Once that work has been done, scholars may read in a critical apparatus how one set of readings relates to others, and come to judgments regarding which to prefer on the basis of a sense, say, of the style or thought of a given work. Scholars of the New Testament are inclined to take for granted the groundwork that used to be called "lower criticism," which needs to be completed before inferences are drawn. But it is vital for the evidence to be evaluated as evidence before it is used in any historical or literary work. Taste is not a reliable criterion for authenticity.

Sometimes scholars confuse what should be the case with what is the case. Claims are frequently made for and against the authenticity of writings that have nothing to do with documentation, but reflect entrenched views of what the writing should say about a given topic. Discussion of Jesus, at any level, is likely to exacerbate the problem. For that reason, provenience is a key category that should be applied early in the assessment of evidence, prior to attempts to use the evidence as if it were valuable. Until we know where a writing has come from, we do not know its value, and should not make surmises on the basis of its assertions.

To illustrate this principle, I review here some cases in which I have been consulted in regard to documentary or epigraphic discoveries across a range of periods, cultures, and subjects. In each case, the soundest approach to the find has been guided by an informed understanding of its provenience. The results are often not clear-cut determinations of authenticity or forgery. Provenience sometimes shows there are possibilities between those extremes, and often simply demands more information than we have to hand. I review the cases in reverse chronological order, according to the alleged date of the writing.

The first example comes from the archives of Bard College, a leather-bound set of pages labeled "George Washington's Manuscript Book of Prayers." The manuscript was identified in 1891 by A. Howard Clark, curator at the National Museum (later known as the Smithsonian), and Lawrence Washington, who wrote, "the Prayers were found in a case in my library with a number of papers in Washington's handwriting (among them the letter to his brother Lawrence, No. 40 in the catalogue) which I inherited from my father, Col. John Augustine Washington, the last private owner of Mt. Vernon."[1]

No reason was found to dispute the discovery, and a trustee of Bard College purchased it to hold on behalf of the Episcopal Church (in which Washington had served as a vestryman). The handwriting became and remains a contentious issue. Further, the case that Lawrence Washington opened in 1891 was not *in situ* at Mount Vernon, but had been in storage and transit for the better part of a century.

No signature appears on the manuscript. Was it written by Washington, or rather for Washington? Did he compose or copy it, or was that the work of a member of his household, or one of the many visitors to Mount Vernon during the general's life? Was it deposited in the case after Washington's death? Did Lawrence Washington connive in a forgery? In the face of so many questions, prompted by basic doubt about how precisely the manuscript came to be in its case, biographers have wisely not used it as evidence. Ron Chernow's recent biography, for example, does not mention "George Washington's Manuscript Book of Prayers."[2] In the

---

1. Lawrence Washington, letter to Williams Everts Benjamin, 12 September 1895, in the archives of the National Cathedral in Washington, DC.

2. Chernow, *Washington: A Life*.

absence of any categorical finding, after I transcribed the work and after visiting the archives of the National Cathedral in Washington in order to study correspondence relative to the prayers, I catalogued my description in the Library of my College.[3]

Perhaps when I read about that trunk being opened long after Washington's death, I should have been wary. Another trunk proved something of a family disappointment. My grandfather was an amateur archaeologist and historian with a keen interest in his own family. The Chilton family had married into the Voorhees family at the beginning of the nineteenth century, and it turns out that Lieutenant John Voorhees served at the Battle of Bunker Hill. Among my grandfather's papers, handed on to my father, were letters from Lieutenant Voorhees to members of his family, including his alleged eyewitness account from a combatant at Bunker Hill. On hot days in summer on Long Island, when conditions were too still for sailing, I transcribed some of the correspondence during my adolescence.

Later consultation with a historian, however, revealed a disturbing fact. The alleged eyewitness account agreed with broadsheets published at the time of the battle, as part of the propaganda of the Continental Congress. That was why it attributed retreat to confusion in regard to orders, rather than to a shortage of powder (a strategic weakness that had to be concealed, even at considerable cost). It is not impossible that Voorhees simply copied the party line in his letter, but other possibilities also need to be considered, and—as in the case of the Washington Prayers—finding manuscripts so distant from their point of origin provokes caution. In this case, my family decided to deposit the correspondence proper with the New Jersey Historical Society and the copied broadsheet with the Charlestown Historical Society, keeping duplicates for ourselves. The odds of coming to a conclusion in regards to the Voorhees Papers seem to me longer than those of determining the provenience of the Washington Prayers.

In one case, I made the initial identification of a find myself. While working at the Bibliothèque nationale in Paris, one hot afternoon I found myself a bit light-headed in the main Reading Room. I moved to the catalogue room of the manuscripts collection, where I knew there was a big window that could be opened. While enjoying a gentle breeze, I read some of the original, Latin catalogue, basically so as not to doze off.

---

3. Incentive for this work came from the previous Archivist, Annys Wilson; the present Archivist, Helene Tieger, fields inquiries regularly.

Ancient Gospel or Modern Forgery?

As I did so, I ran across a description that did not tally with the catalogue's entry as a Hebrew manuscript. It appeared rather to be an Aramaic Targum. When I ordered "HEBR. 75" and it came into my hands, I found a hitherto unknown, complete manuscript, with new readings and an innovative format, in handwriting I have identified as from the thirteenth century. Records at the Bibliothèque nationale indicate it was acquired in Aleppo in 1673 on behalf of Jean-Baptist Colbert, a major contributor to the Library. Owing to those records, the provenience of the manuscript was established and I wrote up this discovery for publication.[4] Since then, I have included its readings in my edition of the Isaiah Targum for the *Comprehensive Aramaic Lexicon*,[5] and the manuscript is now a standard part of the Targumic data base that is agreed internationally.

For the sake of economy, I would like briefly to refer to two controversial claims in which provenience has proven an issue and I have been consulted in some way, albeit tangentially.

When the National Geographic Society (NGS) brought out *The Gospel of Judas*,[6] I pointed out that their advertising was quite unlike the findings of their own consultants.[7] The importance of a Gnostic writing of 300 or 400 CE is skewed by claiming Judas as its author, and the theology of the document is totally obscured. In its release, the NGS repeatedly states that it has "authenticated" the document. Several news agencies have simply repeated those claims. But "authentic" turns out to be a slippery term as used by the NGS. No scholar associated with the find argues this is a first-century document, or that it derives from Judas. The release says the document was "copied down in Coptic probably around A.D. 300," although later that is changed to "let's say around the year 400." Not content with vapid claims of authenticity, the NGS goes on to claim that the *Gospel of Judas* gives "new insights into the disciple who betrayed Jesus." Nonetheless, it is fortunate that, despite the way the manuscript has been hyped, divided up, and carelessly stored, enough remains to say that it is a Gnostic writing.

In the case of the alleged ossuary of James, the brother of Jesus, fortune has been less kind. Because the owner of the ossuary did not adequately or promptly specify where it was discovered and how he acquired it, the possibility of forgery could not be excluded when a publicity

---

4. Chilton, "'HEBR. 75' in the Bibliothèque nationale."
5. Available online at: http://cal1.cn.huc.edu/.
6. Kasser, Wurst, et al., *The Gospel of Judas*.
7. Chilton, "'Gospel of Judas' Called an Authentic Fabrication."

campaign on behalf of the inscription's authenticity was launched in 2002. Several prominent scholars, some of them expert in epigraphy and some not, tried to talk their way around this problem. Their enthusiasm got to the point that a few of them tried to deny that there were inconsistencies in the style of the inscription, that the patina on the ossuary seemed irregular, and that for a Christian ossuary to call James "the brother of Jesus" and not "brother of the Lord (Jesus)" seemed odd. But the principal problem remained that any object whose provenience is unknown cannot be authenticated. The damage to the ossuary inflicted en route between Israel and the Royal Ontario Museum did nothing to encourage confidence in the professionalism of those concerned. Still, advocates of the ossuary enjoyed prominent media coverage. Perhaps that made them incautious in their judgments.[8]

In any case, an investigating panel of the Israel Antiquities Authority reported in June of 2003 that the patina inside the inscription itself did not correspond to the patina around the inscription. In effect, it appeared that the lettering had been cut through the weathering of the stone. In July the owner, Oded Golan, was arrested for fraud. Under the legal powers of the Israel Antiquities Authority, his residence and storage facility had been searched, and several ossuaries were discovered, as well as equipment for engraving, stencils of ancient letters, and dirt from excavations. In a bizarre twist, the "Ossuary of James" was found on a plank atop a toilet. One headline writer could not resist referring to its being "de-throned."[9]

After Golan's arrest, the Royal Ontario Museum put out the statement, "There is always a question of authenticity when objects do not come from a controlled archaeological excavation, as is the case with the James Ossuary."[10] True enough, but reading those words reminded me of my last contact with the Museum. They had invited me to a symposium on the ossuary on the occasion of their exhibition in connection with the 2002 Annual Meeting of the Society of Biblical Literature. I agreed, and they asked for a preliminary sense of my views. I laid out my questions in regard to provenience. The call ended cordially enough, but a few minutes later, the phone rang again: the Museum claimed that inviting me had been a mistake, since enough participants had been secured; my services on the panel were not required, after all. Oded Golan has nonetheless proven

---

8. See Byrne and McNary-Zak, eds., *Resurrecting the Brother of Jesus*.

9. Chilton, "Scholars, Journalists and the Ossuary"; Chilton, "Another Look at the James Ossuary."

10. Royal Ontario Museum, "Royal Ontario Museum Statement: Oded Golan's arrest/ James Ossuary."

Ancient Gospel or Modern Forgery?

resilient, determined, and thorough in his continued insistence upon the ossuary's authenticity.[11] In a legal case, the burden of proof lies with the prosecution; in historical assessment, the burden of proof lies with the assertion of authenticity, an assertion greatly weakened when provenience has not been established.

Sometimes a consideration of provenience does just the opposite of what you might expect. In the spring of 1988, a collector brought me a stone slab that he had purchased at an estate sale in Millbrook, New York. Although it is written in a Greek alphabet, its language is abbreviated Latin. After producing a diplomatic edition of the epitaph, I set about attempting to determine its provenience. The initial discoverer, Raffaele Garucci, had transcribed the inscription *in situ* in 1859, prior to its removal (according to a bookseller's label) in 1873. His transcription accorded precisely with the artifact, including the usage of an Aramaic word that had long been disputed. On the basis of this provenience, I wrote the find up for the *Jewish Quarterly Review*, and it is now an accepted example of ancient Jewish epitaphs.[12]

No such investigation at more than a century's distance from the moment of discovery was necessary in the case of the ossuary of Caiaphas. In that instance, the artifact with its two inscriptions was found and photographed *in situ*. Although complete certainty cannot be claimed that this Joseph Caiaphas was the high priest at the time of Jesus' death, the fact is that the New Testament knows him only as "Caiaphas," while Josephus calls him "Joseph Caiaphas." That fact, alone with the position and decoration of the ossuary, make its association with the high priest the most plausible finding.[13] Again, provenience proved a help.

The last case, before I compare issues of provenience in the case of Morton Smith's claims, alleges to be from an earlier decade still. In 2004 a granddaughter of Alfredo Farace, high-ranking civil servant in the Italian government during the early twentieth century, contacted me concerning what she called "Jesus' death certificate." The document, written in Italian, records Pilate's sentence of death. Its wording agrees with that of a sheepskin with Hebrew writing that was unearthed in 1580, and then published

---

11. See Golan, "The Authenticity of the James Ossuary and the Jehoash Tablet Inscriptions—Summary of Expert Trial Witnesses."

12. Chilton, "The Epitaph of Himerus from the Jewish Catacomb of the Appian Way"; Chilton, "The Epitaph of Himerus at Woodstock."

13. Specter, "Tomb May Hold the Bones of Priest Who Judged Jesus"; Chilton, *Rabbi Jesus*, 212–13.

in Spanish in 1583 by Rodrigo de Yepes.[14] Although de Yepes was accused of forgery, fragments of "The Sentence of Pilate" (as the document has come to be called) have been found from as early as the year 1200.[15] The copy that Alfredo Farace took down, however, is an Italian rendering of the Spanish text deposited in Naples, and represents, at the earliest, a medieval adaptation of the *Acts of Pilate* genre of the Byzantine period.

Provenience is not an abstract criterion that can be applied in the same way to each document or artifact. Unique features are often involved, as in the case of what some have styled the Mar Saba Clement. To begin with, the excerpt from what purports to be a letter of Clement to Theodore, although described by Smith as his discovery at Mar Saba, was actually found inside a Dutch volume published in 1646. Curiously, the volume is Isaac Voss's edition of Ignatius of Antioch, a work that played a key role in the discussion of Ignatian pseudepigraphy.[16]

Not only Morton Smith in 1958, but also Guy Stroumsa in a later visit to Mar Saba in 1976, established that the letter was written in the blank back pages of the volume.[17] Smith took black and white photos, and after Stroumsa's intervention photographs in color were arranged by Kallistos Dourvas. The Greek Patriarchate has, since Stroumsa's visit, cut the page from the volume, and keeps it separately.[18] The inability to examine the manuscript and test its ink is a problem, since otherwise it is impossible to confirm Smith's contention that the writing was done during the eighteenth century.[19]

Even with the question of when the writing was introduced into the volume foreclosed, we still may ask: when did Voss's edition arrive at Mar Saba? Who introduced it, and for what purpose? Was there already writing on the back pages? Stephen Carlson discusses annotations in the catalogue of the Library,[20] which may hold out some prospect that information in regard to the provenience of the volume, if not of the writing, is still available. That book is to Morton Smith's letter what the case from

---

14. See Lyell, *The Sentence of Pontius Pilate*.

15. My notes on the *Sentence* are in my files, for any further consultation with the family of Alfredo Farace. After that I will determine a use or place for them.

16. Voss, *Epistulae genuinae S. Ignatii Martyris*.

17. Stroumsa, "Comments on Charles Hedrick's Article: A Testimony."

18. See the discussion about the manuscript's current status in Hedrick and Olympiou, "Secret Mark."

19. See Ehrman, *Lost Christianities*, 67–89.

20. Carlson, *Gospel Hoax*, 36–39. See further Chilton, "Unmasking a False Gospel," 16. A longer version of this review of Carlson appears in *Review of Rabbinic Judaism*.

Ancient Gospel or Modern Forgery?

Mount Vernon is to the Washington Prayers. Neither the book nor the case closes the question, but they do provide orientation in the discussion of provenience.

In the case of the so-called *Secret Gospel of Mark*, however, the levels of question in regard to provenience are multiple. One might compare scholarly discussion to a shell game that has successfully hidden its pea since Morton Smith claimed in 1960 that he had found a letter quoting *Secret Mark* in the monastic library at Mar Saba. The shells are individually well wrought, and they are shifted around deftly. The letter was written on the end pages of a seventeenth-century volume, but it purports to be from the second-century theologian Clement of Alexandria. This "Clement" speaks of secret teaching that Mark promulgated in Alexandria after Peter's death in Rome, but he also and forcefully attacks the version of this secret gospel advocated by a group called the Carpocratians. And Smith enters the frame again to argue that what "Clement" most complains about is not the false, but the true Mark, and scholars such as John Dominic Crossan and Helmut Koester have championed *Secret Mark* as key to the editorial history of the canonical Gospel.[21]

Each of those claims amount to categorical assertions of provenience that are untested and very far from proven. We can begin by finding out where the book in which the letter was written came from. Until we can do that, we are not dealing with evidence, or even with a stalemate about evidence. We are dealing with an unverified claim, which may remain so for as long as some of the other cases briefly indicated here. Acknowledging uncertainty is not an admission of defeat, but a step in the direction of scholarship.

---

21. Crossan, *Four Other Gospels*, 91–124; Koester, *Ancient Christian Gospels*, 293–303.

4

Morton Smith and the *Secret Gospel of Mark*
Exploring the Grounds for Doubt

Craig A. Evans

IN 1958 MORTON SMITH (1915-1991) visited the Greek Orthodox Mar Saba Monastery in the Judean desert.[1] Among other things, he catalogued a number of old books and documents. At the 1960 annual meeting of the Society of Biblical Literature Smith announced that during his brief visit to Mar Saba he had found three pages of Greek written on the endpapers of a seventeenth-century edition of the letters of Ignatius.[2] These pages comprise a letter attributed to Clement of Alexandria (c. 150-215), in which a mystical, or secret, version of the Gospel of Mark is discussed. What makes the find controversial is that, in one of the passages quoted from this gospel, Jesus teaches a naked young man the "mystery of the kingdom

---

1. Established some 1500 years ago, the Mar Saba Monastery is one of the oldest continuing monasteries in the world. It is situated on the south bank of the Kidron Valley, approximately equidistant from Jerusalem to the west and the Dead Sea to the east. The name is derived from Saint Sabba (Greek: *Hagios Sabbas*; Arabic: Mar Saba), whose remains, it is believed, are preserved at the monastery. Smith visited in the summer, for three weeks.

2. Voss, *Epistolae genuinae S. Ignatii Martyris*.

of God." The passage, along with the discussion in the letter, could imply a homosexual encounter.

Smith published his find in two books, both released in 1973—one a lengthy and learned volume by Harvard University Press and the other a briefer, popular version by Harper & Row.[3] Almost immediately there were suspicions of a hoax. An early and penetrating review was written by Quentin Quesnell, who complained of the lack of testing of the manuscript and several other unanswered questions.[4] Although Smith shot back,[5] many scholars have expressed doubts about the find. In time, two camps formed. One camp contends that not only is the Clementine letter genuine but the longer version of Mark discussed in the letter actually existed and could be the original Mark; if so, this means the Gospel of Mark in today's New Testament is an abridged edition. The other camp either rejects outright the Clementine letter or regards as spurious its claim of a longer version of Mark.

If Morton Smith's Mar Saba find is genuine, then it truly is a significant discovery. At the very least we have recovered a lost letter of an important father of the church, Clement of Alexandria. The Mar Saba *Letter to Theodore*, then, would be the only surviving letter of Clement. This letter, moreover, adds to our knowledge of the Carpocratians, supplementing what Clement says about them elsewhere. Perhaps most important of all, we have evidence of a different, longer edition of the Gospel of Mark, in circulation at least as early as the second century. Accordingly, if genuine, Smith's discovery represents a significant contribution to New Testament and Patristic studies. But was his discovery genuine?

Recent studies have reignited the controversy surrounding the authenticity of Smith's find. Arguing on the basis of handwriting analysis and a number of coincidences, Stephen Carlson concluded in 2005 that the Clementine letter and its quotation and discussion of a longer version of Mark (a.k.a. *Secret Mark*) are a hoax and the hoaxer is Morton Smith.[6] The same year Carlson's book appeared, Scott Brown published his doctoral dissertation, in which he defends the authenticity of Smith's discovery and

---

3. Smith, *Clement of Alexandria and a Secret Gospel of Mark*; Smith, *Secret Gospel*. Smith supplies black and white photographs of the three pages of Greek text. For color photographs, see Hedrick and Olympiou, "Secret Mark."

4. Quesnell, "The Mar Saba Clementine." See also Musurillo, "Morton Smith's Secret Gospel." Musurillo too suspected the Mar Saba find was a modern forgery.

5. Smith, "On the Authenticity of the Mar Saba Letter of Clement." See the rejoinder by Quesnell, "A Reply to Morton Smith."

6. Carlson, *Gospel Hoax*.

offers several interpretations that differ from Smith's interpretation of the find.[7] In a book that appeared in 2007 Peter Jeffrey came to the conclusion reached by Carlson, though he pursued different lines of evidence and nuanced some of the overlapping points of the argument somewhat differently as well. Jeffrey believes he can find ecclesiastical and personal issues of importance to Smith echoed in various ways in the Clementine letter.[8] In 2007 Pierluigi Piovanelli also joined the debate. He too expresses doubts about the authenticity of the find.[9] Brown has responded to the books by Carlson and Jeffrey with lengthy and very negative reviews.[10] And in 2010 Francis Watson published a learned study that offers fresh arguments for concluding that Smith is indeed the author of the Clementine letter.[11]

The controversy has been such that, in recent annual meetings of the Society of Biblical Literature, special sessions have been convened to explore and debate the matter further. At one of these meetings Harvard alumnus and distinguished scholar of Gnosticism Birger Pearson stated that he now believes the Clementine letter to be a hoax.[12] Harvard alumna and distinguished Markan scholar Adela Yarbro Collins has also concluded that in all probability *Secret Mark* is a hoax.[13] However, Pearson's and Collins's distinguished Doktorvater Helmut Koester, who has made extensive use of Smith's find,[14] continues to regard the letter as genuine.

In recent issues of *Biblical Archaeology Review* the question of the authenticity of Morton Smith's controversial Mar Saba find has been revisited.[15] Hershel Shanks and some of the contributors argue that Morton

---

7. Brown, *Mark's Other Gospel*. The dissertation is "The More Spiritual Gospel."

8. Jeffery, *Secret Gospel of Mark Unveiled*. Jeffery contends that what is depicted in the Mar Saba Clementine "cannot be made to fit at any point in the history of the Alexandrian liturgy" (ibid., 90).

9. Piovanelli, "*L'Évangile Secret de Marc*."

10. Brown, "Factualizing the Folklore"; Brown, Review of *Secret Gospel of Mark Unveiled*, by Peter Jeffery. A second review, by J. Harold Ellens (*RBL*), is strongly supportive of Jeffery's book and critical of Brown's review. Also positive of Jeffery's study are the reviews by Webb in *JSHJ*; Foster in *ExpTim*; Harris, "A Bible Fantasy," in *Times Literary Supplement*; and Johnson in *Worship*.

11. Watson, "Beyond Suspicion."

12. Pearson's 2008 SBL presentation has been published as "The Secret Gospel of Mark."

13. See Collins, *Mark*, 486–93.

14. Koester, "History and Development of Mark's Gospel"; Koester, *Ancient Christian Gospels*, 293–303.

15. See the feature "'Secret Mark': A Modern Forgery?" in *BAR* 35.6 (2009). There are several essays on the topic in this issue of *BAR*: Hedrick, "An Amazing Discovery";

Smith was probably telling the truth, that he in fact did find three pages of Greek written in the back of an old book, and that he was not himself the author of these pages, nor was he party to their composition. In short, the late professor of ancient history at Columbia University was not in any way involved in a hoax.

Notwithstanding the position taken in *Biblical Archaeology Review*, several scholars remain quite skeptical of the authenticity of the Mar Saba find. I too remain skeptical, although as recently as fifteen years ago I assumed that the Clementine letter was genuine and that there may well have been a different edition of the Gospel of Mark circulating in the second century. So why now am I so skeptical, even after some recent and not insignificant support for the authenticity of the Mar Saba find?

THE AMUSING AGRAPHON

Let me explain my position by calling attention to an unusual study that appeared in *Catholic Biblical Quarterly* in 1950. Princeton University Associate Professor of Latin Paul Coleman-Norton published a leaf of Greek text that he says he found sandwiched between pages of an old Arabic book in a mosque in North Africa, where he was stationed in 1943 while serving in the US Army during World War II. Coleman-Norton tells us that he copied the Greek text and then left the mosque. Later he returned with a camera, hoping to make a photograph of the text and the old book in which it was found, but he was unable to do so. Eventually he was transferred and so never had another opportunity to see or photograph the text. A few years after the war Professor Coleman-Norton transcribed the text, translated it, and added a number of philological notes and comments. He submitted his brief study to Arthur Darby Nock, editor of the *Harvard Theological Review*, who forwarded it to Bruce Metzger for evaluation. Metzger recommended that the study not be published unless a photograph could be provided. Coleman-Norton next submitted the study to Philip Hyatt, editor of the *Journal of Biblical Literature*, who likewise forwarded it to Metzger for evaluation. Metzger again recommended that the study not be published unless a photograph could be provided. It was submitted to the *Journal of Religion* and was again rejected, this time by editor

---

Shanks, "Morton Smith—Forger"; Koester, "Was Morton Smith a Great Thespian and I a Complete Fool?"; Shanks, "Restoring a Dead Scholar's Reputation." Further discussion is found in Shanks, "First Person."

Amos Wilder. A year or so later the study appeared, as already mentioned, in *Catholic Biblical Quarterly*.[16]

Coleman-Norton's Greek text is an instance of what scholars call an agraphon, that is, a saying attributed to Jesus *not written* (Greek: *a-graph*) in the New Testament Gospels. Coleman-Norton calls this non-canonical saying an "amusing agraphon" and it is not hard to see why. After Jesus warns that the wicked will be cast into outer darkness, where they will weep and gnash their teeth (Matt 25:30), a thick-headed disciple asks Jesus how the toothless will be able to gnash their teeth. To this disciple Jesus replies, "Teeth will be provided."

I doubt many readers of Coleman-Norton's study have entertained the possibility that this agraphon might constitute an authentic utterance of Jesus. Coleman-Norton himself entertained the possibility but did not press it.[17] The question here concerns the authenticity of the find itself, not the authenticity of the humorous saying. In other words, did Coleman-Norton find an ancient text as he claims, or has he perpetrated a hoax?

Some twenty years after the publication of Coleman-Norton's study Bruce Metzger gave the presidential lecture at the 1971 annual meeting of the Society of Biblical Literature, titled "Literary Forgeries and Canonical Pseudepigrapha."[18] He began his address by discussing Coleman-Norton's study, declaring that he firmly believes that the text is a modern forgery and that the story of its being found in North Africa in 1943 is a hoax. Metzger takes this negative position because he remembers Coleman-Norton, years before the Second World War, regaling his Princeton students (of which Metzger was one) with a witticism in which Jesus assures his disciples that the damned who are toothless will receive a set of dentures so that in Hell they may weep and gnash their teeth.[19] Metzger's recommendation that the respective editors of the aforementioned journals require a photo was a delicate way of handling a potentially awkward situation. Instead of accusing Coleman-Norton, his former professor, of

---

16. Coleman-Norton, "An Amusing *Agraphon*."

17. Ibid., 444–45. As to the original of the agraphon Coleman-Norton could only think of two possibilities: "either an ancient wag has been at work here or the incident occurred substantially as recorded" (ibid., 444). Conspicuously absent is mention of a third possibility: a *modern* wag has been at work.

18. Metzger, "Literary Forgeries and Canonical Pseudepigrapha." More personal details will be found in Metzger, *Reminiscences of an Octogenarian*, 136–39.

19. The agraphon reads: "'Rabbi, how can these things be, if they be toothless?' And Jesus answered and said: 'O thou of little faith, trouble not thyself; if haply they will be lacking any, teeth will be provided'" (Coleman-Norton, "*Agraphon*," 443 n. 18).

Ancient Gospel or Modern Forgery?

perpetrating a hoax, he simply suggested to the journal editors that he provide evidence. Of course, Metzger knew that none could be provided. Unfortunately for *Catholic Biblical Quarterly*, the editor did not contact Metzger, and so Coleman-Norton's spurious study was published.

Metzger rightly regarded the amusing agraphon a modern forgery primarily because Coleman-Norton possessed knowledge of its distinctive elements (i.e., the problem of the toothless wicked and the punch line "teeth will be provided") *before making the discovery*. For detectives of forgeries and hoaxes this is the prime criterion: Is there evidence that the discoverer possessed knowledge of distinctive features of the discovery *before* the discovery was made? If the discoverer did possess such knowledge prior to the discovery, it is almost always assumed that forgery is involved.[20] A second, closely related criterion asks if the discovery reflects the interests of the discoverer, interests in evidence prior to the discovery? If it does, forgery is suspected.

To the best of my knowledge all competent biblical scholars agree with Metzger's judgment: Professor Coleman-Norton was the author of the amusing agraphon. He not only composed the Greek text, he also fabricated the entire story of finding a leaf of Greek inserted into an old book amongst old books in a mosque in North Africa while stationed there in 1943. None of it happened; the entire story is fiction.[21]

Coleman-Norton's fictional story of a find may owe its inspiration to another fiction, a novel published in 1940 entitled *The Mystery of Mar*

---

20. See Carlson, *Gospel Hoax*, 72, in reference to both Coleman-Norton and Smith.

21. For a review of other biblical hoaxes and forgeries, see Goodspeed, *Strange New Gospels*. For other examples, see Farrer, *Literary Forgeries*. Two of the forgeries reviewed by Goodspeed may be mentioned. One is known as *Acts 29*, supposedly translated by C. S. Sonnini, from a "Greek manuscript found in the Archives at Constantinople." Publisher T. G. Cole tells us that the text was found "interleaved in a copy of Sonnini's *Travels in Turkey and Greece* [sic], and purchased at the sale of the library and effects of the late Right Hon. Sir John Newport, Bart., in Ireland" (Goodspeed, 59). The alibi is clever, for Charles Sigisbert Sonnini (1751–1812) was a real person, who in fact published *Voyage en Grèce et en Turquie*, which appeared in English as *Travels in Greece and Turkey*. Cole's tale of a Greek text, probably composed in the nineteenth century by an adherent of the British-Israel movement, found "interleaved" in an old (genuine) book matches Coleman-Norton's story. Goodspeed also tells us of a long-lost *Second Book of Acts*, translated and published in 1904 by Kenneth Sylvan Guthrie (1871–1940), who published a number of books on Philo, Plotinus, and neo-Platonism. *Second Acts* narrates Paul's departure from Rome and return to Palestine. It is not clear what the original language was or where the text was supposedly found. Goodspeed (ibid., 101) rightly regards the work as a modern hoax, whose purpose is to prove that Jesus taught reincarnation.

Saba.[22] This story is set in Palestine in the late 1930s, with the European war approaching. To undermine the morale of the British Empire the Nazis plant a leaf of Greek text amongst the rare books in the Mar Saba Monastery's collection, a text that an honest British scholar would subsequently discover. The Greek text, dubbed the Shred of Nicodemus,[23] states that Nicodemus and Joseph of Arimathea removed the body of Jesus from the tomb and reburied it elsewhere. The implication is that Jesus was not resurrected after all; the empty tomb discovered Easter Sunday signified nothing. With faith in the resurrection dashed, the British would have little motivation and courage to fight the Nazis. Fortunately, the nefarious plot was exposed and the Greek leaf was demonstrated to be a forgery.

The Mystery of Mar Saba may well have provided Coleman-Norton with the scenario needed to introduce his spurious agraphon to the public (at least to a public somewhat wider than his Princeton classroom). Coleman-Norton chose North Africa, instead of Mar Saba, for the setting because that was where he was stationed in 1943. But the rest of the details are a match with the novel: Greek text, offering new material relating to Jesus, found in an old book amongst rare books in a religious establishment.

THE PROFESSOR WHO KNEW TOO MUCH

My brief summation of the novel *The Mystery of Mar Saba* probably brought to the minds of most readers Morton Smith's account of his discovery of three pages of Greek text penned in the back of an old book amongst a number of old and rare books and papers in a religious establishment, this time the very establishment and setting of the novel: the Mar Saba Monastery. In the real-life story the discovery is made by *Professor Morton*. In the novel the truth of the discovery is made by Scotland Yard inspector *Lord Moreton*. Just as the Greek text in the novel embarrassed the Christian Church (in supposedly proving that the resurrection did not take place), so Morton Smith's Greek text embarrassed the Christian Church (in supposedly hinting at Jesus' homosexual orientation).

As interesting as these parallels are, and there are more, what I find most troubling is that themes of interest to Professor Smith, as seen in his publications *before* the finding of the Clementine letter, are found in the Clementine letter. And these are not just themes of interest to Professor

---

22. Hunter, *Mystery of Mar Saba*. The book was reprinted numerous times on into the 1960s and 1970s.

23. See ibid., frontispiece, for facsimile and English "translation."

Smith; they are quite unusual themes and, apart from Professor Smith himself, they are themes advanced by no one else. In what follows two unusual themes will be explored: (1) The "mystery of the kingdom of God" and prohibited sex, and (2) Markan materials omitted from Mark that exhibit Johannine traits.

(1) In his doctoral dissertation, written in Hebrew and defended in 1944 and then published in English in 1951,[24] Professor Smith linked Mark 4:11 ("To you is given the mystery of the kingdom of God...") with secrecy and forbidden sexual activity:

> an important part of primitive Christianity was a secret doctrine which was revealed only to trusted members. Such a doctrine is suggested by the words put in the mouth of Jesus, speaking to his disciples: 'To you is given the mystery of the kingdom of God, but to those outside all things are in parables, that they may surely see and not perceive,' etc. . . . A similar distinction was recognized by the Tannaïm between material suitable for public teaching and that reserved for secret teaching, as we learn from Hagigah T 2.1 (233): 'The (passages of the Old Testament dealing with) forbidden sexual relationships are not to be expounded to three (at a time) . . .'[25]

I have quoted about one-half of a lengthy paragraph. It is part of Smith's discussion of human comprehension and what can and cannot be taught openly. The paragraph that has been partially quoted explores the idea that the early Church seems to have held to a doctrine of secrecy. Evidence of this, Smith thinks, is found in Mark 4:11, where Jesus explains to his disciples, "To you is given the mystery of the kingdom of God . . . ," and in Paul, who says that he and other Christian leaders "speak wisdom among the perfect [or mature] . . . the wisdom of God in a mystery" (1 Cor 2:6–7).[26] Following these two New Testament citations Smith suggests a comparison with the rabbinic distinction "between material suitable for public teaching and that reserved for secret teaching." The secret teaching

---

24. Smith, *Tannaitic Parallels*. Below the Preface (vii) Smith provides two dates: 1944 and 1950. The latter refers to the English version, which appeared in 1951 as noted. The 1944 date refers to the original Hebrew version of the dissertation, *Makbilot ben ha-Besorot le-sifrut ha-Tana'im* ("Parallels between the Gospels and the Literature of the Tannaim"). The doctoral degree was conferred in 1948.

25. Smith, *Tannaitic Parallels*, 155–56. See the discussion of this passage in Carlson, *Gospel Hoax*, 71–72. The phrase "not to be expounded to three" means not to expound the teaching to groups of people. Secret teaching may be taught to one or two.

26. Smith (*Tannaitic Parallels*, 156) references 1 Cor 2:1–6, but he actually quotes portions of 1 Cor 2:1–7.

includes forbidden sexual relationships and Ezekiel's vision of God's chariot throne. The paragraph concludes with a further comparison with the Torah, which according to the rabbis was to be taught openly, and the teaching of heretics, which was to be taught secretly. Smith believes the evangelists Mark and John edited and presented the teaching of Jesus in response to this rabbinic teaching.

Smith's linkage of the saying about the "mystery of the kingdom of God" (Mark 4:11) to secrecy and teaching regarding forbidden sexual relationships is to the best of my knowledge unique. Gospel scholars agree that Mark 4:11 fits awkwardly in its context and debate what the original meaning was. But only Smith links it to sex; I know of no commentator prior to the time of Smith (or after, for that matter) who has done this. Smith finds the linkage between secrecy and prohibited sex in the Tosefta tractate *Hagigah* 2.1, which discusses forbidden sexual relationships, as found in Lev 18:6–30.[27] Among these forbidden sexual relationships is homosexual activity (cf. Lev 18:22 "You shall not lie with a male as with a woman; it is an abomination").

In his 1955 review of Vincent Taylor's commentary on the Gospel of Mark,[28] Smith vigorously challenges Taylor's denial that Mark 4:11 envisioned secret rites.[29] Against Taylor, Smith reminds us that Mark represents Jesus "as teaching in secret and commanding secrecy on many occasions," which is based on the "recollection that Jesus (also for a wide variety of reasons) practiced secrecy."[30] The first part of Smith's statement will elicit no objection from those persuaded by William Wrede's interpretation of Mark (wherein the point of secrecy was to hide the messianic identity of

---

27. Although Smith references "Hagigah T 2.1," which is supposed to refer to the Tosefta (as explained in *Tannaitic Parallels*, xi), he seems actually to have quoted the parallel passage from the Mishnah—i.e., the first half of *m. Hag.* 2:1. It should be pointed out that *m. Hag.* 2:1 is partially quoted and expanded upon in *t. Hag.* 2.1–7. The latter passage is concerned with things that should be kept secret from the public. For English translation of this passage, see Neusner, *Tosefta*, 2:312. For an English translation of *m. Hag.* 2:1, see Danby, *Mishnah*, 212–13. That the rabbinic passages in the Mishnah and Tosefta are referencing Lev 18:6–30, see Danby, *Mishnah*, 212 n. 20; Neusner, *Tosefta*, 2:312.

28. Taylor, *Gospel according to St. Mark*; Smith, "Comments on Taylor's Commentary on Mark." Here as well as elsewhere I am indebted to Francis Watson's recent study, which I shall discuss more fully below.

29. Taylor, *Mark*, 255: "it means 'open secret' . . . There is no case in which it connotes secret rites or esoteric knowledge communicated to 'initiates.'"

30. Smith, "Comments," 29.

Jesus),[31] but the second part of Smith's statement is quite another matter. Jesus "practiced secrecy," we are told, "for a wide variety of reasons."[32] What could Smith have had in mind? Could one of those reasons have had to do with teaching regarding prohibited sexual activities, as perhaps hinted at in his dissertation? And as hinted at in subsequent publications, not to mention his remarkable discovery at Mar Saba?

In an article that appeared in March of 1958, just a few months before Smith visited Mar Saba, Smith once again mentions the *Hagigah* passage from the Tosefta. This time, however, he also mentions Clement of Alexandria and cites his work *Stromateis*.[33] This interesting article calls for a few more comments. Twice Smith mentions *Hagigah*, one time in reference to the story of the Jewish sage Aher, who "used the spiritual power acquired by his mystical experience to lead good Jews into heresy."[34] Smith mentions *Hagigah* a second time in reference to "the teaching about the throne of God," which was "to be kept most secret of all."[35] Smith adds that this teaching "quite possibly was not committed to writing." In a footnote to this final part of the statement Smith references Clement of Alexandria,[36] where in *Strom*. I.1.13-14 he discusses secrecy, the secret elements of Jesus' teaching, and how it is incumbent on him (Clement) to omit some of the teaching, and to impart what teachings he thinks he is permitted to impart cautiously, lest his readers "stumble by taking them in a wrong sense." Here we have echoed themes articulated in the paragraph from the 1951 dissertation quoted and discussed above.

To return to the interesting 1958 essay, Smith also talks about the initiate's union with his god. Smith speaks of magical prayers and Jewish mystics, whose favorite prayer was the Qedushah, all of which suggests that "the recitation of the Qedushah was conceived as a means of invoking the deity or a result of union with him."[37] In another context Smith speaks

---

31. Wrede, *Das Messiasgeheimnis in den Evangelien* (ET: *The Messianic Secret*).

32. Smith ("Comments," 29) criticizes the Messianic Secret hypothesis because it tries to explain all of the secrecy phenomena in reference to one motive: the secrecy of Jesus' messiahship. Smith believes that there were additional motives.

33. Smith, "The Image of God," at 507 n. 4 (for the reference to *Hagigah*) and n. 5 (for the reference to Clement of Alexandria and *Stromateis*). This passage is also discussed by Carlson, *Gospel Hoax*, 72.

34. Smith, "Image of God," 505 n. 1. Here the reference is to *t. Hag.* 2.3.

35. Ibid., 507. In n. 4 on this page Smith cites *t. Hag.* 2.1.

36. Ibid., 507 n. 5.

37. Ibid., 480 n. 1.

of God uniting with the holy person.[38] In a reference to the magical papyri, Smith cites Erwin R. Goodenough's discussion of a charm in which appeal is made to the god Eros.[39] This leads Smith to engage Arthur Darby Nock, who doubts that a charm that invokes Eros could be Jewish.[40] Smith counters Nock by remarking: "If a Jew could be supposed to invoke Beelzebub, he could be supposed to invoke Eros."[41] Smith's "Jew" here, of course, is Jesus, whose critics claimed that he had accessed the power of Beelzebul (cf. Matt 12:24; Mark 3:22; Luke 11:15), while "Eros" refers to the Greek god of sexual love.

To conclude, Smith's linkage of Mark's "mystery of the kingdom of God" to secret teaching, teaching that may have included prohibited sexual activity, is highly unusual. It is most unlikely that these words, "the mystery of the kingdom of God," however they were understood by early Christians, had anything to do with sexual activity, prohibited or otherwise. There is no evidence that anyone in the history of the Church thought this. No modern commentator has ever thought this—only Smith. That Smith a few years later at Mar Saba would actually stumble upon a text, an unknown letter of Clement, that also makes this connection is highly suspicious.

(2) The second unusual feature that Smith surmised was that the evangelist Mark may well have omitted materials that contained Johannine traits. In his 1955 review of Taylor's commentary Smith speaks of the possibility that the evangelist Mark may have omitted material.[42] This, of course, is the point at issue in Clement's Mar Saba letter—material omitted from the Markan Gospel. Smith also discusses Mark's use of a source with

---

38. Ibid., 508 n. 3: "when He is united with his saint." On "initiates," see Smith's discussion of Goodenough on 488: "To describe this salvation they certainly used the language of the mystery religions and to achieve it, he thinks, they may have adopted some of the mystery rites ... and called those who agreed with them 'initiates' ..." One might also look at Smith's review of Taylor's commentary on Mark, where Smith refers to τέλειοι as "initiates" ("Comments," 30). See also *Tannaitic Parallels*, 156 and 160 n. 8.

39. Goodenough, *Jewish Symbols in the Greco-Roman Period*, 2:200–202. On the presence of pagan elements in Jewish charms, see Goodenough's discussion on 153–55.

40. Nock, "Religious Symbols and Symbolism I," 570. Nock concedes (and this concession is quoted by Smith) that the Eros charm "might be the work of a Jew who had wholly or partly abandoned tradition."

41. Smith, "Image of God," 485 n. 1.

42. Smith, "Comments," 35: Whatever did not serve Mark's interests, "he would leave out as uninteresting, even if he did not deliberately censor it." Recall also "Image of God," 487, where Smith speaks of material that "has come down to us heavily censored."

"Johannine traits."⁴³ This is precisely what the first and long quotation of *Secret Mark* is—a passage with Johannine traits (cf. John 11, the raising of Lazarus) that had been omitted from public (i.e., canonical) Mark.⁴⁴ Watson comments: "Clement's letter confirms Smith's surmise that Mark may have 'deliberately censored' his source-material, and that this source-material may have included proto-Johannine elements."⁴⁵ Quite so. Watson, of course, also draws attention to Smith's fascination with secrecy and initiation, which has been reviewed above.

In discussing various bodies of evidence (such as biblical literature, Jewish literature, testimonia, and archaeology), Smith reminds us in his publication that appeared in 1958, written before making his Mar Saba find, that,

> the preserved material—even when accessible—represents only a small part of what once existed. By their very existence, they demonstrate how much has been lost; by the variety of the material they preserve, they prove the extent of our ignorance and tacitly warn of the danger of supposing that what is not to be found in them was never to be found at all. This supposition ... is especially dangerous in the study of Judaism, because Jewish material has come down to us heavily censored ... What, then, would have been the testimony of the material which has disappeared? We cannot be sure.⁴⁶

The Mar Saba Clementine, with its quotations and discussion of a longer edition of the Gospel of Mark, vindicates Smith's assumption of lost, censored items. What "would have been the testimony of the material which has disappeared?" In one case we no longer need to ask this question. We now know. The Mar Saba Clementine provides us with some potentially shocking testimony, which almost disappeared, had it not been for Smith's amazing discovery.

To sum up: Prior to the discovery of the Clementine letter at the Mar Saba Monastery Smith had published three studies (1951, 1955, 1958) in which he discusses (1) Mark 4:11 ("the mystery of the kingdom of God"),

---

43. Smith, "Comments," 26: "what one would expect of a source with other Johannine traits" (and earlier on this page: "They have many points of contact with Jn.").

44. See Smith, *Secret Gospel*, 45–62. Smith places the long quotation from *Secret Mark*, in which Jesus raises the dead youth, alongside John 11, where Jesus raises the dead Lazarus. Smith acknowledges that as soon as he read the quotation from *Secret Mark* he recognized it as "a variant of the story of Lazarus" (45).

45. Watson, "Beyond Suspicion," 157–58, with quotation from 158.

46. Smith, "Image of God," 486–87.

(2) secrecy and initiation, (3) forbidden sexual relationships, including union with a god, (4) omitted Markan material with Johannine traits, and (5) Clement of Alexandria (usually in reference to his *Stromateis*), who believed it was necessary to omit some of Jesus' secret (potentially offensive) teaching. It should also be noted that, while at Drew University in 1956–1957, Smith worked with one of the writings of Hippolytus, the *Philosophumena* (or *Refutation of All Heresies*), which includes criticism of the Carpocratians, a Gnostic group notorious for its sexual libertarianism who are also discussed in the Mar Saba Clementine.[47]

Smith's provocative ideas were hardly mainstream in the 1950s. But his two suggestions—that the saying in Mark 4:11 may have had something to do with secret teaching involving prohibited sex and that the evangelist Mark may have omitted material containing Johannine traits—were especially eccentric and, so far as I have been able to ascertain, wholly unique. Yet, not long after the publication of these strange ideas Smith found the Clementine letter at Mar Saba, in which are combined the five elements delineated in the preceding paragraph.[48] The key passage in the Mar Saba Clementine letter is the first and longer of the two quotations of the longer edition of the Gospel of Mark. The quotation reads as follows:

> And they come into Bethany. And a certain woman whose brother had died was there. And, coming, she prostrated herself before Jesus and says to him, "Son of David, have mercy on me." But the disciples rebuked her. And Jesus, being angered, went off with her into the garden, where the tomb was; and immediately a great cry was heard from the tomb. And approaching, Jesus rolled away the stone from the door of the tomb. And immediately, entering where the youth was, he stretched forth his hand and raised him, seizing his hand. But the youth, looking upon him, loved him and began to beseech him that he might be with him. And going out of the tomb they came into the house of the youth, for he was rich. And after six days Jesus gave him instruction, and in the evening the youth comes to him, wearing a linen cloth over his naked body. And he remained with him that night, for Jesus was teaching him "the mystery of the

---

47. Some of this work was published in Smith, "Description of the Essenes in Josephus and the Philosophumena." On Carpocrates and his following, see Irenaeus, *Haer.* 1.25; Hippolytus, *Haer.* 7.20; Clement, *Strom.* III.2–6.

48. These coincidences are dismissed too quickly in Rau, "Weder gefälscht noch authentisch?" 150. Rau is responding to Quesnell's review, which did not take into account the full evidence of Smith's prior interest in the themes found in the Mar Saba Clementine.

kingdom of God." And thence, arising, he returned to the other side of the Jordan.[49]

In this passage and in the discussion relating to it in the Mar Saba Clementine letter we find all five elements that had appeared earlier in Smith's publications:

First, we have a verbatim quotation of part of Mark 4:11: "The mystery of the kingdom of God" (τὸ μυστήριον δέδοται τῆς βασιλείας τοῦ θεοῦ). All that is missing in the quotation is the verb (δέδοται), which does not fit the grammatical context in the Clementine letter.

Second, we find the element of secrecy, which is found explicitly in the word secret or mystery (μυστήριον) in the quotation of Mark 4:11, and also elsewhere in the Clementine letter. For example, we are told that the evangelist Mark did not declare all of Jesus' teachings, nor did he even "hint at the secret ones [μυστικάς]" (or "mystical ones") (*Letter to Theodore* I.16–17). We are further told that Mark "did not divulge the things not to be uttered" (I.22); neither did he "write down the hierophantic teachings of the Lord" (I.23–24). The deeper truths were to be "read only to those who are being initiated into the great mysteries [μεγάλα μυστήρια]" (or "great secrets") (II.1–2). Indeed, "Not all true things are to be said to all men" (II.12–13, quoting Philo, *QG* IV,67). Mark's longer Gospel, the one quoted in the Clementine letter, is twice called a "secret" or "mystical Gospel" (μυστικὸν εὐαγγέλιον) (II.6,12). Accordingly, Clement enjoins that "the light of the truth should be hidden from those who are mentally blind."

Third, forbidden sexual activities are hinted at throughout the Clementine letter, including and especially the first quotation of the longer edition of Mark. Clement complains of the "unspeakable teachings of the Carpocratians" (I.2), who have fallen into a "boundless abyss of the carnal and bodily sins" (I.4). They "have become slaves of servile desires" (I.7). According to the Mar Saba letter, a certain elder of the church in Alexandria, having obtained a copy of the longer version of Mark, has interpreted it "according to his blasphemous and carnal doctrine" (II.5–7). In the context of the letter it is clear that the passage so interpreted is the one quoted above, in which the young man comes to Jesus at night, wearing nothing but a linen cloth over his naked body. After the quotation Clement insists that the words "naked man with naked man" do not occur in the text (III.13–14), thus suggesting that this was the "blasphemous and carnal" interpretation of the elder in the church in Alexandria: Carnal in

---

49. Translation adapted from Smith, *Secret Gospel*, 16–17.

that the reference is to sexual activity, blasphemous in that it is suggested that Jesus was sexually involved with the young man. (Later in the letter, he is described as the "youth whom Jesus loved," III.15.)

Fourth, according to Clement's letter the longer quotation from *Secret Mark* is an example of omitted Markan material, which, as it turns out, possesses Johannine traits.

Fifth, the Mar Saba find claims to be a letter penned by Clement of Alexandria, as the preface makes clear: "From the letters of the most holy Clement, the author of the *Stromateis*" (I.1). Smith's references to Clement in his earlier publications, as we have seen, also are to Clement's *Stromateis*.

Accordingly, we find all five elements—and they are unusual elements—in the Mar Saba find, and Smith himself had discussed these elements in no fewer than three pre-find publications.[50] But there are other remarkable coincidences that call for comment and here I depend on Francis Watson's recent and stimulating contribution to the debate that in important respects has broken new ground.[51]

THE CASE OF THE MAR SABA MYSTERY

Watson observes interesting parallels between Smith's personal narrative of his thoughts relating to his Mar Saba visit and the thoughts of the fictional British archaeologist "Sir William Bracebridge" in James Hunter's Mar Saba novel. In the novel Sir William explains why he visited the Mar Saba monastery: "This monastery... is one of the oldest religious institutions of its kind in the world, and at one time housed many *manuscripts. Most of these were removed*, but I have always had the feeling that *some might have been overlooked and hidden away*. My supposition proved correct" (emphasis added).[52] Smith's explanation and hopes for visiting the monastery are essentially the same: "I had not expected much from the Mar Saba *manuscripts*, since I knew that *almost all of them had been car-*

---

50. See also Smith's description of his interests, in his struggle to "interpret" his find: "What concerned me most was the secrecy of Jesus and particularly 'the mystery of the kingdom of God,' since that phrase appeared in the text... Pauline baptism and the magical background of its peculiarities, the libertine tradition and the Carpocratians—all these subjects, I could see, were directly relevant to my problem." See Smith, *Secret Gospel*, 74–75. These were Smith's interests *prior* to the Mar Saba find. There may be allusions to some of these themes in Smith's correspondence and unpublished papers. On this point, see Pierluigi Piovanelli's contribution in the present volume.

51. Watson, "Beyond Suspicion." See n. 11 above.

52. Hunter, *Mystery of Mar Saba*, 279. Also see Watson, "Beyond Suspicion," 165.

ried off to Jerusalem in the past century and were listed in the catalogue of the Patriarchal library. But there was always the chance that *something had been missed*, or that other manuscripts had been brought in by monks coming from other monasteries" (emphasis added).[53] The parallel is amazing, both in substance and in language. As Watson remarks: "The fictional English scholar and the non-fictional American one visit the Mar Saba monastery with exactly the same expectation."[54] And, of course, they meet with the same results. Each finds something that had been "overlooked." There are still more parallels.

Watson notes that both the fictional scholar and Morton Smith braced themselves for disappointment. The novel's "Sir William" explains: "I was prepared to leave Mar Saba, *reconciled* to the negative results of my research, when a monk told me he had certain manuscripts in his *cell* that had evidently been overlooked . . ." (emphasis added).[55] Similarly, Smith tells us: "I was gradually *reconciling* myself to my worst expectations and repeating every day that I should discover nothing of importance. Then, one afternoon near the end of my stay, I found myself in my *cell*, staring incredulously at a text written in tiny scrawl . . ." (emphasis added).[56] There is more.

Both Sir William and Professor Smith wonder if what they have found could be a forgery, but the documents found alongside their respective and surprising discoveries weigh against forgery. Sir William not only found the embarrassing Shred of Nicodemus, he also found copies of the *Shepherd of Hermas* and the *Epistle of Barnabas*. The finding of the latter two manuscripts, in addition to the Shred, leads Sir William to ask "who would be likely to go to the trouble and expense of forging such manuscripts for no particular purpose we can see?"[57] For this reason he concludes that the Shred is probably authentic. Smith reasons the same way. He concedes that the long quotation from *Secret Mark*, made up of words and phrases from canonical Mark and reflective of Johannine traits, if an imitation, "it is an imitation of the simplest and most childish sort."[58] However, the presence of the quotation *in the Clementine letter* argues for its authenticity, for "Clement's style is often very difficult . . . Without

---

53. Smith, *Secret Gospel*, 11. Also cited by Watson.
54. Watson, "Beyond Suspicion," 165.
55. Hunter, *Mystery of Mar Saba*, 293.
56. Smith, *Secret Gospel*, 12.
57. Hunter, *Mystery of Mar Saba*, 286.
58. Smith, *Clement of Alexandria*, 76.

profound study it could not be imitated with assurance of accuracy . . ."[59] That is, the not-easily-imitated Clementine text argues for the authenticity of the texts quoted in the letter, that is, the passages from *Secret Mark*.[60]

And finally, Watson shows that the Greek text of the novel's Shred of Nicodemus is made up of words and phrases from Mark, along with a few Johannine traits, such as reference to a garden (John 18:1) and the involvement of Nicodemus in the burial of Jesus (John 19:39). Even the respective percentages of words drawn from Mark, found in *Secret Mark* and the Shred, are comparable. Watson concludes: "In view of the other parallels between the work of the popular novelist and the biblical scholar, it is likely that the author of the one text is familiar with the other, finding in it the inspiration for his own production."[61] Watson draws a further inference: "Had *The Mystery of Mar Saba* been first published in c. 1975, the analysis presented here would show it to be heavily dependent on *The Secret Gospel* (1973)" and on Smith's account of his visit to Mar Saba and his find.[62] Of course, we know that Hunter's novel was published in 1940, long before Smith's 1958 "discovery." Since Hunter's dependence on Smith is not an option, Smith's dependence on Hunter appears to be the unavoidable conclusion.

DISPUTED SCIENCE

The debate over handwriting analysis requires a few comments. In his 2005 publication Stephen Carlson, assisted by a professional handwriting expert,[63] concluded that Morton Smith penned the three pages of Greek text found at the back of the seventeenth-century edition of the letters of Ignatius. Other scholars have challenged these findings. Dismissing Carlson's analysis, Hershel Shanks asked two Greek-speaking handwriting experts to compare samples of Smith's Greek with the Greek of the Mar Saba find. One expert concluded that Smith did not write the Clementine letter. The other expert concluded that he did. Shanks has posted their

---

59. Ibid.
60. Watson, "Beyond Suspicion," 167.
61. Ibid., 169.
62. Ibid., 170.
63. She is Julie C. Edison, described as a "professional forensic document examiner who has given courtroom and deposition testimony" in various jurisdictions. See Carlston, *Gospel Hoax*, 112 n. 9.

reports on the Biblical Archaeology Society web page.[64] The appeal to native Greek-speakers has not resolved the controversy.

Although Carlson does not regard himself as a handwriting expert per se, his expertise in evaluating documents, as well as procuring assistance and expert advice, should not be quickly dismissed (as I think Shanks has done). *Novum Testamentum*, a highly respected international journal devoted to the critical study of the New Testament, recently published an article, in which Carlson's conclusion that "Archaic Mark" (Greek NT ms 2427 = Chicago ms 972) is a modern forgery has been vindicated.[65] This manuscript, written on what at one time was believed to be fourteenth-century parchment, deceived the likes of Edgar Goodspeed, Ernest Cadman Colwell, Kirsopp Lake, and Kurt and Barbara Aland, scholars well-versed in ancient Greek manuscripts and hands. "Archaic Mark," under the number 2427, appears in the list of miniscules in the two standard critical editions of the Greek New Testament. In these editions it is dated to the fourteenth century, evidently on the basis of the presumed age of the parchment, as well as the paleography.[66] Carlson, however, concluded that although the parchment is old, perhaps dating to the fourteenth or fifteenth century, the handwriting is modern and the forger, who imitated fourteenth-century Greek penmanship remarkably well, used Philipp Buttmann's 1860 edition of the Greek New Testament as his base text.[67] As reported in the recent issue of *Novum Testamentum*, scientific testing has confirmed Carlson's conclusion. The ink was found to contain a chemical that was not in use prior to 1874 and Carbon 14

---

64. Anastasopoulou, "Experts Report Handwriting Examination." Tselikas, "Agamemnon Tselikas' Handwriting Analysis Report." Both reports are summarized in the magazine as Hershel Shanks, "Handwriting Experts Weigh In on 'Secret Mark.'" Venetia Anastasopoulou has concluded that Smith did not pen the Mar Saba letter. Agamemnon Tselikas has concluded that Smith did pen the letter. Peter Head has raised questions about the credentials of Ms. Anastasopoulou, which are rather thin. In contrast, Mr. Tselikas has authored more than 150 articles on Greek paleography. Moreover, Peter Jeffery ("Response to Handwriting Analysis") faults Anastasopoulou's report for not taking into account important factors that feature prominently in the analysis of Carlson and Edison, such as the appearance of "forger's tremor" and the similarities between some of the letters (esp. *theta*, *lambda*, and *tau*) in the Clementine letter and samples of Smith's Greek.

65. Mitchell, Barabe, and Quandt, "Chicago's 'Archaic Mark' (ms 2427) II." See Carlson, "'Archaic Mark' (MS 2427) and the Finding of a Manuscript Fake."

66. See Aland, Aland, Karavidopoulos, Martini, and Metzger, eds., *Greek New Testament*, 18*; Aland and Aland, eds., *Novum Testamentum Graece*, 17*.

67. Buttmann, ed., *Novum Testamentum Graece* (1860). Buttmann's text is based primarily on Codex Vaticanus.

has dated the parchment to the sixteenth century. It is now believed that the manuscript was produced in the early twentieth century. Once again handwriting analysis was at best uncertain. Internal considerations, including evidence of anachronism, pointed to forgery.[68] Scientific testing provided confirmation.

Where does this leave us with regard to Smith's Mar Saba find? With uncertain and conflicting handwriting analyses, Carlson and two handwriting experts, one English-speaking and one Greek-speaking, think Smith wrote the document in question. Another Greek-speaking handwriting expert thinks he did not. Which conclusion is correct? One is reminded of the sensational scandal involving the notorious Hitler diaries, which came to public attention in 1983. Three handwriting experts and at least one Hitler scholar argued for the authenticity of the more than 60 volumes of diaries.[69] Had the matter been left to handwriting "experts," it would have been necessary to rewrite history. Fortunately, the diaries, initially hailed as the "biggest literary discovery since the Dead Sea Scrolls,"[70] were subjected to scientific study and were shown to be forgeries, mostly produced in the 1970s. Perhaps in this connection readers need to be reminded that Smith's three pages of text have never been subjected to scientific testing, which might be able to determine the age of the paper when the ink was applied and whether the ink dates to the eighteenth century or the twentieth century. In any event, handwriting analysis does not appear to be conclusive.

---

68. In her part of the study, Mitchell, Barabe, and Quandt ("Chicago's 'Archaic Mark,'" 123) praise Carlson's "keen detective work" and find "his thesis convincing."

69. The handwriting experts were Max Frei-Sulzer (Switzerland), Ordway Hilton (USA), and Kenneth Rendell (USA). Hugh Trevor-Roper (UK), an expert on Hitler, also declared the diaries authentic. Curious anachronisms and inconsistencies gave rise to suspicion, but it was the chemical analysis of the paper and bindings, which revealed the presence of whitener and inks not in use until the 1950s, that proved conclusively that the diaries and other documents were forgeries. Eventually career-forger Konrad Kujau confessed that he was the author of the diaries. The astounding story is recounted in Harris, *Selling Hitler*. I thank Bart Ehrman for calling my attention to this book. For a summary of the scientific evidence, see *Selling Hitler*, 354–55. For a photo of one of the pages of the diaries, with the notation that three handwriting experts were deceived by it, see plate 4 (following p. 194). Hitler scholar Trevor-Roper declared: "I *know* Hitler's handwriting. I *know* his signature" (Trevor-Roper's emphasis). He said this even when serious doubts about the diaries' authenticity were being raised. As it turned out, he was quite mistaken. See *Selling Hitler*, 302. See also Ehrman, *Lost Christianities*, 67–89.

70. Harris, *Selling Hitler*, 331.

Ancient Gospel or Modern Forgery?

Whatever the handwriting analysis shows, the remarkable coincidence of the five elements Smith brought together in earlier publications also appearing together in Smith's Mar Saba find justifies suspicion. The additional parallels adduced by Francis Watson add to this suspicion. Some may even say these remarkable parallels and coincidences justify more than suspicion; perhaps they call for a conclusion.

These parallels and coincidences notwithstanding, several scholars continue to defend Smith. They remain convinced that the Mar Saba find is genuine. I wonder what kind of evidence would it take to persuade them that suspicions of forgery are fully justified? It is natural and understandable to assume that our colleagues are completely honest and would never take part in a hoax. Unfortunately, as Christopher Rollston has recently reminded us, this charitable assumption is naïve.[71] Suspicious coincidences need to be taken very seriously.

THE CRITERION OF KNOWING THE FIND BEFORE MAKING THE FIND

Let's return to Coleman-Norton's amusing agraphon. What evidence is there that Coleman-Norton is the author of this agraphon? All we have is Bruce Metzger's claim that he heard Coleman-Norton utter something very similar several years before making the find. For most scholars—perhaps all scholars—this is enough. Coleman-Norton's knowledge of the contents of the agraphon before he allegedly discovered it in North Africa provides more than enough evidence for Metzger to judge it a hoax. But in the case of the Mar Saba find we have the testimony of Morton Smith himself, who writes of the very elements that he later discovers in his Mar Saba find. In this case we do not have to rely on the memory of a former student, who says he heard his professor say such-and-such many years ago. In the case of the Mar Saba find we actually have the publications of Professor Smith—still available for study—publications that we know appeared *before* he made his discovery.

For scholars who remain unconvinced of the probative value of prior knowledge and coincidence as evidence of hoax, and therefore continue to urge us to accept Smith's Mar Saba find as genuine, I suggest they also accept Coleman-Norton's find. After all, the only weighty objection to its

---

71. Rollston, "Non-Provenanced Epigraphs I." After discussing the Coleman-Norton hoax, Rollston states that "to assume that bright, well-trained people are always characterized by professional ethics is belied by 'epigraphic history'" (192–93).

acceptance is Bruce Metzger's claim that Coleman-Norton knew the contents of the agraphon *before* he found the agraphon.

Not only does Smith's scholarly discussion of matters that would *later* be discovered in the Mar Saba find trouble me, his non-usage of his discovery in *subsequent* research, which would have and should have benefited from it, also troubles me. Here I have in mind the arguments, conclusions, and insinuations of his book *Jesus the Magician*.[72] In this work Smith suggests that the historical Jesus was recognized by his contemporaries as a magician, whose practices included "union"—spiritual and/or physical—with his followers.[73] In his two books on *Secret Mark*, Smith discusses secret rituals and union of Jesus with his followers. Yet Smith's *Jesus the Magician* does not depend on the Mar Saba find in any significant way.[74] This curious feature has been remarked upon by scholars, some of whom see it as one more indication that Smith knew perfectly well that the Mar Saba find was not authentic and therefore did not make use of the find in his later, serious work.[75]

At the 2008 annual meeting of the Society of Biblical Literature some of Smith's surviving correspondence was discussed.[76] It was noted that nowhere does Smith hint at his involvement in a hoax. I am not sure how significant this observation is, given the fact that Smith gave instructions in his will to have all of his correspondence destroyed after his death.[77]

72. Smith, *Jesus the Magician*.

73. Ibid., 122–23, 146, 152. On 123 Smith speaks of the believer who "will be united with" Jesus "in love" and of Christians who "adapted his magical rite of union so as to make it also a ritual expression of libertine teaching." Here one would expect some discussion of the Mar Saba Clementine and the passage quoted from *Secret Mark*. Yet, strangely, there is no discussion and not even a reference in the footnotes.

74. In a response to a reviewer of his Mar Saba Clementine books (i.e., *Clement of Alexandria* and *Secret Gospel*), Smith makes it clear that his *Jesus the Magician* does not depend on *Secret Mark*. See Smith, "In Quest of Jesus": The "fragment of secret Mark plays no substantial part" in the argument of *Jesus the Magician*. Smith adds that reviewer Frank Kermode's claim "that *Jesus the Magician* rests on the secret gospel fragment is utterly untrue." Kermode's review appeared as "The Quest for the Magical Jesus."

75. See the discussion in Brown, *Mark's Other Gospel*, 53, 251 nn. 133–34; Carlson, *Gospel Hoax*, 77–78. Smith's virtual non-usage of the Mar Saba find is inconsistent with the usual vanity seen in scholarship, where scholars as much as possible in their footnotes call attention to their previous publications.

76. See also Allan Pantuck's contribution to the present volume.

77. Calder, "Smith, Morton," 602: Smith's "personal and scholarly correspondence was destroyed by Smith's literary executor, David Smith, in accord with his wishes in 1991." For a friendly biography of Smith, see Baumgarten, "Smith, Morton." Baumgarten summarizes the debate concerning the authenticity of the Mar Saba Clementine

Ancient Gospel or Modern Forgery?

Accordingly, we really do not know what may or may not have been hinted at in his correspondence. All that survives is a small sample.[78]

In any case, why should we expect Smith to drop any hints or make admissions during or after the commission of a hoax, assuming *Secret Mark* is a hoax? Bruce Metzger tells us that Paul Coleman-Norton never acknowledged his hoax. Indeed, according to Metzger, years later Coleman-Norton complained of the way his transcription of the Greek text of his amusing agraphon was presented in its published form. He gave no indication to Metzger that his North African find was bogus. Yet, Metzger had no doubt whatsoever that Coleman-Norton's text and story of its finding were fraudulent.[79]

Before concluding this part of the discussion, let me assure readers that I do recognize that innocent coincidences sometimes occur. In 1960, when Morton Smith announced his Mar Saba discovery, Professor A. H. M. Jones, a distinguished British scholar of Roman history, published an essay, in which he argued that the rank of Pontius Pilate, governor of Judea and Samaria, was that of prefect, not procurator, as is stated by the early second-century Roman historian Tacitus in his *Annals* 15.44.[80] The very next year a stone slab was uncovered during an excavation at Caesarea Maritima, on which were inscribed the words: "Pontius Pilate, prefect of Judea."[81] This remarkable coincidence aroused no suspicion for at least three reasons: (1) The Pilate inscription was discovered during a controlled dig; (2) Professor Jones did not discover the inscription, nor was he present at the excavation; and (3) the inscription confirmed a plausible hypothesis, viz., that Pilate's rank was prefect. Not one of these "innocent" details applies to Smith's Mar Saba find.

---

but takes no position.

78. Although from time to time, thanks to the diligence of Allan Pantuck and others, additional items come to light. For discussion of some of these other items, which may have a bearing on this strange case, see the contribution to this volume by Pierluigi Piovanelli.

79. Metzger, *Reminiscences*, 139.

80. Jones, "Procurators and Prefects in the Early Principate," in his *Studies in Roman Government and Law*, 117-25.

81. See Frova, "L'iscrizione di Ponzio Pilato a Cesarea."

Craig A. Evans—*Morton Smith and the* Secret Gospel of Mark

CURIOUS FEATURES ABOUT THE FIND ITSELF

Finally, there are a few other details that raise troubling questions. I begin with some oddities about the old Voss edition, in which Smith says he found the Clementine letter.

First, Isaac Voss's 1646 edition of the genuine epistles of Ignatius stands out among the old books at the Mar Saba monastery. Smith lists ten old printed books, ranging in date from 1628 to 1805. Nine of these books were published in Venice and in the Greek language. But Voss's book was published in Amsterdam and in the Latin language. As Carlson remarks, it "sticks out like a sore thumb."[82] Smith too apparently sensed this problem, offering wholly gratuitous speculations, none of them convincing, that attempt in one way or another to link the book to Venice.[83] Why did he do that? Perhaps because he recognized the non-Greek, non-Venetian publication of the book as a problem, a problem that needed to be mitigated in some way. Would an authentic find occasion this kind of embarrassment?

Second, there is no evidence that the book was at Mar Saba prior to Smith's visit in 1958. It is not listed in the monastery's 1910 catalogue of books.

Third, I find it odd that Smith worked on the Clementine letter for some fifteen years (1958–1973) and never returned to Mar Saba to examine Voss's book itself. Smith was content to work from his black and white photographs. Why did Smith make no effort to subject the book to scientific analysis?[84]

And *fourth*, there is the striking coincidence of the subject matter of the Clementine letter and the last printed page of Voss's book, the printed page that lies opposite the first handwritten page. Clement's letter is concerned with inauthentic interpolations in the Gospel of Mark. So is Voss, with respect to the letters of Ignatius and the pseudepigraphal *Epistle of Barnabas*, into which "impudent fellows" insert "all kinds of nonsense."[85] Bart Ehrman has called our attention to this interesting coincidence.[86] On the assumption that Smith forged the Clementine letter, his choice of Voss's book was brilliant. Selecting the Voss book, because of its last page, was a humorous, almost poetic touch.

82. Carlson, *Gospel Hoax*, 38.
83. Ibid., 38–39.
84. This question is raised by Ehrman, "Response to Charles Hedrick's Stalemate," 160.
85. Voss, *Epistolae genuinae*, 318.
86. Ehrman, "Stalemate," 162.

Ancient Gospel or Modern Forgery?

There are also internal oddities. Skeptical scholars have remarked that the vocabulary of *Secret Mark* is too Markan and the vocabulary of the Clementine letter is too Clementine, which suggests the composer of the letter, who probably made use of Otto Stählin's concordance of Clement's vocabulary,[87] overdid his imitation.[88] Charles Murgia has compared the Clementine letter to other forgeries of antiquity and concludes that the Mar Saba document reads as an autograph, not as a copy.[89] If it is an autograph, then it cannot be a copy of an authentic letter of Clement. Watson has also observed in the Mar Saba Clementine dependence on the language and syntax of the Papias fragments concerned with the authorship of the Gospels of Mark and Matthew. Clement does this nowhere else. Indeed, as Watson remarks, "The compositional procedure is more plausibly ascribed to a modern author than to a second-century one. Clement of Alexandria would not require this degree of assistance from Papias. A modern author might well."[90] On top of this, as Ehrman and others have noted, the Mar Saba letter at points actually contradicts the authentic Clement.[91]

---

87. See Stählin, ed., *Clemens Alexandrinus*, 4 vols. Smith's personal volumes of this work were among the books he donated to the Jewish Theological Seminary. The volumes are heavily annotated by Smith. Volume 4, which appeared in 1936, is a concordance of Clement's vocabulary, thus greatly facilitating efforts to imitate Clement, should anyone wish to do so. In "Image of God," 482 n. 2, Smith references Clement of Alexandria and cites Stählin's work.

88. For example, see Ernest Best, *Disciples and Discipleship*, 199–205, as well as the comments in Ehrman, "Stalemate," 161. Ehrman appeals to Criddle, "On the Mar Saba Letter." Some of the early reviewers of Smith's books made similar observations.

89. Murgia, "Secret Mark: Real or Fake?" Murgia observes that the Mar Saba Clementine seems to exhibit trademarks of literary forgeries. His argument is accepted by Ehrman, "Stalemate," 156, 161; and Carlson, *Gospel Hoax*, 54–55.

90. Watson, "Beyond Suspicion," 148–51, with quotation from 150. I find Watson's observations and reasoning here especially compelling. He remarks that these parallels "betray the work of a modern forger who has used the Papias excerpts as a template for his own work" (148). And later: "The reuse of the Papias template corresponds to a certain poverty of invention" (150). Watson finds it odd too that in his learned and detailed *Clement of Alexandria* Smith did not reference the parallels with Papias. See "Beyond Suspicion," 151 n. 61.

91. Ehrman, "Stalemate," 160–61. Ehrman cites discrepancies in attitudes toward and understanding of gnosis and in telling the truth. The latter point is especially pertinent, for in the Mar Saba letter Clement urges Theodore to deny, "on oath," the existence of *Secret Mark*. Where in the genuine writings of Clement do we find Clement urging the faithful to swear falsely, in flat contradiction to the teaching of Jesus (cf. Matt 5:33–37)?

Craig A. Evans—*Morton Smith and the* Secret Gospel of Mark

Finally, I find it unlikely that a different edition of Mark, whether a second-century expanded edition, or a first-century edition perhaps expanded by the Markan evangelist himself, could leave no traces in the manuscript tradition. I also find strange the absence of discussion, polemic, and apologetic related to the passage from *Secret Mark* that is quoted in the Mar Saba Clementine, the only letter of Clement to have survived. It is hard to believe that a story (no matter how secret it was supposed to be) in which Jesus (in the nude?) instructs a new convert did not generate controversy, controversy that would have left traces in the writings of the Fathers. It is very curious that such a story managed to survive only in a letter written in the back of a seventeenth-century book, which Morton Smith, whose previous publications showed interest in this very topic, just happened to find in the Mar Saba Monastery.

CONCLUSION

Although not the intention of its author, the novel *The Mystery of Mar Saba* seems to have spawned at least two Gospel-related hoaxes that more or less adapted the setting and circumstances of the hoax described in the novel. In the case of the first, the best that the hoaxer (Coleman-Norton) could do was "find" a page of Greek in an uncatalogued rare book in a mosque in North Africa. In the case of the second, the hoaxer (Smith) could do better—he could "find" pages of Greek in an uncatalogued rare book in the very monastery in the Judean wilderness in which the novel's fraudulent page of Greek was planted. To be sure, the sites actually visited by the hoaxers placed limits on where they could make their respective "finds." The first hoaxer had visited North Africa (but not Palestine); the second had visited Palestine, the location of the Mar Saba Monastery.

In my opinion Morton Smith's Mar Saba discovery is a hoax. I cannot prove this, of course, so I concede the point made by Hershel Shanks in his summation in *Biblical Archaeology Review*.[92] In my view the evidence that Smith possessed knowledge of distinctive elements of the Mar Saba find prior to his finding it, is more than sufficient for viewing the find with grave suspicion.[93] The same can be said with respect to

92. Shanks, "Restoring a Dead Scholar's Reputation," 90. Shanks calls into question, perhaps even refutes, some of the arguments put forward by Carlson and Jeffrey.

93. Shanks makes this point in a cordial note sent to me 22 October 2009: "To my mind you may have ground for suspicion, but not proof of a very serious crime." There is indeed ground for suspicion. Rau ("Weder gefälscht noch authentisch?" 186) believes that the available evidence is ambiguous and that not until the actual document

Ancient Gospel or Modern Forgery?

Coleman-Norton's amusing agraphon. No one can prove that Coleman-Norton perpetrated a hoax. But most would agree that he probably did. The reason most regard it as a hoax is that before making the find he had spoken in jest of dentures being supplied to the toothless damned, so that they might gnash their teeth. The reason many New Testament scholars, perhaps even *most* New Testament scholars, will continue to view Smith's find as a hoax is that, before making his find at Mar Saba, he too spoke of the mystery of the kingdom of God, secrecy, prohibited sexual relationships, and Clement of Alexandria. That this unusual combination of elements just happens to appear in a document that Smith himself found should serve as a warning to scholars that in the case of the Mar Saba Clementine and its quotations and discussion of a longer edition of the Gospel of Mark we may well be dealing with a hoax.[94] However, we should speak cautiously in this matter, not simply out of fairness to the late Morton Smith but also out of professional courtesy for our colleagues who have reached a different conclusion.[95]

---

is properly tested can a firm decision be reached. Perhaps in a scientific sense, then, "proof" is still lacking. But Watson, as the title of his recent study reflects, believes the internal evidence and parallels are "beyond suspicion." He is convinced that Smith's Mar Saba find is a hoax.

94. Historians who are not biblical scholars have reached the same conclusion: Akenson, *Saint Saul*, 87: "Secret Mark is a forgery..."; 89: "Morton Smith... has to be the most likely prankster, and he could only have enjoyed watching the most powerful figures in the liberal wing of the Quest establishment... take the bait."; 89: "there exist many very solid scholars who are not besotted with the gimcrack false-antiquities of the sort exemplified by Secret Mark..."; Jenkins, *Hidden Gospels*, 102: "there are unresolved rumors of forgery. The location of the find is fascinating, since this was the scene of the forgery described only a few years before in the then-popular novel *The Mystery of Mar Saba*." Akenson is Professor of History at Queen's University, Kingston, Ontario, Canada. Jenkins is Distinguished Professor of History and Religious Studies at Pennsylvania State University. Evidently Metzger also regarded the Mar Saba find as a hoax, for he placed his discussion of it in the chapter entitled "Literary Forgeries." See Metzger, *Reminiscences*, 128–32.

95. I wish to add that if conclusive evidence should finally materialize that proves Smith's Mar Saba find is indeed a hoax and that Smith is himself the hoaxer, this does not make Professor Helmut Koester or any other scholar a fool. Koester, like many of us, was willing to give Smith the benefit of the doubt and, like many of us, finds it difficult to imagine someone expending so much energy in the commission of such a grotesque hoax.

5

Craig Evans and the *Secret Gospel of Mark*
Exploring the Grounds for Doubt

Scott G. Brown and Allan J. Pantuck

CRAIG EVANS HAS PRODUCED a well-written and comprehensive explication of his latest grounds for doubting the authenticity of the *Letter to Theodore*. In this reply, we examine each of his main arguments with the same degree of scepticism espoused by Evans and show that his grounds for doubt are themselves groundless.

THE AMUSING AGRAPHON

Evans's case against the authenticity of the *Letter to Theodore* begins with a look at a probable hoax by Paul R. Coleman-Norton consisting of a lost saying of Jesus that he published in an article titled "An Amusing *Agraphon*."[1] Allegedly a response to one of Jesus' references to that place where there will be weeping and gnashing of teeth, the saying runs as follows:

---

1. Coleman-Norton, "An Amusing *Agraphon*."

Ancient Gospel or Modern Forgery?

> And, behold, a certain one of his disciples standing by said unto him: "Rabbi (which is to say, being interpreted, Master), how can these things be, if they be toothless?" And Jesus answered and said: "O thou of little faith, trouble not thyself; if haply they will be lacking any, teeth will be provided."[2]

Although Coleman-Norton reported that he witnessed a manuscript that contains this humorous saying in a town in Morocco, after his death, Bruce Metzger, one of his former students, claimed that Coleman-Norton told a form of this joke to his students at Princeton prior to the alleged discovery.[3] Evans cites this incident as a case of knowing the discovery before finding it and uses it to illustrate the principle that forgery must be suspected whenever a discovery substantiates the ideas of its discoverer or reflects that person's interests. That such was the case with Morton Smith and the *Letter to Theodore* is a recurring theme of Evans's paper.

Before making this argument, Evans pauses to propose that James Hunter's novel *The Mystery of Mar Saba*[4] "may well have provided Coleman-Norton with the scenario needed to introduce his spurious agraphon to the public (at least to a public somewhat wider than his Princeton class room)" (p. 81). Evans acknowledges that Coleman-Norton's alleged discovery occurred in a location that is very different from the setting of the manuscript discovery in Hunter's book, but surmises, "Coleman-Norton chose North Africa, instead of Mar Saba, for the setting because that was where he was stationed in 1943. But the rest of the details are a match with the novel: Greek text, offering new material relating to Jesus, found in an old book amongst rare books in a religious establishment" (p. 75). Evans elaborated this characterization of the similarities between the two finds a bit earlier, describing both texts as isolated leafs of Greek text found among old books:

> Princeton University Associate Professor of Latin Paul Coleman-Norton published a leaf of Greek text that he says he found sandwiched between pages of an old Arabic book in a mosque

---

2. As translated by Coleman-Norton, ibid., 443 n. 18.

3. Coleman-Norton himself noted the existence of a modern version of this joke (ibid., 444 n. 21). In its contemporary form, a preacher's dire warning of weeping and gnashing of teeth elicits the inappropriately rational question, forcing the preposterously serious response "Teeth will be provided." That joke is at least as old as 1885. It appears in the magazine *Our Corner* 5 (1 February 1885) 120 (edited by Annie Besant and published in London by Freethought Pub. Co.).

4. Hunter, *Mystery of Mar Saba*.

in North Africa, where he was stationed in 1943 while serving in the US Army during World War II. (p. 78)

To undermine the morale of the British Empire the Nazis plant a leaf of Greek text amongst the rare books in the Mar Saba Monastery's collection, a text that an honest British scholar would subsequently discover. (p. 81)

These similarities in the discoveries are not very strong, but they are essential to Evans's proposal, for without them there is nothing to suggest that Coleman-Norton read Hunter's book. When you check that book itself, however, you find that Evans's description is mostly erroneous. Evans describes the fictional forgery, called the Shred of Nicodemus, as "a leaf of Greek text" that was "plant[ed] . . . amongst the rare books in the Mar Saba Monastery's collection" for Sir William Bracebridge to "discover." In Hunter's story, however, a monk simply hands Bracebridge a stash of manuscripts that he himself pretended to discover "in an old chapel buried behind a movable stone."[5]

This is how Hunter presents the situation. He first describes the instructions that Heimworth, the mastermind behind the deception, gives to a monk:

> "Is everything in readiness?"
> "Ja."
> "You have all the manuscripts?"
> The other nodded.
> "Put this one among them. You know your instructions. If Sir William asks any questions you know nothing except that the manuscripts have been here to the best of your knowledge since the monastery was built, and must have been overlooked when the others were removed.["][6]

Bracebridge's time at the monastery is not narrated. Instead, Hunter later has Bracebridge recount the discovery to the chief of the Palestinian police, Colonel Alderson:

> He [Alderson] turned from the window and came back to his seat.
> "May we see the manuscript, Sir William?"
> The archaeologist nodded, and opened a brief case he had in his hand.
> "By the way," said Alderson, "how did you discover it?"

5. Ibid., 281.
6. Ibid., 235.

Ancient Gospel or Modern Forgery?

> "In almost the same way in which Tischendorf found the Sinaiticus. One of the monks found them in an old chapel buried behind a movable stone. They took them out, and being unable to read them, and hearing I might be coming there, kept them for me. I am acting, as you know, for the British Museum, and I told them we would likely buy them from them."[7]

Evans is correct that both accounts involve a single page of Greek containing new material about Jesus. Apart from that parallel, which itself resembles several real discoveries, the parallels are not real, so neither are the grounds for suggesting that Coleman-Norton was inspired by Hunter's book.

THE PROFESSOR WHO KNEW TOO MUCH

Evans's erroneous description of how Bracebridge finds the Shred of Nicodemus in *The Mystery of Mar Saba* is also important to Evans's case against Smith, for Evans goes on to note that the story of discovery in Hunter's novel is just like Smith's account of his own discovery:

> My brief summation of the novel *The Mystery of Mar Saba* probably brought to the minds of most readers Morton Smith's account of his discovery of three pages of Greek text penned in the back of an old book amongst a number of old and rare books and papers in a religious establishment, this time the very establishment and setting of the novel: the Mar Saba Monastery. (p. 81)

It would not be surprising if Evans's summation of Hunter's novel reminds his readers of Smith's account of his discovery, because Smith's account appears to be the basis for Evans's misrepresentation of Hunter's book.

Evans goes on to note that "In the real-life story the discovery is made by *Professor Morton*. In the novel the truth of the discovery is made by Scotland Yard inspector *Lord Moreton*" (p. 81). This alleged parallel is puzzling, for Professor *Smith* had the name Morton for twenty-five years before Hunter published his novel. It is really only Evans's utilization of parallel sentence structure, made possible by a sliding use of the word "discovery" and the substitution of Smith's first name for his last name, that creates the impression of a parallel. In any event, it is not Lord Moreton who discovers the truth about the manuscript. The hero Medhurst learns

---

7. Ibid., 281–82.

the true situation directly from the forger Yphantis sixty pages before Lord Moreton learns the news, which he merely receives from Alderson over the phone.[8] There was no detective-like discovery, and Lord Moreton is not even an active inspector (note the title Lord) but "Chief of the Metropolitan Police."[9] Evans finds these parallels "interesting" and a bit "troubling" (p. 81). So do we.

These parallels lead up to Evans's principal objection to the letter's authenticity: "what I find most troubling is that themes of interest to Professor Smith, as seen in his publications *before* the finding of the Clementine letter, are found in the Clementine letter. And these are not just themes of interest to Professor Smith; they are quite unusual themes and, apart from Professor Smith himself, they are themes advanced by no one else" (pp. 81–82). Evans specifies two such unusual themes, namely, "(1) The 'mystery of the kingdom of God' and prohibited sex, and (2) Markan materials omitted from Mark that exhibit Johannine traits" (pp. 87–87). At the conclusion of this section, however, he lists five themes:

> Prior to the discovery of the Clementine letter at the Mar Saba Monastery Smith had published three studies (1951, 1955, 1958) in which he discusses (1) Mark 4:11 ("the mystery of the kingdom of God"), (2) secrecy and initiation, (3) forbidden sexual relationships, including union with a god, (4) omitted Markan material with Johannine traits, and (5) Clement of Alexandria (usually in reference to his *Stromateis*), who believed it was necessary to omit some of Jesus' secret (potentially offensive) teaching. (X-ref)

Later on, Evans similarly refers to "the remarkable coincidence of the five elements Smith brought together in earlier publications also appearing together in Smith's Mar Saba find" (p. 94). Since the reader is likely to be confused about what Evans is claiming to demonstrate in this section, we should explain that in the paper he presented at the symposium, he argued that Smith had "linked" together (not just "discuss[ed]") points 1, 2, 3, and 5 *in all three* of these pre-find publications, which is something that could indeed be described as "quite unusual" and even unique—were it in fact true. It is not, and Evans has since revised his argument in response to the concise reply that Pantuck delivered during the symposium, but some

---

8. Ibid., 344–45 (cf. 386–87), 404. Craig S. Keener borrows Evans's error about Lord Moreton in *Historical Jesus of the Gospels*, 60.

9. Hunter, *Mystery of Mar Saba*, 303.

Ancient Gospel or Modern Forgery?

traces of the earlier thesis remain. The present, fuller reply now responds to the revised argument that Evans submitted for this book.

Evans first argues that "Smith linked Mark 4:11 ('To you is given the mystery of the kingdom of God . . .') with secrecy and forbidden sexual activity" (p. 82). For evidence he quotes part of a paragraph of Smith's 1951 book *Tannaitic Parallels to the Gospels*.[10] In the reproduction of this passage below, the words in gray are ones that Evans omitted using ellipses:

> Further I think the passage in Sifre on Deut. to have been based on the fact that an important part of primitive Christianity was a secret doctrine which was revealed only to trusted members. Such a doctrine is suggested by the words put in the mouth of Jesus, speaking to his disciples: "To you is given the mystery of the kingdom of God, but to those outside all things are in parables, that they may surely see and not perceive," etc. And Paul himself wrote in I Cor. 2.1–6 "And I, coming to you, brethren, came not proclaiming the testimony of God in lofty words or wisdom . . . that your faith might not be in the wisdom of men, but in the power of God. But we speak wisdom among the perfect, and a wisdom not of this age . . . but we speak the wisdom of God in a mystery." A similar distinction was recognized by the Tannaïm between material suitable for public teaching and that reserved for secret teaching, as we learn from *Hagigah T* 2.1 (233): "The (passages of the Old Testament dealing with) forbidden sexual relationships are not to be expounded to three (at a time,) but may be expounded to two; and the account of creation not to two, but it may be expounded to a single hearer; and (Ezekiel's vision of) the chariot may not be expounded to a single hearer unless he be learned in the Law and of good understanding."

The paragraph continues beyond this quotation. On this passage Evans comments, "Smith's linkage of the saying about the 'mystery of the kingdom of God' (Mark 4:11) to secrecy and teaching regarding forbidden sexual relationships is to the best of my knowledge unique. Gospel scholars agree that Mark 4:11 fits awkwardly in its context and debate what the original meaning was. But only Smith links it to sex; I know of no commentator prior to the time of Smith (or after, for that matter) who has done this" (p. 83).

Although Evans does not explain what he means by the words "linkage" and "links," he clearly intends his quotation to demonstrate that, in

---

10. Smith, *Tannaitic Parallels*, 155–56.

Smith's mind, the mystery of the kingdom of God is somehow associated with forbidden sex. And certainly someone reading Evans's abbreviated quotation might get that impression. But someone who sees the full quotation will be apt to form a different impression of what Smith is saying. Most notably, one sees that the reference to Tosefta, tractate *Hagigah* 2.1 is not concerned specifically with the Torah's regulations concerning forbidden sexual relations (i.e., incest, intercourse during menstruation, adultery, homosexuality, and bestiality) but with all the scriptures that the Tannaïm thought should be discussed in secret. If we follow Evans's logic, then, we would have to infer that Smith "linked" the mystery of the kingdom of God to all of them. The unsuitability of that notion to Evans's argument readily accounts for the abrupt end of his quotation.[11]

Smith's actual point becomes apparent when all the omitted words are put back in. Smith is illustrating the fact that both the Christians and the Tannaïm drew a distinction between exoteric and esoteric teaching. Smith chose Mark 4:11 and 1 Cor 2:1–7 as familiar and explicit examples of the public/private distinction, without implying that Mark and Paul were talking about the same matters that the Tannaïm taught in private.[12]

The second pre-discovery paper that Evans cites is Smith's 1955 review of Vincent Taylor's commentary on the Gospel of Mark.[13] Evans finds in this article evidence that Smith interpreted Mark 4:11 as a secret rite. Specifically, Evans states, "Smith vigorously challenges Taylor's denial that Mark 4:11 envisioned secret rites" (p. 83).

We find no support for this statement in Smith's article, but its actual source was not hard to locate. Evans's argument in this section relies heavily on Quentin Quesnell's characterizations of these pre-1958 articles, and on this subject Quesnell wrote, "He [Smith] insisted against Taylor that

---

11. Evans is making the same point as Carlson, *Gospel Hoax*, 71–72, with the same ellipses. The difference is that Evans also adds ellipses at the beginning and omits more words using the middle ellipses. Quesnell had similarly summarized this passage in "Mar Saba Clementine," 60. Scott G. Brown already responded to this misrepresentation in "The More Spiritual Gospel," 112–13; and Brown, "Factualizing the Folklore," 322–25. Evans has added to the final, published form of his paper a paragraph describing the parts that he omitted from the quotation, but this sequestering of the elements contained in the ellipses does not address our point that their unnecessary removal from the quotation is the very thing that creates the impression that Smith linked Mark 4:11 with sex.

12. Other scholars who have discussed this page of Smith's *Tannaitic Parallels* have better understood his point. See Jónsson, *Humour and Irony in the New Testament*, 180–81; Nock, "Hellenistic Mysteries and Christian Sacraments," 207.

13. Smith, "Comments on Taylor's Commentary on Mark."

the *mysterion* of Mk 4:11 could connote 'secret rites' as well as 'esoteric knowledge communicated to "initiates."'"[14] The difference between the two statements is interesting. Quesnell pictures Smith insisting that the mystery of the kingdom of God *could* involve secret rites *as well as* esoteric knowledge, whereas Evans pictures Smith insisting that this mystery involves only secret rites. In any case, the present authors see no indication that Smith argued against Taylor that the mystery of the kingdom of God refers to secret rites. Smith's three-page discussion is too long to reproduce here, so we will instead present a summary of Smith's arguments and ask the reader to compare it against Smith's discussion.

Smith is responding to the following statements written by Taylor:

> In the NT, and especially in the Pauline Epp., it [μυστήριον] means an "open secret" made known by God, and is used of the Gospel, or the inclusion of the Gentiles. There is no case in which it connotes secret rites or esoteric knowledge communicated to "initiates." In the present passage [Mark 4:11] and its parallels [in Matthew and Luke], it is used of a knowledge concerning the Kingdom of God which has been imparted to the disciples, but not to the people in general.[15]

Smith first remarks that the second and third sentences appear contradictory. He conjectures that Taylor might have intended to use the word "Elsewhere" at the beginning of the first sentence—that is, to state that although *elsewhere* in the New Testament μυστήριον means an open secret, here in Mark 4:11 it connotes secret rites or esoteric knowledge communicated to initiates. As an alternative explanation, Smith conjectures that Taylor is not equating the terms *disciples* and *initiates*, and therefore is presuming that the knowledge that Mark 4:11 reserves for disciples is not esoteric knowledge (like that of the mysteries) that is communicated to "initiates." In other words, Smith does not know what Taylor means here. However, he is certain that Taylor's first statement that μυστήριον always denotes an open secret in the New Testament is incorrect, and he cites "1 Cor. 2.6 f.

---

14. Quesnell, "Question of Evidence," 60. Evans does not cite Quesnell, nor does he mention what Smith wrote in reply to this statement in Smith, "On the Authenticity," 198. Smith wrote, "Quesnell says (p. 60 and n. 28) that I 'insisted against Taylor that the *mystērion* of Mk 4:11 could connote "secret rites."' This statement, too, is false. In the passage he cites—*HTR* 48 (1955) 29, contradicting Taylor's claim that *mystērion* 'in the NT . . . means an "open secret" . . . There is no case in which it connotes secret rites,'—I said nothing of secret rites, but merely insisted that traditions about Jesus' secrecy may be partially accurate."

15. Taylor, *Gospel according to St. Mark*, 255.

(cf. 3.1–3); Col. 2.2; Eph. 5.32" as passages that disprove the statement.[16] He then adds, "In 1 Cor. Paul says plainly that there is a wisdom which he preaches among the 'initiate' (τελείοις), but which he cannot yet preach to the Corinthians because they are still 'carnal.' Paul, therefore, claimed to have a secret doctrine."[17] Smith does note that the word "initiate" exists in Paul's statement, because this word contradicts Taylor's second sentence, but he does not apply this observation to Mark 4:11 (which does not use the word). He is simply demonstrating that Taylor's generalizations are contradicted by several passages in the Pauline writings.

Smith then returns to the depiction of Jesus privately teaching his disciples a mystery in Mark 4:11. Smith notes that Mark depicts Jesus "as teaching in secret and commanding secrecy on many occasions" and that the reasons for this were likely more diverse than the umbrella motives proposed as solutions to the supposed "Messianic secret": "Actually, the early Church had a wide variety of motives for attributing secret doctrine to Jesus, and among them may well have been the recollection that Jesus (also for a wide variety of motives) practiced secrecy. Every such attribution, therefore, must be judged individually."[18] To illustrate this point, Smith offers his own interpretation of Mark 4:11–12. The saying reads, "And he said to them, 'To you has been given the [mystery] of the kingdom of God, but for those outside everything is in parables; so that they may indeed see but not perceive, and may indeed hear but not understand; lest they should turn again, and be forgiven.'" Smith writes:

> Mk. 4.11–12 is probably an answer to Jewish polemic. The Jews are saying, "Jesus was not the Messiah, because if he had been he would have been recognized by our scholars. He was heard and rejected." The Christian answer is, "They never heard his true teaching. He revealed the mysteries of the Kingdom only to his disciples; for outsiders he had only parables. Thus he fulfilled God's command to prevent the Jews from believing."[19]

This is the point at which Smith starts to argue vigorously. He seems offended by what he sees as Taylor's apologetic attempt to read 4:12 in a way that evades the implication that God intended the Jews not to believe. Smith's interpretation of 4:11–12 is obviously important to the question of whether he thought that this saying refers to either sex or secret rites. And

16. Smith, "Comments," 29.
17. Ibid.
18. Ibid.
19. Ibid., 29–30.

we learn some very important things here. First, the logic of Smith's argument requires "the mysteries" (sic, pl.) to refer to "[Jesus'] true teaching" which, if the Jewish scholars had heard it, would have convinced them that he was the messiah. Thus, Smith was thinking of the mysteries of the kingdom of God as teachings, not rites. Second, he thought that this saying emerged *after* Jesus' time, as a Christian answer to Jewish polemic. Smith likely already assumed as much when he wrote *Tannaitic Parallels*, for he introduced Mark 4:11–12 as "words put in the mouth of Jesus."[20] Third, Smith's post-Easter origin for these two verses would disqualify "the mystery of the kingdom of God" as evidence pertaining to the life of the historical Jesus.[21]

Evans does not inform his reader that Smith actually interpreted "the mysteries of the kingdom of God" in his article. Instead, Evans proceeds to link this mystery with "prohibited sexual activities" by speculating about what sort of secrecy Smith was talking about:

> Jesus "practiced secrecy," we are told, "for a wide variety of reasons." What could Smith have had in mind? Could one of those reasons have had to do with teaching regarding prohibited sexual activities, as perhaps hinted at in his dissertation [*Tannaitic Parallels*]? And as hinted at in subsequent publications, not to mention his remarkable discovery at Mar Saba? (X-ref)

This unnecessary speculation about what Smith might have meant evades what Smith actually wrote. Had Evans informed his readers that Smith read Mark 4:11–12 as post-Easter Christian apologetic and that the secrets it implies concern teachings that would have convinced the Jews of Jesus' messiahship had they heard them, it would be clear to everyone that these secrets do not involve forbidden sexual behaviour. In fact, there is no need to speculate about what Smith might have had in mind, for he discussed Jesus' secrecy in several places in this article:

> In [Mark] 4.11 f. the concern is to explain the rejection by the Jews, in 4.34, to discredit outside teachers and justify the disciples' claim to a monopoly of the true, secret doctrine. (p. 31)

> Jesus' failure to produce a sign of his Messiahship was evidently one of the strong points of Jewish polemic . . . it appears that

---

20. Smith, *Tannaitic Parallels*, 156 (the same passage from this book that was quoted earlier).

21. That conclusion would imply that the reference back to 4:11 in the mystic gospel is also unhistorical and that the gospel story Smith discovered cannot be used to reconstruct a rite of the historical Jesus. Cf. Brown, "Factualizing the Folklore," 324–25.

even for his followers Jesus did no "sign" during his lifetime. His opponents knew this and made the most of it. . . . His followers . . . may also have tried to contradict it by circulating a story that he gave his "sign" (the Transfiguration) in secret to his three most intimate disciples, but forbade them to speak of it till after his resurrection (Mk. 9.9). (pp. 39–40 n. 26)

But it seems easier to explain the apparent distinction [between Jesus and "the Son of man" in Mark 8:38] as a product of one of the secrecy themes of Mk.'s sources (possibly reflecting the behavior of Jesus himself). Certainly that is indicated by the structure of 8.27–9.1: Jesus reveals his rank to the disciples by treating Peter's guess [that Jesus is the Messiah] as correct. He then begins to teach them further secrets about the Messiah, especially his destined suffering. Peter protests. Jesus rebukes him and shuts off any possible questions or objections by calling the crowd and teaching them the same thing, keeping concealed only the identity of the Messiah. (p. 43)

In sum: These two sorts of prediction were current in the early Church. Both were useful. (On the one hand: To *us* have been revealed the secret signs of the End. On the other: Do not despair, it may come any minute, better repent now.) So both were preserved. (p. 42)

The only element of Jesus' apocalyptic teaching which would certainly have had to be changed, "explained" or suppressed before 70 A.D. would have been a false prophecy of specific events for a date prior to 70. (Can it be that Jesus' unusually clear and emphatic refusal, in Mk., to set a date, contradicts some deliberately lost tradition of a date which he did set?). (p. 52 n. 43)

Therefore they had to explain the somewhat humiliating fact that Jesus had not revealed the exact date, even to his closest followers. They passed on the humiliation to Jesus and made him explain in Mk. 13.32 that this is a secret kept by the Father to Himself. (pp. 53–54 n. 45)

These statements show us that Smith pictured a situation in which the church had to defend its belief in Jesus' messiahship against counterarguments from unpersuaded Jews. In Smith's view, Mark 4:11–12 explains Jewish disbelief in a general way and gives a scriptural rationale for it. The transfiguration explains why the Jews did not witness any sign of Jesus' messiahship and are only hearing about this sign now. Jesus' rebuke of Peter explains that Jesus never announced his messiahship to the crowds but taught them only the doctrine that the messiah would have to suffer. Hence only his disciples knew that Jesus was the messiah. Christians also had secret knowledge of the coming End and appealed to secrecy in order to account for their lack of a date for the End.

These messianic and eschatological secrets are the ones that Smith is actually writing about. Smith himself said as much when Quesnell originally asserted that Smith was talking about secret rites: "I said nothing of secret rites, but merely insisted that traditions about Jesus' secrecy may be partially accurate. The other passages cited by Quesnell from the same article deal with eschatological and messianic secrets and have nothing to do with any secret rite."[22] So contrary to Evans's claims, we have found no evidence that Smith thought that the mystery of the kingdom of God referred to either sex or secret rites before 1958, *only clear evidence that he did not.*

At best we can affirm that Smith linked the mystery of the kingdom of God to secret *teachings* here. This should not surprise anyone. Together with Mark 4:33–34, these verses indicate that Jesus spoke to the crowds in parables in order to prevent them from understanding what he was saying, but privately explained everything to his disciples. The notion of secret teachings that Jesus withheld from everyone but his disciples *is explicit in the text.*

We now come to the third paper discussed by Evans, Smith's essay "The Image of God," which he wrote in 1955, updated in 1956, and published in 1958.[23] Evans points out that Smith mentions both the *Hagigah* passage from the Tosefta and Clement of Alexandria and his *Stromateis* as examples of esoteric teaching. Evans then devotes a paragraph to demonstrating that "Smith also talks about the initiate's union with his god" (p. 84). By this Evans means to imply that this 1958 publication contains something resembling the interpretation that Smith later offered of the mystery of the kingdom of God in the "secret" Gospel of Mark in terms of a rite that produces union with Jesus' spirit and maybe involves physical union as well. The way Evans argues this point is worth reflecting on, for this is one of the few original arguments in his paper and it typifies his use of evidence.

First, Evans takes the word "initiate" for the person who unites with his "god" (lowercased, implying something like a pagan god, divine man,

---

22. Smith, "Authenticity," 198.

23. Smith, "The Image of God." The paragraph in question appears on pp. 144–45 of the Brill reprint. (Smith, *Studies 1)*

or a magician) from a paragraph on page 488 (of the original publication), which is nineteen pages before the footnote citation of Clement. Here Smith is describing Erwin R. Goodenough's thesis in *Jewish Symbols in the Greco-Roman Period*[24] that Jews in the Greco-Roman world borrowed the language of the mystery religions to describe their understanding of salvation. Smith writes,

> As to the significance of these [archaeological] remains [of Greco-Roman Judaism], Goodenough finds that most of the religious Jews in the Greco-Roman world (which for him includes, as it did in fact, Palestine) were primarily concerned about salvation, by which they meant spiritual peace in this life and the assurance of happiness hereafter. To describe this salvation they certainly used the language of the mystery religions and to achieve it, he thinks, they may have adopted some of the mystery rites, particularly those involving a cup of wine which brought some special blessing. They gave a mystic interpretation to the Sabbath and the festivals and called those who agreed with them "initiates," as contrasted with those who did not. That some Jews went further than this, Goodenough says, is possible, but unsubstantiated . . .[25]

This information illuminates the way Goodenough interpreted the symbolism contained in the archaeological remains of Greco-Roman Judaism. Reading these remains in the light of Philo's mystical Judaism, Goodenough argued that a similar kind of Judaism existed throughout the Greco-Roman world. According to Smith's description of Goodenough's position, the adherents of this mostly hypothetical Judaism referred to themselves as "initiates." There is no reference to union with a god, and Smith himself is not even endorsing Goodenough's position. In fact, Smith very clearly pronounced this thesis a failure.[26] Smith is not even

---

24. Goodenough, *Jewish Symbols in the Greco-Roman Period*, 13 vols.

25. Smith, "Image of God," 128–29.

26. Smith, "Goodenough's *Jewish Symbols* in Retrospect"; see particularly 58–59: "But with his [Goodenough's] failure to demonstrate the prevalence of a belief in sacramental salvation the main structure of his argument was ruined. That the Jews *commonly* took over pagan symbols for a mystic significance which those symbols did not *commonly* have, is incredible. So the borrowing of these symbols cannot *commonly* be evidence of a mystic Judaism. Individual mystics there doubtless were. Philo *may* have been one (though Goodenough's interpretation of him is by no means certain; contrast Wolfson!). But the difficulties in the supposition of a *widespread, uniform* mystical Judaism are formidable. How did it happen that such a system and practice disappeared without leaving a trace in either Jewish or Christian polemics?"

responsible for the wording of this description of Goodenough's position. A letter that Goodenough wrote to Smith reveals that Smith showed this paper to Goodenough prior to publication, and Goodenough edited precisely this paragraph so that it described his position in these exact words.[27] So Evans's citation of the word "initiate" in this context to prove that "Smith also talks about the initiate's union with his god" in this article is illegitimate on many levels.

Evans further notes that in a footnote twenty-seven pages prior to the reference to Clement, "Smith speaks of magical prayers and Jewish mystics, whose favorite prayer was the Qedushah, all of which suggests that 'the recitation of the Qedushah was conceived as a means of invoking the deity or a result of union with him'" (p. 84). Evans neglects to note that Smith was summarizing the thesis and evidence in a paper by E. Peterson.[28] In any event, we must recall that the union that Evans wishes us to picture is sexual ("forbidden sexual relationships, including union with a god"), and Peterson's theory evidently refers to mystical union with the divine, a well-known spiritual state which does not involve a penis or render one guilty of sexual misconduct.

Next, Evans states, "In another context Smith speaks of God uniting with the holy person" (pp. 84–85). In this instance the word "union" does indeed represent an idea that is undeniably Smith's, but Smith was referring to religious symbols that can have more than one reference, and the word *union* here refers to a particular symbol that simultaneously represents God and the saint. It is the symbol that unites God and the holy person by representing both simultaneously, not God and the holy person that are united. By no stretch of the imagination could this use of the word *union* be construed as sexual.

In the last of his examples, Evans plumbs another footnote for an indication that Smith associated Jesus with sex. The footnote in question develops the following argument: (1) A. D. Nock believes that a particular Jewish charm noted by Goodenough "cannot be Jewish, because it is part of a technique to obtain Eros as a familiar spirit," but concedes that it might derive from "a Jew who had wholly or partly abandoned tradition." (2) Smith objects, "If a Jew could be supposed to invoke Beelzebub, he could be supposed to invoke Eros." (3) Therefore, Smith concludes, the

---

27. Goodenough, letter to Morton Smith, 5 December 1955. Manuscripts and Archives, Yale University Library.

28. Smith, "Image of God," 121–22 n. 29.

charm could be Jewish.²⁹ About this argument Evans writes, "Smith's 'Jew' here, of course, is Jesus, whose critics claimed that he had accessed the power of Beelzebul (cf. Matt 12:24; Mark 3:22; Luke 11:15), while 'Eros' refers to the Greek god of sexual love" (p. 85). In this way Evans finds Smith connecting Jesus to a small-g god of sex.

This is certainly the most plausible aspect of this particular argument. The problem with this reasoning, however, is that the two individuals are not the same. For while Jesus is certainly the example of the Jew who was thought by some to be possessed by Beelzebub, the person who "could be supposed to invoke Eros" is the unknown individual who composed the charm. Smith is not suggesting that Jesus authored this charm. He is suggesting that the author could be a Jew.

Clearly, Evans's demonstration that "Smith also talks about the initiate's union with his god" is a fabrication produced by drawing together scattered, unrelated, and misrepresented words and phrases.

Evans now turns to the second unexpected theme that he finds in Smith's pre-find writings. Relying on Francis Watson (who is relying on Stephen Carlson),³⁰ Evans writes,

> The second unusual feature that Smith surmised was that the evangelist Mark may well have omitted materials that contained Johannine traits. In his 1955 review of Taylor's commentary Smith speaks of the possibility that the evangelist Mark may have omitted material. This, of course, is the point at issue in Clement's Mar Saba letter—material omitted from the Markan Gospel. Smith also discusses Mark's use of a source with "Johannine traits." This is precisely what the first and long quotation of *Secret Mark* is—a passage with Johannine traits (cf. John 11, the raising of Lazarus) that had been omitted from public (i.e., canonical) Mark. Watson comments: "Clement's letter confirms Smith's surmise that Mark may have 'deliberately censored' his source-material, and that this source-material may have included proto-Johannine elements." (pp. 85–86)

There are two elements in this argument with which we agree. First, the *Letter to Theodore* does refer to Mark omitting materials. Second, Smith did draw attention to Johannine qualities in the group of controversy stories in Mark 2:1—3:6 and suggest that at this point Mark may have

---

29. Ibid., 126 n. 46.
30. Watson, "Beyond Suspicion."

used a source that contained "Johannine traits."[31] However, we believe that the rest of this argument is mistaken. Evans finds it suspicious that Smith's discovery confirmed his conjecture about Mark's use of a source with Johannine traits, but it actually does not. As Smith himself demonstrated, the long quotation from *Secret Mark* completely lacks Johannine traits. Brown confirmed this in *Mark's Other Gospel*.[32] The evidence in the letter suggests that we are dealing, not with a situation in which Mark uses a source with Johannine traits, but with a situation in which Mark and John work independently of each other. The Gospels of Mark and John relate many of the same incidents, and when they do, they lack each other's distinctive traits. So the absence of Johannine traits in *Secret Mark*'s extant story is what we would expect if Mark himself wrote it and did not rely on a source that had Johannine elements.[33]

The issue of censorship is likewise confused. Following Watson, Evans cites this comment in Smith's review of Taylor:

> Mk. was remote from the historical situation, his interests were those of the Church of his day, and whatever did not serve those interests—e.g., whatever historical framework his sources may have contained—was just what he would leave out as uninteresting, even if he did not deliberately censor it.[34]

Watson and Evans find the words "deliberately censor" very interesting, but seem not to notice the word that precedes them. In order to understand this sentence, we need to read it in context.

These words conclude Smith's remarks on Taylor's reasoning that, since Mark's account of Jesus sending out the twelve (6:7–13) displays no real knowledge about what they did, it is probably redactional. Smith first notes that this conclusion does not sit well with Taylor's opinion that Mark was Peter's close associate. Smith then suggests that "the tradition which governed the ordering of events in this part of Mk. may have been more

---

31. Smith, "Comments," 26.

32. Smith, *Clement of Alexandria*, 152–58; Smith, *Secret Gospel*, 53–56; Brown, *Mark's Other Gospel*, 85–92. On a liberal estimate, roughly 41 of the 54 verses in John's account (76%) contain features that are *possibly* secondary or Johannine (ibid., 86). None of these features appear in the mystic gospel's account. Pantuck already addressed the issue Evans raises here in "Solving the *Mysterion* of Morton Smith and the Secret Gospel of Mark."

33. See Brown, "Longer Gospel of Mark and the Synoptic Problem."

34. Smith, "Comments," 35.

reliable than T. believes."[35] Smith offers the following reconstruction of its historical framework:

> Rejected at home [i.e., Nazareth in 6:1–6], Jesus might well send out the disciples to prospect for friendlier villages [6:7–13]. Such missionary activity would bring his name to Herod's ears [6:14]. If Herod's execution of John [6:15–29] was motivated, as Josephus says it was (Ant. 18.118), by fear of a rising, then the knowledge that a former disciple of John's was sending preachers about the countryside would have been just the thing to touch it off. It would also have motivated Herod's plan to kill Jesus [Luke 13:31]. Jesus' reported courage [in Luke 13:32] may well have been sobered by the arrival of John's followers [Matt 11:2–3?], from his obsequies (Mt. 14.12), and the return of the disciples with nothing much to report (Mk. 6.30). It would then be understandable that Jesus should take to the open country for a little rest (6.31). It is equally understandable that [as Taylor observes] "Mark himself does not represent the movements of Jesus as a flight from Herod" (p. 308) [in contrast to Matt 14:13].[36]

The sentence that Evans and Watson quote directly follows. Seen in its context, it is clear that Smith is trying to account for the missing historical framework in Mark 6 that Mark's sources seem to presuppose. Appealing to the common wisdom of his day, Smith explains that Mark's interests were not historical but ecclesiastical, and those Church interests influenced what Mark included or left out. Hence Mark was apt to omit such "uninteresting" things as "whatever historical framework his sources may have contained . . . even if he did not deliberately censor it."

This is not a conjecture about Mark deliberately censoring things that he finds problematic. It is an explanation for Mark's lack of interest in the historical framework, in what his sources likely told him about why one event leads to the next. Smith made the same point about the narratives in the Hebrew Scriptures:

> Even when there is a historical framework, as in Kings, the interest of the author is not in this framework, but in the miracles of the prophets and, more generally, in the miraculous management by Yahweh, who used natural and supernatural events alike to punish Israel for its sins. To explain away a miracle by imagining some sequence of natural events which might have

35. Ibid., 34.
36. Ibid., 34–35.

produced the same effect is to misunderstand the genre of the story and to thwart the author's purpose in telling it; his primary concern was not to report what happened, but to give glory to Yahweh.[37]

So how does this unexceptional appeal to the insights of redaction criticism turn into proof for a supposedly unusual belief about Mark censoring "problematic" materials? And how do those problematic materials come to include Johannine traits or proto-Johannine elements? The process is interesting to watch. After properly quoting Smith, Watson paraphrases Smith as suggesting that "reliable but irrelevant or problematic material in [Mark's] sources may actually have been 'censored.'"[38] In the space of two sentences, Watson has reinterpreted the word "uninteresting" as meaning "irrelevant *or* problematic" and recast Smith's "he did not deliberately censor it [the historical framework]" as "these sources may actually have been 'censored' [by Mark]," thus inverting Smith's meaning. Further down the same page, Watson simply excises the word "irrelevant": "Already in 1955, Smith envisages the possibility that Mark may have 'deliberately censored' material in his sources that he finds problematic, and that at least one of those sources is common to Mark and John."[39] In this statement Watson additionally juxtaposes the issue of Mark omitting details with the separate issue of Mark possibly knowing a source with Johannine traits. By the end of the paragraph these separate issues become a single "surmise": "Clement's letter confirms Smith's surmise that Mark may have 'deliberately censored' his source-material, and that this source-material may have included proto-Johannine elements."[40] Again, a few pages later: "He [Smith] had already surmised that Mark may have omitted or censored material present in the older authentic tradition he inherited—tradition shared in part with the Fourth Evangelist."[41] Evans subsequently continues the trend by foregrounding Watson's characterizations of Smith's statement, relegating Smith's original statement to a footnote, and explicitly conflating the separate issues: "The second unusual feature that Smith surmised was that the evangelist Mark may well have omitted materials that contained Johannine traits" (cf. "Markan materials omitted from Mark that exhibit Johannine traits"; "omitted Markan mate-

37. Smith, "Present State of Old Testament Studies," 20.
38. Watson, "Beyond Suspicion," 157.
39. Ibid., 157–58.
40. Ibid., 158.
41. Ibid., 161.

rial with Johannine traits"; p. 85). If it were true that *Secret Mark* exhibits Johannine traits, the evidence could now fit the theory.

Smith's further comment, cited by Evans, to the effect that "Jewish material has come down to us heavily censored" (p. 86)[42] does not bring us any closer to demonstrating Smith's prior knowledge of his discovery.

We may now summarize what we believe Evans has successfully demonstrated with respect to Smith's prior knowledge of his discovery:

- Smith mentioned the mystery of the kingdom of God as an example of secret teaching in 1951 and 1955.
- Smith mentioned Clement and his *Stromateis* as examples of secret teaching in 1958.

The results are meagre. Yet we may still ask whether these particular themes are what Evans's thesis requires them to be, namely, "quite unusual themes" that, "apart from Professor Smith himself, . . . are themes advanced by no one else" (p. 82).

Clearly that is not the case. These were not new and unusual ideas that lacked textual substantiation. Rather, to scholars of early Christianity and Judaism, they were simply common knowledge. Mark himself describes the mystery of the kingdom of God as a secret that Jesus expounded only to his closest disciples (4:10–12), and Clement's secrecy is a prominent theme in the *Stromateis*. Clement himself used Mark 4:11 to justify his own secrecy (*Strom.* V.12.80.6), thereby implicating himself in Smith's discovery. The standard nature of this knowledge is readily illustrated. As Brown had already noted,[43] the third chapter of Joachim Jeremias's *The Eucharistic Words of Jesus* (published in German in 1935 and significantly revised and enlarged in 1960)[44] contains a subsection in which Jeremias illustrates how "The whole environment of primitive Christianity knows the element of the esoteric." In the space of six pages (pp. 125–31) Jeremias discusses the examples of Clement and his *Stromateis*, *Hagigah* 2.1, the mystery of the kingdom of God, 1 Cor 2:6, and Paul's use of the word τέλειοι.

---

42. Citing Smith, "Image of God," 486–87 (repr. in *Studies*, 1:127–28).

43. Brown, "Factualizing the Folklore," 323.

44. Jeremias, *Abendmahlsworte Jesu*, 3rd ed. (1960). I am referencing the 1966 English translation by Norman Perrin, which was based on the 1960 German edition and contains Jeremias's additions up to 1964 (London: SCM).

Ancient Gospel or Modern Forgery?

THE CASE OF THE MAR SABA MYSTERY

Returning to the matter of *The Mystery of Mar Saba*, Evans discusses two parallels noted by Watson between Smith's account of his discovery and Hunter's novel. In the novel, Sir William Bracebridge observes that "most of [the manuscripts] were removed [from Mar Saba], but I have always had the feeling that some might have been overlooked and hidden away. My supposition proved correct."[45] In his popular book, Smith wrote: "I had not expected much from the Mar Saba manuscripts, since I knew that almost all of them had been carried off to Jerusalem ... But there was always the chance that something had been missed."[46] Watson finds it remarkable that both Smith and Bracebridge should "visit the Mar Saba monastery with exactly the same expectation."[47] Furthermore, while Bracebridge reports that "I was prepared to leave Mar Saba, *reconciled* to the negative results of my search, when a monk told me he had certain manuscripts in his *cell* that had evidently been overlooked ..." (italics added),[48] Smith reports that he was "gradually *reconciling* myself to my worst expectations and repeating every day that I should discover nothing of importance. Then, one afternoon near the end of my stay, I found myself in my *cell*, staring incredulously at a text written in tiny scrawl ..." (italics added).[49] Evans joins Watson in affirming that "Smith's dependence on Hunter appears to be the unavoidable conclusion" (p. 91).

While these similarities are interesting, one can imagine scenarios other than direct causation to explain them. Take for instance the realities of manuscript hunting. Smith "became interested in Greek manuscripts and manuscript hunting" "under the influence of Professor Werner Jaeger,"[50] and by 1958 he had already spent a lot of time scouring the holy lands for rare and unknown manuscripts. He spent a year from 1951 to 1952 visiting minor Greek monasteries to catalogue their manuscript holdings, several months in 1958 in Palestine and Turkey during which he visited Mar Saba, and some time in 1966 in Syria searching for Hebrew manuscripts. There is no need to appeal to a fictional book to explain Smith's expectations of what he might find when his real-life experiences

---

45. Hunter, *Mystery of Mar Saba*, 279.
46. Smith, *Secret Gospel*, 11.
47. Watson, "Beyond Suspicion," 165.
48. Hunter, *Mystery of Mar Saba*, 293.
49. Smith, *Secret Gospel*, 12.
50. Ibid., 8.

had taught him how much hunting is needed to find anything of value. As he noted in 1959, "the Classical texts of the monasteries were systematically hunted out by both eastern and western European collectors or dealers" and accordingly "a great deal of comparatively worthless material must be gone through in the hope of finding a few things of value."[51] So it should not surprise us that when he came to Mar Saba he was not particularly hopeful and that his hope was waning with each passing day.

Whereas Smith was a real manuscript hunter, Hunter's character Bracebridge is a fictional one, an invention that Hunter consciously patterned after one of Smith's famous predecessors, Constantin von Tischendorf. This is clear when Bracebridge states that his discovery happened "In almost the same way in which Tischendorf found the Sinaiticus" and later states,

> "You will recall, gentlemen, that when Tischendorf visited the monastery of St. Catherine at Mount Sinai on his last journey in 1859, he was on the point of leaving, disappointed at his failure to find the remnant of the manuscript, some pages of which he had rescued from being burned some fifteen years previously. On his last evening there a young monk showed him a Greek manuscript which turned out to be the famous Sinaiticus, of which you are now the custodians for the people of the Empire and the world. I recall these facts to show how history has repeated itself in my case."[52]

The discovery in Hunter's novel is a clear case of art imitating life. Smith lived that life and therefore had similar expectations.

DISPUTED SCIENCE

In this section Evans retreats from his previous claims that the science of handwriting analysis has proved the letter to be a forgery. When Carlson's book *The Gospel Hoax* came out, Evans promoted Carlson's analysis of the manuscript's handwriting as a triumph of science, even volunteering his own promotional blurb:

> With his expertise in the legal and forensic aspects of exposing forgeries . . . Carlson has shown persuasively, [that] the handwritten document is not written at all—it is drawn, as forgers

---

51. Smith, "Monasteries and Their Manuscripts," 175, 177.
52. Hunter, *Mystery of Mar Saba*, 281, 293.

inevitably do when imitating a hand not their own. All of the usual indicators of forgery are present, including the "forger's tremor." ... These telling details and many more have been laid bare by Carlson, with the result that the controversy surrounding this unverified discovery has finally been laid to rest. Scholars owe Stephen Carlson a word of thanks.[53]

Concerning the identity of the forger, Evans likewise declared,

> the recently published clear, color photographs of the document have given experts in the science of forgery detection the opportunity to analyze the document's handwriting and compare it with samples of handwriting from the late Professor Smith. The evidence is compelling and conclusive: Smith wrote the text.[54]

Evans's present contribution, however, presents the practice of questioned document examination as a fallible enterprise: "Had the matter [of the Hitler diaries] been left to handwriting 'experts,' it would have been necessary to rewrite history" (p. 93). The main reason for this extraordinary reversal is likely the fact that Venetia Anastasopoulou, a professional Greek questioned document examiner, has now offered a thirty-six page analysis of the letter's handwriting and found no evidence favouring forgery but did find abundant evidence favouring authenticity (i.e., she believes that the handwriting was not imitated but was rendered quickly, naturally, and unconsciously). She also compared Smith's Greek handwriting with that of the letter and concluded that he was very far from capable of imitating a hand of this calibre.[55]

Responding to this turn of events, Evans now suggests an uneven split: "Carlson and two handwriting experts, one English-speaking and one Greek-speaking, think Smith wrote the document in question. Another Greek-speaking handwriting expert thinks he did not" (p. 93). Here at least Evans tacitly acknowledges that Carlson himself is not a handwriting expert—or, as Evans would prefer to put it, that "Carlson does not regard himself as a handwriting expert per se" (p. 92). In actual fact, Carlson has no credentials, training, or even prior experience in this field, and

---

53. Danny Zacharias, a student of Evans, posted this blurb on the internet 6 November 2005. It is presently available at "The Gospel Hoax."

54. Evans and Tov, eds., *Exploring the Origins of the Bible*, 169. Cf. Evans, *Fabricating Jesus*, 95; Evans, "How Scholars Fabricate Jesus," 144; Evans, interview in Strobel, *Case for the Real Jesus*, 49, 50.

55. Anastasopoulou, "Experts Report Handwriting Examination." See also Shanks, "Handwriting Experts Weigh In on 'Secret Mark.'"

the fundamental mistakes he made are a matter of public record.[56] Still, Evans claims that the English-speaking questioned document examiner Julie Edison arrived at the same conclusions as Carlson through a joint investigation. But that is not so. Carlson implied that Edison validated his analysis, but when the authors contacted Edison directly, she indicated that she did not express "a professional opinion regarding Morton Smith's Letter of Clement,"[57] that she is in fact not qualified to do so due to her unfamiliarity with Greek, and that she met with Carlson for only a few hours on a single afternoon,[58] after which she wrote a letter assessing his methods (not his competence in employing them) and never heard from him again. Carlson posted excerpts of that letter on the internet[59] but omitted everything in it that was critical of his method or otherwise unhelpful, including her statement "Although my undergraduate degree is in history, my knowledge of ancient Greece, Rome, and early Christianity is basic at best. And I have a limited knowledge of the Greek alphabet." It was this omission that allowed Evans and others to infer that she is qualified to assess the document and in fact did so—an inference that Carlson has to date done nothing to correct.

Edison's letter, moreover, offers no indication that she thought that "Smith wrote the document" (Evans's words) or even examined Smith's handwriting. Nor did she examine the colour photographs. Instead, she recalls, "We only looked at a book containing writings attributed to Clement; and possibly a sheet containing symbols of the 18th century Greek alphabet."[60] Presumably the book that Edison saw was Smith's *Clement of Alexandria and a Secret Gospel of Mark*, which contains the halftone reproductions of Smith's own black-and-white photographs that Carlson

---

56. See Brown, "Factualizing the Folklore," 293–306; Pantuck and Brown, "Morton Smith as M. Madiotes"; Viklund, "Tremors, or Just an Optical Illusion?; Brown and Pantuck, "Stephen Carlson's Questionable Questioned Document Examination"; Brown, "My Thoughts on the Reports by Venetia Anastasopoulou" (see the last five pages).

57. Julie Edison, e-mails to Allan J. Pantuck, 2 and 3 March 2010.

58. Ibid., 3 and 7 March 2010.

59. Carlson posted Edison's letter on the Yahoo Group Textual Criticism (http://groups.yahoo.com/group/textualcriticism/message/1224) and on his blog: Carlson, "Some Initial Reviews and a Second Opinion."

60. Edison, e-mail to Pantuck, 5 March 2010. Carlson never borrowed the colour photographs from their owner, Charles W. Hedrick, nor asked Hedrick to provide him with prints or scans (Hedrick, e-mail to Scott G. Brown, 25 June 2005). Smith's own black-and-white photographs of the manuscript were then still unavailable inside Smith's archive at the Jewish Theological Seminary, which had not yet been catalogued.

based his handwriting figures on. The difference between halftone reproductions and actual photographs is very significant. Halftone reproductions of the kind used in Smith's book modify the information that exists in a photograph, reducing the full tonal range to a grid of dots that differ from each other only in size and shape (the largest dots fill their section of the grid and become squares). At an ordinary viewing distance, these dots merge in our perception with the white space around them (the paper) to produce the illusion of continuous tone (grayscale). The illusion of seeing shades between white and black disappears as soon as one magnifies the image to the point that the dots become visible. At that point, one is looking at the binary halftone apparatus, which is not at all an accurate representation of the illusion it creates. As we noted in an earlier study:

> What up close appears as a jagged line [in a halftone image] might appear as a smooth gray line in the original photo. Curved lines and straight lines angled away from the orientation of the screen have a stepped appearance that resembles a halting pen movement. The result is phantom tremors and blobs and disconnections that do not exist in the original photographs.[61]

Accordingly, halftone reproductions have long been deemed unacceptable as the basis for questioned document examination.[62] But this is precisely what Carlson and Edison based their observations on.

In any event, despite viewing unreliable evidence, Edison never claimed to see a forger's tremor in the handwriting, again contrary to Evans's statement. Evans's narrative about Carlson studying "large color photographs of the text" and "bringing in handwriting experts [*sic*, pl.]" who "examined the magnified photos" and discovered "what they call 'forger's tremor'" is apologetic fiction.[63]

This leaves Agamemnon Tselikas as a handwriting expert who is on Evans's side.[64] Tselikas is certainly a well-respected expert in Greek palaeography. Like Anastasopoulou, he had scans of the original photographs (both black-and-white and colour) at his disposal. The fundamental problem, however, is that palaeographers are not questioned document examiners. As Tom Davis notes, "Palaeographers and document analysts have curiously little in common. . . . Palaeographers and forensic scientists

---

61. Brown and Pantuck, "Stephen Carlson's Questionable Questioned Document Examination," 3.

62. Hilton, *Scientific Examination*, 282–83.

63. Evans, interview in Strobel, *Case for the Real Jesus*, 49–50.

64. Tselikas, "Agamemnon Tselikas' Handwriting Analysis Report."

read and write for different journals, attend different conferences, work in different environments, and do not communicate with each other."[65] Questioned document examiners spend most of their time attempting to answer the two questions that most interest us: Is this disputed document (or amendment, or signature) a forgery? And could this suspect have written this document? By contrast, palaeographers study the history of a form of handwriting, often with the goal of deciphering old documents and bringing their contents to light. Palaeographers do not normally encounter imitated handwriting in the course of their work, so their training does not extend to the detection of forged handwriting. Moreover, according to Davis, "nowhere in the literature of their subjects [is] there an agreed and established methodology for testing the hypothesis of common authorship by examining handwriting."[66] It is the questioned document examiners who have well-established methods for identifying authors and forged handwriting. Anastasopoulou followed these methods when she looked for signs of both forgery and authenticity in the manuscript's handwriting and when she systematically compared how Smith and the writer of Mar Saba 65 form each letter. Tselikas did not.

In our opinion, only one properly qualified expert in questioned document examination has thus far studied suitable images of Mar Saba 65 and rendered a knowledgeable opinion on the matters of whether this writing is imitated and whether Smith could have produced it. This expert's observations indicate that the manuscript most likely contains someone's natural handwriting, which in turn implies that it is from the eighteenth century (or possibly a bit earlier).[67]

THE CRITERION OF KNOWING THE FIND BEFORE MAKING THE FIND

After offering a summary of his previous arguments pertaining to prior knowledge and some advice for "scholars who remain unconvinced," (p. 94) Evans, again following Carlson, now suggests that "Smith knew perfectly well that the Mar Saba find was not authentic and therefore did not make use of the find in his later, serious work" (X-ref). Setting aside the notion that Smith's eight years of research on the letter differs from his other research in not being serious, we think the reason Smith relied little

65. Davis, "Practice of Handwriting Identification," 251.
66. Ibid., 252.
67. See Brown, "My Thoughts on the Reports by Venetia Anastasopoulou."

on his discovery in his later research is implied in a letter that he wrote to John Dart on September 24, 1977. Replying to Dart's observation (in a letter of September 19) that many of Smith's arguments about Jesus in his books on the secret gospel could have been supported by gnostic texts, Smith wrote:

> I'm happy that you've noticed the many similarities between my picture of Jesus and the traditions of early gnosticism, and I think you're quite right in supposing that you're onto something significant. I deliberately kept gnostic parallels out of my book on the secret gospel because I was trying to defend my opinion that this gospel tradition went back to the practice and teaching of Jesus himself. For this purpose the later parallels would not have been useful, and they would have given aid and comfort to the obscurantists who were sure to try to dismiss the new material as "gnostic and apocryphal." So the case for the contrary had to be made as far as possible from canonical material. But the gnostic parallels are undeniably there and I think they indicate that the gnostics were not late offshoots from the main stem of orthodox Christianity (as the Church fathers represented them), but were survivals of independent lines of early Christian tradition, and in some important aspects preserved the teaching and practice of Jesus more faithfully than did the orthodox (whose "orthodoxy," of course, came to them as a result of their victory in the contest for adherents, and before that victory—i.e., before the third century—was merely a claim they had in common with all other groups). I tried to demonstrate this fact of survival for the one gnostic I had to deal with in some detail—Carpocrates, see <u>Clement</u>, pp. 266-278—but of course the new gospel and the material about Jesus got all the attention, so nobody nobody [sic] noticed the question of survivals in gnosticism.[68]

This explanation for his avoidance of gnostic gospels may be compared to an observation Smith made to A. D. Nock in a letter from the winter of 1961: "Of course . . . [some of those] working on the [secret] Gospel text take it for granted that anything similar to the canonical gospels is derivative, and anything not similar, secondary. Thus they cover the field completely with only two false assumptions."[69] These remarks show that Smith was ever cognisant of the fact that his peers generally do not place non-canonical gospel evidence on a par with canonical gospel evidence.

68. Smith, letter to John Dart, 24 September 1977.

69. Smith, *Secret Gospel*, 67. The first pair of brackets is Smith's clarification, the second ours.

If he was going to convince his peers about anything related to Jesus, "the case ... had to be made as far as possible from canonical material."

We can see this approach in Smith's book *Jesus the Magician*, which relies mainly on the canonical gospels for its Christian ("insiders") evidence about Jesus.[70] This explanation might not satisfy Evans, however, who in a footnote remarks with astonishment that Smith neglected to mention the secret gospel on pages 122–23, 146, and 152 of this book, where "Smith speaks of the believer who 'will be united with' Jesus 'in love' and of Christians who 'adapted his magical rite of union so as to make it also a ritual expression of libertine teaching'" (p. 95 n. 73). Evans protests, "Here one would expect some discussion of the Mar Saba Clementine and the passage quoted from *Secret Mark*. Yet, strangely, there is no discussion and not even a reference in the footnotes" (p. 95 n. 73). The reason for this will be apparent to anyone who checks Evans's documentation. On those pages Smith was discussing the Eucharist, a different rite of union with Jesus than the one that Smith thought the "secret" gospel incident depicts (baptism). He discussed the secret gospel on pages 134–35 and 138 of that book in relation to the mystery of the kingdom of God, and he juxtaposed this presumed rite of union with the Eucharist on page 138.

CURIOUS FEATURES ABOUT THE FIND ITSELF

In this section Evans reshuffles various arguments from Carlson, Watson, Bart Ehrman, and Charles E. Murgia in an effort to demonstrate that Mar Saba 65 is odd in itself.[71]

---

70. Smith, *Jesus the Magician*.

71. This section originally began with the observation that "the book is speckled with mildew and mold spots, which is not what one would expect in a book preserved in a monastery in the arid Judean desert." Evans removed this point from the final paper, but since he has made this point elsewhere, and we took the time to research it, we will take the opportunity to respond. Here we have a deduction based on commonsense, but commonsense cannot tell us anything about the actual conditions in which this book was kept between its publication in Amsterdam in 1646 and Smith's arrival at Mar Saba 312 years later. Fortunately, various firsthand descriptions of Mar Saba exist from this period, some of which refer to dampness. The account by Henry Martyn Field, published in 1884, described this monastery as "dark, dingy, and musty" (*On the Desert*, 257). Henry Octavius Coxe's 1858 report on its manuscripts noted that the staircase leading up to the other library (the one attached to the chapel) seemed "admirably calculated to preserve its contents from damp and plunder," which likewise implies a problem with dampness in some parts of the monastery (*Report to Her Majesty's Government on the Greek Manuscripts Yet Remaining in Libraries of the Levant*, 11–12). The extensive water damage revealed in Smith's photograph of handwriting

Ancient Gospel or Modern Forgery?

Evans begins by amplifying Carlson's arguments concerning the printed book into which Mar Saba 65 was written. Evans writes,

> *First*, Isaac Voss's 1646 edition of the genuine epistles of Ignatius stands out among the old books at the Mar Saba monastery. Smith lists ten old printed books, ranging in date from 1628 to 1805. Nine of these books were published in Venice and in the Greek language. But Voss's book was published in Amsterdam and in the Latin language. As Carlson remarks, it "sticks out like a sore thumb." Smith too apparently sensed this problem, offering wholly gratuitous speculations, none of them convincing, that attempt in one way or another to link the book to Venice. Why did he do that? Perhaps because he recognized the non-Greek, non-Venetian publication of the book as a problem, a problem that needed to be mitigated in some way. Would an authentic find occasion this kind of embarrassment? (p. 97)

Evans describes three grounds for suspicions here: the book's origin in Amsterdam, Smith's excessive embarrassment over this non-Venetian origin, and its Latin and "non-Greek" text.

As to the first point, it is necessary to note that the ten books Smith lists comprise only the few printed books in the tower library that contained manuscript additions. These appear in his published catalogue precisely because they contained manuscripts. Smith actually came across at least 489 books in this library. So the 2 percent of the library's books that we happen to know about cannot tell us what the other 98 percent should look like (not to mention the books in Mar Saba's other library, which Smith did not catalogue). We actually do know of one other book that Smith found in the tower library. His Mar Saba notes in his archive at the Jewish Theological Seminary mention a book published in Leipzig in 1768.[72] And Agamemnon Tselikas's report for *Biblical Archaeology Review* notes a 1715 Oxford edition of Clement's works. This particular book might actually be a Paris reprint of that Oxford edition. In any case, Tselikas found it listed in a catalogue of "263 old printed books that patriarch Nicodemus sent to the monastery of St. Sabba in 1887."[73] Tselikas included a photograph of the first page of this catalogue, where this book appears

---

in another printed book from the tower library (Mar Saba 22) is consistent with these observations. See the image in Pantuck and Brown, "Morton Smith as M. Madiotes," 117, 118.

72. Pantuck and Brown, "Morton Smith as M. Madiotes," 116 n. 28.

73. Tselikas, "Handwriting Analysis Report," sections "D. Textological observations" and "G. Anexe 4. List of books 2." On the place of publication, see n. 75.

as no. 6. The titles of eleven other books appear on this page. The list does not include the details of publication, but based on the titles and the date of the catalogue, we can determine that five of these books were published in Paris (nos. 1, 2, 3, 5, 8), one was published in Moscow (no. 9), and one in Jerusalem (no. 11).[74] So a "non-Venetian publication" is not unusual.

Nevertheless, Evans points to psychological evidence that Smith knew that this book was out of place, specifically, Smith's "wholly gratuitous speculations, none of them convincing, that attempt in one way or another to link the book to Venice" (p. 97). Reportedly, the speculations in question appear on page 1 of Smith's book *Clement of Alexandria and a Secret Gospel of Mark*. Here is the first paragraph:

> The pages on which the text is written are reproduced in actual size on Plates I–III. The book in which they are found is an exemplar of Isaac Voss's edition of the *Epistulae genuinae S. Ignatii Martyris* (Amsterdam: J. Blaeu, 1646). Its front cover and title page have been lost, but Voss's name is given at the end of the dedication; I was able to identify the edition by photographing the first preserved page (p. 2) and the last numbered page (p. 318) and comparing these photographs with the corresponding pages of complete copies. The manuscript was written over both sides of the last page (which was blank) of the original book and over half the recto of a sheet of binder's paper. The binding was of that heavy, white paperboard so often found on books bound in Venice during the seventeenth and eighteenth centuries. From the remains of it, I should guess that it was approximately contemporary with the book itself. Therefore the date of the book, plus about fifteen or twenty years (1660 or 1665), may be taken as the date *after* which the manuscript insertion was probably made.

The next paragraph on this page describes various experts' opinions on the date of the manuscript's handwriting, and the final line on that page introduces a paragraph outlining Smith's reasons for thinking that the scribe was a scholar. So where is Smith's embarrassment over the book's origin in Amsterdam? Where are the painful rationalizations of this fact? The answer lies in Evans's footnote documentation for this statement, which simply cites pages 38–39 of *The Gospel Hoax*. Here is what Carlson wrote:

74. The titles that we cannot place with certainty are nos. 4 (Ἑρμηνεία εἰς τ[ὴ]ν Ἱερ[ὰ]ν Ἀποκάλυψιν Ἰωάννου τοῦ θεολόγου), 7 (Συναγωγ[ὴ] τῶν Θεοφθόγγων ῥημάτων τῶν θεοφόρων Πατέρων ἤτοι Εὐεργετινός), 10 (Συμεὼν Ἀρχιεπισκόπου Θεσσαλονίκης), and 12 (Εὐθυμίου τοῦ Ζιγα[β]ηνοῦ Ἑρμηνεία εἰς τούς Ψαλμούς), although no. 10 could be vol. 155 in the series Patrologiæ Græcæ (Paris: J.-P. Migne, 1866).

Ancient Gospel or Modern Forgery?

The book containing *Secret Mark*, no. 65, sticks out like a sore thumb. It is the only book printed in Amsterdam; all the others were published in Venice. The most that Smith could do to link the book to Venice is to suggest that its 'heavy, white paperboard' binding was common in Venice (*Clement* 1), but paperboard binding was also common throughout Europe in the seventeenth century.

The mystery quickly unravels. Smith wrote nothing that indicates that he thought that the book's city of publication posed a problem. Instead, Carlson chose to bolster the impression that the book "sticks out like a sore thumb" by matter-of-factly characterizing Smith's reference to the book's binding as a dubious response to this supposed problem. Evans then accepted Carlson's unlikely inference as a fact—quite naturally since Carlson presented it as one—and then appears mistakenly to have inferred from Carlson's phrase "the most that Smith could do" that Smith made several other even less plausible speculations, the dubiousness of which Evans proceeds to describe for us as if he had actually read them. The result of this two-part invention is a new fallacious reason to doubt Smith's integrity.

Evans's statement that the Voss book is "non-Greek" is inaccurate. The book's critical text of Ignatius's letters is in Greek, and the translation and analysis are in Latin. It is an academic work, and Latin was the preferred language of scholarship at that time. More to the point, the edition of Clement noted by Tselikas is precisely this kind of book. The photograph that he provided shows it listed as Κλήμεντος Ἀλεξανδρέως τὰ εὑρισκόμενα πάντα, which is the Greek title to John Potter's critical edition of Clement's works, *Clementis Alexandrini Opera quæ exstant*.[75] Like the Voss book, it presents printed Greek text (with ligatures and abbreviations) and Latin translation in parallel columns, with academic analysis and commentary in Latin. The same applies to the aforementioned books published in Paris, which belong to the series *Patrologiæ Græcæ* by the Catholic publisher J.-P. Migne. Like Voss's edition of Ignatius and Potter's edition of Clement, these are critical editions of church fathers set out in parallel Latin and Greek columns (their Latin titles begin with *Sancti Patris Nostri*); these particular books present the extant works of Basil of Caesarea, John of

---

75. The information that this is the 1715 Oxford edition comes from Tselikas and is not in the list itself. That Oxford edition, however, lacked the word πάντα in the title, which was added to the J.-P. Migne reprint of Potter's book in 1857. If this book is in fact the reprint, the place of publication would then be Paris, and the book would be part of the series Patrologiæ Græcæ.

Damascus, Dionysius the Areopagite, Justin Martyr, and Athanasius. So Carlson's reasoning that the Voss edition would be an oddity at Mar Saba because a book with a "facing Latin translation of the Greek would not have been useful for the Greek Orthodox monks" is confuted by the facts, as is his claim that "the presence of any Latin text at Mar Saba would have been remarkable."[76]

Evans continues: "*Second*, there is no evidence that the book was at Mar Saba prior to Smith's visit in 1958. It is not listed in the monastery's 1910 catalogue of books" (p. 97). It is true that the 1910 catalogue containing 191 entries does not list the Voss book. But it is also true that Smith found nearly five hundred books when he arrived; so the "catalogue" was largely incomplete.

"*Third*," Evans asks, "Why did Smith make no effort to subject the book to scientific analysis?" (p. 97). We do not actually know whether or not he attempted to do this. But one thing we do know is that the normal procedure in questioned document examination is for the person alleging forgery to arrange and pay for the analysis, not for the accused to prove him- or herself innocent. Quesnell was the first to cast suspicion upon Smith and to assert the necessity of forensic examination, so it was incumbent upon Quesnell to arrange for the testing. And that is something he attempted to do. His first written request to the Patriarch to see the manuscript, mailed on November 21, 1973, received no reply.[77] Eventually, in the summer of 1983, he was permitted to examine the manuscript in Jerusalem, but was refused permission to arrange for any tests.[78] Guy Stroumsa likewise raised the issue of testing in 1976 and was turned down.[79] As far as the authors know, the librarians at the Patriarchal library have refused even to show the manuscript to everyone else who has asked about it; for years they offered different excuses for its unavailability and

---

76. Carlson, *Gospel Hoax*, 39.

77. Quesnell, "Question of Evidence," 49 n. 4.

78. Peter M. Head informed Timo Paananen that Quesnell wrote the following statement to Head in 1987: "As to the availability of Smith's document: it was retrieved from Mar Saba about 1976[.] (I printed a note to that effect in *CBQ* at the time . . .) It is now in the library of the Greek Orthodox Patriarchate in Jerusalem. Several scholars have reported being turned away when they asked to see it, but in the summer of '83 I was allowed to examine it. I was not allowed to have any of the basic scientific [tests] done on the ink." See Paananen and Viklund, "Per Beskow and the Elusive MS"; and Paananen, "Short Interview with Quentin Quesnell."

79. Stroumsa, "Comments on Charles Hedrick's Article," 148.

Ancient Gospel or Modern Forgery?

finally claimed that they do not know where it is.[80] So the likelihood is that if Smith did try to arrange for tests, he received the same treatment.

For his last "curious feature," Evans, now relying on Ehrman, notes that the book by Voss into which the manuscript was written is concerned with interpolations into the letters of Ignatius while the *Letter to Theodore* is concerned with interpolations into the Gospel of Mark. Evans considers this coincidence suspicious and even "humorous," but is aware that it is such only "on the assumption that Smith forged the Clementine letter" (p. 97). In other words, the agreement is suspicious only if one chooses to interpret it that way. Other interpretations are possible, and the correct one is impossible to know. One can imagine, for instance, a Greek manuscript hunter finding the exemplar of the letter at the monastery and, wishing to take the manuscript away with him, selecting the endpapers of a book with similar contents as an appropriate place to leave a copy for the monks.

Evans turns now to "internal oddities" about the contents of the letter. The present authors and others have responded to all but one of these alleged oddities elsewhere, so we direct the readers to the discussions listed in this footnote.[81] The remaining argument that requires a reply is Watson's hypothesis that the author inexplicably depends "on the language and syntax of the Papias fragments concerned with the authorship of the Gospels of Mark and Matthew" (p. 98).[82] The letter states that Mark wrote an account of "the Lord's doings" (τὰς πράξεις τοῦ κυρίου, I.16). Watson considers this an obvious echo of Papias's phrase "the things either said or done by the Lord" (τὰ ὑπὸ τοῦ κυρίου ἢ λεχθέντα ἢ πραχθέντα). Knowledge of Papias's phrase is certainly possible: there are enough similarities between one of Clement's accounts of Mark's activities in the *Hypotyposeis*

---

80. Brown, *Mark's Other Gospel*, 25; Paananen and Viklund, "Per Beskow and the Elusive MS."

81. On the notion that "secret" Mark is too Markan and the letter too Clementine, see the paper by Hedrick in this volume as well as Brown, *Mark's Other Gospel*, 54–57, 105–11, and the observations of Pantuck reported in Brown, Review of *The Secret Gospel of Mark Unveiled*; and Brown, "The *Letter to Theodore*," 536–37. On Charles Murgia's opinion that the "Mar Saba document reads as an autograph, not as a copy," see Brown, *Mark's Other Gospel*, 32–33. On Ehrman's contention that "the Mar Saba letter at points actually contradicts the authentic Clement," see Brown, "More Spiritual Gospel," 89–91, 99 n. 101; Brown, *Mark's Other Gospel*, 30–31, 67–69; and Burgess, "'Whatever Makes for Progress Towards Gnosis.'"

82. Watson, "Beyond Suspicion," 148–51.

and Papias's account to suggest that Clement might have known Papias's account or an oral tradition that derives from it.[83]

What Watson deems most surprising is a "structural" similarity in the syntax. Both traditions about Mark have sentences that contain "not ... nor ... but." Watson represents the Greek parallels so:

> *Theodore*: οὐ μέντοι ... οὐδὲ μήν ... ἀλλ' ...
>
> Papias: οὐ μέντοι ... οὔτε γάρ ... οὔτε ... ὕστερον δέ ...

They need to be seen in context:

> *Letter to Theodore*: Mark ... wrote an account of the Lord's doings, *not, however*, declaring all of them, *nor yet* hinting at the mystic ones, *but* ...[84]
>
> Papias: Mark ... as many things as he remembered accurately wrote—*not, however*, in order—the things by the Lord which were either said or done. For *neither* had he heard the Lord, *nor* had he followed him, *but later* ...[85]

Watson interprets this structural similarity as evidence that the letter's author needed help from Papias in order to construct his own account, which Watson cannot picture the real Clement requiring.

It should be apparent, however, that the actual verbal agreements here are limited to οὐ μέντοι and that a compelling case for inexplicable literary reliance cannot be built on such a small foundation. It should also be apparent that the words οὐ . . . οὐδέ in the letter ("not ... nor") are part of the same syntactical construction, unlike the words οὐ . . . οὔτε γάρ in Papias ("not. . . . For neither"), which belong to different clauses. Although similar, the "neither ... nor" construction in the Papias passage (οὔτε . . . οὔτε) is not the construction used in the letter. How, then, could the author of the letter have borrowed from Papias a construction that Papias was not using? And how does the premise of

---

83. Both accounts are cited by Eusebius in *Hist. eccl.* 3.39.15; 6.14.6. See Hill, "What Papias Said about John (and Luke)," 592. He outlines the parallels in 586 n. 11.

84. As translated by Smith (except the word "mystic," which he translated as "secret").

85. Eusebius, *Hist. eccl.* 3.39.15: Μάρκος μὲν ἑρμηνευτὴς Πέτρου γενόμενος, ὅσα ἐμνημόνευσεν, ἀκριβῶς ἔγραψεν, οὐ μέντοι τάξει, τὰ ὑπὸ τοῦ κυρίου ἢ λεχθέντα ἢ πραχθέντα. οὔτε γὰρ ἤκουσεν τοῦ κυρίου οὔτε παρηκολούθησεν αὐτῷ, ὕστερον δὲ, ὡς ἔφην, Πέτρῳ. Our very awkward translation attempts to preserve the syntax and word order.

dependence account for the fact that the letter uses different words after οὐ μέντοι (οὔτε is not the same word as οὐδέ)?

One might detect an echo of Papias in the letter's sequence describing what Mark did write followed by "not, however" and a description of what Mark did not do, but the syntax οὐ ... οὐδὲ ... ἀλλά is a different syntactical construction. It is one that Clement himself used in *Protr.* 1.2.4:

> What my Eunomos sings is *not* the measure of Terpander *nor* that of Capito *nor* the Phrygian or Lydian or Dorian, *but* the immortal measure of the new harmony which bears God's name— the new, the Levitical song.
>
> Ἄιδει δέ γε ὁ Εὔνομος ὁ ἐμὸς **οὐ** τὸν Τερπάνδρου νόμον **οὐδὲ** τὸν Κηπίωνος, **οὐδὲ** μὴν Φρύγιον ἢ Λύδιον ἢ Δώριον, **ἀλλὰ** τῆς καινῆς ἁρμονίας τὸν ἀίδιον νόμον, τὸν φερώνυμον τοῦ θεοῦ, τὸ ᾆσμα τὸ καινόν, τὸ Λευιτικόν[.]

There seems to us little justification in alleging that the ordinary Greek construction found in the letter depends on a text that does not use it. Watson's repeated censuring of Smith for concealing the letter's dependence on Papias is quite unjustified.[86]

CONCLUSION

We agree with Evans that the *Letter to Theodore* potentially "represents a significant contribution to New Testament and Patristic studies" (p. 76). And we fully appreciate the need to vet important discoveries with a hermeneutics of suspicion. For his part, Evans has scrutinized the secondary literature of the last half century and brought together what he considers to be the best reasons for doubting the letter's authenticity, adding some new arguments in the process. In response, we have applied the same scepticism to Evans's arguments, systematically compared them to the facts, and found these arguments sorely wanting.

It is one thing to be provisionally skeptical about a discovery for the purpose of ensuring its authenticity. It is another thing to manufacture doubt through a cavalcade of invention, innuendo, and pretext.

---

86. Watson, "Beyond Suspicion," 149 n. 56, 150 n. 57, 151–52 nn. 61, 62, 64.

6

Was Morton Smith the Bernie Madoff of the Academy?

Hershel Shanks

I COME BEFORE YOU to consider a single issue—whether Morton Smith is guilty of forging the *Secret Gospel of Mark*. I don't care whether you disagree with Smith's interpretation of the document. I don't care if you think he was misguided or even stupid. And I don't care if you conclude that the document was forged in the eighteenth century or even that it was forged in the second century. The only question I wish to explore is whether Morton Smith, distinguished professor at Columbia University and universally admired for his scholarship, is a forger of the Clement letter.

I wonder if the good men who accuse Smith of forging this document realize what they are saying. They are, in effect, saying that Smith is the Bernie Madoff of the academy. They are charging him with a fifteen-year Ponzi scheme—from the time of his alleged discovery of the document until his publication of two books on the results of his research concerning the document. During that time Smith deceived a bevy of the world's most distinguished scholars into investing their time and scholarship in a document that had no reality.

Let us consider the question. At least theoretically, it is much easier to prove that *Secret Mark* is a modern forgery than that it is authentic. The

Ancient Gospel or Modern Forgery?

reason for this is simple. There are, at least theoretically, an infinite number of flaws that would prove it a modern forgery. A single one of these, if proven, will damn it as a forgery. On the other hand, no matter how you may demonstrate that it is authentic, there is always another theoretical test that you failed to apply that would prove it a forgery. You just haven't applied that test. Thus, a single flaw can prove it a forgery, but it is impossible to prove 100 percent that it is authentic. Let's see how this paradigm applies in this case.

It is claimed that *Secret Mark* has been unmasked as a forgery on a very large number of grounds. My friend Peter Jeffery has written a thick book that purportedly proves the case for forgery.[1] Some of his arguments are so dense and arcane that no ordinary human being can follow them to refute them. Take two of them that I can at least understand: The views about homosexuality reflected in *Secret Mark* are those of the 1950s rather than the eighteenth century (when this copy of the letter was allegedly penned) or the second century when it was supposedly written.[2] You have to be an expert in the history of homosexuality to refute Jeffery's charge. If the charge is true, the letter is clearly a forgery. If it is not true, however, and you do succeed in refuting Jeffery's argument based on the history of homosexuality, Jeffery is not bothered. He simply says, "Well, I've got another argument," and he trots out another reason why he believes the document is a forgery.

Another alleged flaw presented by Jeffery is easier to understand, namely his claim that there is an anachronistic reference to Christian liturgy in the Clement letter. That is, the letter refers to an aspect of Christian liturgy that did not appear in the liturgy until *after* Clement died in about 215.[3] Smith failed to notice this, says Jeffery, when he forged this reference in the letter. Well, you've got to be an expert in the history of Christian liturgy to refute this argument, which, clearly, few of us are. And Jeffery admits that the history of Christian liturgy is like a "labyrinth."[4] However, one of the world's leading liturgiologists, Thomas Talley, unfortunately now deceased, disagrees with Jeffery.[5] But even if you get Jeffery to agree that this argument has been refuted, he would simply say, well, let me

---

1. Jeffery, *Secret Gospel of Mark Unveiled*.
2. Ibid., 185–212.
3. Ibid., 60–70.
4. Ibid., 72.
5. Talley, "Liturgical Time in the Ancient Church," 43–48.

introduce you to my friend Stephen Carlson, a bright graduate student, who has uncovered a number of other flaws.

For example, this handwriting expert (Mr. Carlson)—he has read a book on the subject and talked to an American handwriting professional—has found some telltale signs of forgery in the letter, such as pen lifts and forger's tremor, that expose *Secret Mark* as a forgery.[6] Well, you refute this by showing not only Carlson's blatant lack of expertise, but also by the very different assessment of a true Greek handwriting expert. *Biblical Archaeology Review* retained Venetia Anastasopoulou, who compared Smith's Greek handwriting with the Greek handwriting of the Clement letter.[7] Anastasopoulou concludes that Smith writes Greek *not* like a native Greek writer, but like a student learning how to write the language. Anastasopoulou concludes that Smith did not himself pen the Clement letter. I would also point out that it is especially important to realize that the Clement letter is presented not as the original, but as an eighteenth-century copy. The eighteenth-century copier had another document before him that he was trying very carefully to copy; hence, what may appear to be pen lifts and forger's tremors could be the result of the eighteenth-century copyist's effort to be careful with what he was copying.

Well, says Carlson, I've got more flaws in my bag of tricks: Smith was trying to play a joke on his scholarly buddies, not only by fooling them with this supposed copy of a letter of Clement, but also by burying some clues that he, Smith, was actually the author. What a joke! The scholarly world couldn't catch him even though he put his name in the forgery. One clue Smith buried as a joke, says Carlson, is a play on his first name: Morton. Smith planted in the letter, says Carlson, a reference to salt that has lost its savor.[8] This cannot be, says Carlson, because there was no such thing as granulated salt until its invention by the Morton Salt Company. Get it? Smith was playing on his own name. But the fact that Carlson alleges is just plain wrong. Granulated salt was not invented by the Morton Salt Company. There are numerous ancient references to granulated salt and adulterated salt that can be found in ancient sources.[9] And the Morton Salt Company sold granulated salt long before inventing the process on which they base their advertising motto, "When it rains, it pours."

6. Carlson, *Gospel Hoax*, 23–47

7. Anastasopoulou, "Experts Report Handwriting Examination." See also Hershel Shanks, "Handwriting Experts Weigh In on 'Secret Mark.'"

8. Carlson, *Gospel Hoax*, 59–62.

9. For a few examples see the discussion in Shanks, "Restoring a Dead Scholar's Reputation," 60.

Ancient Gospel or Modern Forgery?

If you think that is the last of the reasons upon which Smith's detractors rely as proof of forgery, you would be badly mistaken. There are many, many more. Indeed, Professor Francis Watson has recently come to Carlson's rescue.[10] Smith wasn't inserting a pun on Morton, Watson says, but a pun on his last name, Smith—again, as a joke on his fellow scholars. The forged Clement letter contains a Greek word meaning "to forge." The Latin equivalent is *fabricare*, which can refer to a metal object forged by heating and hammering. This kind of forging is done by someone called a smithy or, better yet, by a Smith—aha! Morton Smith! Get the joke?

My point is this: No matter how many arguments for forgery that you refute, you can never prove that the letter is authentic. There will always be some other flaw that you haven't yet found that would expose the letter as a modern forgery. Let me illustrate this with the work of a man I admire, even though I disagree with him in this case. He is a distinguished Greek philologist in Athens. I contacted him at the same time I retained Venetia Anastasopoulou. He too has a good Greek name: Agamemnon Tselikas. Tselikas came to a different conclusion from Anastasopoulou. He concluded that Smith very probably forged the Clement letter. He sent quite a lengthy report, which I put on the *Biblical Archaeology Review* website,[11] but I admit I had difficulty following it, as did some others. I have a very good relationship with Agamemnon Tselikas, and I urged him to write a more understandable summary of his report. It was especially important, I told him, because of this conference. This month I finally received his summary and I am passing it out as a handout here (see the appendix below).

Tselikas starts from the fact that he has been unable to find in the Mar Saba library, where Smith found the Clement letter on the blank pages at the back of an eighteenth-century book, any other document penned by this same scribe. Therefore, Tselikas concludes, the Clement letter was not written at Mar Saba. However, Tselikas found a similar handwriting at a monastery on the small Greek island of Cephalonia. He also learned that Smith had studied the documents at this monastery. Tselikas concludes that the handwriting of this scribe at the Cephalonia monastery provided the exemplar that Smith would use to forge *Secret Mark*. Either Smith or someone at his behest wrote *Secret Mark* in the back of the eighteenth-century book which Smith had purchased. Smith then took this book with the forged letter in it to Mar Saba where he pretended to have found it, says

---

10. Watson, "Beyond Suspicion," 152–55.
11. Tselikas, "Agamemnon Tselikas' Handwriting Analysis Report."

Tselikas. Smith did this whole thing to prove how important he was, to become "known and significant," to quote Tselikas's report. Tselikas admits his case is not 100 percent, but very near. I do not find Tselikas's reasoning at all convincing—to say nothing of the fact that his report and even his summary is extremely difficult to follow. However, I will leave it to others to analyze his report in greater detail.

Incidentally, Tselikas made an extensive effort to find the Clement letter that Smith allegedly forged. As you know, it was written in the back of an eighteenth-century book. After Smith published his claim, the book was taken to the library of the Greek Patriarchate in Jerusalem. There the pages of the letter were cut out of the book to study them and photograph them. Then they disappeared.[12] Tselikas often works in this library and knows it very well; he also knows the people there very well. He says he made every effort to find the pages, but he was unsuccessful. So there is no opportunity to examine the ink for whatever indication this might give as to forgery *vel non*. But it is worth noting that it is the Greek Orthodox Patriarchate, not Morton Smith, that has prevented the manuscript from undergoing this kind of analysis.

On the other hand, depending on how gullible you are, you may conclude that Smith himself stole the two pages from the Patriarchate Library in order to prevent anyone from scientifically examining the ink, which would demonstrate it to be a twentieth-century ink thereby unmasking Smith.

I know that the scholars who have put forth the various proofs of Morton Smith's forgery will not agree with me that I have demolished their arguments. But that is not my point. Even if I have, that would not prove that *Secret Mark* was authentic. In short, it is possible to prove the document a forgery, but it is not possible to prove that it is authentic. There is always one more test that you didn't think of that would have proved it a forgery. And any one test may theoretically prove the document a forgery. But it is impossible to prove that it is authentic.

Since I freely admit that authenticity cannot be proven, why then do I conclude that the letter is authentic? My reasons are based not on logic, but on an expertise that I believe I do have: an understanding of human nature. Morton Smith was a distinguished, tenured scholar at Columbia University. He spent fifteen years studying this document and discussing it extensively with his closest colleagues. After fifteen years of grappling with the issues, he published both a scholarly book and a popular book on the

---

12. See Hedrick and Olympiou, "Secret Mark," 7–9.

Ancient Gospel or Modern Forgery?

letter.[13] He knew, of course, that if he forged the letter and it was exposed, his career and his life would be ruined. He would have been disgraced and driven from the academy. What was the upside, according to those who believe he forged the letter? He would have played a joke on his colleagues; he would successfully have fooled them—although they would not even know that he fooled them. It would even be a better joke, say those who contend the letter is a forgery, because he planted clues in the letter that would expose him as the forger, like the puns on Morton and Smith.

To me, it is just not believable that Morton Smith would forge this letter. He may have been crazy, but not *that* crazy. A joke that would ruin his entire life? But it is more than this. It is a matter of character. Is there any hint that Smith was of a character that would allow him to do this horrendous thing? I think not. And I am confirmed in my belief by the like judgments of the other scholars who have pronounced it authentic and not the work of Smith. In my work as editor of *Biblical Archaeology Review* for the last 36 years, I have daily contact with the world's greatest scholars. In the case of *Secret Mark*, I admit that I am influenced by these people, especially by the people who knew Smith well and vehemently reject the charge that he is a forger. I myself knew Morton; he was on my editorial advisory board. But I cannot say that this is the only basis of my judgment.

Many other scholars knew Smith intimately and can speak much more authoritatively of his character—and their judgment also influences me. The first is Harvard's Helmut Koester. Helmut spent a week with Smith discussing problems in interpreting the Clement letter.[14] Was Smith just playing with Helmut Koester, one of the world's greatest New Testament scholars, just to fool him? To this day, Koester firmly believes the Clement letter is authentic and that Smith did not forge it. (Whether it could have been forged in the eighteenth century or the second century is another matter, which has not received adequate attention.)

But Koester is not the only one. Gershom Scholem was one of the brightest stars in the firmament of Jerusalem scholars. He was one of Smith's closest mentors when Smith was studying for a Ph.D. there. The two continued to be close thereafter. Their correspondence over the years reveals how Morton labored to understand the Clement letter. Guy Stroumsa, formerly of Hebrew University who now holds a chair at Oxford, has studied

---

13. Smith, *Clement of Alexandria and a Secret Gospel of Mark*; and Smith, *Secret Gospel*.

14. Discussed by Koester in "Was Morton Smith a Great Thespian and I a Complete Fool?" 58.

this correspondence and reports that it reveals how Smith struggled to understand the text of this letter.[15] Let me quote Stroumsa's judgment: "[These letters between Smith and Gershom Scholem] are enough to convince even the most skeptical reader about [Morton] Smith's honesty,"[16] and "no one can seriously deny that [Smith's] discovery of the Clementine letter was genuine."[17]

More recently, I received a letter from another very distinguished scholar, Jeffrey Tigay of the University of Pennsylvania.[18] It is worth quoting Jeff's letter at some length:

> My college major was essentially Morton Smith—I took every course of his that I could—and we kept in contact for the rest of his life. He was so rigorous in his scholarship, and honest to a fault, that it is just inconceivable to me that he would have resorted to fraud, nor can I believe that he would have diabolically used and defrauded such teachers and friends of his as Elias Bickerman, Henry Cadbury, Judah Goldin, Saul Lieberman, Arthur Darby Nock, Gershom Scholem and Krister Stendahl, to all of whom he was deeply indebted for advice on [his scholarly *Secret Mark*] book and for other kinds of support. A while ago I asked my colleague Robert Kraft, emeritus professor of religious studies at the University of Pennsylvania and an expert on early Christianity who was in regular contact with Morton over the years, what he thought about the issue. His assessment of Morton was identical, and he added that practically the only people accusing Morton of fraud are people who didn't know him. That sums it up well!

Let me end with a few remarks about the position of those who maintain Morton Smith was a forger. They each tend to rely on different flaws that prove the document is a forgery. Indeed, each one of these scholars' positions is different. It reminds me of a statement of a very great and famous American judge, Judge Learned Hand, who once wrote of a distinguished lawyer: "He dared to rest his case upon its strongest point, and so avoided that appearance of weakness and uncertainty which comes

---

15. Stroumsa, ed., *Morton Smith and Gershom Scholem, Correspondence 1945–1982*.
16. Ibid., xvii.
17. Stroumsa, "Comments on Charles Hedrick's Article," 153.
18. Published as Tigay, Letter to the Editor in "Queries and Comments," *BAR* 37.3 (2011).

of a clutter of arguments."[19] If uncertainty comes from a clutter of arguments, that is certainly the case here.

And one final point: None of Morton Smith's detractors address the matter of his character. To me, Morton's character is the central issue. Does anyone really believe that a man of this sterling character and reputation and scholarly achievement would be a Bernie Madoff to the academy?

APPENDIX: SUMMARY REPORT OF AGAMEMNON TSELIKAS[20]

Based on extensive report I sent you on the letter of St. Clement I expose here a summary of my remarks.

I noticed several grammatical errors in the text which we can divide into two categories: Those which are due to the "author" and those which are due to the copyist. The first category concerns syntactic and meaning errors, which St. Clement would not be possible to make. The second category concerns the wrong dictation of some words. This phenomenon is frequent in the Byzantine and post-Byzantine manuscripts and we can not give particular importance. However, if the scribe generally appears as an experienced and very careful, some of these mistakes show that he had not sufficient knowledge of the language.

The main palaeographical observation is 1) that a big number of lines of the letters and links are not continuous, fact which means that the hand of the scribe was not moving spontaneously, but carefully and tentatively to maintain the correct shape of the letter. 2) That there are some completely foreign or strange and irregular forms that do not belong to the generally traditional way and rule of Greek writing.

Morton Smith had described some manuscripts of eighteenth century in the island of Cephalonia in Greece, whose handwriting has several similarities with that of Clement's letter.

The history of the text of the works of St. Clement offers no evidence of an earlier copy of the letter. In none of the manuscripts that transmit the Clement's texts the letter is contained. So this letter is the only attributed to Clement. The way in which the letter is transmitted to us is not normal,

---

19. Dillard, ed., *The Spirit of Liberty*, 98.

20. The summary report was circulated at the *Secret Mark* Symposium. All grammatical errors are original to the report. It is now available also online at the opening page of Tselikas' more extensive handwriting report: see Tselikas, "Handwriting Analysis Report."

it generally not agrees with the codicological practice. The scribe could incorporate the text into a collection or an anthology of patristic texts, if not a volume of works of Clement. The printed book in which the letter is found might contain patristic text (Ignatius of Antioch), but this has nothing to do with the texts of Clement. Obviously raises the question of the place where the letter was copied. The most logical answer is that the text was copied in the monastery of St. Sabba in the date mentioned. Indeed the collection of manuscripts of the Monastery of St. Sabba have enough evidences of copying manuscripts inside it since very old times (thirteenth–seventeenth centuries), but also in modern times primarily in the late eighteenth century. The manuscripts which were written at different times in the monastery are mostly liturgical, catechisms and lectures, which were in use for the daily practice of the monastery. Many other manuscripts dating from the seventeenth and eighteenth century, according to their notes, entered in the monastery after dedication of the monks who chose to live there or people who became monks there, or manuscripts sent from Jerusalem. From the examination I made of the manuscripts of collection of St. Sabba, and the Archive of the Patriarchate I did not find any script that is written by the same scribe of the Clement's letter. Even in the correspondence of the monastery with the Patriarchate until the nineteenth century was not met the same handwriting. Already by the mid-nineteenth century the style of Greek the writing has changed and has abandoned the traditional form. If the scribe of the letter had any codicological activity at the Monastery, it is reasonable to have copied other books too, like other scribes in the monastery.

Interesting is the case of the existence of old printed books in the Library of St. Sabba. According the catalogue of 263 old printed books that patriarch Nicodemus sent to the monastery of St. Sabba in 1887 and derived from the multiple ones of the Central Library, the edition of the works of Ignatius is not included. Nor is it in the record of the books of the monastery dating from 1923. In opposite, between these books is the edition of Clement's works of Oxford in the year 1715. Therefore the edition of Ignatius entered into the library of the monastery after the year 1923.

Following the ascertainment of the above observation, it is to exclude that the letter was written in the edition of the Ignatius inside the Monastery of Saint Sabba before 1923.

A question is when the printed book of Ignatius works entered in the monastery? The text of the letter was written before the entrance of the volume in the monastery, or it was written inside the monastery after its entrance? At this point one could make several assumptions.

I think that is impossible for someone to write this text inside the monastery since 1923. It was not allowed to anyone to have access to the books and, if he had, he was under the constant supervision (as now). No one could easily use an old book to write on white leaves such a text. And even, on what original, since there was not such in the monastery?

From this point onwards I express some thoughts about Morton Smith involvement in the discovery of Clement's letter. Morton Smith has certainly earned the trust of the abbot during his stay in the monastery, in the first as in the second time. But to move freely in the library and use the edition of Ignatius to copy the Clement's letter I find it impossible.

Most convincing is that the edition of Ignatius with the letter already written by Morton Smith or by someone else was placed in the library by Morton Smith himself.

Once we prove that the handwriting of the letter is alien to the genuine and traditional Greek, we can accept that it is an imitation of an older script.

A comparison of the handwriting of the Greek letters of Morton Smith with the handwriting of Clement's letter can not give significant evidence that Morton Smith is the scribe, and this because as imitation, certainly the scribe of the letter would not use his own personal style. Nevertheless, some factors point to Morton Smith. My conclusion is that the letter is the product of a forgery and all the evidences suggest that the forger can not be other person than Morton Smith or some other person under his orders. Morton Smith was able to do it. He had the model (the described manuscripts), the appropriate and famous place for the discovery (St. Sabba Monastery), the reason (to become known and significant).

7

The Young Streaker in Secret and Canonical Mark

Marvin Meyer

FOR A VERY LONG time the young man, or *neaniskos*, streaking through the Gospel of Mark, chapter 14, has proved beguiling to students of the New Testament. Even before more instances of a Markan *neaniskos* turned up in the fragments of the *Secret Gospel of Mark*, scholars suggested interpretations that might shed light on this enigmatic character. Vincent Taylor aptly dubbed many of these efforts as "desperate in the extreme."[1] Maybe, it was said, this is Mark's adaptation of Joseph fleeing, *sans* cloak, from Potiphar's wife in Genesis, or of the brave fleeing naked on that eschatological day in Amos. Or maybe this *neaniskos* was an unnamed historical disciple, some eyewitness to the arrest of Jesus. My personal favorite among the suggested interpretations: maybe this is Mark's way of inserting himself into the narrative of the gospel, rather after the manner of Alfred Hitchcock positioning himself unobtrusively somewhere in his films. Now, since the discovery of *Secret Mark* in 1958 and its publication in 1973, there are more examples of a *neaniskos* turning up, clothed and unclothed, in the Markan tradition.

---

1. Taylor, *Gospel according to St. Mark*, 561.

Ancient Gospel or Modern Forgery?

I have attempted to track down this streaking *neaniskos* since 1983, when I presented my first academic paper on the youth in Mark.[2] The paper was published, along with other subsequent articles—most recently a piece on the beloved disciple in early Christian literature. In that 2009 essay, entitled "Whom Did Jesus Love Most? The Beloved Disciple in John and Other Gospels," I discuss the place of the *neaniskos* in canonical Mark and *Secret Mark* in the company of the several disciples said in different early Christian texts to be particularly beloved.[3] As we now see in texts from the Nag Hammadi library and elsewhere, there are plenty of followers of Jesus designated as beloved—almost too many—and the anonymous Markan *neaniskos* is one of them. Apparently, in early Christian communities there were claims and counterclaims about who might have been Jesus' favorite among the disciples, and the texts proclaiming this or that disciple as especially beloved assert, in effect, "Jesus loved our disciple more than your disciple." Mark's *neaniskos*, I believe, is a part of this ongoing discussion in early Christian texts.

As we know very well, almost from the moment when the books of Morton Smith on *Secret Mark* appeared in 1973, the authenticity of the secret gospel fragments and the place of the figure of the young man were attacked. The early review by Quentin Quesnell is familiar to many of us, and it set the tone for a number of subsequent contributions.[4] On the other hand, such scholars as Helmut Koester, Hans-Martin Schenke, and John Dominic Crossan assumed the authenticity of the letter of Clement of Alexandria with the fragments of *Secret Mark*, and the letter was included in the second edition of Otto Stählin's *Clemens Alexandrinus*.[5] In a review essay by Smith, he summarizes "the score at the end of the first decade" among scholars addressing the letter of Clement: "[T]wenty-five have agreed in attributing the letter to Clement, six have suspended judgment or have not discussed the question, and only four have denied the attribution."[6]

The recent appearance of three more books and several articles has resurrected old debates and fanned new flames of controversy over *Secret*

---

2. Meyer, "The Youth in the *Secret Gospel of Mark*." This and other essays of mine have been published in Meyer, *Secret Gospels: Essays on Thomas and the Secret Gospel of Mark*. The present paper builds upon the contributions made in these essays.

3. Meyer, "Whom Did Jesus Love Most?"

4. Quesnell, "The Mar Saba Clementine."

5. Stählin, ed., *Clemens Alexandrinus*, vol. 4, register 1. The epistle was added "provisionally ... to further discussion" (viii).

6. Smith, "Clement of Alexandria and Secret Mark," 450.

Marvin Meyer—The Young Streaker in Secret and Canonical Mark

Mark.[7] In 2005 Scott Brown published a version of his Toronto dissertation, *Mark's Other Gospel*, and Stephen Carlson countered with *The Gospel Hoax*. Carlson formulated arguments concerning the supposed forger's tremor, M. Madiotes the "bald swindler," and the "Morton" Salt Company and salt technology to indicate that Morton Smith forged the text of Clement's *Letter to Theodore* and *Secret Mark* and dropped hints of his forgery. In 2006 Peter Jeffery produced *The Secret Gospel of Mark Unveiled*, with arguments for a Smith forgery based on issues of liturgy, homosexual lifestyle, and Oscar Wilde's seven veils. Since the publication of the books by Carlson and Jeffery, Scott Brown and Allan Pantuck, with others, have attempted to refute the arguments raised by Carlson and Jeffery. A session at the 2008 Annual Meeting of the Society of Biblical Literature in Boston featured a panel with Brown, Carlson, and Pantuck (as well as Bart Ehrman, Charles Hedrick, and Birger Pearson) among the presenters, and emotions ran hot.

I find it rather distasteful to see in these exposés what seem to be inappropriate attacks upon one of our late colleagues, Morton Smith, and my perception that some scholars are inclined to "pile on" concerns me. The renewed debate is not simply a matter of interpretation; we scholars thrive in the world of honest debate. What is being charged is that Morton Smith, a distinguished member of our profession and a colleague and friend in religious, historical, and textual studies, deliberately violated some of the most precious tenets of scholarship, and his character is under attack. Some of the charges seem almost libelous. Many of us knew Morton Smith, some very well; and while we are not unaware of his sly and sardonic side, we know many stories of his generosity of spirit, his commitment to excellence, and his integrity as a scholar.

Here, as elsewhere, I join with colleagues who assume the authenticity of the letter of Clement citing the fragments of *Secret Mark*. I appreciate the statement of John Dominic Crossan about the question of authenticity, and I concur with his perspective: "The authenticity of a text can only be established by the consensus of experts who have studied the original document under scientifically appropriate circumstances."[8] Nonetheless, while caution is called for, I am convinced that as a working hypothesis the authenticity of Clement's letter and the antiquity of the fragments of *Secret Mark* may be affirmed. Part of my argument is based on Morton Smith's

---

7. The three books are: Brown, *Mark's Other Gospel* (2005); Carlson, *Gospel Hoax* (2005); and Jeffery, *Secret Gospel of Mark Unveiled* (2007).

8. Crossan, *Four Other Gospels*, 100.

own interpretation of the Markan fragments. I maintain that a careful reading of the fragments of *Secret Mark* within the context of canonical Mark would suggest that Smith, with his suspicion of form critical and redactional critical methods, may in fact have misunderstood and misinterpreted *Secret Mark*. And I cannot comprehend how a person could simultaneously create ("invent," "forge") and misunderstand the same text. Smith was gifted, he was clever, but I am not sure anyone is that clever.

As I read canonical Mark and the fragments of *Secret Mark*, placed appropriately within the narrative of the Gospel of Mark, the (slightly) longer text of Mark now makes better sense, but it does so in a way that is very different from the interpretation of Morton Smith. I understand that in the longer, restored text of Mark, narrative themes regarding the *neaniskos* as paradigmatic disciple become more apparent, and the *neaniskos* functions as a literary rather than a historical figure. By the time the reader or hearer comes to chapter 16 of the Gospel of Mark, I propose, the challenge of discipleship is front and center in the place and the speech of the *neaniskos*, now in the tomb of Jesus.

If the figure of the unnamed Markan youth is a literary figure in the text, it should be profitable to pursue other youths, fleeing and sometimes leaving their clothes behind, in ancient literature. To that task we turn.

YOUTHS, FLIGHT, AND NUDITY

In the literature of the Bible and beyond, there are figures of youths, sometimes called *neaniskoi*, who resemble the youth in the Gospel of Mark and the fragments of *Secret Mark*. Sometimes these youths are on the run, sometimes they are naked. The instances of Joseph and the eschatologically courageous in the Jewish scriptures have already been noted. In the New Testament and early Christian literature, the term *neaniskos* is used occasionally. In the Gospel of Luke, where the dead son of the widow of Nain is raised by Jesus, the youth is addressed as a *neaniskos*, and there are a few general parallels with the story of the raising of the *neaniskos* in *Secret Mark*. In the Acts of the Apostles the term *neaniskos* is employed several times; the term also occurs in 1 John, the *Gospel of Peter*, and the Visions and Similitudes of Hermas.[9]

More interesting, and probably more important for our Markan interests, are depictions of youths fleeing and sometimes abandoning their robes in Greco-Roman sources. Four instances merit our consideration:

9. Cf. Meyer, "Youth in the *Secret Gospel of Mark*."

Marvin Meyer—The Young Streaker in Secret and Canonical Mark

1) Dennis MacDonald, who has proposed that the Gospel of Mark is a literary adaptation of themes in the epic poems of Homer, understands the figure of the Markan youth to be based on a certain young man named Elpenor, who is described in Homer's *Odyssey*.[10] According to book 10 of the *Odyssey*, Elpenor drank an inordinate amount of wine at Circe's dinner, and he paid the price:

> There was a certain Elpenor, the youngest (νεώτατος) in our ranks,
> none too brave in battle, none too sound in mind.
> He'd strayed from his mates in Circe's magic halls
> and keen for the cool night air,
> sodden with wine he'd bedded down on her roofs.
> But roused by her shouts and tread of marching men,
> he leapt up with a start at dawn but still so dazed
> he forgot to climb back down again by the long ladder—
> headfirst from the roof he plunged, his neck snapped
> from the backbone, his soul flew down to Death. (552–60)[11]

Thus Elpenor's soul departs to Hades. As MacDonald observes regarding Mark's streaking youth and Homer's Elpenor, "The garment the youth left behind thus may symbolize the flight of the naked soul from the body; if so, it corresponds to the flight of Elpenor's soul to Hades."[12] MacDonald goes on to mention an artistic presentation of Elpenor on a vase at the Boston Museum of Fine Arts, on which Elpenor is portrayed as a naked youth—a soul without a body. Later in the *Odyssey*, Odysseus visits the soul of Elpenor in Hades and provides his body a proper burial, and MacDonald sees these interests paralleled in the account of the youth in the tomb in Mark 16, where the Markan text is preoccupied with issues of death and resurrection.

While I find Dennis MacDonald's theory that Homer's Elpenor lurks literarily behind Mark's *neaniskos* to be interesting and thought-provoking, I do not share MacDonald's Homeric preoccupations and convictions. I have strong misgivings about his interpretation of the story of Mark's *neaniskos* as an imitation or emulation of Homer. His interpretation seems forced, and at the end of the day I do not consider his evidence convincing. Still, the similar concerns about death and life in the two stories show that such accounts may have come to expression in a variety of ways in the literature of the Greco-Roman world.

10. MacDonald, *Homeric Epics and the Gospel of Mark*.
11. Robert Fagles, trans., cited in MacDonald, *Homeric Epics*, 128–29.
12. MacDonald, ibid., 129.

2) In an article entitled "Why the Youth Shed His Cloak and Fled Naked," Howard Jackson enumerates several tales of fleeing unclothed youths in Greco-Roman literature, and he raises the issue of a possible connection between these accounts and the Markan *neaniskos*.[13] Thus, in the speech of Demosthenes against Meidias in *Oration* 21, Demosthenes recounts an incident that left him in a state of near-naked embarrassment:

> But now this would be the hardest blow for me to bear, if, when the offenses were fresh in your memory, you displayed such anger and indignation and bitterness that, when Neoptolemus and Mnesarchides and Philippides and another of these very wealthy men were interceding with you and me, you shouted to me not to let him off, and when Blepaeus the banker came up to me, you raised such an uproar, as if I was going to take a bribe—the old, old story!—that I was startled by your clamor, Athenians, and let my cloak drop so that I was half-naked (μικροῦ γυμνόν) in my tunic, trying to get away from his grasp ... (215–16)[14]

Jackson rightly notes the parallels between this account and the story of the Markan streaker: both figures are startled, grabbed, stripped, and eventually get away. Jackson understands this to be a "commonplace image," recognizable in a world in which clothing did not have buttons, zippers, and other clasps.[15] I would suggest that this "commonplace image" also functions as a literary motif.

3) Another tale of a fleeing youth in Greco-Roman literature mentioned by Howard Jackson is to be found in the speech of Lysias against Simon in *Oration* 3. In this speech an account is given about Simon and friends, while inebriated, attempting to seize a young man for their pleasure. A passage in the speech of Lysias relevant for our purposes reads as follows:

> It was at this moment that I arrived from Piraeus, and since I was passing, I called at Lysimachus's house. After a little while we came out. These men, who were by now drunk, jumped on us. Some of those present refused to join this attack, but Simon here, together with Theophilus, Protarchus, and Autocles, began dragging the young man (μειράκιον) off. But he threw off his cloak and ran away (ὁ δὲ ῥίψας τὸ ἱμάτιον ᾤχετο φεύγων). (12)[16]

13. Jackson, "Why the Youth Shed His Cloak and Fled Naked."
14. Demosthenes, *Orations*, vol. 3, 144–45.
15. Jackson, "Why the Youth Shed His Cloak and Fled Naked," 285.
16. *Lysias*, trans. S. C. Todd.

Later in the speech Lysias describes the flight of the young man in similar terms: "As soon as the young man realized what was happening, he threw off his cloak and ran away" (τὸ γὰρ μειράκιον ὡς ἔγνω, ῥῖψαν θοἰμάτιον, φεῦγον ᾤχετω) (35). While the young man here is referred to as a μειράκιον, basic features of the account call to mind the literary description of the Markan *neaniskos* in flight.

4) These speeches of Demosthenes and Lysias address features of a person fleeing naked, à la the Markan youth, but they do not address the full extent of the motifs surrounding the *neaniskos* in canonical Mark and *Secret Mark*. Another ancient youth may come closer to embracing the several themes we recognize in the Markan tradition: a naked youth, and flight, to be sure, but also the initiation of a candidate for sacred mysteries. Such initiation into the divine mysteries is made explicitly clear in the first fragment of *Secret Mark*: "And after six days Jesus told him what to do and in the evening the youth comes to him, wearing a linen cloth over his naked body. And he remained with him that night, for Jesus taught him the mystery of the kingdom of God" (II.6–10). The Greco-Roman youth I have in mind comes not from a literary source, but from an artistic source—from the walls of the so-called Villa of the Mysteries at Pompeii.[17]

Painted on the walls of a triclinium in this famous suburban villa stands a naked youth, nude except for boots. He is reading from a scroll, and his face betrays a look of astonishment. He is in the company of women and mythological figures: Dionysos, Ariadne, satyrs, satyresses, sileni. There is evidence of fear, flight, and ecstasy. The scenes in these frescoes have prompted a number of different interpretations, but it is clear to nearly all interpreters that these enigmatic scenes reflect images from the myths and mysteries of Dionysos. In the Villa of the Mysteries, the focus of the Dionysian interests seems to be upon sexuality, understood in a domesticated manner and presented in a sequence of scenes directing the eye of the viewer around the triclinium and eventually through the door of the cubiculum, very possibly a bedroom, where the mysteries of Dionysian ecstasy may be experienced. The women depicted in the frescoes seem to be in charge of sexual matters and enlightened in sexual mysteries. The only mortal in the room is the naked young man, who apparently is being introduced to—we might even say initiated into—sexual mysteries. As his expression indicates, the youth is excited and surprised

---

17. Cf. Meyer, "The Naked Youths in the Villa of the Mysteries, Canonical Mark, and *Secret Mark*," in Meyer, *Secret Gospels*, 149–67.

by what he is discovering from the women. Like the youth in Mark, he is discovering the mysteries, and he is amazed.

THE YOUTH IN SECRET AND CANONICAL MARK

In his study of secret and canonical Mark, John Dominic Crossan writes, "I consider that canonical Mark is a very deliberate revision of *Secret Mark*."[18] I agree with this assessment. Yet, in order to account for the parallels in terms and themes within passages in secret and canonical Mark, Crossan proposes a peculiar theory of dismemberment and scattering to explain the revision. "It is now impossible to tell the full scope of that revision," he states, "but two features seem certain. First, canonical Mark eliminated both SGM (*Secret Gospel of Mark*) 2 and 5 (i.e., the quotations peculiar to *Secret Mark*) as discrete literary units. Second, canonical Mark scattered the dismembered elements of these units throughout his gospel."[19] In this manner Crossan accounts for features of Mark in such passages as Mark 10:17–22 (the story of a rich inquirer), 14:51–52 (the naked youth in flight), and 16:1–8 (the youth and the women at the tomb).

Crossan is quite correct, I believe, in taking a comprehensive look at similar themes in secret and canonical Mark, but his supposition that elements in canonical Mark come from the dismemberment of passages in *Secret Mark* is most curious. I prefer the simpler solution of Helmut Koester, also based on a conclusion he considers unavoidable: "Canonical Mark is derived from *Secret Mark*. The basic difference between the two seems to be that the redactor of canonical Mark eliminated the story of the raising of the youth and the reference to this story in Mk. 10:46."[20] Nonetheless, I believe that Crossan's awareness of the connections among the several Markan passages featuring a *neaniskos*, or a young man, leads in the right interpretative direction.

In earlier studies I have argued that a careful reading of *Secret Mark*, with the restored passages placed within the text of canonical Mark, exposes what I have called a subplot in *Secret Mark* that is present in only a truncated form in canonical Mark. In retrospect, it could be that I have been somewhat too enthusiastic in suggesting that the succession of passages can be called a subplot; perhaps a more modest designation—maybe, scenes or vignettes in the life of discipleship—would be more appropriate.

---

18. Crossan, *Four Other Gospels*, 108.
19. Ibid.; cf. 119–20.
20. Koester, "History and Development of Mark's Gospel," 56.

Marvin Meyer—The Young Streaker in Secret and Canonical Mark

The passages in the succession of scenes are the passages mentioned above, in conjunction with the analysis of Dom Crossan. They are five in number, and they are connected to one another by means of a series of terms and themes. And they all feature a *neaniskos*.

1) The first passage, Mark 10:17–22, narrates the story of a rich inquirer who is a candidate for discipleship. He is unnamed, and is described only as a rich man who "had great possessions" (ἔχων κτήματα πολλά, 10:22), and who claims to have kept the commandments "from [his] youth" (ἐκ νεότητός μου, 10:20). Luke describes his wealth with words nearly identical to those in *Secret Mark*; Luke reads, "for he was very rich" (ἦν γὰρ πλούσιος σφόδρα, 18:23; *Secret Mark* reads, ἦν γὰρ πλούσιος, II.6). Matthew calls him a *neaniskos*, twice, the only times Matthew employs the term in his gospel. Mark says that Jesus "looking upon him, loved him" (ἐμβλέψας αὐτῷ ἠγάπησεν αὐτόν, 10:21), in the same words employed in fragment one of *Secret Mark* to describe the love of the youth for Jesus (III.4). Fragment two also refers to the fact that this is the youth Jesus loves (III.15). The rich youth of Mark 10, however, is scandalized by the cost of discipleship, and he turns away in sadness, unwilling to follow Jesus.

2) The second passage is fragment one of *Secret Mark*, to be located after Mark 10:34. It describes the raising of a *neaniskos* in terms reminiscent of the raising of Lazarus in the Gospel of John.[21] When raised, it is said, "the youth, looking upon him (Jesus), loved him" (ὁ δὲ νεανίσκος ἐμβλέψας αὐτῷ ἠγάπησεν αὐτόν, III.4), and they went together to the house of the youth, "for he was rich" (ἦν γὰρ πλούσιος, III,15). Six days later Jesus gave him instructions, and at night the youth came to Jesus "wearing a linen cloth over his naked body" (περιβεβλημένος σινδόνα ἐπὶ γυμνοῦ, III.8). The wording of this clause is precisely the same as the clause in Mark 14:51 (περιβεβλημένος σινδόνα ἐπὶ γυμνοῦ), and some scholars have seen allusions here to the ritual garb of early Christian baptism, or formal initiation into discipleship.[22] The unnamed youth in Mark has become a disciple of Jesus.

3) The third passage is fragment two of *Secret Mark*. It is short, and simply reads as follows: "And the sister of the youth whom Jesus loved and his mother and Salome were there, and Jesus did not receive them" (III.14–16). Placed within the context of Mark 10:46, this brief passage explains what happened when Jesus came to Jericho, without the brusqueness

---

21. Cf. Meyer, "Youth in *Secret Mark* and the Beloved Disciple in John."

22. Cf. Smith, *Clement of Alexandria and a Secret Gospel of Mark*; Crossan, *Four Other Gospels*; Scroggs and Groff, "Baptism in Mark"; Jonathan Z. Smith, "The Garments of Shame."

of the version in canonical Mark. According to canonical Mark, nothing happened at Jericho: "And they came to Jericho; and as he (Jesus) was leaving Jericho with his disciples and a great multitude . . ." This passage from *Secret Mark* also reiterates the love of Jesus for the youth, but it goes on to indicate that Jesus did not receive or accept the women. Could that comment be a hint about what will be disclosed about women at the tomb in Mark 16?

4) The fourth passage is Mark 14:51–52, the passage with the young streaker. The young person is depicted as "a young man . . . with nothing but a linen cloth about his body" (νεανίσκος τις . . . περιβεβλημένος σινδόνα ἐπὶ γυμνοῦ), as in the earlier passage from *Secret Mark*, and when he is seized, he runs for his life, naked. In their study of this passage, Robin Scroggs and Kent Groff maintain that here "the believer is symbolically baptized" and dies with Christ as he leaves his linen garment behind, only to appear dressed in white baptismal clothing in Mark 16:5.[23] Morton Smith responded to this interpretation with his typically sharp wit: "This interpretation neglects only the main facts: this young man deserted Christ and saved himself."[24] The linkage made by Scroggs and Groff between the *neaniskos* in Mark 14 and the *neaniskos* in Mark 16 is correct, in my opinion, but Smith's critique remains essentially right. In Mark—*Secret Mark*, restored—the disciple Judas betrays Jesus, the disciple Peter denies Jesus, the other disciples flee from the cross—and the unnamed youthful disciple runs away. What the women will do is explained at the end of the gospel.

5) The fifth and final passage in the succession of scenes or vignettes on the *neaniskos* and discipleship is Mark 16:1–8. According to this passage, the women, including Salome, go to the tomb to anoint the body of Jesus, and what they see there amazes them. Inside the tomb is the *neaniskos*, now "dressed in a white robe" (περιβεβλημένον στολὴν λευκήν, 16:7). He is the youthful disciple, and no angel, in spite of what Matthew and Luke may make of him in their edited accounts. The youth is portrayed like the faithful of the book of Revelation, who are "wearing white robes" (e.g., περιβεβλημένους στολὰς λευκάς, 7:9), and he proceeds to announce the good news about how they and the other disciples may see the risen Christ in Galilee. The women, alas, flee from the tomb, and they say nothing to anyone. The Greek in this passage is especially

---

23. Scroggs and Groff, "Baptism in Mark," 548.
24. Smith, "Clement of Alexandria and Secret Mark," 457.

strong: οὐδενὶ οὐδὲν εἶπαν, literally, "They said nothing to no one."[25] The gospel then ends, in 16:8, with the famous clause and its dangling conjunction: ἐφοβοῦντο γάρ, "For they were afraid." Previously the men had all fled from Jesus and the cross, and now the women also flee from the tomb in fear. It is no wonder that, as we have seen in the second fragment of *Secret Mark*, Jesus refuses to accept the women who are with the *neaniskos*. At the conclusion of the Gospel of Mark, only the youth in the tomb is left to proclaim the crucified and risen Christ. The tension between the call of the gospel and the lack of response begs to be resolved.

READING AND HEARING MARK'S MESSAGE OF DISCIPLESHIP

In the latter part of the first century of the Common Era, somewhere in the Mediterranean basin, followers of Jesus are gathered in a house church to worship and learn about the life of discipleship. They are fortunate to hear the reading of a scroll of the Gospel of Mark—the *Secret Gospel of Mark*. Throughout the gospel the vicissitudes of the life of discipleship are recounted. The disciples, named and known, are a difficult and quarrelsome bunch, and often they seem not to understand who Jesus is and what he is trying to do. Peter, arguably the alpha disciple, cannot comprehend the prospect of the cross for Jesus, and he is practically exorcized by Jesus, who scolds him with harsh words: "Get behind me, Satan! For you are not on the side of God, but of men" (Mark 8:33). In the face of the arrest, trial, and crucifixion of Jesus, the disciples betray, deny, and abandon their master and rabbi. So where is the good news, where the *evangelium*?

In the latter half of the gospel, another figure appears, unnamed, unknown, who seemingly is unconnected to the actual historical events themselves, but who moves in and out of the narrative in a sequence of scenes. This is a youth, the sort of character we have seen who crops up in ancient literature in stories of fear and flight as well as scenes of initiation and discipleship. The youth, presented with familiar literary images, may function as everyman, everywoman, everydisciple, in a manner that recalls aspects of the presentation of the beloved disciple in the Gospel of John.[26] Mark's youth, termed a *neaniskos*, is a rich inquirer who hesi-

---

25. On οὐδενὶ οὐδέν, cf. Aeschylus, *Agamemnon*, 1212: ἔπειθον οὐδέν' οὐδέν, ὡς τάδ' ἤμπλακον. From *Aeschyli septem quae supersunt tragoedias*.
26. Cf. Meyer, "Youth in *Secret Mark* and the Beloved Disciple in John"; also Raymond E. Brown, *Gospel according to John*, xciv–xcv, and 924: "There is little doubt that

tates but eventually turns to Jesus as a disciple that loves Jesus and is loved by him. He is brought from death to life by Jesus. Still, his uncertainties follow the uncertainties of the other disciples, and as they flee from the crucifixion, so also he flees. But at the end of the gospel it is the youth, and only the youth, who is in the tomb, identifying with Jesus in death and life.

The tension at the end of the Gospel of Mark, as read from the scroll in the house church, is not easily resolved. On the one hand, most of the male and female disciples in the gospel account have fled in fear and dismay in the face of the scandal of the cross and the demands of the cross in their lives. On the other hand, the voice of the youth, who is now in the tomb of Jesus, continues to cry out. This is the same youth who earlier in the gospel was raised to life by Jesus, was taught by Jesus, and ran away from Jesus when Jesus was arrested. At the end of the gospel the youth has come back to Jesus in his death; he is joined to Jesus in his death, and he even looks and sounds rather like Jesus: "Do not be amazed; you seek Jesus of Nazareth, who was crucified. He has risen, he is not here; see the place where they laid him. But go, tell his disciples and Peter that he is going before you to Galilee; there you will see him, as he told you" (Mark 16:6–7).

The reading of the Gospel of Mark is finished, and the scroll is rolled up. Now only the hearer, the implied hearer or reader, can resolve the tension created in the gospel. Will the hearer or reader flee from Mark's theology of the cross and resurrection, like the twelve and even the women? Or will the reader see himself or herself in the *neaniskos*, and also take up the costly life of discipleship? With such a challenge the Gospel of Mark—the *Secret Gospel of Mark*—abruptly, but fittingly, comes to a conclusion.

---

in Johannine thought the Beloved Disciple can symbolize the Christian."

8

Halfway Between Sabbatai Tzevi and Aleister Crowley

Morton Smith's "Own Concept of What Jesus 'Must' Have Been" and, Once Again, the Questions of Evidence and Motive[1]

Pierluigi Piovanelli

DE-ESSENTIALIZING THE STUDY OF EARLY CHRISTIAN APOCRYPHAL TEXTS

ONE OF THE PHENOMENA most characteristic of the modern rediscovery of Christian apocryphal texts is the tendency to make exceptional claims about their value for the reconstruction of early Christian history only to have them counterbalanced with more critical interpretations that end up practically denying their worth outright—at least for the history of the first-century Jewish sectarian communities and movements that

---

1. I would like to express my sincere gratitude to the organizers, Tony Burke and Philip Harland, for inviting me to participate in this highly stimulating conference on the *Secret Gospel of Mark*. My thanks are also due to Robert Edwards for his constant efforts to improve the quality of my English style.

progressively metamorphosed into the variety of second- and third-century Christian churches.² This is exemplified by the ongoing debate over the famous (or infamous) *Gospel of Judas* which was recently rescued from the oblivion of time and the injuries suffered at the hands of a gang of less than scrupulous antiquities dealers.³ Even more amazing, however, is the polarization that exists between specialists who believe that every scrap of apocryphal text preserves traditions as old and valuable as those of their canonical counterparts and, at the other end of the spectrum, scholars who hold that they are no more than secondary rewritings of New Testament texts. John Dominic Crossan is one of the most outstanding representatives of the first group, while Craig Evans can legitimately be considered the new champion of the second trend.⁴ Everyone, however, hopefully will agree that reality cannot so easily be reduced to a black and white picture without any nuance of grey. Thus, a few years ago, following the path of a scholar so competent and circumspect as Jean-Daniel Kaestli,⁵ I started examining the material evidence and the arguments put forward in order to substantiate the various interpretations proposed—notably on the *Gospel of Thomas*, the *Gospel of Peter*, and the so-called *Secret Gospel of Mark*—by the proponents of the two conflicting schools of thought.⁶ Not surprisingly, the *Gospel of Thomas* appeared to be the finest and largest fish ever caught by the last two generations of "wise fishermen" of apocryphal texts, while the *Gospel of Peter* was a nice specimen but not quite as extraordinary as some (Irish) anglers would have one believe. As for the *Secret Gospel of Mark*, though it was not an old shoe that someone had thrown into the water that looked like some type of aquatic being, it has proved finally to be an extremely sophisticated fishing lure.

---

2. A development pertinently described by Räisänen, *Rise of Christian Beliefs*.

3. See the volumes published by Scopello, ed., *The Gospel of Judas in Context*; and DeConick, ed., *Codex Judas Papers*.

4. Contrast, e.g., Crossan, *Four Other Gospels*; Crossan, *Historical Jesus*, 427–34; with Evans, *Fabricating Jesus*, 52–99 and 252–60; Evans, "Gospel of Judas and the Other Gospels." On the ideological presuppositions underlying contemporary indiscriminate criticism of non-canonical texts, see Burke, "Heresy Hunting in the New Millennium."

5. See especially Kaestli, "L'utilisation de l'*Évangile de Thomas*"; Kaestli, "L'*Évangile de Thomas*"; and Kaestli, "L'*Évangile secret de Marc*."

6. Piovanelli, "Pre- and Post-canonical Passion Stories"; Piovanelli, "L'*Évangile secret de Marc* trente trois ans après"; Piovanelli, "'Un gros et beau poisson'"; Piovanelli, "Thomas in Edessa?"

ONCE AGAIN, THE QUESTION OF EVIDENCE

The Wrong Document, at the Wrong Place . . .

It is well known that the debate over the authenticity of the fragmentary *Letter to Theodore* attributed to Clement of Alexandria, and discovered by the late Morton Smith (1915–1991) in an annex of the Mar Saba Library in the summer of 1958, was reopened by Stephen C. Carlson in 2005 with a short book in which he was able to highlight a series of anachronisms and technical anomalies—including codicological, paleographic, and graphological examples—that would betray not only the forged nature of the document but also its modern, Smithsonian origins.[7] He was promptly followed in 2007 by Peter Jeffery, whose study of the ritual and liturgical use—if any—of *Secret Mark* in Alexandria seems to have brought even more anachronisms and inconsistencies to light.[8] More recently, in 2010 Francis Watson detected some troubling verbal and conceptual correspondences between Morton Smith's retelling of his own discovery in 1973 and James Hunter's popular novel, *The Mystery of Mar Saba*, published in 1940.[9]

In reaction to the offensive against the authenticity of the *Letter to Theodore*, Scott Brown has not hesitated in assuming the valiant task of refuting, in detail and at length, almost every point of Carlson's and Jeffery's criticisms—particularly the question of the anachronisms and the riddles supposedly embedded within the text.[10] In this endeavor Brown has also

---

7. Carlson, *Gospel Hoax*. In doing so, Carlson has taken on and radicalized many of the critiques already formulated by Quesnell, "The Mar Saba Clementine"; Quesnell, "Reply to Morton Smith." See Piovanelli, "L'Évangile secret de Marc," 63–66 (Quesnell) and 242–45 (Carlson), as well as Alain Le Boulluec's penetrating remarks in his review of both Brown, *Mark's Other Gospel*, and Carlson's book in *Apocrypha*. As for the reception of Carlson's theses by German scholarship, see Klauck, *Die apokryphe Bibel*, 62–93; Rau, "Weder gefälscht noch authentisch?"; Rau, "Das Geheimnis des Reiches Gottes."

8. Jeffery, *Secret Gospel of Mark Unveiled*. The highly polemical nature of Jeffery's work has been variously appreciated by the reviewers: see Brown on *RBL*; Foster in *Expository Times*; Johnson in *Worship*; Ellens in *RBL*; Kelly in *Magic, Ritual and Witchcraft*.

9. Hunter, *Mystery of Mar Saba*. See Watson, "Beyond Suspicion," 161–70. The connection with Hunter's work of fiction was initially made by Jenkins, *Hidden Gospels*, 101–2, and Price, "Second Thoughts on the Secret Gospel."

10. Brown, "Factualizing the Folklore"; Brown, "Question of Motive in the Case against Morton Smith"; Brown, "The *Letter to Theodore*"; Pantuck and Brown, "Morton Smith as M. Madiotes"; Brown and Pantuck, "Stephen Carlson's Questionable

received the support of some Scandinavian bloggers who have pointed out other weaknesses in the line of reasoning followed by the advocates of the modern forgery approach, such as the poor quality of the pictures used by Carlson to carry out his graphological analysis.[11] However, the most serious attempt to vindicate Smith's academic honor and reputation was the 2008 publication of a corpus of one hundred and twenty letters exchanged by Smith and his mentor and friend, the great Israeli specialist of Jewish mysticism, Gershom Scholem (1897–1982), between 1945 and 1982.[12] Thus, in the opinion of Guy Stroumsa, its editor, "[t]he correspondence should provide sufficient evidence of his [i.e., Smith's] intellectual honesty to anyone armed with common sense and lacking malice."[13] Sadly enough, as I will clarify below, this was just wishful thinking on his part and, in spite of their undisputable interest, the content of some of Smith's letters serves to make his position more ambiguous and fragile than ever.

Before reviewing this new evidence, it would be best to remember briefly at least two incontrovertible facts that are going to play, cumulatively with other considerations, a decisive role in the validation or invalidation of the authenticity and historical reliability of the *Letter to Theodore*. The first is that Clement's fragment was found, so to speak, in the wrong place—this means that it was discovered in a location in which it would be both unnatural and even suspect to find such an amazing document. Actually, in spite of Smith's efforts to convince his readers to the contrary,[14]

Questioned Document Examination."

11. Viklund, "Reclaiming Clement's Letter to Theodoros"; Viklund, "Tremors, or Just an Optical Illusion?"

12. Stroumsa, ed., *Morton Smith and Gershom Scholem, Correspondence 1945–1982*. Stroumsa announced the discovery of these letters at the Jewish National and University Library in Jerusalem in his essay, "Comments on Charles Hedrick's Article," 149–53. For a critical review of Stroumsa's edition and a first evaluation of the data, see Piovanelli, "Une certaine 'Keckheit, Kühnheit und Grandiosität.'" Also see the important reviews by Campanini, "A proposito di un carteggio recente"; and Accorinti in *Gnomon*.

13. Stroumsa, *Correspondence*, xv.

14. Thus, examples from Mar Saba of the practice of recycling older fragments of parchment in the bindings of more recent volumes were presented by Smith, "Monasteries and Their Manuscripts," 174–75, 177; Smith, "New Fragments"; Smith, *Secret Gospel*, 37. However, this is not exactly the same as finding an unknown ancient text and copying it at the end of a modern printed book. In order to explain such a unique phenomenon, Smith had to imagine a chain of exceptional events—i.e., that 1) a codex containing no fewer than twenty-one letters of Clement was kept at Mar Saba, because it was probably there that John of Damascus had seen and cited it in the first half of the eighth century (but see below, n. 21); 2) this codex had been almost completely

this is the only case in the history of not only Greek but also Latin, Hebrew, Aramaic, Coptic, Syriac, and other ancient classic and late antique literature in which an important text by a major author would have been found copied at the end of a European book—in this case, Isaac Voss's edition of the *Epistulae genuinae S. Ignatii Martyris*, published in Amsterdam in 1646—at a date as late as the first half of the eighteenth century.[15] Moreover, the volume in question was found in a library where, in the absence of any rigorous control, almost anybody could have fraudulently introduced it between ca. 1750 and 1958. In other words, if a new, revolutionary text attributed to a classic author were to be discovered outside of a manuscript found in an old cemetery, an ancient cache, or a well-kept and organized library, but instead penned by a modern hand on the back pages of an old volume of, e.g., Migne's *Patrologia Graeca*, even if such a volume was retrieved from the shelves of the library of a very remote Armenian or Georgian monastery, it would be more than legitimate to be suspicious about its provenance and to adopt an extremely prudent attitude with respect to its authenticity.

The second problematic fact is that, in the opinion of some of the most qualified specialists, the information provided by the *Letter to Theodore* does not fit very well with what we presently know about Clement of Alexandria and the history of the Egyptian Church. I am referring here to the doubts recently expressed by Attila Jakab, Alain Le Boulluec, and Annick Martin, three French (or French-speaking) historians of early

---

destroyed by the terrible fire which devastated the library of Mar Saba at the beginning of the eighteenth century; and 3) someone—probably a learned Greek monk with an excellent knowledge of patristic literature—found a folio of the codex containing the first part of the *Letter to Theodore* and, intrigued by its content, hastily copied it on the blank pages at the end of a printed edition of the letters of another illustrious Father of the Church. See Smith, *Clement of Alexandria and a Secret Gospel of Mark*, 1–4, 285–90; Smith, *Secret Gospel*, 22–23, 143–48. One should note that the motif of a manuscript fragment miraculously being found among the smoking ashes of a prestigious library was already used to justify the "rediscovery" of the famous Adagio in G minor attributed to Tomaso Giovanni Albinoni (1671–1751), actually "reinvented" by the Italian musicologist Remo Giazotto (1910–1998), who claimed in 1945 to have received a fragment of its score recovered from the ruins of the Sächsischen Landesbibliothek in Dresden. Ironically enough, Giazotto published it in 1958!

15. Not to mention the extremely troubling detail—emphasized by Ehrman, "Response to Charles Hedrick's Stalemate," 162–63; Ehrman, *Lost Christianities*, 87—that the *Letter to Theodore* was copied on the blank pages that follow the very last sentence of the edition, in which Voss denounces the impudence of "that scoundrel" who had dared to write down Ignatius's apocryphal letters "filling so many pages with such trifles" ("Plures enim paginas nugis istis implerat impudentissimus iste nebulo" [Voss, *Epistulae genuinae*, 318]).

Ancient Gospel or Modern Forgery?

Christianity in Egypt who have been involved, at different times and to varying degrees, with the Association pour l'étude de la littérature apocryphe chrétienne (AELAC).[16] Thus, Jakab points out that the author of the letter seems to know the Carpocratians much better than Clement, who apparently thought that Epiphanes, Carpocrates' son, was the true founder of the school (*Strom.* III.2.5).[17] In the same vein but in a more articulated manner, Martin argues that, 1) the revised chronology of Athanasius's *Festal letters* does not confirm Thomas Talley's reconstruction of a "primitive" Alexandrian liturgy for the baptism of the catechumens that would have been based on the chronology suggested by the initiation rite ("after six days") described in the first episode of *Secret Mark* quoted in the *Letter to Theodore* (III.6–7); 2) for Clement the baptism seems to be the only way to obtain illumination, sonship, perfection, and immortality (*Paed.* I.6), without the need for more advanced initiatory stages that would have been devoted to the specific study of a single, more mystical gospel; and 3) moreover, even the eventual presence of Carpocratians in Alexandria—at least at the end of the second century—is doubtful, since Clement does not mention either Carpocrates or Epiphanes among the founders—Marcion, Basilides, and Valentinus—of the main heretical sects of the day (*Strom.* VII.17).[18]

Jakab and Martin also note that the *Letter to Theodore* gives a description of the earliest Christian community in Alexandria as already being in existence and having diversified prior to the arrival of Mark. This report is at odds not only with Clement's silence on Mark's involvement with Alexandria, but also with the account of Eusebius, who accepts the tradition ("some say") that attributes the first conversions in Alexandria to the evangelist (*Hist. eccl.* II.16).[19] Concerning the origins of the church

---

16. See especially Le Boulluec, *La notion d'hérésie*; Le Boulluec, *Alexandrie antique et chrétienne*; Le Boulluec, *Clément d'Alexandrie. Stromates VII*; Le Boulluec and Voulet, *Clément d'Alexandrie. Stromates V*; Martin, *Athanase d'Alexandrie*; Jakab, *Ecclesia Alexandrina*.

17. Jakab, "Une lettre 'perdue' de Clément d'Alexandrie?" 13–14.

18. Martin, "À propos de la lettre attribuée à Clément d'Alexandrie," 282–88. On the question of the Alexandrian liturgy and its sequence, see Camplani, *Le lettere festali di Atanasio di Alessandria*, 171–83; Camplani, "Sull'origine della Quaresima in Egitto"; Camplani, *Atanasio di Alessandria*, 178–81. For other problems inherent to Talley's and Smith's baptismal interpretation of the initiation to "the great mysteries" required of those who would have been allowed to read *Secret Mark*, see Brown, *Mark's Other Gospel*, 147–50 and 266–67.

19. Jakab, "Une lettre 'perdue,'" 14–15; Martin, "À propos de la lettre," 292–95 (the legend of the Markan origins could date from the years 220–30).

in Alexandria, the real question is not to determine which of the two versions of the story is more ancient and historically plausible, but to explain why Eusebius, who constantly relies on the work of Clement, seems to ignore useful information found in one of Clement's letters that he could have consulted easily in bishop Alexander's library in Jerusalem (*Hist. eccl.* VI.20)[20]—at least if any manuscripts containing Clement's correspondence existed and were kept there. This is the final and most fatal blow to the house of cards making up the connection between a postulated collection of Clementine letters and Mar Saba. Actually, as Martin makes perfectly clear, on the one hand John of Damascus lived and worked, until 742, in Jerusalem and not, as his later biographers claimed, at Mar Saba; on the other hand, it is not certain that Clement was the author of the three citations attributed to him, in the midst of other biblical and truly Clementine excerpts, in the *Sacra parallela* anthologies made in the ninth century or later from John of Damascus's presently lost *Hiera*. In other words, the existence of a corpus of letters of Clement could be but the result of an erroneous medieval attribution.[21] Thus, in spite of the remote possibility of a late antique falsification, Martin is compelled to acknowledge that "the hypothesis of a modern forgery starts again with renewed vigor" and that "the scientific reliability" of the *Letter to Theodore* "should be called into question," at least, until it is possible to recover the original document and analyze the ink used by its scribe[22]—a judgment also shared by Jakab and Le Boulluec[23] with such agreement that it makes any previous statements about a growing consensus among Clementine scholars concerning the authenticity of the Mar Saba letter look obsolete.[24]

20. As Smith himself (*Clement of Alexandria*, 285–86) admits. Compare Martin, "À propos de la lettre," 296–97.

21. Martin, "À propos de la lettre," 299–300. Already in the opinion of their first editor, Holl, *Fragmente vornicänischer Kirchenväter*, these fragments were "dubious."

22. Martin, "À propos de la lettre," 300. It is, then, extremely surprising to read in Stroumsa, *Correspondence*, xv, n. 19, that in her essay Martin makes "a convincing argument about the letter's authenticity"!

23. Jakab, "Une lettre 'perdue,'" 15. As for the position of Le Boulluec, contrast his initially cautious appreciation of the *Letter to Theodore* in "La lettre sur l''Évangile secret' de Marc," 41, with his current reservations in "L''école' d'Alexandrie," 547–48, n. 107, and the review mentioned above, n. 7.

24. See, e.g., Hedrick, "Secret Gospel of Mark," 141, concerning the inclusion of the *Letter to Theodore* in the second edition of Clement's writings published by Treu, *Clemens Alexandrinus*, xvii–xviii. Obviously enough, this does not mean that some scholars, like Jay, "A New Look at the Epistolary Framework of the *Secret Gospel of Mark*," are still defending—N.B. on stylistic and literary grounds that are always the easiest to imitate—the attribution of the letter to Clement.

Ancient Gospel or Modern Forgery?

... Discovered by the Wrong Person!

The publication of Smith's letters adds decisively to the aforementioned difficulties, specifically because the author of the discovery was already familiar with, and well trained, prior to 1958, in the main fields of research, topics, and methods that he would later find inextricably intertwined in the study of the *Letter to Theodore*. Thus, we learn that in 1948 he devoted the first six months of the year to the study of Gregory of Nyssa's "background—giving half of [his] time to classical literature and half to the early Fathers, especially Clement of Alexandria."[25] In 1951-1952, thanks to a Fulbright grant, he spent an entire year in Greece exploring monastic libraries in search of new manuscripts of the epistles of Isidore of Pelusium—the initial topic of his Harvard doctoral dissertation—and "brought back about 5,000 photographs of manuscripts (i.e. about 10,000 pages)" from "places like Patmos and Mount Athos" with the hope of putting them to use for his "Th.D. thesis on St. Isidore of Pelusium, an edition of St. Maximus's *Centuries on Love*, and some studies of patristic catenae."[26] According to the title of the unpublished catalogue that Smith compiled and deposited in the Brown University Library in 1952, the passages he had selected were taken "from Greek manuscripts of the tenth to nineteenth centuries found mainly in monastic libraries"[27]—a chronological span that should betray Smith's familiarity, at that time, not only with medieval, but also with modern Greek handwritten materials.[28]

Among the various publication projects that he undertook in 1947 were, "a book, two big articles, and a book review which should be almost an article, on strictly New Testament subjects";[29] a "book on the lives of Jesus";[30] "a book on Mark," which he had almost finished in 1955-1956;[31]

---

25. Letter 11 of 17 August 1948 (Stroumsa, *Correspondence*, 28).

26. Letter 31 of 26 January 1953 (Stroumsa, *Correspondence*, 63). The same information is repeated in the "Account of Advanced Studies" that Smith submitted to the Guggenheim foundation in 1962 (ibid., 195).

27. See the bibliography appended to Smith, *Studies in the Cult of Yahweh*, 2:259.

28. Compare the comments on the "completely chaotic" situation of the seventeenth century and eighteenth century patristic florilegia in Smith, "Manuscript Tradition of Isidore of Pelusium," 209-10.

29. Letter 8 of 9 May 1947 (Stroumsa, *Correspondence*, 22).

30. Letter 9 of 12 December 1947 (Stroumsa, *Correspondence*, 23).

31. Letters 40 of 1 August 1955 (Stroumsa, *Correspondence*, 81); 42 of 27 October 1955 (ibid., 85); 45 of 28 February 1956 (ibid., 89). In this regard, one should also note a perhaps significant slip when Smith designates, in 1968, his *Clement of Alexandria* then in press as "[t]he book on Mark" (letter 86 of 5 July 1968 [ibid., 144]).

and a new anthology of Jewish Pseudepigrapha in translation for 1957–1958.[32] If such announcements were not the result of a vague desire to explore ever new avenues of research—and a few works published in those years seem to demonstrate that this was not the case[33]—, we should conclude that Smith was, from an intellectual point of view, perfectly equipped to deal with both the content and the form of the amazing Clementine fragment that he was later to discover at Mar Saba.[34] In this regard, we should also remember that, from the first steps of the historico-critical school in nineteenth-century German universities, one of the most sensitive cases in the debate about the differences between the Gospel of John and the Synoptics was the absence in the latter of any mention of "Jesus' greatest miracle," the raising of his friend Lazarus of Bethany as narrated in John 11. Since the uncompromising analysis of David Friedrich Strauss, this episode has become a locus classicus for discussions of the Johannine question and the reliability of the Fourth Gospel's evidence for the reconstruction of Jesus' deeds.[35] Now, what Smith was going to discover in the first passage of *Secret Mark* quoted in the *Letter to Theodore* (II.23—III.11) was precisely the missing link between the Synoptics—in this case, an *Ur-Mark*—and the Gospel of John that a good number of exegetes had dreamt of for more than a century. A scholar as meticulous and well-prepared as Smith, already conversant in New Testament criticism, would hardly have ignored this.[36]

---

32. Letters 55 of 9 December 1957 (Stroumsa, *Correspondence*, 106–7); 59 of 12 January 1958 (ibid., 110–11); 61 of 4 December 1958 (ibid., 112).

33. I am especially thinking of Smith, "Comments on Taylor's Commentary on Mark"; Smith, "The Jewish Elements in the Gospels"; Smith, "Aramaic Studies and the Study of the New Testament." Earlier materials were also updated and recycled in Smith, "Prolegomena," 174–99 (repr. in Smith, *Studies*, 2:3–27).

34. On this point, one cannot but agree with Carlson, *Gospel Hoax*, 74–76 and 128–29.

35. Contrast Strauss, *Life of Jesus Critically Examined*, 476–95, for whom, "[i]f the authors or collectors of the three first gospels knew of this [i.e., the raising of Lazarus], they could not, for more than one reason, avoid introducing it into their writings" (491), with, e.g., Meier, *A Marginal Jew*, 2, 798–832, who laboriously tries to reconstruct the original content of the story before concluding that "the silence of the Synoptic Gospels about the raising of Lazarus says nothing one way or the other about the ultimate historicity of the tradition" (832).

36. A point cleverly made by Price, "Second Thoughts," 130–31.

Ancient Gospel or Modern Forgery?

ONCE AGAIN, THE QUESTION OF MOTIVE

In the Beginning, a Hoax?

Smith's correspondence with Scholem also sheds a new light on the circumstances that compelled him to interrupt his collaboration with Brown University sooner than he had expected. In 1953 Smith was apparently doing well at Brown, where he was even planning to have Scholem invited as a guest professor with the help of some faithful friends such as William G. Braude, the well-known specialist of rabbinic literature. Unhappily, in spite of the prospect of tenure that they had used to lure him two years earlier,[37] another candidate received the position left vacant at the Department of Biblical Literature and History of Religions. As a result, at the beginning of 1954 Smith was informed that his contract was not going to be renewed:

> They are "letting me go" allegedly because the teaching here is almost entirely of undergraduates and they think me better qualified to teach graduate students. The real reason, however, seems to be that the University, because of financial difficulties, depends heavily on current contributions from alumni and the religious group among the alumni have therefore been able to press the administration to support a religious revival. (I don't think it took much pressure, really, but the capacity for pressure was there.) One step of this revival requires that a dynamic popular preacher of Christianity be placed in the Department of Biblical Literature. There are only two chairs in the department, and the man in the other one [i.e., Professor William Robbins] has "tenure"—i.e. has been employed so long that he can't be fired except for grave scandal—so out I go.[38]

Even if, from a technical point of view, Smith was not "denied tenure" at Brown[39]—at least, not at the end of a formal process of internal and external evaluation by his peers—the final issue was still his dismissal in favor of a colleague who was, according to Smith himself, theologically more correct in an institution—we can add—with a strong, foundational,

---

37. "After accepting the Yale scholarship I was persuaded to change my mind and stay in at Brown for security's sake; since here [i.e., at Brown University] there is a full professorship in the offing and there [i.e., at Yale University], after finishing the research, I should be out of work and still on the level of an instructor" (letter 30 of 13 June 1951 [Stroumsa, *Correspondence*, 61]).

38. Letter 36 of 14 May 1954 (Stroumsa, *Correspondence*, 72).

39. As Carlson, *Gospel Hoax*, 8 and 80, incorrectly claims.

Baptist orientation.[40] Moreover, in spite of the gentlemen's agreement that allowed him to remain—as is usual in these cases—at Brown for one more year, until June 1955,[41] Smith harbored a long-term grudge against William J. Robbins (1913–2007), the professor of Old Testament and, from 1950, chair of the department, who had undeniably played a key role in the entire affair. According to Smith, Robbins was guilty of nothing less than not knowing the Hebrew language!

> One fly has crept into the ointment: The present Professor of Old Testament has expressed regret that your seminar [a "Survey of Jewish Mysticism (Main Points of its History and Teachings)" that Scholem was planning to give during his invitation as visiting professor at Brown University, in 1956–1957] will require a reading knowledge of Hebrew. He says he thinks there would be a number of students who would like to take a seminar with you, but who could not meet that requirement. (He is right at least as to one student—himself, and I think his regret is due to the fact he thinks such a seminar as proposed might call attention to his deficiency in this matter).[42]

Tactfully, Scholem immediately expressed his sympathy to Smith in quite eloquent terms: "It is bitterly disappointing to hear that you are leaving Brown, and I wish you find a place where your tenure is not dependent on churchmen's interests. That's a bitter pill and I understand how you must feel."[43] At the same time, however, Scholem was displaying more tolerance and magnanimity toward the former colleagues of his protégé.[44]

In January 1950 it had already been necessary for Scholem to comfort the young Smith following a failure at Bryn Mawr (Pennsylvania). The

---

40. Neither Smith, in his published letters, nor Pantuck, in his notes, disclose the name of this scholar. The most probable candidate seems to be Ernest S. Frerichs, who in 1953 was hired at Brown as professor of Religious and Jewish Studies. However, contrary to Smith's all-too-negative description and pessimistic expectations, Frerichs quickly became a highly respected specialist of biblical archaeology and Second Temple Judaism, who eventually also contributed an article to Smith's *Festschrift*: Frerichs, "Contemporary Ecclesiastical Approaches to Biblical Interpretation" (a rejoinder to Smith's study mentioned below, n. 51).

41. Letter 38 of 19 June 1954 (Stroumsa, *Correspondence*, 76–77).

42. Letter 52 of 15 June 1956 (Stroumsa, *Correspondence*, 102).

43. Letter 37, not dated but presumably of 6 June 1954 (Stroumsa, *Correspondence*, 73).

44. Letter 53 of 26 June 1956 (Stroumsa, *Correspondence*, 104). One should note, however, that neither Smith nor Scholem ever mention Robbins's name. His identity was revealed by Pantuck (ibid., 72, n. 206) and Stroumsa (ibid., 102, n. 241).

college was initially "looking for a potential Professor of the Philosophy of Religion,"[45] but Smith quickly realized that he had "no great hope of getting the chair, which seems likely to be reserved for someone with an 'inspirational message.'"[46] On that occasion, Scholem's reply had been, so to speak, prophetic: "Your expanding scholarship makes me wonder—where will all that lead to? The gentlemen at Bryn Mawr had apparently no use for an intelligent man. Meanwhile you will know too much for America, too much of the Fathers of the Church and out of sheer boredom with this world will become a Manichean."[47] Six years later, after the troubles at Brown and a fruitless attempt at Yale—where Smith was interviewed by what Erwin R. Goodenough (1893–1965) did not hesitate to define as "a committee of preachers"[48]—with the announcement of a new application, this time at Cornell University (Ithaca, New York),[49] Scholem cried out: "How the American Universities let a scholar like yourself sit around and wait for a good appointment is above my understanding."[50]

It is certainly difficult to evaluate the psychological impact of such negative experiences, and this is in spite of the unshakeable support that Scholem and other influential scholars such as Goodenough and Arthur D. Nock (1902–1963) constantly offered to Smith. It was, perhaps, because of what he perceived as being a hostile attitude from a guild of theologians that Smith started developing—and making more and more obvious—an uncompromising dislike for what he would later call the "pseudorthodoxy" of Biblical studies, that is, "apologetic and anachronistic scholarship recruited for the defense of certain religious beliefs about the Bible."[51] Thus, it is not surprising if many distinguished specialists became the victims of

---

45. Letter 16 of 10 March 1949 (Stroumsa, *Correspondence*, 35).
46. Letter 20 of 30 March 1949 (Stroumsa, *Correspondence*, 38).
47. Letter 24 of 17 January 1950 (Stroumsa, *Correspondence*, 43–44).
48. Letter 42 of 27 October 1955 (Stroumsa, *Correspondence*, 85).
49. Letter 52 of 15 June 1956 (Stroumsa, *Correspondence*, 103).
50. Letter 53 of 26 June 1956 (Stroumsa, *Correspondence*, 104).
51. Stroumsa, *Correspondence*, 147, n. 349. This is Stroumsa's summary of Smith, "The Present State of Old Testament Studies" (repr. in Smith, *Studies*, 1:37–54), a polemical essay in which Smith describes the Hebrew Bible as being "largely a tissue of miracle stories" (20) and Old Testament studies as being dominated by apologetic perspectives whose main goal is to defend the "'essential' truth" of the Scriptures (29–30). To this Frerichs, "Contemporary Ecclesiastical Approaches," 225, replied that, "[i]f the views of these scholars are judged to be 'pseudorthodox' in a secular setting, their views are 'controrthodox' in an ecclesiastical setting." For other appreciations of "Smith's beliefs and opinions about the piety of the Establishment," see Carlson, *Gospel Hoax*, 84–85 and 130.

Smith's fearsome polemical talent, his "caustic and sometimes devastating criticism of some of our contemporaries," as Scholem will acknowledge after the reading of "the first volume of [the] Secret Gospel discovery."[52]

Could such a cluster of misfortunes have pushed Smith to take a foolish revenge upon his supposedly incompetent pseudo-orthodox rivals? Did he compose the *Letter to Theodore* at "a point in his life" that was, as Carlson puts it, so "vulnerable"?[53] Was his main goal, according to the same critic, "to test the establishment, whether to expose flaws in the gatekeepers of authenticity, to exhibit [his own] skill and cunning, or to take pleasure in the failure of self-appointed experts to pass the test"?[54] In other words, did Smith commit what Carlson considers to be "an academic hoax" in order to ridicule those "preachers" with no philological and linguistic skills who had dared to humiliate him? In my opinion, the absence of any clearly identifiable "joke" embedded within the *Letter to Theodore*,[55] along with Smith's sincere commitment to true scholarship[56] and, especially, his perseverance in defending the authenticity of his discovery without concessions until the very end, are all elements that tend to militate against Carlson's overly simplistic hypothesis of a hoax.

Finding the "Evidence" for a Mystical Libertine Jesus

Smith's extraordinary discovery at Mar Saba is mentioned for the first time in a letter written at the beginning of August 1959, in which he simply tells Scholem: "The material by Clement of Alexandria . . . is turning out to be of great importance, and as soon as I get all minor nuisances off my hands I must work hard at it."[57] By the end of October of the same year, however, he was able to tell Scholem about his project of "the edition of [a] fragment

---

52. Letter 94 of 3 July 1973 (Stroumsa, *Correspondence*, 155). In his correspondence with Scholem, Smith is sometimes inclined to make statements as provoking as, "Why is it that the study of religion attracts so many nitwits?" (letter 84 of 15 August 1967 [ibid., 141]). While in the case of Scholem, even if he is not always charitable towards the colleagues that he thinks are less than competent (see what he writes about Amos Funkenstein in letter 91 of 5 June 1972 [ibid., 151]), he is generally more detached, not to say a little ironic.

53. Carlson, *Gospel Hoax*, 79–80 and 85.

54. Ibid., 78.

55. Brown and Pantuck have convincingly dismissed the majority of Carlson's claims in this sense in the studies quoted above, n. 10.

56. A quality acknowledged even by Carlson, *Gospel Hoax*, 85.

57. Letter 63 of 7 August 1959 (Stroumsa, *Correspondence*, 115).

of a letter allegedly by Clement of Alexandria, . . . which contains some amazing information about the Carpocratians and the Gospel according to Mark."[58] The mention of the disciples of Carpocrates, well-known for their libertinism (real or imagined), had the immediate effect of arousing Scholem's curiosity. He promptly replied: "I am amazed to hear that there is still unknown information about the Carpocratians to be found. *Those are the Frankists of Antiquity.* Produce it [i.e., the edition of the fragment attributed to Clement] as soon as possible!"[59]—an understandably predictable reaction for anyone minimally familiar with the work of the great Israeli specialist of Jewish mysticism, who had already voiced his conviction that *the Frankists were the Carpocratians of modern times.*[60]

From that point on Smith kept Scholem informed about the progress of his work on the *Letter to Theodore*, sending him at the end of January 1961 what seems to be a copy of the manuscript together with "a summary of [his] report on the parallelisms to Clement's style, and a couple of other recent publications."[61] In any case, at the beginning of 1963 Scholem apparently had already received and read the draft of the fourth chapter, on the historical background to *Secret Mark*, of the future *editio maior* to be released in 1973.[62]

---

58. Letter 65 of 28 October 1959 (Stroumsa, *Correspondence*, 117–18).

59. Letter 66 of 30 December 1959 (Stroumsa, *Correspondence*, 119 [emphasis added]).

60. Scholem had explicitly made such a connection in his seminal study on "Redemption through Sin" (on which see Wasserstrom, *Religion after Religion*, 215–24, 340–45), originally published in Hebrew in 1937 and devoted to the controversial figures of Sabbatai Tzevi (1626–1676) and Jacob Frank (1726–1791), and in his groundbreaking monograph, *Major Trends in Jewish Mysticism*, whose first edition was published in English in 1941. See Gershom Scholem, "Redemption through Sin," in Scholem, *The Messianic Idea in Judaism and Other Essays on Jewish Spirituality*, 132–33; Scholem, *Major Trends in Jewish Mysticism*, 316. In this regard, one should also note that the "final manuscript" of *Major Trends* had been read, among others, by "Mr. Morton Smith, S.T.B. (Harvard), a research student at the [Hebrew] University" (ibid., xxvii).

61. Letter 68 of 30 January 1961 (Stroumsa, *Correspondence*, 123). Two months later, Scholem thanked his friend "for the three reprints" he had just received in Jerusalem, "especially the two on Clement's letter on the Carpocratians," congratulating him for the discovery of such "an unexpected testimony!!" (letter 71, not dated but posted 31 March 1961 [ibid., 126–27]). The two articles were, most likely, Smith, "Monasteries and Their Manuscripts," and Smith, "Ἑλληνικὰ χειρόγραφα ἐν τῇ Μονῇ τοῦ ἁγίου Σάββα" ("Greek Manuscripts in the Monastery of St. Saba").

62. For the review mentioned by Scholem (letter 81 of 3 March 1963 [Stroumsa, *Correspondence*, 138]), see Smith, *Clement of Alexandria*, 240. The other specialist to whom Smith submitted a draft of the same chapter (ibid., 195) was the patristics

Suddenly, between January 31 and June 12, 1961, Smith realized the scope of the impact that the two excerpts of *Secret Mark* cited in the *Letter to Theodore* would have on the continuing search for the historical Jesus:

> Though I haven't been able to work on the letter [to Theodore], I've been thinking a good deal about it, and about the possibility that Jesus may actually have taught a libertine gospel—Libertinism is so widespread in the New Testament, almost every book combats it, it cannot all derive from Paul, there are a lot of libertine sayings in Jesus' mouth (The Law and the Prophets were until John, since then! [Matt 11:13//Luke 16:16a]).
>
> Do you think the body and blood eaten and drunk can be a ritual expression of libertinism? (Eating a human sacrifice was a way of binding conspirators together; Apollonius of Tyana was charged with it). I talked about it with [Elias] Bickerman the other day and he was rather enthusiastic, saying this background would explain the reaction to the crucifixion, which I think it would. Any comments you may make on *Mitzvah habaa b'avera* [i.e., "a commandment which is fulfilled by means of a transgression"[63]] in or before the Tannaitic period will be most welcome.[64]

In spite of the doubts and reservations immediately expressed by Scholem,[65] one year later Smith was back, so to speak, on the offensive: "I am really beginning to think Carpocrates and the sort of things he represented (and especially the ascent through the heavens) were far closer to Jesus than has ever been supposed. What's more, *I have the evidence.*"[66] This "evidence" that enabled Smith to make an argument for a libertine Jesus who

---

scholar Cyril C. Richardson (1909–1976), Professor of Church History at the Union Theological Seminary in New York.

63. As Scholem, "Redemption through Sin," 99, aptly renders it. Actually, *Mitzvah ha-Ba'ah ba-'Averah* is the original title of the 1937 Hebrew essay, then freely translated as "Redemption through Sin." On this and other aspects of "transgressive theurgy," one should now refer to Mopsik, *Les grands textes de la cabale*, 524–46.

64. Letter 72 of 13 June 1961 (Stroumsa, *Correspondence*, 127–28). This early mention of the theory of a libertine Jesus performing rituals of erotic magic contradicts Stroumsa's assumption that Smith first expressed such a view to Scholem no earlier than 1974 (ibid., xiv).

65. "About libertinism in the New Testament I do not feel competent to comment although there may be something in what you say regarding libertine sayings put in Jesus' mouth. But I admit to an amount of skepticism regarding the hypothesis about the body and blood formula as a ritual expression of libertinism, Bickerman's enthusiasm notwithstanding" (letter 73 of 3 July 1961 [Stroumsa, *Correspondence*, 129]).

66. Letter 76 of 6 October 1962 (Stroumsa, *Correspondence*, 132 [emphasis added]).

practiced ascent to heaven as an initiatory rite was, undoubtedly, the long passage from *Secret Mark* relating the resurrection of a young rich man in Bethany and his nocturnal initiation into "the mystery of the kingdom of God." This was a major turning point in Smith's research on the historical Jesus, a line of interpretation from which he would never depart and that would lead him to the publication, in 1978, of his famous, and controversial, monograph entitled *Jesus the Magician*.[67]

It is reasonable to conclude that Smith had written the first draft of the pages that, in his commentary, would be devoted to the magical, esoteric, antinomian, and libertine dimensions of the Jesus movement and other early Christian groups as early as 1961-1962—or, at the very least, if our chronological reconstruction is accurate, before March 1963.[68] As for Scholem's friendly but, at the same time, firm reaction to his American friend's radical theses, we have to wait until June 1974, following the publication of Smith's two monographs on the *Letter to Theodore* and *Secret Mark* in 1973.[69] On the one hand, Scholem claimed that he was convinced by Smith's demonstration of "the authenticity of the letter by Clement of Alexandria" and his reconstruction of the Markan question, while, on the other hand, concerning "the libertine character of Jesus' teachings for

67. On Smith's "own concept" of Jesus' activities, see in particular Smith, *Clement of Alexandria*, 237; Smith, *Secret Gospel*, 80-81, 113-14; Smith, *Jesus the Magician*, 134-35, 138; Smith, "Two Ascended to Heaven," 293-94, 300. Smith announced to Scholem the project of writing *Jesus the Magician* (letter 104 of 27 September 1976 [Stroumsa, *Correspondence*, 171]); its imminent publication (letter 108 of 24 November 1977 [ibid., 176]); and finally, his "hope to hear what [Scholem] think[s] of *Jesus*, and especially any correction" (letter 111 of 13 September 1978 [ibid., 179]). Scholem's comments, however, were not, or are no longer, documented.

68. According to Koester, "Was Morton Smith a Great Thespian and I a Complete Fool?" 58, Smith had already suggested "that the initiation rite in the Secret Gospel indicated some homosexual ritual" in a lecture he had given in 1960 (most likely at a meeting of the Society of Biblical Literature covered by *The New York Times*, 30 and 31 December 1960, and mentioned in Stroumsa, *Correspondence*, 200 ["Appendix A"]). Koester recollects Smith's visit to the University of Heidelberg, on the occasion of a sabbatical, in 1963, and the long discussions they had there about "details of the interpretation of Secret Mark" (ibid.). Smith himself had no difficulty admitting that Koester agreed with Scholem and shared the same reservations about his interpretation of *Secret Mark* (letter 97 of 12 July 1974 [Stroumsa, *Correspondence*, 162]).

69. Scholem first received Smith's *Secret Gospel*, whose perspectives he found "indeed very exciting . . . The Jesus of the Sermon on the Mountain and Jesus the Magician, suppressed by the church tradition—what perspectives!" (letter 94 of 3 July 1973 [Stroumsa, *Correspondence*, 155-56]). Smith then personally gave him a copy of his *Clement of Alexandria*, most likely when they met during Scholem's stay in New York, from 17 to 27 September 1973 (mentioned in letters 95 of 13 July 1973 [ibid., 157]; and 96 of 9 June 1974 [ibid., 158]).

initiates," he made it clear that, in his opinion, "it is a hypothesis which remains rather vague" and he admitted that he had "not been convinced."[70]

> That there were groups who drew libertinist consequences from the teachings about the kingdom of God, I take it as firmly established by you and some of your predecessors. The further step to relate it to Jesus himself remains to me a hypothesis for which no hard evidence can be produced.
>
> The doubts about your interpretation of the story on the new Gospel of Mark which I expressed in our talk in New York,[71] have remained with me. I am not sure whether you proposed as a possible hypothesis or an unavoidable consequence of the context of this story within the background which you have described. My admiration for the scholarship and insight demonstrated in your book is enormous and I cannot imagine that it will not have its repercussions on future discussions. [...] But there seems to me a great difference between the stringency of your other deductions and the hypothetical character of *your assumption of Jesus as a mystical libertinist*.[72]

Thus, Smith's attempt to reduce the historical Jesus to the status of a libertine miracle-maker worthy of the *Toledot Yeshu* was met with Scholem's flat refusal. Interestingly enough, Scholem did not qualify Smith's Jesus as a miracle worker/magician, but "as a mystical libertinist," as though such an image of Jesus was more or less identical with his own depictions of Sabbatai Tzevi and Jacob Frank.[73] In a certain sense, through the use of this expression the Israeli scholar was painfully signaling to his American friend that the latter's equation of Jesus with modern, antinomian Jewish messianic claimants was, at best, vague and speculative.

Smith immediately replied, thanking Scholem for his benevolent approval of a large part of the theses he had defended in the *Clement of Alexandria* volume, but reacting in a rather nervous manner to the not-so-veiled criticism raised against the reconstruction of the career of the historical Jesus that he had proposed.

---

70. Letter 96 of 9 June 1974 (Stroumsa, *Correspondence*, 158).

71. See above, n. 69.

72. Letter 96 of 9 June 1974 (Stroumsa, *Correspondence*, 158–59 [emphasis added]).

73. To the bibliography cited above, n. 60, one should add at least Gershom Scholem's monumental biography, *Sabbatai Tzevi*, as well as the entries he devoted to "Shabbetai Tzevi and the Shabbatean Movement," "Jacob Frank and the Frankists," "The Doenmeh," "Nathan of Gaza," and other prominent Sabbatian figures in the *Encyclopaedia Judaica* (1971–1972), conveniently reprinted in Scholem, *Kabbalah*.

Ancient Gospel or Modern Forgery?

> As to Jesus, I should perhaps have emphasized more strongly that *all* accounts of his teaching and practice are conjectural, and I claim to my conjectures only that they fit the reports as well as any and better than most. Of course nothing can be *proved* about this subject. For practical purposes the Gospels are our sole substantial evidence. And they are two generations later than the events and contradict both themselves and each other. Therefore every school of criticism concerned about consistency begins by forming arbitrarily its own concept of what Jesus "must" have been—a pious 'am ha'aretz, a Hillelite rabbi, an eschatological preacher, a prophet like Elijah, etc. etc.—and then declares authentic the material that supports its predetermined conclusion, forces as much neutral material as possible into the picture, and brands the rest "secondary." The strength of my position, I think, is that, into this arbitrary guessing game, I have introduced the common-sense observations that (a) *it is more likely than not* that a man's teachings are reflected by the practices of his disciples, and (b) *it is plausible to suppose* that disputes and divisions found almost universally in the earliest attested forms of the movement (the churches known from the Pauline letters) go back to some peculiarity in its origin. Now I have made my case, the next moves are up to my opponents. Let *them* explain: *If Jesus did* not *practice magic*, how does it happen that the central ritual of the *earliest* known Christianity is a rite of erotic magic (the eucharist)? *If elements of Jesus' teaching were* not *libertine*, how does it happen that the libertinism was epidemic in Christian congregations, *by the time of Paul? If Jesus did not give his followers access to the kingdom*, where do the gospel passages that represent them as in it, come from? And so on, for all the questions I have raised, which *all* point back to the sort of figure I've hypothecated.[74]

These kinds of methodological questions have rarely been raised—at least, not in such a direct and uncompromising way—and legitimately should be included in any serious anthology devoted to the research on Jesus of Nazareth.[75] They "*all* point back to the sort of figure" Smith had been "hypothecat[ing]" for years, even decades—actually, well before his

---

74. Letter 97 of 12 July 1974 (Stroumsa, *Correspondence*, 160–61 [emphasis in the original]). Smith had probably forgotten that Scholem had already expressed, thirteen years earlier, serious doubts about such an interpretation (see above, n. 65). In any case, he reiterated his views in *Jesus the Magician*, 122–23, 152, 201.

75. As, e.g., in the incredibly rich volume—with no fewer than 343 excerpts!—published by Ford and Higton, eds., *Jesus*.

discovery of the amazing document which would finally provide the "evidence" for his claims.

In the End, a Learned Forgery?

Smith retrospectively recognized that Scholem's depiction of Sabbatai Tzevi—or, more to the point, his perception of that characterization—was one of the main inspirational sources for his own reconstruction of Jesus. This happened at the end of September 1976, when Smith wrote to Scholem in order to thank him for the sending of the Hebrew edition of his *Zur Kabbala und ihrer Symbolik*, originally published in 1960.[76]

> Your work is always invaluable, even to those like me who are working in fields quite other than the kabbalah, because of its illumination of the profundities of the religious mind (or whatever it is that the religious use[s] instead of a mind) . . . "I have read you with an eye to the deeper problems," and *I think I've learned more about Jesus from you and Shabbatai Zvi* (I'm sometimes not sure which is which) *than I have from any other source except the gospels and the magical papyri.*[77]

One should not be surprised by such an appraisal for a book in which Sabbatai Tzevi and other mystical nihilists are rarely mentioned. The fact is that Smith had not yet found the time to read it because he had just started working on his own *Jesus the Magician* and "[g]ospels and papyri ha[d] kept [him] busy all summer."[78] Accordingly, the time was ripe to make a more general statement and acknowledge the intellectual debt that he owed to his mentor and friend: Smith's Jesus had been (at least, in part) modeled after Scholem's Sabbatai Tzevi.[79]

Far from being a shift toward reductionism, the identification of possible convergences between the figures of the two illustrious religious leaders is one of the true marks of Smith's genius and ability to anticipate the future evolution of the research on the historical Jesus. In other words, Smith's exposure to Scholem's studies on Sabbatai Tzevi had enabled him

---

76. English translation: Scholem, *On the Kabbalah and Its Symbolism*.

77. Letter 104 of 27 September 1976 (Stroumsa, *Correspondence*, 170, [emphasis added]).

78. Ibid. (Stroumsa, *Correspondence*, 171).

79. Smith's explicit confession thus confirms the hypothesis of a Sabbatian influence that I put forward in Piovanelli, "L'Évangile secret de Marc," 247–50, prior to the publication of Stroumsa, *Correspondence*.

Ancient Gospel or Modern Forgery?

to see Jesus as a truly Jewish messianic figure, a flesh and blood Jew whose conduct and teachings (in this order) need to be reconstructed with the help of both friendly and unfriendly testimony and contextualized within the social framework of first-century Palestine.[80] Every sensitive student of the Kabbalah who also paid attention to Sabbatai Tzevi, from Elijah Benamozegh (1823–1900) to Scholem, immediately noticed the commonalities between the ancient rabbi from Nazareth and his modern colleague from Smyrna.[81] What is really amazing is that New Testament scholars and specialists of the historical Jesus were apparently unaware of such an analogy, and this in spite of the Albert Schweitzer Memorial Lecture that the late William David Davies (1911–2001) delivered at the meeting of the Society of Biblical Literature and the American Academy of Religion, November 1, 1975 in Chicago.[82] Smith, however, was not an ordinary New Testament scholar, but an enthusiastic disciple of the most renowned specialist of Jewish mysticism and messianism, whose "concern" for Kabbalistic, Sabbatian, and Frankist "ideas" dated at least as far back as 1947–1950,[83] thus largely predating not only the writing of *Jesus the Magician*, but also the discovery of the *Letter to Theodore* and *Secret Mark*.

80. See, in this sense, Smith, *Jesus the Magician*, 1–20 (albeit without mentioning Sabbatai Tzevi).

81. In his 1863 unpublished monograph, *Essai sur les origines des dogmes et de la morale du christianisme*, the rabbi from Livorno wrote: "Shabbetai is a modern image which reflects in its most essential traits Jesus' older depiction. Accordingly, he is a precious tool for the study, in a situation more accessible to modern (scholars), of an older phenomenon which was provoked by the same causes and the same abuses of the same doctrine" (Benamozegh, *La kabbale et l'origine des dogmes chrétiens*, 65 [my translation]). On Benamozegh's fascinating perspectives, see Guetta, *Philosophy and Kabbalah*. As for Scholem's more balanced position, see *Sabbatai Tzevi*, 795–99.

82. Davies, "From Schweitzer to Scholem." Davies's essay has been incorporated (alas, without the footnotes) in anthologies like Blum, ed., *Gershom Scholem*, 77–97; or Kriegel, ed., *Gershom Scholem*, 200–13 (French translation), but it is conspicuously absent from historical Jesus studies, including the groundbreaking monograph of Davies's former student Sanders, *Jesus and Judaism*.

83. In 1947, Scholem had made an interesting proposal to Smith: "A lot of my small stuff has appeared both in the Kabbalistical and Sabbatian Heretical field, and if you tell me you are interested, I will be glad to send you some of it . . ." (letter 7 of 23 March 1947 [Stroumsa, *Correspondence*, 20]), to which Smith promptly replied, "Thank you also for the pamphlets you sent me . . . Please continue to send me such Kabbalistic and Sabbatian things as you think will interest me, remembering that *my concern is the ideas* and I am content to leave the bibliographical details to experts" (letter 8 of 9 May 1947 [ibid., 22–23 (emphasis added)]). Three years later he even declared, "[W]hat I should most like to translate would be a volume of your essays in Sabbatianism and Frankism: Could you and would you send me a suggested list of titles and places of publication?" (letter 25 of 16 March 1950 [ibid., 46]).

Certainly by the time of his first contacts with Scholem in 1940–1944, Smith had developed an interest in the *Hekhalot Rabbati*, one of the most important "macroforms" (as Peter Schäfer qualifies these texts) of late antique and early medieval Jewish mystical literature of the Hekhalot (the heavenly "palaces" visited by the "descenders to the Merkavah") pseudepigraphically attributed to the sage Ishmael ben Elisha (ca. 90–135 CE).[84] Smith had translated it into English from a preliminary edition of the Hebrew-Aramaic text prepared by Scholem and Chaim Wirszubski (1915–1977).[85] Then, having left the first draft of it in Jerusalem, he spent the next thirty-seven years in a series of cyclical attempts to retrieve and have it revised for a publication that only saw the light posthumously, thanks to Don Karr's efforts, in 1995.[86] Nonetheless, Smith was able to crystallize his reflections on *Hekhalot Rabbati* in a conference paper he gave in 1960, in which he also reacted to the publication of the Israel Goldstein lectures on *Jewish Gnosticism, Merkabah Mysticism, and Talmudic Tradition* that Scholem had delivered at the Jewish Theological Seminary of America in New York, in 1957.[87] A few passages that manifestly anticipate Smith's later ideas about ascents to heaven[88] deserve to be quoted in full:

> As suggested in the course of the outline it [i.e., the text of *Hekhalot Rabbati*] breaks quite distinctly into two parts, chapters 1 to 12, the spells which are to be said by one who desires to see the *Merkabah*, and chapters 13 to 30 (the end), an account of the ascent through the palaces of heaven, culminating in a

---

84. The bibliography on Hekhalot texts and Merkavah mysticism is too large to be mentioned here. For a critical review of the main schools of thought and interpretation, see Boustan, "The Study of Heikhalot Literature"; Schäfer, *The Origins of Jewish Mysticism*, especially 243–330; Piovanelli, "Pratiques rituelles ou exégèse scripturaire?"

85. See Stroumsa, *Correspondence*, 195 ("Appendix A").

86. *Hekhalot Rabbati*, 1–43. For "the hapless course—as Karr defines it—of Smith's translation" through his letters, see the index in Stroumsa, *Correspondence*, 205, sub voce "Hekhalot."

87. Smith, "Observations on *Hekhalot Rabbati*." In spite of a certain delay in the publication of the volume, Smith had already finished his paper and sent it to Scholem by the end of January 1961 (letter 68 of 30 January 1961 [Stroumsa, *Correspondence*, 121–22]). As for Scholem's contribution to the study of *Hekhalot Rabbati* and Hekhalot mysticism, see his *Major Trends*, 40–79 ("Merkabah Mysticism and Jewish Gnosticism"), and *Jewish Gnosticism, Merkabah Mysticism, and Talmudic Tradition*, especially 31–35 ("Some Old Elements in the Greater Hekhaloth").

88. Smith, *Clement of Alexandria*, 237–48 ("The rite was a means of ascent to the heavens"); Smith, "Ascent to Heavens and the Beginning of Christianity," 415–29 (repr. in Smith, *Studies*, 2:47–67); Smith, "Two Ascended to Heaven," 290–94.

session with the Cherubim, the Ophanim, and the Holy Beasts, "[and they are called by the appellation of gods] being throned together," as Clement of Alexandria said [*Stromata* VII,10], "with the other gods, who were first established in their orders by the Saviour." [Footnote 3: This is the goal of Clement's gnosis; *Opera*, ed. Stählin, III, 41, lines 24f.].[89]

Scholem's study of the materials in the hekhalot tradition... has just led us to conclusions amazingly close to those reached by Goodenough from his study of the archaeological remains: to wit, the Hellenistic period saw the development of a Judaism profoundly shaped by Greco-Oriental thought, in which mystical and magical... elements were very important. From this common background such elements were derived independently by the magical papyri, Gnosticism, Christianity, and Hellenistic and Rabbinic Judaism. I may add that in all of these traditions *such material was passed on as secret doctrine*.[90]

The magical papyri occasionally prescribe the use of a medium, usually an uncorrupted boy, who, under the magician direction, sees the gods and describes what he sees. [Footnote 28: Such mediums appear in *The Demotic Magical Papyrus of London and Leiden*, ed. F. Griffith and H. Thompson (Oxford, 1921), I. 8, 18f., II. 1ff., and in *Papyri Graecae Magicae*, ed. K. Preisendanz, vol. I (Leipzig, 1928), pap. IV, lines 89ff.].[91]

Thus, as early as 1960, Smith was already associating the apotheotic traditions of the Hekhalot literature with "the goal of Clement's gnosis." He also detected within Second Temple Judaism and early Christianity the presence of Hellenistic "mystical and magical... elements" of the kind of those found in the so-called *Mithras Liturgy* and other magical papyri.[92] Among those phenomena, he had singled out "the use of a medium, usually an uncorrupted boy"—albeit not a νεανίσκος, "young man," as in *Secret Mark*, but a παῖς, "child"!—in order to acquire a divine assistant. In his opinion, such teachings and practices were "passed on as a secret doctrine." This was precisely the cluster of basic "elements" that he would soon put to use in order to make sense of the strange gospel excerpts quoted in the *Letter to Theodore*.

Finally, Smith's epistolary reveals an early and unexpected concern for a contemporary charismatic personage as anticonformist and

---

89. Smith, "Observations on *Hekhalot Rabbati*," 148.
90. Ibid., 153–54 (emphasis added).
91. Ibid., 154.
92. A point criticized by Jeffery, *Secret Gospel of Mark Unveiled*, 102–6, 290–92.

controversial as Aleister Crowley (1875–1947), the famous British writer and occultist so well-known for the rites of "sex magick" that he customarily performed with his followers.[93] Even if in his letter of November 1945 Smith acknowledged that these kinds of distractions were but "nonsense," he had manifestly appreciated the reading not only of "a selection of [Crowley's] poetry and one of his plays,"[94] but also of a "book about his life" published in 1930 by a certain Percy R. Stephensen—not "Stephenson," as in the edited volume of the Smith–Scholem correspondence—, whose undeniable "purpose was to whitewash" Crowley.[95] Smith used this work to compile a relatively well-documented list of Crowley's most significant achievements, which covers no fewer than fourteen lines of the printed letter. He even attempted to track him down after his expulsion from Italy subsequent to the accidental death, in 1923, of one of his disciples, where Stephensen's book stops.

Smith's concluding remarks are particularly enigmatic and intriguing:

> Crowley was in England in the thirties when Stephenson's [sic] book was published. When was the article you have about the Mittel-Danj [?] "zwischen Schopenhauer und Busch" written?
> Why am I interested in a fool like him? I cannot say. I just am. He has a certain "Keckheit, Kühnheit und Grandiosität" (as Goethe said about Byron)[[96]] which I find lacking in your usual research student and your average Anglican minister.[97]

Smith seems to establish a connection between Crowley's presence "in England in the thirties" and a mysterious "Mittel-Danj"—the editor's choice of not publishing the original Hebrew text of the letter makes any

---

93. An interest already noticed by Jeffery, "Secret Gospel of Mark Revisited." In this regard, we could add that Crowley and the poet Victor B. Neuburg (1883–1940), a young disciple of his initiated in the Algerian desert in 1909, had at that point a devastating experience which is not so far from the kind of homoerotic encounter that Smith presupposed behind the rite described in the first excerpt of *Secret Mark*. See Owen, "The Sorcerer and His Apprentice."

94. Crowley, *Mortadello*.

95. "Apparently either Crowley or one of his disciples had Stephenson [sic] write it when Crowley was growing old and wanted to return to England and quit his youthful ways" (letter 3 of 26 November 1945 [Stroumsa, *Correspondence*, 10]). See Stephensen, *The Legend of Aleister Crowley*.

96. More precisely, "Byron's Kühnheit, Keckheit und Grandiosität, ist das nicht alles bildend?" See Eckermann, *Gespräche mit Goethe*, 2:52 (after a conversation held on 16 December 1828).

97. Letter 3 of 26 November 1945 (Stroumsa, *Correspondence*, 11).

attempt to understand such a bizarre German-Slavic[98] (Yiddish?) expression even more difficult—, apparently a tragic-comic figure ("between Schopenhauer and Busch") about whom Scholem had written an article earlier. It was not a secret, however, that self-proclaimed specialists of Kabbalah such as Eliphas Lévi (born Alphonse Louis Constant [1810–1875]) or Frater Perdurabo (i.e., Aleister Crowley) were, in the eyes of the greatest twentieth-century scholar of Jewish mysticism, but "charlatans and dreamers."[99] Thus, Smith had to anticipate his correspondent's possibly dismissive reaction and candidly confess his fascination for Crowley's "boldness, audacity, and grandeur" à la Byron.

We have no means of ascertaining how long a figure as colorful and transgressive as Crowley retained Smith's interest. Did Smith notice the superficial, but still evident parallels between the biography of the modern magician of Thelema and the life of the ancient miracle worker of Nazareth?[100] Did he dare to compare the declared goal of Stephensen's booklet to "whitewash" Crowley from all of his detractors' allegations to the Gospels' equally apologetic attempts to exonerate Jesus from all of his adversaries' accusations? Although we cannot provide any definitive answer, the evolution of Smith's career tends to demonstrate that those parallels were duly noticed and played a determinant role—consciously or unconsciously, we do not know—in his magical and libertine reconfiguration of a historical Jesus halfway between Sabbatai Tzevi and Aleister Crowley.

In conclusion, a plausible reconstruction based on circumstantial evidence suggests that, as early as 1940–1944, Smith was exposed to Scholem's revolutionary theories about Jewish mysticism and Sabbatian/Frankist antinomian messianism and started thinking about the historical Jesus as a truly Jewish messiah à la Sabbatai Tzevi. Back in the United States, he pursued his work on *Hekhalot Rabbati* and discovered the dark side of Aleister Crowley's magical practices. Since 1947, he carried out a series of studies on both primary (the writings of Clement of Alexandria

---

98. The word "Danj" sounds almost Slavic to my distinguished colleague Agatha Schwartz, who informs me that *dan* in various Slavic languages means "day" and suggests that "Mittel-Danj" could mean "in the middle of the day," or the like.

99. See Scholem, *Major Trends*, 2 and 353, n. 3; Scholem, *Kabbalah*, 203; Scholem, *Alchemy and Kabbalah*, 12–13.

100. As Stephensen certainly did, when he wrote that Crowley "laid himself open to the ridiculous charge of establishing a 'love cult' or a 'free love' colony. Women, it should be noted, including Mary Magdalene, formed part of the entourage of an earlier Master, whose word was 'God is Love'" (*Legend of Aleister Crowley*, 27).

and the Gospel of Mark) and secondary sources ("the lives of Jesus"). After the terrible disappointment of losing his position at Brown University, in 1955–1956 he intensified his research not only on the Jesus movement, but also on its Greco-Roman background and, more generally, the question of Hellenistic influences in Palestine, a topic to which he devoted his Harvard ThD dissertation in 1957.[101] Perhaps he also realized that, in order to make a stronger proposal about the historical Jesus as a miracle worker/magician, he was in need of more consistent proof. He finally found such "evidence" in 1958, when he discovered the truncated fragment of the *Letter to Theodore* at Mar Saba.

Contrary to the overly simplistic view held by those who believe that Smith crafted, so to speak, the biblical hoax of the century in order to fool his naïve colleagues, we should conclude that the overwhelming evidence points towards the making of an extremely sophisticated forgery "used by Smith as a tool for promoting ideas that existed beforehand in his own head."[102] If this was—as I believe it really was—the case, in doing so Smith would have been guilty of the most inexcusable act of professional misconduct that a scholar could perpetrate. However, the ideas that he was trying to promote were extremely innovative and far in advance of his time. They paved the way for, among others, Ed Parish Sanders's full reevaluation of Jesus' Jewishness[103] and, more recently, Bruce Chilton's depiction of Jesus as a Kabbalah *chasid*.[104] They eventually contributed to

101. Revised and published later as *Palestinian Parties and Politics That Shaped the Old Testament*. Interestingly enough, the original impetus of such a study probably lies in a discussion with Nock in the summer of 1955. The latter was not convinced by Smith's hypothesis that "the group which put together [the] collection [of miracle stories recycled in the Gospel of Mark] conceived Jesus as a healing god, by analogy with Asclepius and Sarapis." According to Nock, "the miracle stories unquestionably come mostly from Galilee, and . . . the Galilean Jewry of Jesus' time was so thoroughly cut off from gentile influence that any such conception or influence was highly improbable" (letter 40 of 1 August 1955 [Stroumsa, *Correspondence*, 81]; see also letter 42 of 27 October 1955 [ibid., 85]). In the following years Smith published two substantial studies on the Hellenization of Second Temple and early Rabbinic Judaism: "Palestinian Judaism in the First Century" (repr. in Smith, *Studies*, 1:104–15), and "The Image of God" (repr. in Smith, *Studies*, 1:116–49).

102. Beskow, *Strange Tales about Jesus*, 103.

103. As explicitly acknowledged by Sanders (*Jesus and Judaism*, 6). To the bibliography cited by Piovanelli, "L'Évangile secret de Marc," 253 n. 100, we need to add now Bertalotto, *Il Gesù storico*, 53–60.

104. See Chilton, *Rabbi Jesus*. In his latest, more popular, book on Jesus, *The Way of Jesus*, Chilton is even more explicit when he (anachronistically) evokes the Kabbalistic (Lurianic) notion of *tiqqun*. As for Smith's groundbreaking role in the recovering of Jewish and Christian mystical practices, see, e.g., Idel, *Ascensions on High in Jewish*

a radical change in Jewish Christian relations. Thus, in the end a more plausible and noble explanation for Smith's hypothetical forgery would be that, in doing so, he decided to perform the best possible *maʿaśeh zar*, "strange—i.e., antinomian—deed," available to him *le-taqqen ʿolam*, "in order to repair the world"—the small world of early Christian studies or the entire universe, we do not know.

THEN, WHAT ARE WE SUPPOSED TO DO WITH A DISCOVERY SUCH AS THIS?

Recently, Timo Paananen, a young and enthusiastic Finnish student, wrote in his Master's thesis on the *Letter to Theodore* in contemporary scholarly debate and controversy, "If Smith performed *the best possible hoax* with the Theodore-letter, the Academy can do nothing but use the *Secret Gospel of Mark* as a valid historical source, as is appropriate for the current paradigm in the field of Biblical studies."[105] I must confess that I find such a position extremely debatable because the cumulative amount of circumstantial evidence mentioned above—the wrong document, at the wrong place, discovered by the wrong person, who was, moreover, in need of exactly that kind of new evidence to promote new, unconventional ideas—raises the worst suspicions about the authenticity of Smith's finding. Biblical studies are not an exception and do not escape the general rule of historical and literary studies that specifies that the scientific value of any reconstruction which relies on dubious evidence is, in turn, unreliable too. Therefore, at this point we should agree that, in the case of a text as dubious as the *Letter to Theodore*, the only possible scholarly attitude to adopt is simply not to use it in any reconstruction of the history of early Christian traditions, texts, individuals, and groups, be they the Gospel of Mark, the historical Jesus, Alexandrian Christians, the Carpocratians, or Clement of Alexandria. Paraphrasing legal terminology, the recommendation I would give to my students is, "You shall not rely on any information, materials, opinions or content found on or delivered through the so-called *Letter to Theodore*."

Certainly, it would be naïve to imagine that this and other contemporary learned forgeries that have achieved such an iconic status, both in academia and in popular culture, will suddenly disappear from the screen

---

Mysticism, 27–28, 58 and 60 ; Pilch, *Flights of the Soul*, 163–67.

105. Paananen, "Conspiracy of the Secret Evangelist." The full text of the Finnish original is available at https://helda.helsinki.fi/handle/10138/21710.

of our scholarly radars. As the comparable cases of other successful falsifications abundantly testify,[106] rare are the specialists who dare to challenge the authenticity of supposed masterpieces of the past on which entire new fields of research have been built, while other colleagues are caught in the Gordian knot of personal and/or political loyalties that impair their freedom of judgment. It takes a certain time to put things into perspective. Be that as it may, my personal wish is that in the future specialists will meet less frequently to discuss the *Letter to Theodore* and *Secret Mark*. Instead, I would like to see more conferences devoted to the emergence of early Jewish mysticism and the historical Jesus in which the positive role that Morton Smith played in the development of such studies would finally be acknowledged and taken into due account.

---

106. I am especially thinking here of some controversial artistic and cultural artifacts widely talked about in academic milieus and medias: the Ludovisi and Boston Thrones (possibly the work of sculptors Santo Varni [1807–1885] or Adolf von Hildebrand [1847–1921]), the Artemidorus Papyrus (attributed to the Greek forger Constantine Simonides [1820–1867?]), and the writings of the seventeenth-century Ethiopian philosopher Zär'a Ya'qob (actually written by the Italian missionary Giusto da Urbino [1814–1856]). On these highly instructive cases, see Franco, *Falso d'autore*; Canfora, *True History of the So-called Artemidorus Papyrus*; Canfora, *Il viaggio di Artemidoro*; Canfora, *La meravigliosa storia del falso Artemidoro*; Brodersen and Elsner, eds., *Images and Texts on the "Artemidorus Papyrus"*; Condello, "'Artemidoro' 2006–2011" (kindly brought to my attention by Claudio Zamagni); Trozzi, *Lo Hatata Zar-a Yaiqob*; Pietruschka and Bausi, "Urbino, Giusto da." For another intriguing case and a promising new method to detect modern forgeries which could be applied to the Mar Saba letter as well, see Kiernan, "Source of the Napier Fragment of Alfred's Boethius."

9

A Question of Ability: What Did He Know and When Did He Know It?
Further Excavations from the Morton Smith Archives[1]

Allan J. Pantuck, MD

"'You look terrific!' is not a translation of 'Shall I compare thee to a summer's day? Thou art more lovely and more temperate...' The basic unit of translation. What is it? It cannot be the single word. That seldom has a life of its own. A word I can look up, but I cannot translate it." —Judah Goldin[2]

THE THEORY THAT MORTON Smith forged the *Letter to Theodore* presupposes that he possessed all the expertise needed to create it prior to "discovering" it in 1958. This theory is possible to test by considering whether,

---

1. Thanks to Charles Hedrick and Timo S. Paananen for helping to correct at least some of my more egregious mistakes and to Scott G. Brown for his expertise in finding the correct words and their proper arrangement. The mistakes that remain are my own. This paper is submitted with apologies to Morton Smith, a great scholar who wished to be remembered only for his scholarship, and who had only disdain for biographical studies. Said Smith to the author in 1986, "private history is the worst kind."

2. Goldin, "Reflections on Translation and Midrash," 93.

prior to 1958, Smith possessed the knowledge and abilities that would have been required for such a feat. While there is no doubt that Smith was an extremely competent scholar, was proficient in reading various ancient languages, and was acquainted with Greek manuscripts, the extant evidence suggests that Smith did not possess the facility in patristic Greek required to compose this writing. Further, it has been adequately established by a native Greek questioned document examiner that Smith lacked the paleographic skills needed to physically write the letter's natural, free flowing, native eighteenth-century cursive Greek hand. Finally, a global survey of archival Smith papers and correspondence suggests both that Smith lacked the expertise in Clement's thought, vocabulary, and writing style needed to forge the *Letter to Theodore* and that during the five years between 1958 and the completion of the first draft of *Clement of Alexandria and a Secret Gospel of Mark* in June 1963 he was in fact acquiring his proficiency in Clement and his understanding of the letter, doing the groundwork research that he later presented in this book.

HOW GOOD WERE SMITH'S ABILITIES IN GREEK?

Smith is widely acknowledged as a brilliant scholar of ancient history, as an academician of wide ranging expertise marked by great erudition and philological precision, as "a man who worked comfortably in Greek, Latin, and Hebrew, and had a good working knowledge of Syriac," and as one who preferred to read ancient sources in their original languages rather than in translation.[3] However, the degree of language fluency required to read, understand, and translate into English a document written in a foreign language is not the same as the language mastery Smith would have needed in order to compose an original three-page document in the style of a known ancient Greek author. During childhood, a person acquires language naturally, whereas second language acquisition in adulthood requires a painstaking intellectual endeavor that rarely, if ever, results in the fluency or competence of a native speaker of that language, regardless of one's ability or motivation.[4] According to the "critical period" hypothesis, there is a cut-off at about twelve years of age after which learners lose the

---

3. Cohen, "In Memoriam Morton Smith," 283. Smith felt that a scholar must have sufficient command of a language to read primary documents in their original language in order to avoid being a second hand repeater of second hand information.

4. Krashen, *Second Language Acquisition and Second Language Learning*.

ability to achieve native fluency.[5] Among foreign language skills such as reading, listening, or speaking, composition is considered the most difficult skill for non-native speakers to master.[6] Moreover, processing of complex syntax in adults acquiring foreign languages continues to be non-native even after many years of exposure,[7] and those who learn Greek as adults often have difficulty achieving native mastery of its complex morphology and free word order, particularly when the primary language is a language with simple morphology and strict word order such as English.[8]

To compose a letter of Clement of Alexandria, an early Christian writer whose other works date to the late second century CE, Smith must necessarily have mastered not only the contents of Clement's thought, but also his distinctive vocabulary, rhetorical techniques, and style, and to have been able to have done so in a way that did not rely on any close verbal imitation or direct quotation. The skill required is well summed up by Judah Goldin, in a paper dedicated to Smith for his fifty-eighth birthday, in which he reflects that "the test of translation is met or missed—despite learning and despite virtue—in the choice of the right word, the exact word, and the proper arrangements of the language one translates into, not the language one translates from ... The language translated into is the test we must pass. And it is only a slight exaggeration (if that!) to say that a knowledge of that is more important than a knowledge of the original."[9] Therefore, one must ask: How good was Smith's Greek?

We can get some initial perspective on this issue by first considering how well Smith could write in Hebrew, a language that he spent numerous years acquiring through formal instruction while living in Jerusalem. Moreover, Smith was required to pass examinations that included his ability to compose in Hebrew, and he was required to submit his PhD thesis to the Hebrew University in Hebrew.

Morton Smith attended the college preparatory Academy of the New Church in Bryn Athyn, Pennsylvania from 1928 until 1932. As a freshman, Smith was required to take a year of Hebrew—essentially a class in religion providing background for the Old Testament and an understanding of the New Church's Hebrew hymns.[10] After graduating magna cum laude in

---

5. Penfield and Roberts, *Speech and Brain Mechanisms*.
6. Richards and Renandya, eds. *Methodology in Language Teaching*.
7. Clahsen and Felser, "How Native-like Is Non-native Language Processing?"
8. Andreou, Karapetsas, and Galantomos, "Modern Greek Language."
9. Goldin, "Reflections," 98–99.
10. Gregory A. Jackson, Archivist Bryn Athyn College & Glencairn Museum,

1936 with a Bachelor of Arts degree from Harvard University majoring in English Literature, Smith became a student of the New Testament at the Harvard Divinity School from 1937 to 1940, studying New Testament under Henry Cadbury[11] and rabbinics under Harry A. Wolfson.[12] In his second year, Smith approached Wolfson and expressed a desire to further study Hebrew:

> My troubles seem to be over for the summer, I have settled down as librarian here in the Divinity School, and I am actually beginning to read Hebrew—that is to say I spend three hours a day on it—one on review, one on reading ahead in the Midrashim, and one on the Bible—so I hope for nothing more but that you will assign me an hour when I can come weekly and mistranslate at you.[13]

Many who picture Smith capable of forging a letter in ancient Greek base this proposition in part on the folklore that Smith was capable of mastering rabbinic Hebrew in a year.[14] In fact, after two years of dedicated study with Wolfson, Smith's Hebrew remained very basic. Leo Schwartz describes the process as follows:

> Knowing him [Smith] to be a brilliant student, Wolfson suggested that he study rabbinic Hebrew for the background of the New Testament and that he would teach him by his own method. The first reader was the Sefer Ha-Aggadah ... Wolfson read each sentence and translated it and parsed each word, Smith then studied it by himself, and following the rabbinic doctrine that knowledge of a text is assured by repeating it 101 times, he virtually memorized each passage. Wolfson also gave Smith one

---

e-mail to author, 19 December 2011.

11. Henry Joel Cadbury (1883–1974), influential New Testament scholar at Bryn Mawr and then at Harvard.

12. Harry Austryn Wolfson (1887–1974), influential historian of philosophy and medieval religious thought at Harvard University, and author of many works on Philo, patristic thought, medieval philosophy, Islamic theology, and Spinoza.

13. Smith, letter to Harry A. Wolfson, 26 June 1938. All letters from Smith to Wolfson from the Papers of Harry Austryn Wolfson, Correspondence ca. 1900–1974, in Harvard University Archives, call number HUGFP 58.7, Boxes 16, 24, 31, 39, 41. Courtesy of the Harvard University Archives.

14. For example: "He learned Hebrew in a year," Calder, "Smith, Morton," 600. See also Calder, "Morton Smith," 229: "Wolfson urged that Smith learn rabbinic Hebrew as background for the New Testament. This Smith did in a year."

pisgam, maxim, to memorize each week. By the end of the year Smith could read Hebrew.[15]

Under Wolfson's influence, Smith was granted a Sheldon Travelling Fellowship from Harvard Divinity School in 1940. Smith elected, again under the influence of Wolfson, to continue his studies of Hebrew as background to the New Testament at the Hebrew University in Jerusalem. Stranded in Jerusalem for four years due to the closure of the Mediterranean during World War II, Smith ultimately earned a PhD, which he wrote in Hebrew, applying source and form criticism to analyze parallels between the Gospels and early rabbinic literature. The state of Smith's proficiency in Hebrew upon his arrival in Jerusalem, following his two years of dedicated study of Midrash with Wolfson at HDS, can be judged by his very first letter to Wolfson, written July 1, 1940:

> Since I don't want to write bad Hebrew to you and can't write good, I shall confine myself to English . . . Since RDK has become my patron I have been trying to learn Hebrew grammar in Hebrew. Just now I am reading a child's grammar by [unclear]. In this I have the help of a young university student, who doesn't know much Hebrew, but suffices for the purpose and has a lot of information about bus-routes, restaurants, and the price of eggs, which cannot be gotten out of Gesenius. Not that I am getting much out of Gesenius. I have the grammar and the dictionary, in old editions, and, am using them for commentaries. I have been reading and re-reading Judges and Samuel, but I should rather memorize the Bible than understand it, and I shall probably do neither . . . What I think of doing with Klausner is a study of the Hebrew translation of the New Testament—but all this depends on my first learning to feel at home in Hebrew.[16]

By the end of 1940, Smith wrote Wolfson on his progress:

> After Arabic I do most work for my course in the Talmud. The class is reading *Baba Bathra* (slowly, thank Heaven) and before each lesson I must translate both the Mishna and the Gemara

---

15. Schwarz, *Wolfson of Harvard*, 121-24.

16. "Gesenius" is a reference to William Genesius, *Gesenius' Hebrew Grammar*, considered one of the definitive reference works on Hebrew grammar. Joseph Gedaliah Klausner (1874-1958) was Professor of Hebrew Literature and History at Hebrew University. Smith later changed the focus of his studies from Hebrew Literature under Klausner to Classics under Professor Mosche Schwabe, pleading his "ignorance of Hebrew" and lack of interest "with any modern Hebrew literature except the translations of the New Testament."

to be read. The Mishna is not so difficult, thanks to my reading in the Aggadah, but the Gemara keeps me up to all hours of the morning and then my translations are as often incorrect as not. My reading in Hebrew, apart from the Mishna and Jeremiah, has been limited to *Avodah Israel*, which I am working through with my tutor.[17]

Having been in Jerusalem nearly a year, Smith wrote to Wolfson:

The more I hack away at the Talmud the more discouraged I get. I have been working on the Gemara now for half a year and I can read almost a page an hour. When I look at the twenty folio volumes of the Shas and calculate the hours . . . I sometimes think I would have done better to have taken up football.[18]

And three months later:

Just now I am giving almost all my time to Hebrew grammar, since I have decided to take the examinations at the end of the month in both the elementary & the advanced course on Hebrew composition. The examination in the advanced course I expect to fail, but I hope from my failure to learn my weaknesses, for I must pass the same examination this fall.[19]

In fact, Smith failed both the spring and fall examinations on Hebrew composition, and finally acknowledged this to Wolfson only in June, 1942:

For the past six months I have not dared to write you because in December I failed to eliminate the remaining quarter of my requirement in Hebrew—the essay—and while I did not think you would be angry I knew you would be disappointed. I was very much disappointed, and equally surprised . . . I took the examination again today. When it was over that particular instructor I had been most afraid of chose to read my paper and after reading it told me that, though he could not, of himself, say (for the grades are given by the instructors as a body) he thought I would certainly pass . . . Incidentally, you see I am not vain enough to try my Hebrew style on you; as a matter of fact, it's a sort of bad stew in which Biblical phrases and Talmudic expressions and bits of modern slang and rank Anglicisms

---

17. Smith, letter to Harry A. Wolfson, 12 December 1940.
18. Ibid., 16 March 16 1941.
19. Ibid., 1 June 1941.

drift around in a curious colorless liquid I am quite unable to define.[20]

By the middle of 1942, Smith was able to boast that he found himself able to talk and read in Hebrew "almost anything I wanted with *tolerable fluency*."[21] By the end of 1942, Smith passed the last of his Hebrew examinations, and wrote that he had at least "an official knowledge of the language."[22] And by 1944, Smith had completed his dissertation for Hebrew University, written in Hebrew, *Makbilot ben ha-Besorot le-sifrut ha-Tana'im* ("Parallels Between the Gospels and the Literature of the Tannaim").[23] In his last letter written to Wolfson from Jerusalem in 1944, Smith described how the thesis required not only corrections and additions to the content required by Schwabe, but also corrections for mistakes to its Hebrew.[24] It is likely not due to an oversight alone that Smith, even in this last letter from Jerusalem, still elected to write to Wolfson in English rather than in Hebrew. When Smith returned to the U.S. in 1944, he began a remarkable, life-long correspondence with his Hebrew University professor, and later friend, Gershom Scholem.[25] Smith's first two letters of this correspondence, composed within six months of having left Jerusalem, were written in Hebrew, and reveal both the proficiency he had achieved as well as the limitations that remained when it came, not to reading a foreign language or in translating from a foreign language into English, but to writing original compositions in a non-native language; for in just these two letters, translated back into English by a native speaker of Hebrew (Yonaton Moss), there are at least seven footnoted instances where Smith's Hebrew is described as "elliptical," "strange," "unclear," "obscure," and in one case possibly "intending the reverse" of what Smith had actually written.[26] Moreover, five years later, working as an Assistant Professor of Biblical Literature for Brown University, Smith still felt compelled to meet weekly with William Braude (1907–1988), a Reform rabbi and Juda-

20. Ibid., 22 June 1942.

21. Ibid., emphasis mine.

22. Ibid., 15 October 1942.

23. In fact, the doctoral degree required additional changes requested by Saul Lieberman, who was on Smith's thesis committee, and the degree was not conferred finally until 1948. The thesis was later translated back to English by Smith as *Tannaitic Parallels to the Gospels*.

24. Smith, letter to Harry A. Wolfson, 22 June 1942.

25. Now published by Stroumsa, ed., *Morton Smith and Gershom Scholem, Correspondence 1945–1982*.

26. Ibid., 1–8.

ic scholar living in Providence, to work at reading and translating Hebrew in order to maintain the proficiency he had previously attained. In 1951, Smith wrote Scholem:

> One of the unexpected advantages of working at Brown is that there is in the neighborhood a Rabbi who not only reads Hebrew but is really a devoted reader of the midrashim. He is about 10 years older than I—I should judge, perhaps less—took a Ph.D. from Brown (under Casey,[27] for a study of proselytism in Rabbinical Literature)[28] and is now making a translation of *Midrash Tehillim* for the Yale Judaica series.[29] He is a very earnest student and Wolfson and Lieberman both admire him highly. I have been seeing him once a week or so, all winter, to read the Hebrew text along with his translation . . . At all events, there are not many places in America where I should have so good an opportunity to go on with reading in Rabbinical literature.[30]

What about his Greek? I have focused on Smith's Hebrew abilities because it is possible to demonstrate, in Smith's own words, using archival documents from the period, the efforts required and the challenges and limitations that presented themselves to Smith in working in a foreign language, and to establish a realistic sense of how much work Smith would have had to have done to become even more proficient in Greek. In addition to his year of required Hebrew at the Academy of the New Church, Smith was also required to complete a minimum of three years of Latin and two years of French, but in the years Smith attended, Greek was not offered as part of the school's curriculum.[31] Furthermore, unlike Hebrew, for which Smith had the advantage of having spent four years immersed in a Hebrew-speaking country, working often daily with a private Hebrew tutor, and being required to pass examinations in Hebrew, Smith's Greek appears to be have been primarily self-taught. Indeed, no one else at Hebrew University at that time appears to have had proficiency in both Hebrew and Greek, and though he had found tutors for private instruction in Hebrew, Arabic, and Armenian, he does not seem to have had one for Greek. Even in the case of Arabic and Armenian, for which Smith made

---

27. Robert Pierce Casey (1897–1959), head of the Department of Biblical Literature at Brown University in 1934.
28. Braude, *Jewish Proselyting*.
29. Braude, *Midrash on Psalms*.
30. Letter 28 of 31 March 1951 (Stroumsa, *Correspondence*, 55–56).
31. Jackson, e-mail.

great efforts with formal class instruction and with private tutors, Smith acknowledged in 1944, as he looked back over the four years he had spent in Jerusalem, that "I have almost forgotten what Arabic and Armenian I once knew, even to the alphabet."[32] One of Smith's goals during his time in Jerusalem was not only to extend his Hebrew skills, but also to do the same for Greek.[33] In 1941, he expressed his hope to Wolfson that,

> whether or not I can carry through my plan and get a degree, I shall at least be able with another year of hard labor, to make myself at home in Greek and Hebrew ... I plan to spend eight hours a day on Hebrew (three on the Mishnah, three on the Gemara which I count as Hebrew, and two on the Tenach), four hours a day on Greek (two on the New Testament, one on Plato, and one on grammar), an hour a day on Arabic and an hour a day on Armenian ... After six months of this life I hope to be so familiar with Hebrew and New Testament Greek that I can go through the commentaries and translations quickly ... My greatest difficulty will be to hold myself to my schedule, day in and day out, for the next year.[34]

Smith's self-designed program of reading in Greek appears to have been necessitated by the fact that he was the only person at Hebrew University who was at least nominally capable of speaking both Hebrew and Greek. In 1942, Smith wrote a letter to Wolfson describing an incident in which the military police came to Hebrew University seeking a person with both Greek and Hebrew skills, for "it seemed they needed, badly, someone who could talk both modern Greek and Hebrew, and who could act as interpreter for a person of so great importance that his name could not be disclosed."[35] The self-assessed state of Smith's Greek abilities can be deduced by his reply: "I tried to explain to them that the Greek I talked was hopelessly literary and generally *ungrammatical* at the same time."[36] However, having no better options, Smith was chosen by the police and sent to

---

32. Smith, letter to Harry A. Wolfson, 13 May 1944.

33. In fact, Smith writes of trying at various times during his years in Jerusalem to learn Hebrew, Greek, Arabic, Aramaic, Persian, Ethiopic, German, and Italian. In both a letter dated Christmas 1941 and in his final letter of 1944, Smith admits that his ignoring Wolfson's advice and attempting to learn so many languages at once was a mistake.

34. Smith, letter to Harry A. Wolfson, 16 March 16 1941.

35. Ibid., 14 October 1942.

36. Ibid. Emphasis mine. Ungrammatical: not conforming to the rules of usage accepted by native speakers.

Haifa, though due to a further comedy of errors, he returned to Jerusalem having not had the opportunity to serve as translator. Moreover, despite the ambitious program Smith set for himself, which he acknowledged was the result of the "romantic enthusiasm which always, with me, precedes the opening of the school year," Smith's letters are comically full of excuses for why his "prophecies should be taken with a handful of salt" and for "the differences between my plans and my accomplishments."[37] Unable to maintain the program, Smith was forced to acknowledge that "my Greek and Armenian have suffered equally . . . in the former I have read only a few pages of the Phaedo and the vespers according to the [Jerusalem] Orthodox liturgy."[38] By the end of 1941, Smith promised Wolfson that in "January I shall spend time, chiefly on Greek, as in February I go down to a monastery in the desert where I shall have to speak Greek or starve,"[39] again an assessment of his abilities that can suggest only that, at least at the time, Smith struggled with Greek.

In the intervening years between his time in Jerusalem in the 1940s and his second visit to Mar Saba in 1958, Smith does not appear to have devoted any concentrated time to formal Greek instruction or study. Returning to Cambridge in 1944, Smith completed examinations to be awarded the Bachelor of Sacred Theology degree in 1945. Then, after a two-year period working as an Episcopal priest in Philadelphia and Baltimore, he requested from Bishop Powell and was granted in 1947 an indefinite leave of absence from his clerical duties to return to academics at Harvard Divinity School. There he worked on a Doctor of Theology degree from 1948 to 1950[40] while also working as research assistant to Arthur Darby Nock[41] in his course on the History of Religions. During these years, Smith began a study of the textual tradition of the manuscripts of Saint Isidore of Pelusium, the fifth-century ascetic church father, under the guidance of Professors Nock and Werner Jaeger.[42] In 1950, having completed his formal course work, Smith accepted a position for one year

---

37. Smith, letter to Harry A. Wolfson, 12 December 1940.

38. Ibid., 25 December 1941.

39. Ibid. The monastery in the desert refers to the monastery of Mar Saba where Smith would discover the letter of Clement sixteen years later.

40. The degree was not granted until 1957.

41. Arthur Darby Nock (1902–1963), English classical philologist and historian of religions. Nock served as a primary mentor to Smith at Harvard Divinity School, and Smith later dedicated his *Clement of Alexandria* to him.

42. Werner Wilhelm Jaeger (1888–1961), classical philologist, editor of the writings of Gregory of Nyssa.

as Instructor in Biblical Literature at Brown University. In the middle of that year, Smith wrote to Scholem:

> I'm very much in the air as to what I shall or should try to do in the near future. The only thing clear to me is that I must get time for a great deal of reading in both Greek and Hebrew, in order to consolidate and somewhat extend my present bridge-heads on those languages. How this had best be done, I'm in doubt. On the one hand, I might stay here, teach, and have a good deal of spare time for reading—though there would be an increasing burden of administrative work, and also I should be expected to turn out a lot of scholarly papers, which would mean wasting a good deal of time on secondary material. On the other hand, I have good reason to expect a fellowship for study in Greece, at the end of this year, and *that* I should like very much—but it probably would do no immediate good to my knowledge even of Greek, let alone Hebrew.[43]

After completing his year as Instructor in Biblical Literature, Smith was offered a three-year contract with generous terms to remain at Brown as an Assistant Professor rather than take a five-year research fellowship at Yale under Erwin Goodenough. Goodenough was one of Smith's closest friends and colleagues, and a scholar in the history of religion at Yale University best known for his multi-volume book *Jewish Symbols in the Greco-Roman Period*. Smith was able to include in his contract negotiations with Brown a leave of absence without pay from 1951 to 1952 for a year of post-doctoral research in Greece to photograph manuscripts related to Isidore, supported by a Fulbright Grant. Jaeger and Nock helped arrange for Smith to work based at the American School of Classical Studies in Athens. Ultimately, in addition to collecting photographs of all the major Isidore-related manuscripts in Western Europe, including seventy-eight manuscripts, mainly in excerpts, from Greece, Smith also published notes on minor manuscript collections from smaller monasteries and libraries in Cephalonia, Dimitsana, Skiathos, and Epirus that had previously not been well catalogued.[44] During this period, Smith wrote to Wolfson: "I've been trying, myself, to write about the idea of incarnation and the way something of the sort turns up in almost every part of the theology as well as in pagan philosophical systems . . . and you will be amused to know

---

43. Letter 26 of 4 December 1950 (Stroumsa, *Correspondence*, 48–49).
44. Smith, "Σύμμεικτα."

that, just to make it worse, I'm writing in Greek."[45] Though Smith does not explicitly say why Wolfson would have been amused by the idea of him writing in Greek, one can only assume that it was not because of his fluency. More than a year later, Smith wrote to Scholem about the difficulties he was having: "For the time being my struggle with my Greek essay on the concept of incarnation goes on."[46] Ultimately, Smith neither completed nor published this essay.

Though Smith never published anything that he had written in Greek, he had at least two opportunities to do so—the first in 1958, the year he discovered Clement's *Letter to Theodore*, and the second in 1959, one year after his discovery. In 1958, Smith published a short essay in the periodical of the Greek Archdiocese of North America.[47] In the essay, titled "Hebrew—Why Not Greek?" Smith made the case for increasing the opportunities for students to learn Greek since "Greek is a language so complex and so subtle that it can hardly be mastered by those who do not begin it early."[48] Though the *Orthodox Observer* is now an English language journal, in 1958 it was exclusively Greek, and it was quite unusual for it to publish a piece written in English. The second opportunity for Smith to publish in Greek was for the catalogue of the manuscript material he had found at Mar Saba in 1958. The list of his findings was translated and edited from Smith's English into Greek by Archimandrite Constantine Michaelides.[49] Thus, Smith's only publication in Greek was written by Smith in English and only later translated into Greek by a native Greek speaker. The fact that Smith, on two occasions, representing immediate bookends on either side of his discovery of the *Letter to Theodore*, declined the opportunity to have composed in Greek when it would have been expected and appropriate, speaks against the notion that Smith was capable of composing in Greek with the same degree of fluency as a native speaker. Anyone who wants to argue that Smith was capable of composing the vastly more complex composition of *Letter to Theodore* must explain how Smith was able to go from having only a "bridgehead" on the Greek language in 1951 to a mastery of second-century patristic Greek such as to be able to compose in 1958 a three-page document containing not one

---

45. Smith, letter to Harry A. Wolfson, 18 February 1952.
46. Letter 32 of 7 June 1953 (Stroumsa, *Correspondence*, 64).
47. Smith, "Hebrew—Why Not Greek?"
48. Ibid., 198.
49. Smith, "Ἑλληνικὰ χειρόγραφα ἐν τῇ Μονῇ τοῦ ἁγίου Σάββα" ("Greek Manuscripts in the Monastery of St. Saba").

but two very different authorial styles, one embedded into the other, and in which are featured, not only the vocabulary and verbal associations of Clement of Alexandria, but with correct linguistic and stylistic usage, including his syntax, euphony, and rhythm.

Before doing so, one should consider the words of someone who worked on translating Greek with Smith, Roy Kotansky:

> I am a scholar of magic, and though I did my Ph.D. on magic at Chicago (1988) under Dieter Betz, I asked Morton Smith, a longtime colleague and friend, to be my principal reader, outside of Chicago. My work, on the magical lamellae, has long since been published in a Cologne papyrological series. As a managing editor of Betz's *Greek Magical Papyri in Translation*, years ago, I also read, and critiqued, all of the contributors' translations, including those of Morton Smith. What strikes me most about the issue of forgery with SM, is not that Morton would have done this at all (he wouldn't have, of course), but rather that he COULD NOT have done it: his Greek, though very good, was not that of a true papyrologist (or philologist); his translations of the big sections of PGM XIII did not always appreciate the subtleties and nuances of the text's idioms, I believe, and he seemed very appreciative of my corrections, at that time. He certainly could not have produced either the Greek cursive script of the Mar Saba ms., nor its grammatical text, as we have it. There are few up to this sort of task . . . I was with him once at the Getty Museum examining magical gemstones in the collection in the '80s, and many times I had to gently correct his misreadings of rather obvious readings. Morton was not a paleographer/epigraphist, nor a papyrologist. I don't think that he read these kinds of Greek texts very well.[50]

PALEOGRAPHY

The *Letter to Theodore* was written on the end pages of a seventeenth-century book[51] in a style of Greek handwriting characteristic of the eighteenth century, which leads one to wonder both whether Smith was physically capable of such a feat and whether his knowledge of paleography was sufficient to fool a dozen experts in Greek paleography with whom he consulted on dating the *Letter*. Regarding the former question,

---

50. Roy Kotansky, e-mail to Scott Brown, 17 August 2006.
51. Voss, *Epistulae genuinae S. Ignatii Martyris*.

in April 2010 Venetia Anastasopoulou, a native-Greek questioned document examiner, submitted a thirty-nine-page report for the website of the *Biblical Archaeology Review*.[52] After comparing the writing characteristics of the *Letter to Theodore* against sufficient samples of Smith's Greek handwriting, including his Greek handwriting from the 1950s, she concluded that Smith lacked the ability required to produce the rhythmic and skilful handwriting in the *Letter to Theodore*, for his own proficiency in Greek

Morton Smith in Greece circa 1951–1952. Smith presented a photo album of his trip to his father in April 1953 on the occasion of his father's eighty-second birthday. Photograph provided by The Archives of The Jewish Theological Seminary Library.

was "like that of young school children,"[53] a natural state of affairs for one who learned how to write Greek as an adult rather than as a child. According to Anastasopoulou, the calligraphic handwriting of the *Letter to Theodore*, with its many complex abbreviations and ligatures,

---

52. Anastasopoulou, "Experts Report Handwriting Examination," and published in summary in the magazine as Shanks, "Handwriting Experts Weigh In on 'Secret Mark.'"

53. Anastasopoulou, "Experts Report Handwriting Examination," 37.

looks like an artistic design of good quality. Although it is a difficult style of writing and needs a lot of practice in order to be able to write in this way; the text is written spontaneously with an excellent rhythm. The letters and their combinations are curved fluently while at the same time the grammatical rules are followed. The movement of the writing indicates a hand used to writing in this manner. The letters are written unconsciously.[54]

Her conclusion is that the writing of the *Letter to Theodore* "shows freedom, spontaneity and artistic flair. It also shows a skilful penmanship of a well educated and trained writer who uses the language effectively in expressing his thoughts."[55] Moreover, as Scott G. Brown has observed, Anastasopoulou judged the *Letter to Theodore* to demonstrate the hallmarks of spontaneous writing without any of the characteristics that normally appear in forged documents.[56]

What about Smith's expertise in paleography? In 1973, Smith wrote in his account of his discovery fifteen years earlier: "though I knew a little about paleography, I had no pretence to be an expert on the dating of hands."[57] Archival documents from the 1950s appear to confirm this impression. In 1950, while in his last months at Harvard Divinity School, Smith wrote Scholem: "Now that my examinations are over I must begin work on a thesis, but the subject has not yet been decided, and as it will probably be the edition of some classical text I shall have in any case to begin by learning something about paleography."[58] Smith's personal papers[59] include notes he took in the 1950s on Edward M. Thompson's *An Introduction to Greek and Latin Paleography* that can only be described as rudimentary,[60] such as noting the difference between a *biblos* and a *biblion*. According to Stephen Carlson, Smith's article "Notes on Collections of Manuscripts in Greece" constitutes evidence of his "expertise in

---

54. Ibid., 9.

55. Ibid., 13. A different conclusion has been reached by Agamemnon Tselikas, a well-respected expert in Greek paleography: "Agamemnon Tselikas' Handwriting Analysis Report." For the crucial differences between paleographers and questioned document examiners, see the further discussion in "Craig Evans and the *Secret Gospel of Mark*: Exploring the Grounds for Doubt" elsewhere in this volume.

56. Brown, "My Thoughts on the Reports by Venetia Anastasopoulou."

57. Smith, *Secret Gospel*.

58. Letter 23 of 6 January 1950 (Stroumsa, *Correspondence*, 42).

59. Archived at the library of the Jewish Theological Seminary in New York City.

60. Thompson, *Introduction to Greek and Latin Paleography*.

eighteenth-century handwriting" in 1952.⁶¹ However, according to Smith's own notes and records of the manuscripts he photographed in Greece, which Smith later sent to Werner Jaeger, most of the manuscripts were already dated by the libraries and monasteries in which they were found, and his "dating of MSS in uncatalogued libraries is based on very hasty guesses."⁶² In sum, the little evidence that exists on Smith's expertise on paleography in the 1950s suggests that his knowledge fell far short of the expertise required to forge an eighteenth-century manuscript.

ANCIENT EPISTOLOGRAPHY

There is no evidence that Smith had any expertise in the highly relevant area of ancient epistolography. Though Smith did note in his commentary some of the general conventions of letter-writing that appear in the *Letter to Theodore*, he does not appear to have had any knowledge of specific elements of construction and formulae characteristic of letters in the late second or early third century, and he never made any arguments for the authenticity of the *Letter to Theodore* on that basis. However, Jeff Jay has recently demonstrated that the *Letter to Theodore* coheres in form, content, and function with a genre of literature in antiquity in which authors issued accounts of the composition and transmission of their works in order to combat the confusion that arose when premature, stolen, or conflicting copies of their works reached the public.⁶³ As this coherence cannot have occurred purely by chance, Jay's study suggests that either the *Letter to Theodore* is an authentic letter of Clement's time, or it is a forgery from a more recent time created by an unknown author having a more sophisticated expertise in ancient epistolography than Smith appears to have possessed.

CLEMENT AND MARK

There is very little evidence that Smith possessed any significant knowledge of Clement prior to 1958, and the times he mentions Clement before finding the letter are so rare in number and so superficial in content that

---

61. Carlson, *Gospel Hoax*, 44.

62. Smith's manuscript catalogue, and all quotations from letters from Smith to Jaeger, are from the papers of Werner Jaeger, 1934–1961, Harvard University Archives, call number HUG 4464.5. Courtesy of the Harvard University Archives.

63. Jay, "New Look at the Epistolary Framework of the *Secret Gospel of Mark*."

Ancient Gospel or Modern Forgery?

it takes little more than a minute to list them: Smith's 1955 article "Comments on Taylor's Commentary on Mark" includes Clement's name in a footnote enumerating a list of seven of the ante-Nicene fathers;[64] and Smith's 1958 article "The Image of God" cites Clement four times in footnotes.[65] On p. 482 one finds the following:

> 2 Clem. Alex., Strom. 1.150.1 f. (= 22, end), quotes from Aristobulus a statement that Greek translations of parts of the Old Testament had been made before Alexander's conquest of the Persians (omitting *kai*, with Stählin).

Page 501 contains this sentence and its accompanying footnote:

> Accordingly it is not surprising to find in Philo that the menorah is the symbol of "heaven" and its lights, of the planets; in Clement of Alexandria³ that the lights symbolize the seven planets and the menorah itself is "the sign of Christ."
>
> 3 *Stromata* 5.6.34.9—35.2.

Page 507 contains this footnote:

> 5 Cf. Clement of Alexandria, *Strom.* 1.1.13–14 etc.

And page 511 has this note:

> 5 Cf. Clement of Alex., *Paed*, ii.8.63.4: The Kings of the Jews used an elaborate crown composed of gold and precious stones, but the Christians symbolically wear Christ upon their heads.

As far as the question of ability is concerned, these five references to Clement demonstrate only that Smith was *familiar* with Clement of Alexandria before he discovered the letter, which is something we already knew from Smith's own comments in *The Secret Gospel*.[66] A complete lack of familiarity with Clement is almost inconceivable for someone studying New Testament and early church history under Jaeger, Nock, and Wolfson. Finally, in the preserved collections of letter correspondence that I have seen thus far, Smith privately mentions Clement just a single time prior to his discovery, in a letter to Scholem written in 1948:

> Last February I came back to Harvard to work for the degree of Doctor Theology, for which I am to make a special study of the

---

64. Smith, "Comments on Taylor's Commentary on Mark."
65. Smith, "The Image of God."
66. Smith mentioned his prior familiarity with Clement in *Secret Gospel*, 12.

New Testament and of Church history down to 400 and, for a thesis, probably produced under Jaeger's direction, an edition of one of the minor works of Gregory of Nyssa. For the past six months I have been working on the background—giving half my time to classical literature and half to the early Fathers, especially Clement of Alexandria.[67]

If we take Smith literally, this indicates that he spent only a part of three months reading Clement, and even then only incidentally as background for a study of Gregory of Nyssa. However, if estimates are correct that it takes a minimum of 10,000 hours of intense and steady effort to develop expertise in a skill or subject of knowledge,[68] Smith would have had to have spent at least three hours a day, every day, for the entire ten years from 1948 to 1958 to have become an expert on Clement. Two years later, however, again in a letter to Scholem, Smith acknowledged that he had made very little progress even on his thesis:

> With all this miscellaneous activity I've done nothing on my new thesis—a proposed edition of the funeral orations of Gregory of Nyssa . . . My present schedule calls for an edition of Gregory of Nyssa's two short funeral orations before the end of this year, then the trip to Greece to photograph the manuscripts of St. Isidore of Pelusium, then either the edition of that ancient worthy (all 1600 pages of him) or at least a study of—say—his textual tradition. But I don't see how I can finish the funeral orations before June (especially since I haven't yet been able to read one through without falling asleep), and after reading a couple of hundred pages of St. Isidore my private opinion is that our knowledge of his text is altogether as good as its content deserves.[69]

Overall, these citations certainly do show that Smith was familiar with Clement, as he was familiar with a great number of topics; however, both

---

67. Letter 11 of 17 August 1948 (Stroumsa, *Correspondence*, 27–28). Smith received the ThD from Harvard in 1957. His dissertation topic, which changed from Gregory of Nyssa to Isidore of Pelusium to Judaic History, was "Judaism in Palestine I: To the Maccabean Revolt." It was remodelled later as a series of lectures for The American Council of Learned Societies, and was published as: *Palestinian Parties and Politics that Shaped the Old Testament*, which Smith dedicated to Wolfson.

68. Ericsson et al., eds., *Cambridge Handbook on Expertise and Expert Performance*.

69. Letter 26 of 4 December 1950 (*Correspondence*, 48–49). Although Smith never published on Gregory of Nyssa, he did publish two articles on Isidore. The first is "The Manuscript Tradition of Isidore of Pelusium." This paper grew out of a lecture Smith delivered at Oxford in 1951 during his one-year leave of absence from Brown (1951–1952). The second is "An Unpublished Life of St. Isidore of Pelusium."

his personal and professional writing on Clement before 1958 amount to a few sentences—none of which show evidence of detailed study or of focused interest. One struggles in vain to find any evidence prior to 1958 for the years of dedicated research that would have been required to attain the level of knowledge and expertise needed to forge the *Letter to Theodore*.

When one considers all the topics of potential relevance to the *Letter of Theodore*, it appears that Smith had the most documented expertise with the Gospel of Mark. Smith's 1955 article "Comments on Taylor's Commentary on Mark" was an extensive forty-three-page review of Vincent Taylor's *The Gospel according to St. Mark*;[70] its detailed critique demonstrates Smith's erudition on the contents of the Gospel of Mark. Moreover, supported by a Guggenheim grant, in 1955 Smith began working on a monograph arguing that the first half of Mark was based on a collection of miracle stories modelled on a pagan aretalogy. Set aside in 1956 for Smith to begin a study of the Hellenization of Palestine that became the basis for his 1957 ThD thesis, Smith's monograph on Mark was read and extensively annotated by Krister Stendahl,[71] Nock, and Cadbury,[72] and finally published in 1973 as *The Aretalogy Used by Mark*.[73] However, despite demonstrating an interest in Mark in the 1950s, Smith himself made the point, in response to Quesnell's accusation of forgery,[74] that a comparison of this earlier work on Mark with his later work on the *Letter to Theodore* demonstrated just how much his thinking on Mark had been affected by his discovery.[75]

Though Smith's *The Aretalogy Used by Mark* fails to reveal any hint of the ideas he would later develop as a result of his discovery, the question remains whether Smith would have had the ability to compose the *Secret Mark* fragments contained within the *Letter to Theodore*. Mark's Greek is not nearly as difficult as Clement's. Smith himself thought the passages attributed by Clement to Mark to be "an amateurish imitation of Mk full of phrases

---

70. Taylor, *Gospel according to St. Mark*.

71. Krister Stendahl (1921–2008), Swedish theologian and New Testament scholar, and professor and professor emeritus at Harvard Divinity School.

72. His annotated draft is among his archived papers at Jewish Theological Seminary in New York City.

73. Smith, *Aretalogy Used by Mark*.

74. Quesnell, "Mar Saba Clementine."

75. Smith, "On the Authenticity of the Mar Saba Letter of Clement": "Although my interpretation of the text followed the general lines of my earlier thought, the changes produced were enormous" (ibid., 198). The notion that Smith's pre-discovery views are expressed in the *Letter to Theodore* has been debunked elsewhere, including Allan J. Pantuck, "Solving the *Mysterion* of Morton Smith and the Secret Gospel of Mark."

found in the gospels."[76] At face value, it is harder to rule out the possibility that Smith, with his knowledge of Mark and his ability to read Greek, could have composed these passages. However, there are other aspects of these narratives that Smith likely could not have imitated. For example, Helmut Koester has argued that Smith did not have sufficient understanding of form criticism needed to produce this story.[77] Further, as convincingly shown by Brown, Smith never developed any grasp of Mark's literary techniques necessary to have imitated his style. Indeed, throughout his life Smith refused to believe that Mark was capable of literary sophistication.[78]

WHAT DID HE DO AND WHEN DID HE DO IT?

According to Smith's own account in *Clement of Alexandria* and *The Secret Gospel*, he spent two years following his discovery of the *Letter to Theodore* in the summer of 1958 studying the letter, comparing its style and vocabulary to that of the generally-accepted works of Clement of Alexandria, before announcing his discovery and presenting his findings at the December 1960 meeting of the Society of Biblical Literature. Next, in 1961 his attention shifted to the study of the Marcan "Secret Gospel" fragments quoted by Clement. Finally, from 1962 to the middle of 1963 his focus turned to the background of the letter and its relationship and meaning for early Christianity. Five years of work performed in discrete phases, therefore, culminated in Smith's first draft of *Clement of Alexandria*. What evidence is there that this work indeed was done from 1958 to 1963 and not before the discovery?

In 1955, after five years working in the Department of Biblical Literature at Brown, Smith spent 1955–1956 producing studies of the manuscripts of Isidore of Pelusium, supported by a Guggenheim fellowship. In 1956, Smith took a position as Visiting Professor of the History of Religions at the Drew Graduate School, teaching a lecture course and a seminar on the history of Palestine, while also completing his ThD thesis. Smith was then appointed as Assistant Professor at Columbia College in 1957, teaching in his first year the following courses: Humanities A, Religion 21, a general survey of ancient history (History 5–6) covering the history of the Mediterranean Basin and Mesopotamia to the expansion of Islam, and two reading courses, one on the sixth century BCE (History 55), and the other on Near Eastern elements in the Roman Empire (History 56).

76. Smith, "Authenticity," 197.
77. Koester, "Was Morton Smith a Great Thespian and I a Complete Fool?"
78. Brown, *Mark's Other Gospel*, 179, 254–55 n. 185.

Ancient Gospel or Modern Forgery?

As these were all classes he had never taught before, his preparation for classes and grading of papers took up most of his time. On December 9, 1957, Smith wrote to Scholem:

> This is an apology for having done nothing on your book since I saw you last, and having every expectation of doing nothing for the next twelve months to come. The fact is that my courses and preparation for courses to come are taking every bit of my time. I have some 95 students in my general course on ancient history, and this has meant a great deal of paper work. That course and another, on classical literature, which I am teaching, I had never given before; the subjects covered lie somewhat outside my former field; and consequently I have had to work constantly on preparation for them. I'm standing the strain all right, but by summer I shall be dead tired, so I am planning to spend the whole of the summer in the Near East.[79]

Smith discovered the *Letter to Theodore* in July 1958—that summer between his first and second years at Columbia when he visited Jordan, Israel, Turkey, and Greece. Arriving in Jerusalem, Smith received permission from the Greek Patriarch to spend two weeks at the monastery of Mar Saba to study and publish a catalogue of its Greek manuscripts and its early printed books containing manuscript material. In the Morton Smith archives at the Jewish Theological Seminary (JTS), one can find the remains of Smith's original handwritten notes, and the negatives and photographs he had taken of the 489 books he catalogued during his stay at Mar Saba, including ninety-six that were manuscripts or books containing significant manuscript additions in a variety of languages. Descriptions of seventy-six of these were later published by Smith in *New Zion*, the periodical of the Patriarchate.[80]

When Smith returned to Columbia in the fall of 1958, he realized that in order to authenticate the *Letter*, he would need to share its contents with other scholars from whom he would need help. In order to prevent the premature disclosure of its contents, Smith prepared a pamphlet titled "Manuscript Material from the Monastery of Mar Saba: Discovered, Transcribed, and Translated by Morton Smith." This handwritten pamphlet, copies of which reside in the Smith archives at JTS, was submitted to the U.S. Copyright Office on December 22, 1958.[81] This document reveals that, a few

---

79. Letter 55 of 9 December 1957 (Stroumsa, *Correspondence*, 105–6).

80. Smith, "Ἑλληνικὰ χειρόγραφα."

81. Library of Congress, Copyright Office, personal communication with the author, 12 February 2007.

months after he visited the monastery in 1958, Smith was unclear about many aspects of the letter's translation and interpretation (see Figure 1). In a number of places, Smith crossed out his own translations and inserted alternatives, and his footnotes include proposed deletions, alternative translations, and notices that some of his insertions are "interpretive and perhaps unjustified" (see Figure 1). For example, though Smith imagined Mark's expanded gospel as a "secret" writing and interpreted the letter as indicating that in Alexandria "it even yet is most carefully guarded" (II.1), his initial translation shows uncertainty about whether guarding is really indicated: "it even yet is kept most carefully <guarded>." This uncertainty disappears in his published studies, which neither place the word "guarded" in parentheses (which is how he distinguished explanatory additions in *The Secret Gospel*) nor question this word's appropriateness; so the brackets in his initial transcription are the only indication that he ever thought that the verb in question (τηρεῖται) might simply mean "kept." If Smith himself authored the *Letter to Theodore* with an intended meaning that suited a particular agenda, why would he do so using language that he initially supposed might not convey that meaning?

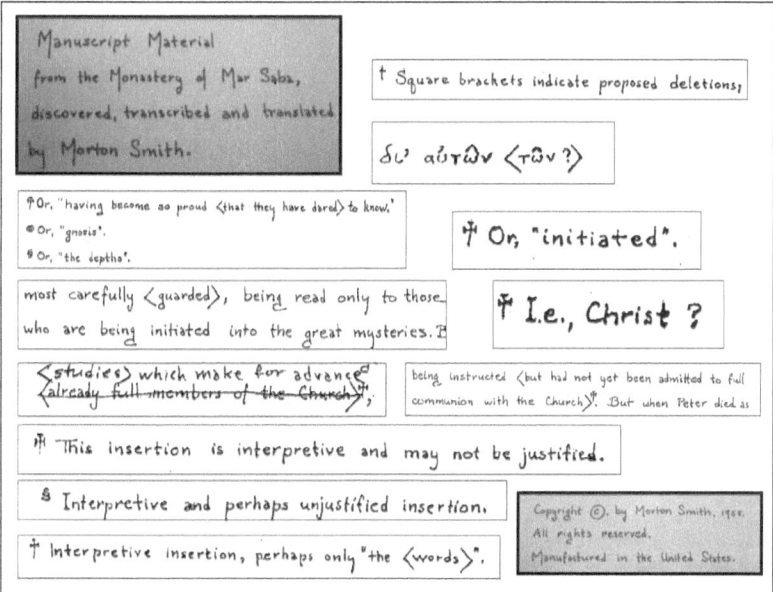

Figure 9.2: "Manuscript Material from the Monastery of Mar Saba: Discovered, Transcribed, and Translated by Morton Smith," submitted for copyright December 1958, containing Smith's original translation of the *Letter to Theodore*. Original document provided by The Archives of The Jewish Theological Seminary Library.

Ancient Gospel or Modern Forgery?

The *Letter to Theodore* was discovered written in the end pages of a book Smith had numbered as 65, an edition of Isaac Voss's *Epistolae genuinae S. Ignatii martyris* published in Amsterdam. Voss's book on Ignatius was first published in 1646, but a second edition was published in 1680 in London. The copy Smith found at Mar Saba was missing its cover and title page; so, in order to date the edition containing the manuscript he had discovered, Smith photographed the first and last pages of the book to compare with complete extant editions, a process he relates in *The Secret Gospel*. The photographs Smith took of pages 2 and 365 of the Voss book still reside in Smith's papers at the JTS archives. Had Smith forged the manuscript, he certainly would have needed to know the book's year of publication before forging the letter into the book. However, evidence shows that it was five months after his return from Mar Saba to Columbia that Smith confirmed the date of the Voss edition by comparing it to the 1646 edition of the book in the rare book collection of the Union Theological Seminary in New York City. The 1646 Voss edition had been acquired by UTS in 1848 as part of a larger purchase of a private book collection (the so-called Van Ess purchase). Notably, when Smith examined the Voss edition on February 26, 1959, it was the first time the book had ever been accessed at UTS from the time it had been acquired one hundred and eleven years earlier.[82] It strains one's credulity to propose that Smith expected the library to keep a record of his examination of the book, which could be used one day to check his story, particularly since the book's signature card is kept separate from the book itself. So Smith's examination of the Voss edition at UTS is best explained as evidence of a meticulous scholar tracking down every detail of his discovery. Moreover, it makes incomprehensible the suggestion of Quesnell, Carlson, and Tselikas that Smith, rather than having discovered the *Letter to Theodore* at Mar Saba, had merely smuggled into the monastery a copy of Voss that he had bought in advance and into which he had forged the letter, intentionally removing the cover and title page to hide any evidence of where Smith had bought it or to use the front pages as "practice sheets."[83] The fact that Smith went to UTS to examine the Voss edition in 1959 suggests that, in fact, he did not know the date of the edition he discovered in 1958.

---

82. Union Theological Seminary, personal communication with the author, 8 March 2006.

83. For example, see the posts by Stephen C. Carlson and Steven Goranson to the Yahoo Group Textual Criticism, archived on The Secret Gospel of Mark Homepage. Online: http://www-user.uni-Bremen.de/~wie/Secret/discussion-hoax.html.

Allan J. Pantuck, MD—*A Question of Ability*

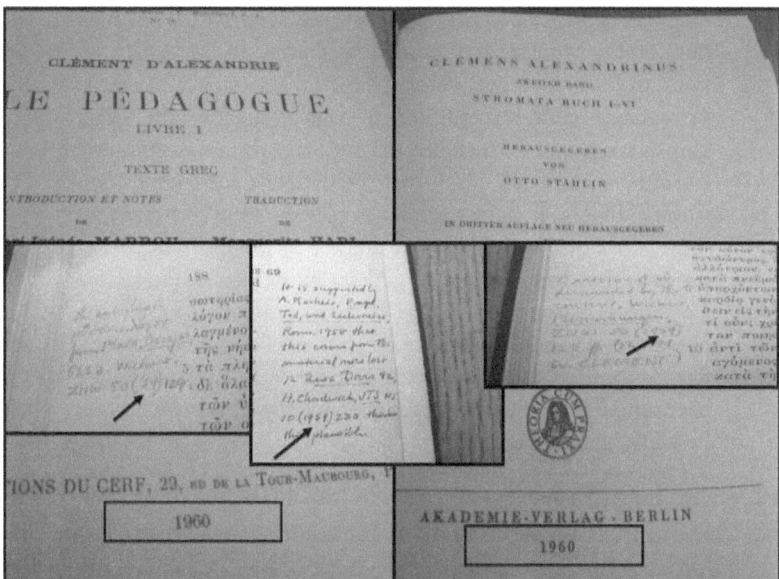

Figure 9.3: Smith's personal copies of critical texts of Clement's writings published in 1960 with marginal notations to scholarship published in 1959.

Evidence supports that Smith spent the next two years laboriously comparing the style, vocabulary, and ideas of the letter point-by-point with Clement of Alexandria's undisputed writings. Had Smith forged the letter, he would have needed to have all his resource material available before 1958. Instead, a number of Smith's personal copies of critical texts of Clement's writings, including *Clement d'Alexandrie, Le Pédagogue*, by Henri Irénée Marrou and Marguerite Harl, and the second volume of Stählin's critical edition,[84] were not published until 1960 and contain marginal notations to related scholarship that had been published only in 1959 (see Figure 2). In the years between Smith's discovery and the announcement of his discovery at the Society of Biblical Literature in December 1960, Smith corresponded with no fewer than nineteen other scholars requesting help on aspects of the letter.[85] For example, in 1960 Smith sent a letter to Werner Jaeger requesting his opinion regarding its source:

---

84. Donated by Smith in his will, and now part of the Bickerman Collection at the Jewish Theological Seminary. The JTS call numbers are BR65.C6 P314 1960 and BR65.C54 1960, respectively.

85. William Calder III is the only scholar in this group who is still alive. Calder, who confirms that Smith was working on Clement in 1959–1960, continues to believe the letter to be Clementine (personal correspondence with the author, 2006).

Ancient Gospel or Modern Forgery?

> The text is an XVIII c. (?) MS appendix to a XVII c. printed book in the Monastery of Mar Saba. The rest of the book contains, so far as I can see, nothing which throws any light on the provenance of the MS addition. The quotations from the 'secret gospel,' not given in the following text, are so close in style and wording to canonical Mark that the date of their composition is quite uncertain, but a number of reasons seem to prove that they were not composed by the author of the letter; whatever his date, they were somewhat earlier. His date, therefore, is the essential question . . . I would be most grateful, also, for any comments you might care to make on points of style or content, and this particularly if you would give me permission to include or summarize them, with appropriate acknowledgements, in the first edition of the text.[86]

Moreover, in April 1960, Smith wrote to Judah Goldin telling him that he was "deep in work on St. Clement of Alexandria. Perhaps I told you that I've found what purports to be part of a letter of his. This takes editing and editing takes all sorts of time."[87] Evidently this generated further discussion between the two scholars, and in December 1960, Smith again wrote Goldin:

> Thank you for your material on secret teachings. As you can imagine, I'm keeping a file, and yours will be a prize entry. I think your observations are completely justified, though I'm not really sure about the significance to be attached to sequence of material in the Midrashim.[88]

In the University Archives of Columbia University, one finds not only the typed and hand-corrected text of the talk Smith delivered on the *Letter to Theodore* at the SBL in December 1960, but also a typed report Smith prepared in January 1961 that summarizes his findings for the scholars he had been relying upon for help. Of note, one learns that the only aspect of the letter that Smith discussed that night was his analysis of the vocabulary and style of the letter in relation to Clement's known writings. Though

---

86. Smith, letter to Werner Jaeger, 1 August 1960.

87. Letter from Smith to Goldin, April 17, 1960. Judah Goldin (1914–1998), Professor Emeritus of Postbiblical Literature at the University of Pennsylvania, was an outstanding Jewish scholar and pioneer of the teaching of Jewish Studies in American Universities. I thank David Goldin, Judah Goldin's son, for permission to examine these documents, and Professor Jeffrey Tigay for making them available to me for study.

88. Letter from Smith to Goldin, December 12, 1960.

Allan J. Pantuck, MD—*A Question of Ability*

Parker Pierson had been invited to offer comments on the *Secret Mark* fragments, Smith himself had not yet begun to study them. However, in 1961 Smith appears to have turned his attention to the study of the excerpts from a longer Gospel of Mark that Clement cited in the letter, and made extensive notes on Marcan vocabulary and usage (which can be found at JTS), including notes as to whether or not certain words from canonical Mark could be found in the "SG" [i.e., Secret Gospel].

The period from 1961 to 1963 finds Smith developing and evolving his interpretation of the meaning of the letter. Just prior to his SBL announcement, Smith wrote again to Jaeger:

> I thank you most sincerely for your invaluable commentary on the letter of Clement. In particular, what you say in conclusion, on the importance of the mystery religions for early Christianity, goes far beyond my own thought on the subject, yet I can see now that it follows from the contents of this letter.[89]

In June 13, 1961, Smith wrote to Scholem:

> Though I haven't been able to work on the letter, I've been thinking a good deal about it, and about the possibility that Jesus may actually have taught a libertine gospel—Libertinism is so widespread in the New Testament, almost every book combats it, it cannot all derive from Paul, there are a lot of libertine sayings in Jesus' mouth (The Law and the Prophets were until John, since then!).[90]

And then in October 25, 1962, again to Scholem:

> I have been sick much of the summer (persistent bronchitis) and the edition of Clement on the Carpocratians creeps along by inches, but quite wonderful things keep turning up. I am really beginning to think Carpocrates and the sort of things he represented (and especially the ascent through the heavens) were far closer to Jesus than has ever been supposed . . . I wish you were here so that I could discuss it with you.[91]

In June, 1962, Smith wrote Erwin Goodenough, telling him that he had decided to take a sabbatical from 1963 to 1964 to study the relationship between magic and early Judaism, Christianity, and Gnosticism.[92]

89. Smith, letter to Werner Jaeger, 4 November 1960.
90. Letter 72 of 13 June 1961 (Stroumsa, *Correspondence*, 127–28).
91. Letter 77 of 25 October 1962 (Stroumsa, *Correspondence*, 132–33).
92. Smith, letter to Erwin Goodenough, 16 June 1962, from Manuscripts and

Ancient Gospel or Modern Forgery?

In the archived papers at JTS, one finds Smith's "Notes on the Gospel Doctrine of the Holiness of Sin," written on the back of a History final examination from 1963, in which Smith appears to be exploring some of the concepts on libertinism he had mentioned the previous year to Scholem. Finally, there is a series of fascinating letters between Smith and Cyril Richardson, professor of church history and director of graduate studies at Union Theological Seminary, dating from 1960 to 1963.[93] Following Smith's public announcement of the *Letter to Theodore* at the SBL, Richardson initiated a close study of it with Smith. For more than three years, Smith and Richardson met regularly to discuss the problems and issues of *Secret Mark*, and in 1963 they discussed for several months how to explain the linguistic and geographical similarities between *Secret Mark* and the Gospel of John. From their letters it becomes clear that Smith did not actually come to propose his theory of a common source lying behind Mark and John as the best way to explain the similarities until June 1963 (Richardson himself did not find this explanation persuasive), nearly five years after his discovery.

Stanley Isser, Professor Emeritus of Judaic and Religious Studies, University of Albany, SUNY, worked on his PhD in ancient history at Columbia University under Smith and Elias Bickerman, and was Smith's research assistant from 1962 to 1964, helping him to prepare the first draft of *Clement of Alexandria*. Isser recounts:

> What Smith introduced me to was a meticulous method for determining authenticity. He took every word and phrase in both the letter and the gospel text and compared them with the manner and frequency of such words and phrases that were used in Clementine literature and in canonical Mark in order to see if they fit the style in those texts. My main job was to go through concordances and critical editions of the literature in question and to recheck his references through every variant reading of the texts. This is work that would now be done with computers. Smith had done it manually. I think this aspect of the book is what took most of his time between his discovery and publication, and I checked through it again.[94]

Archives, Yale University Library.

93. The Burke Library Archives at Union Theological Seminary in the City of New York, C. C. Richardson Papers Series 1, box 5, f9: Correspondence CCR/Morton Smith.

94. Stanley Isser, e-mail to author, 6 May 2010.

Smith completed his first draft of *Clement of Alexandria* in July 1963 and left for Europe to begin his sabbatical. That summer, Smith visited with Helmut Koester, who was visiting professor at the University of Heidelberg in Germany; they spent many days discussing his manuscript.[95] Even then, Smith was still struggling to understand aspects of the letter, including whether or not the *mysterion* mentioned in the letter could refer to baptism.[96] Koester's review of Smith's book reflects the thought that Koester continued to give to that question.[97]

CONCLUSION

A survey of Smith's papers and correspondence, archived in numerous libraries and universities around the world, indicates that Smith lacked most of the exceptional abilities needed to forge the letter. Specifically, this evidence suggests that his Greek had not advanced to the point that he could compose a new work of Clement, that he had not acquired the necessary expertise in Clement's thought and style, and that he lacked the paleographical knowledge and the writing skill needed to produce the Greek script of the manuscript. Further, this archival data corroborates his account that, during the five years between 1958 and the completion of the first draft of *Clement of Alexandria* in June 1963, Smith was in fact acquiring the proficiency in Clement and understanding of the letter that is displayed in that book. Smith's groundwork research came after he discovered the letter, not before.

---

95. Helmut Koester, letter to Scott G. Brown, 14 November 2006. Also described in Koester's "Great Thespian," 58.

96. On the importance of the concept of *mysterion* for the *Letter to Theodore*, see Pantuck, "*Mysterion*."

97. Koester, Review of *Secret Gospel* and *Clement of Alexandria*.

10

Clement's Mysteries and Morton Smith's Magic
Peter Jeffery

IF OUR TWO EXCERPTS from the *Secret Gospel of Mark* had been discovered on papyrus fragments in an antiquities shop, it would be difficult to learn much about the date, provenance, or authorship of this text, since the papyri would be shorn of all historical context—even the location of their discovery might be unknown. As a result, many scholars would confine themselves to noting the text's most obvious feature: that it tells a Lazarus-like story in vocabulary resembling that of the Synoptic gospels.

But in fact the *Secret Mark* excerpts come to us as quotations in an incomplete epistle ascribed to Clement of Alexandria, "the Stromatist," addressed to an unknown Theodore. This means the epistle (whether by Clement or not) is our most important source of evidence regarding the origins and history of *Secret Mark*, since it is the only thing that could potentially link the two gospel fragments to a historical time and place—especially so, in this particular case, since the epistle purports to describe the origin of the gospel, and the uses to which it was being put in the author's own milieu and by another group. Much of the confusion that pervades the secret gospel discussion, therefore, comes from focusing too exclusively on the gospel and too little on the epistle—from trying, that is, to read what we have of *Secret Mark* without reference to its frame, as if it actually had been discovered on papyrus fragments in a dealer's shop. Once *Secret Mark* has been extracted from its only known context (the epistle), there is little historical data left to constrain any hypothesis about it: any number of plausible interpretations can be spun too easily, with little risk of ever being proved or disproved, since hardly any established facts need to be taken into account. Hence much of the research published so far on *Secret Mark* would have been expended more profitably on its framing epistle.[1]

There are good examples of such myopia in some of the reviews of my book.[2] When I argued that the epistle describes *Secret Mark* being used in a resurrection-themed initiation rite (my "fourth stream of tradition"), these reviewers thought I was saying that the ancient author of *Secret Mark* (i.e., in what would be my "second stream of tradition") intended to describe a baptismal service.[3] But anyone who thought I said that was unconsciously assuming that all statements about the Mar Saba text are really about *Secret Mark*, since that is the part of the text most observers are really interested in. But reading the gospel excerpts without reference to their epistolary frame can yield only untestable hypotheses.

Meanwhile, the frame itself, the epistle ascribed to Clement, comes to us with very little contextual evidence of its own. Since the physical artifact is or was a handwritten entry on the rear flyleaves of a seventeenth-century printed book, the date and provenance are also open to a wide range of possibilities, the more so as the leaves in question were lost following the book's removal from the ancient Palestinian monastery at Mar Saba. If they were rediscovered, chemical analysis of the ink (which would likely require partial destruction of the paper) would not necessarily prove conclusive, since the kind of iron-gallotannate ink that was in use as late as the 1940s is easy to make.[4] The dearth of external evidence is all the more regrettable since there is so little consensus on what the internal evidence shows. Despite declarations to the contrary, experts are not in agreement

---

1. Jay, "New Look at the Epistolary Framework of the *Secret Gospel of Mark*," is a start, but it should be pointed out that, contra Jay (596–97), Morton Smith actually did possess the hardly "superhuman" characteristics that "those who argue the letter is a twentieth century forgery must now allow"—particularly "a solid knowledge of epistolography" through his work on Isidore of Pelusium, and a "tremendous insight into the psychology and art of deception" evident throughout his publications.

2. Jeffery, *Secret Gospel of Mark Unveiled*.

3. For example, the review of Foster in *Expository Times*.

4. Hundreds of low-tech recipes were circulated and published over the centuries, many of which are now available on internet sites such as http://irongallink.org/ and https://pacer.ischool.utexas.edu/bitstream/2081/3235/2/2006ANAGPIC_Brewer.pdf. For a brief history and bibliography, see Brunelle and Crawford, *Advances in the Forensic Analysis and Dating of Writing Ink*, 3–8.

that this is an authentic epistle of the Clement of Alexandria who wrote the *Stromateis* (*Strom.*) and died in the early third century.⁵ Nor does it make sense if read as what it most closely resembles: a pseudo-Clementine text written in the Nicene era, around 400 CE.⁶

But there is a way forward if we recognize that the epistle too has a historical frame: the writings of the man who announced the text's discovery and published the first interpretation of it. When the epistle is read as a forgery by Morton Smith, the text comes alive, as it were. Vivid characters emerge, acting out a high-stakes drama that is also an uproarious comedy, and that delivers an unmistakable, truculent message, whether or not we agree with it. Every detail of the text and all of its dramatis personae can be shown to be making a specific contribution to the overall message, which is not the case for any of the proposed interpretations that assume ancient authorship, each of which leaves some features unexplained.

Yet most advocates of an ancient origin strongly resist reading the epistle as one of Smith's writings. There are understandable reasons for this reluctance. Reading widely enough in Smith's oeuvre to understand his idiosyncratic thought requires a daunting amount of time and effort. His publications are exhausting to work through: relentless barrages of irrelevant, distorted, and misinterpreted data, specious links between unrelated sources. Those who try the hardest to understand him are consistently appalled: "it is remarkable to notice how free Morton Smith is with both his translations and his evidence . . ."; "loose translations by Smith skew data that should be presented with great precision." He "lumps together too much disparate material, in too many different categories, and too many widely separated sources, without due concern for dating and historical reliability."⁷ "His misinterpretation of the primary sources is so gross as to be virtually fraudulent."⁸ "The circularity of what passes for argument and the prejudices that shape the reconstruction of the figure of Jesus will be apparent to any careful reader."⁹ And Smith's actual thesis, once exhumed from all the distortion and distraction, is palpably preposterous: that Jesus

---

5. The Greek text has been added to the critical edition of Clement's works, but only "provisionally . . . to further discussion." See Stählin, ed., *Clemens Alexandrinus*. It is listed among Clement's doubtful and spurious works in Geerard, *Clavis Patrum Graecorum* 1: *Patres Antenicaeni*, 140 no. 1397. See also Osborn, "Clement of Alexandria," especially 223–25.

6. See chapter 4 of Jeffery, *Secret Gospel of Mark Unveiled*, especially 77–90.

7. Meier, *A Marginal Jew*, vol. 2, 573–74 nn. 71–72.

8. Casey, *Jesus of Nazareth*, 278; see also 542–43.

9. Kee, *Miracle in the Early Christian World*, 212 n. 69.

initiated his disciples, one by one, through magical nocturnal rites that promised ecstatic experiences of heavenly ascent, but turned out to be homosexual encounters. No wonder so many people would rather leave Smith's publications aside and look for an ancient origin instead! But to do that is to reason like the drunk in the old Vaudeville skit, who, having lost his wallet in a dark alley, insists on searching for it under the lamppost because the light is better there.[10]

Indeed, ruling out Smith's authorship *a priori*, so as to be spared the ordeal of sifting through his writings, actually sets up a circular argument from which there is no escape. To set Smith's own work aside is to set aside most of the evidence that Smith wrote the Mar Saba epistle, creating the illusion that there is no such evidence. And to consider only evidence that is consistent with an ancient date is to guarantee that an ancient date will be the only possible conclusion. Those who ask, therefore, how Smith could have authored the document if he himself did not understand it, are merely asking us to accept that only interpretations supporting an ancient date may be considered, ignoring the possibility that Smith's interpretation is the correct one and the Greek text itself is preposterous. Therefore, those who would argue that I have discredited only Smith's interpretation, and not the document itself,[11] have a substantial burden of proof to meet, for they need to do a much better job than anyone has actually done of demonstrating that the epistle and gospel can in fact be read as ancient texts, without reference to Smith, when my interpretation is the only one that explains every feature of and personage mentioned in the text.

The most extensive such attempt to date has been that of Scott G. Brown, who believes that "Jeffery has confused Morton Smith's misinterpretation of the letter with the letter itself."[12] But Brown's reading of "the letter itself" is actually a demonstration that, by translating the text more vaguely, one can camouflage some of the obstacles to an ancient dating, and thus buy chronological leeway at the price of sacrificing comprehensibility. The reliability of this approach is illustrated by the fact that Brown can push it all the way to the extreme conclusion that the secret gospel is by the evangelist Mark himself, rather than an unknown follower, reader, contemporary, or predecessor of Mark.

---

10. Kolodner, "From Natural Language Understanding," 68; Mamet, *Theatre*, 24.
11. For example Rousse-Lacordaire, "Bulletin d'Histoire des Ésotérismes."
12. Brown, review of *Secret Gospel of Mark Unveiled*, by Peter Jeffery, 14.

Ancient Gospel or Modern Forgery?

Thus, according to Brown, the epistle does not speak of a secret gospel, but of a mystic gospel, whatever difference that makes (121–24).[13] Clement's stern warning that Theodore was not to "concede that the secret Gospel is by Mark, but should even deny it on oath" means much less: "there is no secrecy here, only a half-truth intended to undermine the legitimacy of one particular libertine sect" (139). We are not to think of the gospel itself as "most carefully guarded," as Smith translated, but only "very securely or safely kept" (135–37). There is a difference, according to Brown, and it amounts to the conclusion that we cannot know how it was kept: we should not consider "a church archive" or "physical guarding," or "even whether the text resided in a locked room or even if it was kept in just one place," such as "an ordinary library in a house" (135)—even though the epistle is emphatic that the gospel belonged to "the church of Alexandria" and not to an individual. "Clement's description of how Carpocrates used magic in order to procure a copy," seems far out of proportion to what was actually at stake. It "does imply that this text was carefully regulated," Brown concedes, "but a carefully regulated text is not necessarily one whose existence is kept secret" (137). And the biggest non-secret of all is that the mystic gospel actually does not say much. Its apparent borrowings from the canonical gospels are nothing more than "verbal echoes" (198–214). Though Clement's epistle calls it a "more spiritual gospel," Brown assures us that "the truths conveyed . . . are still available to readers of the canonical gospel . . . featured in 'plain' language in the central section of the Markan gospel" (216). The apparently ferocious conflict between Clement's church and the heretics was all much ado about very little, then, since the mystic gospel was "'safely kept' . . . in the sense that it was not made available to people of unproven character, . . . this text was reserved for mature individuals who were not likely to misinterpret it" (137). Yet the added layer of obscurity that distinguishes the mystic gospel from the canonical one somehow serves to "deepen a reader's appreciation of this gospel's christology and discipleship theology" (216). One is left with the impression that the only way to save this text as an early Christian writing is to destroy it. The harsh language of unspeakable teachings, carnal sins, opposition "in all ways and altogether," falsifications, foul demons, deceitful arts, magical enslavement, utterly shameless lies, and so on, softens into a suburban sit-com in which somebody advises someone else to fudge the truth a bit, so that those pesky neighbors will lack authorization to read a book with a hard-to-translate name that is being safely

---

13. The page references in the following are to Brown, *Mark's Other Gospel*.

kept nowhere in particular, and which basically says nothing anyway that cannot already be found in a widely-available earlier edition (i.e., canonical Mark). That could be the looking-glass version of what my own book says: shoehorn this gospel into the first century, and it disappears.[14]

A genuine attempt to read "the letter itself" without prejudgment would have to deal with its most notable feature, pointed out decades ago by Werner Jaeger: "Most striking is the consistent use throughout the letter of terminology derived from the mysteries; this is found in Clement's other works as well, but is more concentrated in this letter than elsewhere."[15] This ritual terminology originally denoted various aspects of the secretive ceremonies by which new devotees were initiated into the ancient Hellenistic mystery religions. But the same terminology was also adapted by ancient philosophers of Jewish, Christian, Platonist, and Gnostic persuasions (including Clement of Alexandria) where it was applied to such things as initiation into the study of philosophy, the interpretation of Old Testament rituals, and the ritual practices of Gnosticism and early Christianity. Morton Smith had his own interpretation of mystery terminology, shaped by his idiosyncratic theories about the nature of ancient magic, which must be considered by anyone bent on excluding him as a possible author. Therefore the central question in making sense of the Mar Saba epistle is: what kind of initiation or ritual is it describing? Is it utilizing mystery cult vocabulary in the same way(s) that Clement did? Or are we reading yet another of Smith's attempts to reconstruct the rituals of ancient magic? Unfortunately, the field of New Testament studies has not developed precise tools for dealing with ancient ritual language; a de facto culture of "don't ask, don't tell" has developed over the years to avoid facing the fact that no modern Christian denomination worships as the early church did, though all of them claim to do so. Inexperience dealing with the ritual aspects of texts is another reason why, almost forty years after its publication, so many still do not understand what the Mar Saba epistle is saying.

CLEMENT'S MYSTERIES

Traditionally it has been assumed, following Eusebius (*Hist. eccl.* 5.10–11; 6.3.2, 6; 6.14.8–11), that Clement was the head of an official, diocesan

---

14. Jeffery, *Secret Gospel of Mark Unveiled*, 60, 90.

15. Private communication quoted in Smith, *Clement of Alexandria and a Secret Gospel of Mark*, 38.

catechetical school in Alexandria, the successor of Pantaenus and predecessor of Origen. As such, Clement would have had the chief responsibility for all Alexandrians going through the multiple stages of Christian initiation. We have detailed descriptions of such rites in majestic series of catechetical (pre-baptismal) and mystagogical (post-baptismal) sermons by some of the great church fathers of the fourth and fifth centuries: Ambrose, Augustine, Cyril of Jerusalem, Chrysostom, and Theodore of Mopsuestia.[16] But for Clement's own pre-Nicene period the evidence is thinner, more ambiguous, and more diverse, as illustrated in Table 1.

Table 1. The process of becoming a Christian, in five early sources

Hebrews 6.1-5	Revelation 5, 7, 15, 19	Justin Martyr, 1 Apology 61, 66-67	Valentinian Exposition (Nag Hammadi XI,2)	Gospel of Philip (Nag Hammadi II,3) 67,29-30
Elementary doctrines about: repentance, faith, ablutions, laying on of hands, resurrection, judgment	The Lamb reads from the scroll.	Instruction, fasting, repentance	Exposition of Valentinian theology (22,1-39, end)	"The Master [did] everything in a mystery:
	144,000 are sealed (=anointed?)		anointing prayer (40,1-29)	
Enlightenment (after which restoring to repentance is no longer possible)	An innumerable crowd washes their white robes in the blood of the Lamb, then sings the Song of Moses by a glass sea.	Water immersion = illumination	first baptism =forgiveness of sins (40,30—41,38)	Baptism,
			gift of the spirit (42,1—43,19)	Chrism,

16. Yarnold, *Awe-Inspiring Rites of Initiation*, 1-54; Harmless, *Augustine and the Catechumenate*; Satterlee, *Ambrose of Milan's Method of Mystagogical Preaching*; Doval, *Cyril of Jerusalem, Mystagogue*.

		The new Christian joins the assembly; prayers and kisses		
	The wedding feast of the Lamb	Eucharist: Justin's is the earliest detailed description.	eucharistic thanksgiving prayer (43,20–38)	Eucharist,
Tasting the heavenly gift			prayer for receiving food and drink (44,1–37)	
Becoming partakers/ sharers in the Holy Spirit				Redemption,
Tasting the goodness of the word of God and the powers of the age to come				Bridal Chamber."

Justin Martyr, who was writing an apologetic for non-Christians, gives the most concrete description of what his community did. Revelation, being highly symbolic, is the most distant from actual ritual. The author of Hebrews, reminding his readers of the process they themselves had gone through, is the hardest for us to interpret, since his fellow Christians knew, as we do not, exactly what he meant by words like "enlightenment/illumination," "tasting," and "partaking."[17] The texts for anointing, baptism, the gift of the spirit and the eucharist that are appended to the so-called *Valentinian Exposition* (a modern title) have been described as "liturgical readings" but might actually be the texts of prayers to be used in these rituals.[18] The *Gospel of Philip* mentions an organized system of five "mysteries" or sacraments, but with limited detail about what each one

---

17. Recent commentators tend to think the author was not referring specifically to the eucharist, but to Christian community life more broadly. Discussions include: Attridge, *Epistle to the Hebrews*, 166–72; Craig R. Koester, *Hebrews*, 127–29, 302–3, 305–6, 310–11; Witherington, *Letters and Homilies for Jewish Christians*, 203–18.

18. Thomassen and Meyer, "Valentinian Exposition with Valentinian Liturgical Readings."

involved. Thus what some readers of my book did not understand is that, in any discussion of either the Mar Saba epistle or of Clement himself, what is at issue would be the entire process of Christian initiation, not baptism alone in isolation from the other stages.

Clement's own writings never outline the entire sequence in one place, but he mentions many details that can be rearranged in the correct order. In Clement's Alexandrian community, the period of catechesis or pre-baptismal instruction seems to have lasted three or four years (*Strom.* II.18.96.2). It was followed by a three-day baptismal celebration (*Strom.* V.11.73.2), which was not paschal in character but drew its imagery from Jesus's own baptism by John, as can be seen extensively in Clement's *Prophetic Eclogues* (*Ecl.*). This emphasis on the Jordan event, rather than the Resurrection event, is also characteristic of all the other Alexandrian groups we know about.[19] At some point this three-day baptismal celebration became fixed so that it began on Epiphany (i.e., the equivalent of January 6 in the Egyptian calendar),[20] which at least one Alexandrian group was already celebrating in Clement's lifetime as the anniversary of Jesus' baptism.[21] There it has remained in the Coptic and Ethiopian Orthodox Churches ever since.[22]

---

19. *Strom.* I.21.146.2 says the followers of Basilides commemorate the baptism of Jesus every January with a nocturnal vigil of readings that resembles the early Christian baptismal vigil on Epiphany. *Exc.* 77–80 and *Strom.* IV.13.89.2–5 quote Valentinian texts that associate baptism with an abstract, astrological victory of life over death, but the idea is escape from the physical world, not burial and resurrection of the body as in Rom 6:3–11. In any case the *Exc.* section is bracketed by passages (76, 85) invoking Jesus' own baptism as the example to be followed, showing that this was the more pronounced emphasis (trans. in Finn, *Early Christian Baptism*, 185–88). The readings or prayers found in the *Valentinian Exposition* also look to the baptism of Jesus by John as the model (40,30—43,19). *Strom.* II.9.44.1–4 quotes from the *Shepherd of Hermas* (a Roman text) on baptism as a kind of passing through death; however, the passage is about the apostles, after their own biological deaths, preaching to the dead from Old Testament times. No early baptismal rite was built upon this theme. Origen's sermons on Exodus were written after he relocated to Caesarea (texts in Finn, *Early Christian Baptism*, 101–223). The Jordan/Epiphany interpretation remained the dominant one in Egypt even in post-Nicene times, see Day, *Baptismal Liturgy of Jerusalem*, 6–7, 90–92, 137.

20. For a Sahidic Epiphany sermon based on Matthew's account of Jesus' baptism, tentatively dated to the seventh century, see Pearson and Vivian, *Two Coptic Homilies*, 153–55 (on authorship), 157–74 (translation).

21. *Strom.* I.21.146.1. Some of the issues, but not all of the evidence, are discussed in Foerster, "Celebration of the Baptism of Christ."

22. Jeffery, *Secret Gospel of Mark Unveiled*, 78, and the footnotes thereto 282.

Table 2. Four trajectories through the Christian life according to Clement

	type of teaching/knowledge *Paed*. I.1.3.3; *Strom*. IV.7.53.1; VI.8.65.1–5; VII.10.57.1–5	type of person *Strom*. VII.10.57.4	experience of Christ *Paed*. III.12.87.1–4, 97.1–101.3	food/drink metaphor *Strom*. V.8.48.9, 10.66.2–5
Protr., apologetic	persuasion (προτρέπω)	Greeks, Hebrews, Egyptians, ἔθνοι	ἱεροφαντέω (verb only, *Protr*.12.120.1; 12.123.2)	
Paed.	κατήχησις (*Strom*. VI.1.1.3)	children (*Paed*. I.5.12.1–6.52.3), like a maturing seed (*Strom* II.18.96.1–2) κατηχούμενοι and "newly instructed" νεοκατήχητος (*Paed*. I.6.36.3; *Strom* VI.15.130.1)	παιδαγωγός (*Paed*. I.1.1.4–2.1; 1.7.53.1–61.3)	milk
Baptism	φωτισμός (*Protr*.10.94.2; *Paed*. I.6.25.3—31.2) λουτρόν (*Protr*.10.94.2) σφραγίς (*Quis div*. 42.4)	τέλειος: perfect, mature, complete (*Paed*. I.5.18.4, 20.1; 6.25.3—31.2) *Ec. Proph*. 57.4		
eucharist				wine, meat
ordinary believer	πίστις (*Paed*. I.6.30.2)	common faithful (*Strom*. IV.16.101.1; VI.7.60.2; VII.7.49.3), doing μέση πρᾶξις (*Strom*. VI.14.111.3)	διδάσκαλος (*Strom*. VI.15.122.1–4), "merely taste the scriptures" (*Strom* VII.16.95.4)	

Ancient Gospel or Modern Forgery?

	type of teaching/knowledge *Paed.* I.1.3.3; *Strom.* IV.7.53.1; VI.8.65.1-5; VII.10.57.1-5	type of person *Strom.* VII.10.57.4	experience of Christ *Paed.* III.12.87.1-4, 97.1—101.3	food/drink metaphor *Strom.* V.8.48.9, 10.66.2-5
advanced gnostic Christian—*Strom.*	γνῶσις, τελείων μάθησις (*Strom.* V.9.60.2) φωτισμός / μαθητεία (*Strom.* V.10.64.4) ἀπόρρητα (*Strom.* I.1.13.2, 14.3, 2.21.2), true philosophy (*Strom.* I.5.32.4), lesser mysteries (=secular sciences) in preparation for greater mysteries (*Strom* I.28.176.1-2; IV.1.1.1—3.4 [ἱεροφαντία at IV.1.3.1]; V.11.70.7—71.3)	gnostic perfected by: φιλοσοφία (*Strom.* I.5,28.3) εὐστοίια (*Strom.* IV.6.29.2) ἀγάπη (*Strom.* IV.7.53.1) γνῶσις (*Strom.* IV.17.109.3; VII.10.55.2, 11.67.8), πίστις (*Strom.*VII.14.85.1-5), Christ (*Strom.* IV.26.163.2; VI.16.141.4; VII.3.13.2) gnostics not really perfect (*Strom.* IV.21.130.1; IV.21.132.1)	literacy necessary (*Strom.* I.6.35.1) scriptures the "voice of the Lord/Logos" (*Paed.* I.8.71.1; *Strom.* IV.21.134.4; V.6.40.1; VI.15,122.1-4; VII.16.95.4) unwritten traditions from Christ, handed down through apostles (*Strom.* VI.7.59.1—63.1)	
ultimate experience of God, attainable after death	ἀγάπη (*Strom.* IV.6.29.3), ἐποπτεία, θεωρία (*Strom.* I.1.15.1-3; VI.14.108.1)	finished with κάθαρσις and λειτουργία (*Strom.* VII.9,56.4, 57.2) ἐσχάτη τελείωσις =death (*Strom.* V.1.7.7-8)	seventh-day Sabbath rest, face to face with the Lord (*Paed.* I.6.37.1; *Strom.* VI.12.102.2; VII.9,57.5); resting in Christ (*Strom* I.6.32.4)	ἐποπτικὴ θεωρία

Peter Jeffery—Clement's Mysteries and Morton Smith's Magic

As Table 2 shows, at least four trajectories of progress through the Christian life can be traced in Clement's writings, depending on whether the focus is on the types of teaching (second column), developmental stages in the growth of Christian maturity (third column), the Christian's advancing knowledge of Christ (fourth column), or metaphors related to food and drink (fifth column). Reading down through each vertical column, the stages naturally cluster around Clement's three most important writings (first column), which correspond to three levels of instruction. The apologetic *Protrepticus* (*Protr.*) or *Exhortation to the Greeks* seeks to convince adherents of the mystery religions that Christianity is superior. Thus the technical ritual language of the mystery cults, which focused on secretive initiations into esoteric knowledge, is used literally in its original sense, but also applied to Christian worship for the sake of comparison. The *Paedagogue* (*Paed.*) is addressed to new converts who actually are being initiated into Christianity; mystery-cult vocabulary is less common here, while the emergence of a specifically Christian terminology can clearly be seen. The converts are described as children—a classic term (with New Testament roots) for baptismal candidates (*Paed.* I.5.12.1—6.52.3; *Strom.* VI.1.1.3).[23] Early in the book these "little ones" are "being recently instructed" [νεωστὶ κατηχουμένους] and "newly instructed" νεοκατηχήτους (*Paed.* I.6.36.3; cf. *Strom* VI.15.130.1), suggesting they are at an early stage in the catechetical process. In fact Clement appears to be the earliest Christian author to use the word "catechesis" in its technical sense of preparing converts for baptism,[24] though there are references in the NT to people being catechized or orally instructed (Luke 1:4; Acts 18:25; Gal 6:6). But the final chapter of *Paed.* (III.12.87.1-4, 97.1—101.3) informs these "children" that they are close to the end of the process, where they will experience a change: they will be enrolled as adults (*Strom.* VI.1.1.3), enter the school of the church, and experience a transition from knowing Christ as a *Paidagōgos* (the guide of young people) to knowing him as *Didaskalos* (teacher). Thus we should look to *Paed.* as our best source of information as to the content of Clement's catechesis. This is not to say that Clement wrote *Paed.* for catechumens to read; more plausibly it is a

---

23. Ignatius, *Trall.* 5.1. Ysebaert, *Greek Baptismal Terminology*, 150–52. Carlo Nardi found the childlike state to be a major theme in *Paed.* in *Il battesimo in Clemente Alessandrino*, 143–76. The catechumens also practiced fasting, prayer, and alms (ibid., 121–42). See also Schneider, *Theologie als christliche Philosophie*, 268–70.

24. See "κατήχησις," 2.a in Lampe, *Patristic Greek Lexicon*, 733. Van den Hoek, "'Catechetical' School of Early Christian Alexandria and its Philonic Heritage," especially 69.

literary rewrite of the kind of material Clement used in teaching the catechumens orally, comparable to some of the treatises of Ambrose of Milan that originated as "composite works based on his catechetical homilies."[25]

The *Stromateis*, Clement's longest extant work, is aimed at an elite group of already-baptized Christians who are pursuing further study within the school of the church, where Christ is no longer Paedagogue but Teacher: "The all-loving Word, anxious to perfect/initiate [τελειῶσαι] us in a way that leads progressively to salvation, makes effective use of an economy well-adapted to our development: at first, he persuades [προτρέπων], then he educates [παιδαγωγῶν], and after all this he teaches [ἐκδιδάσκων]" (*Paed*. I.1.3.3).[26] These more advanced Christians sought to acquire knowledge or *gnōsis* under Clement's tutelage. They began by studying a Platonic philosophical curriculum, which prepared them to move on to allegorical exegesis, the deeper interpretations of the scriptural texts that were handed down orally from the apostles. The Clement we know from *Strom*., therefore, is not a catechist, but the philosopher-teacher of an elite group who considered themselves "knowers" or gnostics.[27] Mystery-cult vocabulary is more common in *Strom*. than in *Paed*. but it is used in more sophisticated ways than in *Protr*., with philosophical applications derived from Plato, eschatological implications derived from the Septuagint, and typological applications derived from Philo.[28]

In general, Clement's gnostics do not seem to have been members of the clergy, though they apparently did have a teaching role (*Strom*. VII.1.3.1–6). But we should not imagine their meetings as similar to modern Bible study groups, since, like Philo's quasi-monastic Therapeutae,[29] they followed a structured daily cycle that included a number of ritual

---

25. J. Warren Smith, *Christian Grace and Pagan Virtue*, 11.

26. Unless otherwise noted, excerpts of *Paed*. are taken, with some translation modifications, from Clement of Alexandria, *Christ the Educator*, trans. Simon P. Wood. In some places Clement appears to be saying that he has written or intends to write a treatise called *Didaskalos* that would represent his post-baptismal teaching and serve as the sequel to *Protr*. and *Paed*. But no work with that title survives. The recent discussion of this problem, and whether the *Didaskalos* should be identified with *Strom*. is traced in Andrew C. Itter, *Esoteric Teaching in the Stromateis of Clement of Alexandria*, 15–32.

27. For clarity, I capitalize "Gnostic" when it refers to the adherents of religions Clement opposed, such as the Valentinians, but I do not capitalize it when it refers to members of Clement's own elite group.

28. See my paper, "'The Mystical Chorus of the Truth Itself,'" Feulner, *Clemens von Alexandrien*, 200–204.

29. Jeffery, "Philo's Impact on Christian Psalmody."

elements, and which was understood as mirroring the eternal praise of the heavenly host. At the same time, they did not refrain from participation in the worship of the wider church, with Christians who were not elite students of Clement's advanced teaching (*Strom.* VII.7.49.3-4). One thing that separated Clement's gnostics from ordinary or "common believers" (*Strom.* IV.16.101.1; VI.7.60.2) was literacy (*Strom.* I.6.35.2). That implies that the gnostics were drawn from the wealthier, more privileged strata of society, which would be consistent with their concerns about the interpretation of Gospel sayings that seem to deny salvation to the wealthy. Hence the only text we have from Clement that appears to be a sermon is entitled "Who is the rich man that is saved?" (*Quis div.*).[30] But I have found no indication that Clement's gnostic circle had its own initiation rituals, or that anyone exercised a juridical role of deeming applicants worthy or unworthy of admission. We do find such things with the emergence of Christian monasticism in the fourth century, but Clement's group was not monastic in a post-Nicene sense. The final sections of *Paed.* seem to invite all the newly baptized without distinction to pursue gnosis under Christ the Teacher.

Among the reasons that the Mar Saba epistle cannot have been written by the author of *Strom.* is that it is inconsistent with Clement's four trajectories and three kinds of teaching. According to the epistle, "during Peter's stay in Rome [Mark]wrote an account of the Lord's doings, not, however, declaring all of them, nor yet hinting at the secret ones [μυστικὰς], but selecting what he thought most useful for increasing the faith of those who were being instructed [τῶν κατηχουμένων]" (I.15-18). Since κατηχουμένος and related words were technical terms for Clement of Alexandria, "those who were being instructed" would have to be the catechumens who were being prepared for baptism. However, Clement's catechesis, as revealed in *Paed.*, does not focus on the interpretation of Mark's gospel or any other book; it is organized around issues of ethical behavior. Hence the last two chapters of *Paed.* (III.11.53.1—12.101.3) sum up Clement's ethical teaching with many quotations from the Gospels, the Epistles, and the Old Testament. But there are no direct quotations that could come only from Mark's gospel, though a few contain wording that Mark shares with the other Synoptics.[31] In this respect Clement's approach

---

30. See also Pearson, "Coptic Homily *On Riches.*"

31. Clement quoted Matthew most often (Jeffery, *Secret Gospel of Mark Unveiled*, 83, 284 nn. 52–53), a fact that is now confirmed by the statistics in Cosaert, *Text of the Gospels in Clement of Alexandria*, 57–218.

Ancient Gospel or Modern Forgery?

to catechesis was consistent with that of Ambrose,[32] while later in the fourth century catechesis moved toward summaries of salvation history that coalesced in the emergent text of the Creed.[33] The Mar Saba epistle's assertion that catechesis was based on the reading of a specific book (canonical Mark) has no parallel in known early Christian writings, and goes against the general trend.

After Peter's death, the epistle says, "Mark came over to Alexandria, bringing both his own notes and those of Peter, from which he transferred to his former book the things suitable to whatever makes for progress toward knowledge [γνῶσιν]. Thus he composed a more spiritual [πνευματικώτερον] Gospel for the use of those who were being perfected [τῶν τελειουμένων]" (I.18–22).[34] If the epistle were by Clement, "those who were being perfected" (or "initiated" or "completed") would have to be those who, having reached the end (τέλος) of the catechumenate, were receiving the initiatory sacraments of baptism and eucharist, knowing how to "partake of such food in a more spiritual manner (πνευματικώτερον)" (Strom. V.10.66.2–5).[35] All the baptized are perfect, not in the sense that they are sinless, but in the sense that they are mature or complete, because they have gone from being spiritual children to being "enrolled among men," and thus prepared "for the reception of gnostic knowledge [ἐπιστήμης γνωστικῆς]" (Strom. VI.1.1.3). If the Mar Saba epistle were a work of Clement, then the parallelism between "being instructed" and "being perfected" would refer to the distinction between the catechumens and the baptized, for there was no later point in Clement's system at which perfection was conferred. The implication (as described in my book) is that the story of Jesus raising the young man was read at a service like the paschal vigils described in fourth- and fifth-century mystagogical sermons. But that is hardly likely, since resurrection thematics were not prominent in Clement's baptismal thought. In fact Clement's main statement on the conferral of perfection at baptism (Paed. I.6.25.1—26.3) is

---

32. Jeffery, *Secret Gospel of Mark Unveiled*, 279 n. 1; see also J. Warren Smith, *Christian Grace*, and Marcia L. Colish, *Ambrose's Patriarchs*.

33. Drijvers, *Cyril of Jerusalem*, 53–58; Augustine, *De catechizandis rudibus* and *Sermo de Symbolo ad Catechumenos* in Augustine, *De fide rerum invisibilium*, 115–99.

34. Clement's extant writings do not say that Peter died a martyr or that Mark came to Alexandria. See the fragments of the *Hypotyposeis* and the *Adumbrationes* on 1 Peter in *Clemens Alexandrinus*, Bd. 3, *Stromateis VII–VIII*, 197–98, 206.

35. See also the even more explicit parallel at V.8.48.9. Unless otherwise noted, excerpts of *Strom.* are taken, with some translation modifications, from William Wilson in ANF 2.

unmistakably based on Jesus' own baptism by John in the Jordan—exactly what we would expect of a pre-Nicene Alexandrian author.

Clement certainly believed that there were oral traditions preserving things the apostles had taught but not written down—teachings the apostles had received from Jesus. He did not, however, write as if there were specific traditions that could be traced back to individual personages of the apostolic age, because he believed that "the tradition of all the apostles, like the teaching, has been one and the same" (*Strom.* VII.17.108.1).[36] It was the heretics who traced their traditions back to Peter or Paul or Matthias (*Strom.* VII.17.106–108), while Clement had learned from his own teachers "the true tradition of the blessed doctrine in direct line from Peter, James, John, and Paul" (*Strom.* I.1.11.3).[37] Thus Clement of Mar Saba seems to "know" more about Mark, and have a more Gnostic view of apostolic tradition than Clement of Alexandria. Moreover, the apostles were merely following Jesus' own example when they reserved some of his teachings to those who were capable of receiving them. When Clement's disciples received these teachings (*Strom.* I.1.13.1–5), therefore, they were actually being "taught by God's son" (*Strom.* I.12.55.1–4; cf. I.1.13.1–5), an understanding that is completely absent from the Mar Saba epistle. According to Clement, the unspeakable ἀπόρρητα, "like God himself, are entrusted to the Logos, not to writing" (*Strom.* I.1.13.2).[38]

The reason the deeper truths are veiled is that they are unwritten (*Strom.* V.9.57.3—10.64.3). Plato, after all, taught that the safest course was not writing but memorization, for it is impossible to prevent a written text from being published (*Strom.* I.1.14.4; V.10.65.3). It is hard to see how Clement of Alexandria could have written this if his own practice involved keeping certain texts reserved for selected readers or hearers only. Clement did not envision two distinct libraries of texts, for catechumens and believers, or for common believers and gnostics—but two sets of readers who share the same texts, while having different levels of understanding. A person of modest literacy could copy a manuscript written in *scriptura continua*, i.e. with no spaces separating the words,[39] but making sense of the text required a higher level of skill—namely, the ability to group letters into syllables and syllables into words. In the same way, the majority

---

36. Translation here from Oulton and Chadwick, *Alexandrian Christianity*, 163.

37. Translation here from Clement of Alexandria, *Stromateis Books One to Three*, trans. John Ferguson, 30.

38. Translation here from ibid., 31, see also I.1.4.1.

39. Saenger, *Space between Words*; Hurtado, *Earliest Christian Artifacts*, 177–85, 233–41; Jeffery, "Monastic Reading and the Emerging Roman Chant Repertory," 61.

of Christians were only capable of understanding the literal, written text of the scriptures, while the advanced, gnostic readers knew how to get at the true but hidden meaning, the allegories beyond the literal text (*Strom.* VI.15.131.2–3) transmitted by the disciples of the apostles. Since the gnostics were already baptized, their training was not catechesis, but "the learning of the perfect [τελείων μάθησις]" (*Strom.* V.10.60.2).

The Mar Saba epistle, however, does not know of the distinction between ordinary believers and gnostics. Having already been told that the "more spiritual Gospel" was written "for the use of those who were being perfected" (I.21–22), that is, being baptized, we are surprised to read a few lines later that Mark "left his composition to the church in Alexandria, where it even yet is most carefully guarded, being read only to those who are being initiated [μυουμένους] into the great mysteries [μεγάλα μυστήρια]" (I.28–II.2). The word μυέω (μυουμένους), related to μυστήριον, is rarely used by Clement of Alexandria, who applied it not to sacramental baptism but to the post-baptismal acquisition of gnosis (*Strom.* VI.15.129.4). The gnostic's death is also an initiation into the blessed vision of God (*Strom.* VI.12.102.2). In the passage that is verbally closest to our epistle (and apparently served as the Mar Saba author's model), Clement promises to teach his students "to pursue the real gnostic natural science, having been initiated into the lesser mysteries before the greater" (*Strom.* IV.1.3.1). Here, Clement was unambiguously using philosophical jargon to outline the curriculum for his advanced, already-baptized gnostics. One had to study the natural sciences and other secular disciplines (the lesser mysteries) to lay the groundwork for advancing to the study of exegesis and theology (the greater mysteries).[40] There is no initiation ceremony prior to entering upon such a course of study, except baptism, paralleling the Hellenistic cult initiations in which there were purifications before handing over the mysteries (*Strom.* VII.4.27.6). Rather, the philosophical study *is* the initiation into the lifelong post-baptismal pursuit of gnosis.

The epistle's identification of "those who were being perfected" (baptized) (I.22) with "those who are being initiated" (gnostics) (II.2), therefore, makes it clear that the epistle is not by Clement of Alexandria, but by someone else, who stacked up all the ritual terms he could find in Clement's writings (with little understanding of how Clement used them) in order to create the impression of a mysterious initiation rite. Scott Brown

40. *Paed.* I.1.1.1—2.1; III.1.1.1—2.3; *Strom.* I.1.15.1—16.3 (but see *Strom.* I.28.176.1–3); IV.1.3.1–4; V.11.70.7—71.1 See also van den Hoek, *Clement of Alexandria and His Use of Philo in the Stromateis*, 42, 60, 171, 188; Rizzerio, *Clemente di Alessandria*, 181–215.

is right to point out that Clement speaks of the greater and lesser mysteries only in connection with philosophical study, not in connection with baptism. But he is quite wrong to conclude from that that the Mar Saba epistle "says nothing about liturgy"—an unsustainable assertion since the text mentions catechumens and group reading of scriptures.[41] Being unfamiliar with early Christian catechetical and mystagogical texts, and relying on outdated articles that say mystery-cult vocabulary was not applied to the Christian sacraments before the fourth century, Brown has concluded that the epistle describes "a purely metaphorical initiation" limited to advanced biblical instruction.[42] While it is true that Clement did not use the more developed mystagogical language of Chrysostom or the Pseudo-Dionysius, he had no reason to avoid applying mystery-cult terminology to the Christian sacraments, which were encounters with the risen Lord just as scripture reading was. Thus the highest initiatory sacrament (which was not baptism but the eucharist) could, like the highest level of philosophical study, be described as ἐποπτεία—the mystical vision achieved at the climax of the Great Mysteries of Eleusis.[43] Nor did Clement of Alexandria use the word "perfected" in an exclusive sense to mean only the gnostics, apart from the ordinary believers, as Brown's interpretation would require.

Clement did, of course, recognize that gnostics were not entirely perfect (*Strom.* IV.21.130.1, 132.1), but grew in perfection as they approached the "final perfecting" or completion of death (*Strom.* V.1.7.7–8). Clement could describe gnostics as being perfected by something else, such as philosophy, beneficence, love, gnosis, faith, or Christ himself (see the third column of Table 2). But perfection belonged to all the baptized. To ascribe perfection to the gnostics alone would have compromised Clement's polemic against the Valentinians, whose two-level community distinguished the merely baptized "psychics" or "spirituals" from the perfect Gnostics. "When we were reborn [i.e., in baptism], we straightway received the perfection for which we strive," Clement wrote. "For catechesis leads to faith;

---

41. Brown, Review of *The Secret Gospel of Mark Unveiled*, 14. When should an activity be considered liturgy? For humanistic/historical definitions see Schilderman, "Liturgical Studies from a Ritual Studies Perspective." For theological definitions see Chupungco, *What, Then, Is Liturgy?*; or, more briefly, Chupungco, "Definition of Liturgy."

42. Brown, Review of *The Secret Gospel of Mark Unveiled*, 14, cf. 6–10.

43. *Strom.* V.10.66.2–5; I.28.176.1–2. The reference to sacrifice in *Strom.* V.10.66.4–5 shows that Clement is indeed speaking of the eucharist, rather than, say, "feeding on the word."

but faith is trained by the Holy Spirit together with baptism. Indeed, faith is the one universal salvation of humanity, and the equality and participation in the just and loving God are the same for all. . . . Consequently, there are not some who are gnostics, and others who are psychics in the same Logos; but all those who have laid aside the fleshly desires are equal and spiritual before the Lord" (*Paed.* I.6.30.2, 31.2).[44] That is why τέλειος and related words have a very important place in Clement's large glossary of baptismal terms.[45] His gnostics were ideal Christians, but not a separate and higher class of Christians. By identifying baptismal perfection with initiation into the highest philosophical mysteries, as if both were achieved in a single ceremony, the author of the epistle once again seems closer to Gnosticism than to Clement's form of Christianity. That is reason enough to take a closer look at the writings of Morton Smith, in which ritual terminology from all sources is indiscriminately mashed together to construct imaginary initiation rites, and the Carpocratian Gnostics are the ones who maintain the real tradition of Jesus.

MORTON SMITH'S MAGIC

If any single theme runs through the bulk of Morton Smith's publications, it is "magic." Yet he never published a systematic exposition of how he understood the term, which seems notably unconnected to scholarly discussions of the subject that were going on in Smith's time.[46] Smith rarely mentioned such bibliography except to deride it,[47] in stark contrast to his youthful enthusiasm for Aleister Crowley.[48] A full and fair description of

---

44. Translation modified from Procter, *Christian Controversy in Alexandria*, 102; see the larger discussion 96–106; Ashwin-Siejkowski, *Clement of Alexandria*, 123–25.

45. See Ysebaert, *Greek Baptismal Terminology*, 173–76, 395–97.

46. For an introductory bibliography see Jeffery, *Secret Gospel of Mark Unveiled*, 299 n. 20.

47. For example, Smith dismissed Mircea Eliade's book on shamanism for "its total and deliberate neglect of the importance of sham" in "Historical Method in the Study of Religion," 15. He would go on to reject the entire contemporary field of magic research as "colonialist sociology" in "O'Keefe's *Social Theory of Magic*," 301.

48. In a letter to Gershom Scholem (letter 3 of 26 November 1945 in Stroumsa, ed., *Morton Smith and Gershom Scholem, Correspondence 1945–1982*, 10–11), Smith described his interest in Crowley's writings, particularly the little-known play *Mortadello*. Smith's praise of the play's literary quality is difficult to endorse, since its tortuous meter and forced rhymes make for laborious reading. But its central character is a religious hypocrite who, like Oscar Wilde's Salomé, seizes power with an exotic, veiled oriental dance that seduces the duke of Venice (her fiancé!) into drinking poison

Smith's theory of magic would exceed the space allotted to me here, since it would have to include much about Smith's reading, the courses he taught on ancient magic, and his brief and turbulent career as an Episcopal priest, when by his own lights he was working as a professional magician.[49] Here I will mention only the aspects of Smith's thought that bear directly on the problem of the Mar Saba document.

The Meaning of "Mystery"

For Morton Smith, μυστήριον and similar words always designated an initiation ritual. This is basic to his discussion of "the mystery of the kingdom of God" in Mark 4:11.[50] The mystery that is "given" to the apostles but not to others in that passage is usually understood as God's eschatological revelation, the secret of who Jesus really is.[51] But Smith argued that, since the mystery the apostles received that separated them from "those outside" must be a ritual, the mystery of the kingdom of God must be baptism—even though Mark's gospel never mentions the baptism of the apostles. Smith knew that most scholars would disagree with this, not least his own teacher Arthur Darby Nock.[52] But Smith discredited the mainstream view, as he frequently did, by accusing his opponents of blindly following "dogmas" or "orthodoxies," be they religious or scholarly:

> All the above argument on μυστήριον has run counter to the common dogma that μυστήριον in the NT always has the sense of רז or סוד and that these always mean "secret," never "secret rite"; [six authors cited]. But this dogma is false. [Citations from the magical papryi are discussed.] . . . Further, the notion that when Paul does use μυστήριον to mean "secret" he cannot at the

---

49. My forthcoming article, "Morton Smith's Theory of Magic," will present much unpublished and newly-discovered archival material illustrating the development and shape of Smith's ideas on the subject.

50. Smith, *Clement of Alexandria*, 178–81.

51. Marcus, *Mystery of the Kingdom of God*, 45–47; Marcus in fact finds that "the phrase 'mystery of the kingdom of God' fits better into the Markan setting than into the Secret Gospel setting" (86–87 n. 41). See also France, *Gospel of Mark*, 196–99; and Henderson, *Christology and Discipleship in the Gospel of Mark*, 101–26.

52. "Mysterion in Paul's letters and in Mark 4.11 has no relation to its familiar use to denote either pagan initiatory ceremonials (and their symbols or concomitants) or other experiences metaphorically so described. What lies behind it is the meaning, 'secret' (whether natural or supernatural), found in the Greek version of the Old Testament," Nock, "Mysterion," 201.

same time use it to mean "secret process" or "rite," is also false. This has been shown by the examples above . . . [53]

Misrepresented Sources

Smith's "examples above" illustrate his inveterate habit of plucking words and phrases out of context, misinterpreting what they say, and then misapplying them to an inappropriate argument. For example, in 1 Cor 2:6–7 Smith says, "it is utterly implausible to neglect the parallelism and to separate the initiated (τελείοις) from the initiation (μυστηρίῳ) . . . to the ancients, baptism was an initiation—a τελετή as Lucian said (*Peregrinus* 11)."[54] If this last statement were true, it would be the earliest use of τελετή in reference to a Christian sacrament. But what Lucian actually wrote was that Christians "worship the man who was crucified in Palestine for introducing a new cult [τελετήν] into the world."[55] There is no reference to baptism as such, and we would not expect Lucian to have an accurate knowledge of Christian ritual terminology. Misrepresentations of this sort can be found in almost every paragraph of Smith's writings.

> . . . Since the "mystery" of I Cor. 2.7 is baptism, it is not unlikely that in I Cor. 4.1–6, where Paul speaks of himself, Kephas, and Apollos as οἰκονόμους μυστηρίων θεοῦ, he refers to their function not only in general, as agents of the grand secret strategy of God, but also in particular, as administrators of the mystery rites of baptism and eucharist, and thus of the salvation effected by these rites. The same sense can be borne by the interpretation of this passage in Eph. 3.9 and of this in Ignatius, *Trall.* 2.3, where the contrast between the "mysteries" and "food and drink" is that of I Cor. 11 between the eucharist and ordinary eating and drinking.[56]

Another misstatement: Ignatius was not making a distinction between eucharistic and ordinary food, but exhorting deacons to observe high moral standards—not because the foods are holy, but because the community is holy.[57] Willful mendacity is so ubiquitous in Smith's writings that the

---

53. Smith, *Clement of Alexandria*, 180.
54. Ibid., 179.
55. Lucian, *Selected Dialogues*, trans. Desmond Costa, 77.
56. Smith, *Clement of Alexandria*, 179.
57. "Furthermore, it is necessary that those who are deacons of the mysteries of Jesus Christ please everyone in every respect. For they are not merely deacons of food

only responsible way to read them is to walk around the library and actually check every source he cites, line by line and page by page. For those few who have actually made the effort, it is quite impossible to emerge with serene assurance that, for once, Smith should be trusted on his most startling claim of all—the claim to have discovered an ancient epistle by Clement.

"Scattered Indications"

With one misproof piled on top of another, we end up under an avalanche of falsehoods, distortions, and non-evidence. Thus, in the next paragraph we skip from a questionable translation of rabbinic literature, to a doubtful identification between similar-looking Hebrew and Greek words, to the very unlikely assertion that a Jewish mystical tract and an Egyptian text in the Greek Magical Papyri are describing the same ritual, to the supposition that Paul would have used Hebrew words with full awareness of all these alleged semantic relationships.

> Finally, the notion that רז and סוד always refer to secrets and never to secret rites is also false. סוד in particular is not infrequently taken in rabbinic literature as a reference to the rite of circumcision; for example, *Tanhuma, Hayyé Sarah* 4, where Prov. 31.24 ... is glossed (by punning on סוד) with the words ... "this is the circumcision, of which it is said, 'The mystery (סוד) of the Lord is given to those who fear him'"—Ps. 25.14.[58] A contributory element in the exegesis may have been the fact that סדין was the initiation garment, the σινδών; see above).[59] More important is the fact that both סוד and רז appear in *Hekalot Rabbati* (27.1; 28.3; 29.1,2,4; etc.) as the magical technique by which one is enabled to ascend through the heavens and be seated in the throne of God. ... Further I have shown (*Observations* end) that the account of the ascent in the *Hekalot* and that

and drink but ministers of God's church" (Ignatius, *Trall.* 2.3, trans. Holmes, *Apostolic Fathers*, 217).

58. The psalm verse is translated, "The counsel of the Lord is with them that fear Him" in Berman, *Midrash Tanhuma-Yelammedenu*,158.

59. There is no mention of סדין in Fabry, "סוד." No connection is made between the two words in Clines, *Dictionary of Classical Hebrew*, 4:121, 125–27, or Levy, *Wörterbuch über die Talmudim und Midraschim*, 4:479–80, 486–87. Smith actually adduced no evidence at all that a flat linen sheet was ever used as a ceremonial initiation garment, only an intimidating landslide of "scattered indications" distorted to create that impression. See Jeffery, *Secret Gospel of Mark Unveiled*, 111–18.

in the so-called "Mithras Liturgy" (*PGM* IV.475ff) go back to a common source of tradition, if not of writing. The "Mithras Liturgy" describes itself as μυστήρια (476), and means by this "initiation," for it prescribes that one may have a συνμύστης (line 732). The first reference to practice of a technique for ascent to the heavens may be that in Col. 2.18: "the angels whom he saw when going in." Into the heavens? (Cf. *Observations* 156). And ascent to the heavens and session with Christ on the right hand of God are described by Paul in the same context as the potential climax of the consequences of Christian baptism (Col. 3.1ff). So the supposition that רז and/or סוד could have been used by Paul to refer to the rite of baptism as a "mystery" is not unsupported.[60]

By this time, another element has entered the picture. Building on his perennial claim that the "Mithras Liturgy" talks about initiating a συνμύστης or fellow initiate, whom Smith generally takes to be a young male disciple,[61] Smith teases us with double entendres. What is meant by "going in"? In the article mentioned ("*Observations* 156"), Smith speculated about "celestial bodies" and even "the body of God"—while emphasizing that "Paul, like other writers of his time, borrows indiscriminately from the different intellectual traditions of the world around him"—before finally settling where we might have expected: "going in. To what? Presumably, to the palaces of heaven."[62] Indeed.

Of course it is actually Smith who "borrows indiscriminately from the different intellectual traditions of the world around him," a procedure he also described as arguing from "scattered indications."[63] It is in fact his usual mode of argumentation.

Double Meanings

The hint of sexual double meaning at "going in" (and perhaps also "climax") is *de rigueur* in Smith's exegeses. His discussion of "mystery of the kingdom of God" has barely started when it moves almost immediately to Eph 5:32, in which human marriage is a mystery (i.e., a type) representing the Church as bride of Christ (cf. Matt 25:1–13, Rev 19:7–9; 21:2, 9, 17). But Smith says, "The word μυστήριον in Eph. 5.32 probably refers to

---

60. Smith, *Clement of Alexandria*, 180–81.

61. A few of many examples cited in Jeffery, *Secret Gospel of Mark Unveiled*, 103–5. On the interpretation of this term, see Betz, *The "Mithras Liturgy,"* 57, 198–204.

62. Smith, "Observations on Hekhalot Rabbati," 156–57.

63. Jeffery, *Secret Gospel of Mark Unveiled*, 91–116.

the spiritual union effected by baptism ... and thence the rite itself which makes the Church the body of Christ by making Christ's spirit live in the members. To this mystery the writer compares the spiritual union effected by physical intercourse in marriage, and he finds a reference to both of these mysteries in Gen. 2.24."[64] From there it is a quick move to another favorite Smith topic: disrobing.

> Anticipating arguments to be presented later, it may be said that a further reason for understanding the "mystery" in I Cor. 2.7 to be baptism lies in the fact that the "wisdom of God" revealed in it involves the secret of Christ's descent in disguise and his assumption of the body from the cosmic powers, for the purpose of subjugating them: [1 Cor 2:7-8 quoted in Greek]; cf. *Ascension of Isaiah* 10-11. This secret of descent in disguise underlies the Pauline interpretation of baptism in Col. 2.15, where the second half of the process, the stripping off in the ascent, is referred to. . . .[65]

The chapters mentioned from the *Ascension of Isaiah* actually do show Jesus descending in disguise, but the intellectual environment of this text would hardly justify using it to elucidate Paul's thought,[66] and the link from there to disrobing is pure Smith. "Note again, as in the longer text of Mk., the connection of baptism with ἀγάπη," writes Smith, reminding us that "love" is what this is really all about.[67]

Often in Smith's use of quotations and allusions, the sexual aspect is only hinted at; its presence can therefore be denied and attributed to the reader's own prurience. But that is an essential feature of Smith's brand of humor. He was always implying or asserting that unsophisticated people would mistakenly perceive a sexual reference in one text or another, while he himself knew better—even though it was Smith himself who kept coming up with these highly inventive misinterpretations. This element of faux deniability can be seen, for example, in every published mention of his most infamous joke, "Holy man arrested ... naked youth escapes" as a newspaper headline for Jesus' arrest at Gethsemane in Mark 14:46-52.[68] But there are countless other examples. The Corinthians misconstrued

---

64. Smith, *Clement of Alexandria*, 178-79.
65. Ibid., 179.
66. See the discussion in Norelli, *Ascensio Isaiae*, 53-66.
67. Smith, *Clement of Alexandria*, 179.
68. Smith, "Clement of Alexandria and Secret Mark," 458 n. 19; Brown, "Question of Motive," 360; Brown, "Factualizing the Folklore," 321-22.

Ancient Gospel or Modern Forgery?

a Marcan statement that Smith must have known is really about kosher food: "The teaching that sexual acts are morally indifferent could easily have been derived from Jesus' reported saying, 'There is nothing outside a human being which, by entering, can make the recipient impure.'"[69] Another example: "The question, 'What was Jesus doing alone, late at night, with a young man wearing only a sheet?' is apt to elicit a snigger from the modern reader, but the answer implied by the snigger cannot be the one the evangelists intended to suggest," Smith wrote in a missive with the sniggering title "Under the Sheet." What the evangelists intended, of course, was a libertine magical rite.[70] For more examples, we need look no farther than Smith's book on Clement of Alexandria.[71]

Smith was not always satisfied with hinting, however, and at times he frankly stated what he meant, in passages that also illustrate his cavalier syncretism of disparate traditions, if not a penchant for outright fabrication. Thus an argument that the Christian eucharist derived from magical rites intended "for erotic purposes, effected by physical means" cites no sources at all except for unspecified "magical papyri."[72] The idea is picked up again in a particularly egregious publication which asserts that Paul knew the Aramaic word *abba* was meaningless glossolalia, then says, amid much other silliness, "With *abbaabba* compare *hubbahubba* and the like in modern popular songs; ecstatic utterances in western society have probably changed little through the ages."[73] The hit song in this case, "Dig You Later (A Hubba-Hubba-Hubba)" sung by Perry Como and Martha Stewart, is from the 1945 popcorn movie "Dollface," about a burlesque-show stripper trying to make it as a legitimate actress.

And yet, Smith did have a source for the idea that mystery initiations are ultimately sexual: Clement of Alexandria, whose *Protr.* extensively criticizes the mystery cults as "sacred initiations that are really profanities,

---

69. Smith, "Paul's Arguments as Evidence" (repr. in Smith, *Studies in the Cult of Yahweh*, 2:103–9, see 105 [on Mark 7:15]).

70. Smith, "Under the Sheet."

71. Smith, *Clement of Alexandria*, 91 (on Hippolytus, *Trad. Ap.* XXI.11); 154 (on John 11:36); 171–72 (on Mark 10:21 deemed "improper").

72. Smith, "How Magic Was Changed by the Triumph of Christianity," 51–58 (repr. in Smith, *Studies*, 2:210–11).

73. Smith, "Pauline Worship as Seen by Pagans," 247 note 22 (repr. in Smith, *Studies in the Cult of Yahweh* 2: 100 note 22). For the true history of this expression, see: Randall and Butters, "*Hubba-Hubba*,"; Weinberger, "Some Data and Conjectures"; Riordan, "Further Note on 'Hubba-Hubba.'" About 2004, the New Zealand Health Ministry tried to promote condom usage with the slogan "No rubba, no hubba hubba"—see http://www.scoop.co.nz/stories/PA0411/S00477.htm.

and solemn rites that are without sanctity" (*Protr.* 2.22.3).[74] In a Smithian vein, Clement even proposed a polemical etymology for the word μυστήριον as derived from μύσος ("defilement"), citing a widely-practiced mystery rite that commemorated a myth in which the god Dionysus, having promised the dead Prosymnos a sexual experience in exchange for being shown the route to Hades, repaid the debt by carving a wooden phallus and sitting on it over Prosymnos' tomb (*Protr.* 2.13.1, 34.3–5).[75] Thus it is simply not true that the so-called "Gay Gospel Hypothesis" rests on only "one comment" or "tentative conjecture" by Smith;[76] anyone who thinks so has simply not read much of Smith's writing. The notion that μυστήριον always means a sexual initiation comes straight out of Clement's *Protr.* and is fundamental to Smith's notion of magic. It was Clement's more subtle uses of mystery vocabulary in *Strom.* that Smith did not understand, just as the author of the Mar Saba epistle did not.

An author can choose certain words to imply a double meaning, but it is also possible for the double meaning to inhere at the level of plot rather than to individual words. Specialists in American folklore (where such texts are common) have a term for this genre: "extended double entendre."[77] Without bothering to look up the examples I cited in my book, Scott Brown accused me of not knowing what I was talking about,[78] thereby demonstrating that incuriosity about footnotes is a key qualification of Smith's defenders. Extended double entendres can also serve as a form of ridicule:[79] the author of the Mar Saba epistle poses as the Clement of *Protr.* inveighing against the obscene rites of the unspeakable Carpocratians, but "unintentionally" reveals that his own holy mysteries are the real obscenities.

---

74. *Exhortation to the Greeks, The Rich Man's Salvation, and the Fragment of an Address Entitled "To the Newly Baptized,"* trans. George William Butterworth, 45.

75. Csapo, "Riding the Phallus for Dionysus," especially 275–76, 286–87; Burkert, "Der geheime Reiz des Verborgenen," see 92; Noce, "Il Tema della nudità dell' anima."

76. Brown, "Question of Motive," 357.

77. Jeffery, *Secret Gospel of Mark Unveiled*, 37, 93, 129. See also: Dundes and Pagter, *Never Try to Teach a Pig to Sing*, 46–47; Richter, "Reader as Ironic Victim"; Krauss and Miner, "From 'G' to 'PG-13'"; Lowe, *Words and Music of Frank Zappa*, 30–31.

78. Brown, Review of *Secret Gospel of Mark Unveiled*, 28–30.

79. Extended discussion on pp. 2–6 of one of my replies to Brown: "The Secret Gospel of Mark Unveiled: Reply to Scott G. Brown."

Ancient Gospel or Modern Forgery?

HOW THE MAR SABA EPISTLE WAS WRITTEN

A Parallel Example

The detailed listings of parallel phrases, quotations, and "fixed formulas" in Smith's commentaries and appendices, while serving their self-evident purpose of locating the Mar Saba text within the matrix of ancient Greek literature, compile just the sort of information that could be reverse-engineered to forge a text by way of a "scattered indications" approach.[80] Smith can be observed doing just that in a 1981 article,[81] where he assembled another collage of biblical and patristic references with the same message as the Mar Saba text. First, he proposed interpreting John 14:6 ("I am the way") by linking it to two verses that could be read suggestively: "the new and living way which he opened for us through the curtain, that is, through his flesh" (Heb 10:20) and "You shall see the heavens opened and the angels of God ascending and descending on the Son of Man" (John 1:51). In the same way, *Secret Mark* is constructed from passages like "looking upon him, [he] loved him (Mark 10:21, 27), ". . . and began to beseech him that he might be with him" (Mark 5:18), and "[the man] whom Jesus loved" (John 13:23; 19:26; 21:7, 20).[82] Even the phrase "for he was rich" (Luke 18:23), though it has obvious resonances with the writings of Clement,[83] reveals a new meaning when we know that Smith regarded the word "rich" as a synonym for "libertine."[84]

Since John 1:51 alludes to Jacob's ladder (Gen 28:12), Smith's 1981 article could introduce a comment by an early church father, Aphrahat, much as he introduced terms, phrases, and concepts from Clement and Papias in the Mar Saba epistle.[85] Aphrahat's statement should be translated,

---

80. Smith, *Clement of Alexandria*, especially chapters 2 and 3, and 351–91. The attempt even to bring in Milman Parry's oral-formulaic theory of Homeric poetry (144, 370–79), while not uninteresting, is an extreme step for something that is supposed to be an epistle by the highly literate Clement, quoting a prose gospel by the more modestly educated Mark.

81. Smith, "Ascent to the Heavens and the Beginning of Christianity," cited from the reprint in Smith, *Studies*, 2:47–67; for what follows see 59–60.

82. The most complete list of canonical parallels used to construct *Secret Mark* is Watson, "Beyond Suspicion," 139–42.

83. See Le Boulluec, "La lettre sur l'"Évangile secret' de Marc."

84. On Luke 19:2–6 compare Smith, *Clement of Alexandria*, 188, 211; and Smith, *Jesus the Magician*, 133–34; for the word "rich" as a synonym for "libertine," see *Jesus the Magician*, 138.

85. For the dependence on Papias see Watson, "Beyond Suspicion," 148–51.

"The ladder that Jacob saw is also the mystery of our Savior, by which just men ascend above from below" (*Dem.* 4.5, my translation).[86] The Syriac word "mystery (*rāza*)" in this passage actually means "type" in the sense of a typological exegesis: in dreaming of a heavenly ladder Jacob foresaw the Christ to come.[87] But by tilting the translation of "above" and "below," and adding the words "initiated by" in square brackets, Smith turned Aphrahat's typological mystery into a rite of heavenly ascent:

> Aphraates, one of the earliest Christian writers of Mesopotamia, declared, "The ladder is the mystery [initiated by] our saviour, by which righteous men ascend from the lower world to the world above." What mystery he had in mind is not known. It would seem to have included a technique for ascent. We may have a reflection of it in the story of the Transfiguration . . .[88]

The transfiguration story, as Smith wrote at every opportunity, shows that,

> Jesus taught a 'mystery of the kingdom of God' in which, by means like those known from contemporary magic, initiates were given what they thought was an experience of entering the heavens and they were thus trained to have such visions as those reworked in the transfiguration and resurrection stories.[89]

Thus *Secret Mark* looks like nothing so much as the lost "writings from Jesus and his immediate disciples" that Smith supposed were deliberately suppressed by later Christians because of perceived "libertine" content.[90] That is why the young man's nocturnal encounter with Jesus took place, like the transfiguration, "after six days" (Mark 9:2).

The Mar Saba epistle is a *tour de force* of scattered indications and double meanings; indeed it concentrates into a few sentences "more rare words and phrases scattered throughout the authentic works of Clement than are compatible with Clementine authorship."[91] Thus Mark,

---

86. *Patrologia Syriaca*, 2 vols., ed. René Graffin, 1.1:145–46. See also *The Demonstrations of Aphrahat, the Persian Sage*, trans. Adam Lehto, 130–31.

87. Murray, *Symbols of Church and Kingdom*, 45, cf. 21. In Dalmais, "'Raza' et sacrement," Dalmais tries hard to make *rāza* mean "sacrament" in this passage (see 174–75), but without success.

88. Smith, "Two Ascended to Heaven," 290–301 (repr. in Smith, *Studies*, 2:77).

89. Ibid.

90. Smith, *Clement of Alexandria*, 263–64.

91. Criddle, "On the Mar Saba Letter," 218.

did not divulge the things not to be uttered [ἀπόρρητα], nor did he write down the hierophantic teaching [ἱεροφαντικὴν διδασκαλίαν] of the Lord, but to the stories already written he added yet others and, moreover, brought in certain sayings of which he knew the interpretation [ἐξήγησιν] would, as a mystagogue, lead [μυσταγωγήσειν] the hearers into the innermost sanctuary of that truth hidden by seven veils [τὸ ἄδυτον τῆς ἑπτάκις κεκαλυμμένης ἀληθείας] (*Letter to Theodore* I.22–26).

Particularly unexpected here is the word "hierophantic," after the pagan priest who taught initiates how to carry out the mystery rites.[92] Clement called Moses a hierophant once, in a passage indebted to Philo (*Protr.* 2.26.1). Otherwise the various forms of the term were reserved for Orpheus, Dionysiacs, and other pagan teachers (*Protr.* 7.74.3; 2.22.7, 34.5). Twice in the apologetic *Protr.* (12.120.1, 123.2) it is used analogously of Christian teaching, and once it refers to philosophical study as a route to the knowledge of divine revelation (*Strom.* IV.1.3.1). But in Clement's authentic works the secret oral traditions of apostolic Christian teaching are never called "hierophantic" as they are in the Mar Saba epistle.

The noun *mystagogue*, which originally referred to the person who led the blindfolded candidate through the nocturnal initiation ceremonies of the mystery religions, was used by Clement only for Orpheus, pagan deities, and heretical Christian teachers (*Protr.* 2.21.1; *Strom.* V.14.130.3; VII.3.17.2). The verb was used only once for Christian teachers (*Quis div.* 3.2), twice for biblical theophanies (*Strom* V.12.79.1 on 2 Cor 12:2–4; *Strom.* V.11.73.4 on Gen 22:13), and once in a passage that describes the teaching of "the Savior himself" with quotations from Euripides' *Bacchae* (*Strom.* IV.25.162). However, personified abstractions never appear in Clement as the subject of μυσταγωγέω ("lead through the initiation"), the way "exegesis/interpretation" does in the Mar Saba epistle. Nor do hierophancy and mystagoguery ever occur in the same sentence except here. The epistle's author was simply stringing together every word he could find in Clement that suggested an esoteric ritual.

The word ἀπόρρητα ("unspeakable things") is used in Clement's writings for the cult of the earth goddess and the teachings of pagan martyrs and philosophers (*Protr.* 2.22.5; *Strom.* IV.8.56.1; V.9.58.1), but also for secrets handed down orally from the apostles (*Strom.* I.1.13.2, 14.2, 2.21.2), teachings of the Savior himself (*Strom.* V.1.7.8; *Quis div.* 5.4), secrets

---

92. For this and other mystery-religion terminology see Cosmopoulos, *Greek Mysteries*, 50–78, 197 and elsewhere.

known to angels (*Strom*. V.1.10.2), and "the unspeakable heritage of the spiritual and perfect man" that the Jewish High Priest received when he entered the Holy of Holies (*Strom*. V.6.40.1, my translation). This last is part of an extended typology of the Jerusalem Temple, much indebted to Philo,[93] which makes use of some of the other terms found in the Mar Saba epistle. But the typology in the epistle is skewed.

For the Holy of Holies in the Jerusalem Temple, Clement used the word *aduton* (ἄδυτον), which literally means a place not to be entered. But in Greek literature the *aduton* seems often to have meant "a location for a mysterious religious event, such as an oracular pronouncement or a healing experience"[94] rather than a physical structure. The *aduton* in Jerusalem, which only the High Priest could enter, represented to Philo and Clement the world of the mind, and was covered by a curtain [παραπέτασμα]. The outer temple was covered by a veil [κάλυμμα], which shut out the world of the senses, where ordinary men congregated in the Court of the Israelites. In between the curtain and the veil was the Court of the Priests, which contained the altar of incense (*Strom*. V.6.32.3—34.7). Hence "the simply sacred word, being truly divine and most necessary for us, is deposited in the *aduton* of the truth," which was symbolized for the Egyptians by the structures called *aduta* that were found in their temples, for the Jews by the curtain covering the Holy of Holies (*Strom*. V.4.19.3, my translation).

Clement's phrase "the *aduton* of the truth" is expanded in the *Letter to Theodore* to "the *aduton* of the seven-veiled truth" (I.26, my translation). But since no known ancient source confirms that the *aduton* in the Jerusalem Temple was hidden by seven καλύμματα, commentators from Smith onwards have sought out comparisons with other symbolic uses of the number seven.[95] Clement resorted to numerology when he found a number in a scriptural text, but was not so interested in numerology that he would often introduce it without such a cue. The number seven for Clement, as for Philo,[96] primarily recalls the days of the week, expanding

---

93. van den Hoek, *Clement of Alexandria*, 116–47.

94. Mary B. Hollinshead, "'Adyton,' 'Opisthodomos,' and the Inner Room of the Greek Temple," 207. See also Clement of Alexandria, *Protr*. 2.11.1.

95. The parallels cited in Smith, *Clement of Alexandria*, 40–41 are inexact, referring to the area external to the Temple, not to the inner sanctum where theophanies occur. Andrew C. Itter reviews proposed interpretations in *Esoteric Teaching*, 43–47. However, Itter's own interpretation goes too far afield, losing sight of the biblical background of Clement's numerological symbolism.

96. Leonhardt, *Jewish Worship in Philo of Alexandria*, 23, 33–37, 39–41, 43, 46, 49, 53–66, 90–95.

from there to include creation (hence the seven planets), or the Sabbath rest ("the holy hebdomad" in *Strom.* VII.9.57.5) superseded by the eschatological eighth day.[97] Temple typology can find sevens in the furnishings or the clothing and purifications of the priests (*Strom.* IV.25.157.3—159.3; VI.4.37.1–3). But only the Mar Saba epistle reports seven veils around the *aduton*. And no genuine text of Clement mentions *hierophants* or *mystagogues* in the context of Temple typology.

However the epistle's tightly-packed kaleidoscope of ritual imagery does have interesting Clementine resonance if we understand "unspeakable" to mean profane rather than sacred, as in "the unspeakable [ἀρρήτους] teachings of the Carpocratians" (I.2) that Theodore did well to silence. Clement of Alexandria used ἀπόρρητα for the unmentionable parts of the body (*Paed.* II.6.51.1; III.3.20.2, 22.1). Moses veiled his face to hide the glory from those who looked at him carnally (*Strom.* IV.18.117.1). The heretics believed that their sex crimes were leading them hierophantically to the kingdom of God (*Strom.* III.4.27.5), a near-parallel to the mystery of the kingdom of God that Jesus taught the young man after six days. Women who wear jewelry and make-up are like elaborate Egyptian temples:

> They adorn the enclosure of the flesh to lure lovers who stand in superstitious dread of the goddess. But if anyone draw back the curtain [καταπέτασμα] of this temple ... to discover the true beauty that is within, I am sure he will be disgusted. He will not find dwelling within any worthy image of God, but, instead, a harlot and adulteress who has usurped the *aduton* of the soul (*Paed.* III.2.5.1–3).

Women like that should hide their shame under a κάλυμμα (*Paed.* III.2.11.3). Abortion is also a kind of κάλυμμα that women use to hide adultery (*Paed.* II.10.96.1). For a reader who is deeply familiar with Clement's writings, therefore, finding Oscar Wilde's Salomé in the *aduton* of seven-veiled truth is less far-fetched than some are inclined to believe.

The more so if we consider what is said in the very next sentence of the epistle: "Thus, in sum, [Mark] prepared matters, neither grudgingly nor incautiously, in my opinion, and, dying, he left his composition to the church in Alexandria" (I.26—II.1). What is communicated by the phrase "neither grudgingly (φθονερῶς) nor incautiously (ἀπροφυλάκτως)"? Neither adverb appears in Clement's genuine writings, though Clement did use the noun φθόνος and adjective φθονερός for inappropriate reluctance

---

97 *Strom.* IV.25.158.4—159.3; V.6.34.8—35.2, 37.1–38.1; VI.16.137.4—145.7; VII.10.57.5.

Peter Jeffery—Clement's Mysteries and Morton Smith's Magic

to divulge secret teachings.⁹⁸ Thus the meaning could be that Mark was neither overly reticent nor overly careless in deciding what teachings to reveal in *Secret Mark*, though Clement did not elsewhere treat this matter as one of balance between grudging refusal and caution. On the other hand, if the epistle were read as an extended double entendre by Smith, it would be saying that, immediately after the exegesis leading mystagogically to the seven-veiled truth, "he prepared in advance, neither jealously (φθονερῶς) nor without a condom (ἀπροφυλάκτως),⁹⁹ as I suppose, and, climaxing,¹⁰⁰ he left his written composition to the church in Alexandria." Those who hope this is only an illusion on my part will find no reassurance in Smith's commentary, where the only citation for the adverb φθονερῶς (should we bother to look it up and read it) is Plato's *Phaedrus*: "For if any man of noble and gentle nature, one who was himself in love with another of the same sort, ... had happened to hear us saying that lovers ... are jealously (φθονερῶς) disposed ..." (243c).¹⁰¹ There's just no getting away from this topic.

In the *Letter to Theodore*'s two references to "the church in Alexandria," by the way, we find another non-Clementine expression that suggests the post-Nicene period. The "Christian schools and study circles" of Clement's time seem to have given way to "the imposition of episcopal control"¹⁰² and the emergence of a metropolitan see of Alexandria, with Clement as principal of the archdiocesan catechetical school and Theodore as another church official. *Secret Mark* seems not to be a book in the library of Clement's study group, but a holy relic of St. Mark kept in the diocesan treasury.

---

98. Citations in Smith, *Clement of Alexandria*, 41.

99. The earliest use of "prophylactic" as a synonym for "condom" listed in the OED dates from 1934.

100. The Latin *morior* and other words for dying and killing were used euphemistically for orgasm; see Adams, *Latin Sexual Vocabulary*, 159. Comparable usage in ancient Greek is not easy to find; there is no mention of it, for example, in Henderson, *Maculate Muse*. However it is frequent in Renaissance poetry in several languages, supported by a long tradition of reading orgasmic "death" into Plato's views on love, with help from Sappho and Marsilio Ficino. See La Via, "*Eros* and *Thanatos*"; Ciavolella, "Eros/Ereos'"; and Wolters, "Ficino and Plotinus' Treatise 'On Eros'"; Irwin, "Thomas Campion and the Musical Emblem"; Starks, "'Immortal Longings'"; and Llewellyn, "Deadly Sex and Sexy Death in Early Modern French Literature." The OED, at "die" I.7.d., cites eight examples of such usage, from Shakespeare, *Much Ado About Nothing*, iii.ii.62, to John Denver's 1974 hit "Annie's Song."

101. Smith, *Clement of Alexandria*, 41–42. Plato, *Euthyphro; Apology; Crito; Phaedo; Phaedrus* (trans. Harold North Fowler), 463.

102. Russell, *Doctrine of Deification in the Greek Patristic Tradition*, 115, 164; see also 120–21.

Ancient Gospel or Modern Forgery?

Though Scott Brown would interpret "the church in Alexandria" as "the group of inter-related Christian communities that existed in Alexandria,"[103] the known facts favor "pluriformity in the Alexandrian Church, encouraged by an ecclesiastical structure that was considerably looser and less 'monarchic' than in Antioch and elsewhere."[104] Even Antioch was not as "monarchic" as some would infer from the letters of Ignatius,[105] and the city had four competing bishops as late as the fourth century.[106] The earliest Christian texts from Alexandria express very different views of Christology and of the Church's relationship to Judaism, after all,[107] and surely these reflect distinct communities in what was one of the largest cities in the ancient world. The transition from diverse "voluntary associations"[108] or house churches to an orthodox patriarchate is likely to have been difficult and riven with conflict,[109] much as it also was in Rome.[110]

The True Truth

According to Smith, the transfiguration story was really "propaganda for a Jewish-Christian libertine group—a group that thought the Law and the Prophets had vanished from 'the freedom in which Christ has set us free,' as Paul put it (Gal 5:1)."[111] Smith even posited an anonymous early

---

103. Brown, *Mark's Other Gospel*, 135.

104. Ruina, *Philo in Early Christian Literature*, 120.

105. Slee, *Church in Antioch in the First Century C.E.*; Bockmuehl, "Syrian Memories of Peter"; Brent, *Ignatius of Antioch*.

106. Marcel Metzger, trans., *Les Constitutions apostoliques*, 1:61–62. See also Shepardson, "Controlling Contested Places."

107. Pearson, "Earliest Christianity in Egypt." Pearson believes that "Alexandrian Judaism itself was a variegated phenomenon in the first century, and that early Christianity there also would have displayed a degree of religious and theological variety, leading to the varieties of Christianity that appear more clearly in our second-century sources" (ibid., 155).

108. Kloppenborg and Wilson, eds., *Voluntary Associations in the Graeco-Roman World*; see especially Mason, "*Philosophiai*: Graeco-Roman, Judean and Christian," particularly 54–55; Ascough, "Translocal Relationships among Voluntary Associations and Early Christianity."

109. Russell, *Doctrine*, 163–66; Christopher Haas, *Alexandria in Late Antiquity*, especially 215–44; Layton, *Didymus the Blind and His Circle in Late-Antique Alexandria*.

110. Brent, *Hippolytus and the Roman Church in the Third Century*; Lampe, *From Paul to Valentinus*, especially 359–65, 381–408 on "fractionation."

111. Smith, "The Origin and History of the Transfiguration Story," 42 (repr. in Smith, *Studies*, 2:84).

transmitter of the transfiguration story who would have been a "libertine apologist," and a "creative thinker, not to say 'liar,'" which means he was "as might be expected, a theologian."[112] Magical initiation into celestial experience, in other words, turns out to be a lie by "libertine" theologians and apologists who consider themselves exempt from the moral law. The Mar Saba epistle presents us with just such a lying theologian: Clement, the purported author, who falls all over himself arguing that,

> even if they should say something true, one who loves the truth should not, even so, agree with them. For not all true things are the truth, nor should that truth which merely seems true according to human opinions be preferred to the true truth, that according to the faith (I.8–11).

It is implausible that any ancient author could have written the phrase "the true truth," which clearly reflects modern Perspectivism, the belief that truth is socially constructed so that there can be no objective universal standard.[113] I have found no such expression in the on-line Thesaurus Linguae Graecae.[114] In any case Clement of Alexandria did not agree with Clement of Mar Saba, but readily admitted that his opponents' opinions were partly true (*Strom* I.13.57.1–6). *Strom.* VII.9.53.2–3 became entangled in a nineteenth-century debate about the morality of lying to promote the Church's interests,[115] but Clement himself advocated no such thing.

Moreover the Mar Saba epistle seems to show Clement opposing the wrong libertines. Clement knew of a group (the followers of Basilides) who recognized a category of non-heterosexual men (*Strom.* III.1.1.2–3). He also opposed an unnamed group that seems more deserving of the "libertine" characterization (*Strom.* III.4.34.1—39.3), and actually did "corrupt boys" (*Strom.* III.4.36.5). But the vice Clement ascribed to the Carpocratians was heterosexual wife-swapping, the sharing of wives like common property as in Plato's *Republic* (*Strom.* III.2.5.1—10.2; III.4.25.5; III.6.54.1). The notion that the Carpocratians had a particular interest in naked men, preserving a ritual tradition going back to Jesus himself, was Morton Smith's invention, based on Gershom Scholem's identification of the Carpocratians with certain antinomian sects descended from the

---

112. Ibid., 43 (*Studies*, 2:85).

113. Solomon, "Nietzsche ad hominem"; König, "Perspektive, Perspektivismus, perspektivisch."

114. Online: http://www.tlg.uci.edu/.

115. Jeffery, *Secret Gospel of Mark Unveiled*, 175–80.

seventeenth-century Jewish heresy of Sabbatai Tzevi. Scholem's opinion that these sects believed in "redemption through sin" appears to explain Smith's statement that "Carpocrates was said to have taught that sin was a means of salvation."[116]

In short the author of the Mar Saba epistle, though he worked by accumulating vocabulary and phraseology borrowed from Clement of Alexandria, canonical Mark, and other sources, is actually showing us a modern Clement with the wrong doctrine of truth, condemning the wrong group of libertines, amassing too much of Clement's ritual terminology to describe the wrong kind of initiation rites, misidentifying Clement's secret oral traditions with an alleged written text, all in an ecclesiastical environment that looks post-Nicene. The simplest and most logical interpretation of all this is that the Mar Saba epistle and its secret gospel must have been written by the same enigmatic figure that composed Morton Smith's publications.

For those who desire to get to the bottom of the Mar Saba epistle, or at least *Secret Mark*, there is no way to avoid wading into the quicksand of Smith's writings. Arguments about word frequency or Smith's facility with Greek are simply suppressing evidence if they do not also consider Smith's "scattered indications" technique of reassembling words and phrases from ancient writings. Indignant denials of the double entendres merely advertise one's own unfamiliarity with both Smith's and Clement's works. Of course liars occasionally tell the truth, and a chronic abuser of primary sources might really discover a new one. But the burden of proof rightly falls on those who would argue in spite of everything that that is what happened in this case. Such a proof must include a demonstration that, somewhere in the historical past—the past that really happened—an author or milieu can be found that provides a better historical frame for the Mar Saba epistle than Smith's writings do: better because it affords a more comprehensive explanation than my book offers of who all the characters in this text are and what they are saying.

---

116. Smith, *Secret Gospel*, 14, where communication with Scholem is mentioned but no specific publication cited. Smith apparently read Scholem's interpretation into Irenaeus's account of the Carpocratians (*Haer.* 1.25.45). He did not acknowledge any dependency on Scholem in *Clement of Alexandria*, 266–78, but he did do so in private correspondence with Scholem (see Stroumsa, *Corespondence*, 119, 158, 160, and especially 170). See also Smith, "The Reason for the Persecution of Paul and the Obscurity of Acts," 261–68 (repr. in Smith, *Studies*, 2:87–94). Scholem's characterization of the Carpocratians is found in Scholem, "Sabbatianism and Mystical Heresy," in *Major Trends in Jewish Mysticism*, 316 and 420 n. 60; and Scholem, "Redemption through Sin," in Scholem, *Messianic Idea in Judaism and Other Essays on Jewish Spirituality*, 78–141, especially 132.

11

Behind the Seven Veils, I
The Gnostic Life Setting of the Mystic Gospel of Mark[1]

Scott G. Brown

FIFTY-ONE YEARS AGO, AT the 1960 meeting of the Society of Biblical Literature, Morton Smith announced his discovery of a letter of Clement of Alexandria describing and excerpting a longer, "mystic" form of the Gospel of Mark (τὸ μυστικὸν εὐαγγέλιον), which Smith called the secret gospel.[2] Two weeks later, Cyril Richardson, a respected church historian who was in attendance, sent Smith a letter outlining "a possible thesis" to explain the gospel pericope that is quoted in the letter, a very brief and typically Markan variant of John 11 in which Jesus raises a dead man in Bethany at the behest of his grieving sister and after six days teaches this young man the mystery of the kingdom of God. Richardson conjectured that this narrative was part of a baptism lection that was read during "the Paschal vigil in Clement's church." Noting Clement's statement that this "more spiritual" version of Mark's gospel was read "only to those who are

---

1. My profound thanks to Roy Kotansky for his invaluable help.

2. The session occurred on Thursday, 29 December 1960, in the Horace Mann Auditorium, Teacher's College, Columbia University. See Smith, *Secret Gospel*, 30. The text of this presentation is available in the Columbia University Archives.

being initiated into the great mysteries" (II.1–2), Richardson wrote, "I take this to mean baptism, to which Clement applies all degrees of mystery language."[3] A year or two later Richardson clarified to Smith that he understood "τὸ λουτρόν as baptism administered alone and τὰ μεγάλα μυστήρια as the entire paschal ceremony, including baptism."[4]

Richardson eventually changed his mind. In his 1974 review of the two books on "secret" Mark that Smith published the previous year, Richardson noted that "there are passages in Clement where he views baptism as very preliminary to the lesser and greater mysteries (*Strom.* 5,11,7,1)."[5] Whereas Smith had argued that the letter describes two levels of catechetical readers—the catechumens proper, who heard the (canonical) gospel that Mark wrote in Rome, and "those being baptized," who heard the more spiritual gospel that Mark produced in Alexandria—Richardson proffered that "the contrast between *katēchoumenoi* and *teleioumenoi* in the letter" was actually between "*simpliciores* . . . and the true gnostics."[6] Thus the actual audience of the mystic text was not the neophytes but "the graduate students," as Massey H. Shepherd put it a year later.[7] These advanced students would have been baptized years before they first heard this text. Hence it cannot be a baptism reading. Unfortunately, this recognition came much too late, for Smith had accepted the baptismal thesis and made it the basis of his interpretation of the mystic gospel and the origin of Christian baptism.[8] Likewise most subsequent scholars, while highly critical of Smith's reconstruction of a magical and libertine baptism rite of the historical Jesus, readily accepted the baptismal life setting of the mystic text. This basic misconception prevailed in studies of "secret" Mark for the next five decades.

Since most scholars who have studied the subject have fundamentally misconstrued what the letter is talking about, it is not surprising that

3. Quoted in Smith, *Secret Gospel*, 65. Smith quotes from Richardson's letter on 64–65.

4. Richardson's opinion is paraphrased in Smith, *Clement of Alexandria and a Secret Gospel of Mark*, 168. I assume that Richardson made this remark while commenting on the first draft of Smith's commentary, during the years 1962–1963 (noted on 87).

5. Richardson, Review of *Secret Gospel* and *Clement of Alexandria*, by Morton Smith, 574. Richardson's citation should actually read: *Strom.* V.11.70.7—71.1.

6. Ibid., 575.

7. Shepherd, "Response to Reginald H. Fuller," 47–51. I quoted from a comment he made during the colloquy (68).

8. For Smith's thesis, see *Secret Gospel*, 66, 68–69, 89–114, 115–21; and Smith, *Clement of Alexandria*, esp. 167–88, 205–20, 235–40, 248–54, 264–65.

some of them see it as incongruous for the historical situation. A case in point is the recent book by Notre Dame musicologist Peter Jeffery, who reads the letter as describing a gospel used for baptism but argues that the quoted gospel pericope is incompatible with what (little) we know about the history of Alexandria's baptism liturgy and theology.[9] This argument allows him to seek the actual life setting of the mystic gospel elsewhere, in the intellectual milieux of twentieth-century Anglican scholarship on early Christian baptism and a homosexual academic subculture in which he would situate the text's discoverer. I addressed these arguments in an essay review of Jeffery's book, where I endeavoured to show that "the great mysteries" do not refer to baptism and the gospel pericope does not depict baptism.[10] Since then I have come to realize that the *Letter to Theodore* contains another, less direct and entirely overlooked indication of the life setting of the mystic gospel. This is found in the detail that Mark created it by adding "certain traditions (λόγια) of which he knew the interpretation would, as a mystagogue, lead the hearers into the innermost sanctuary of the sevenfold veiled truth" (I.24–26).[11] When we examine what the imagery of entering the innermost sanctuary denotes in Clement's writings we realize that this "space" was inaccessible to catechumens and ordinary believers; like the great mysteries that it contains, this sanctuary was accessible only to the Christian equivalent of the Jewish high priest, which Clement called the true gnostic. This overlooked evidence from Clement's writings verifies the gnostic life setting of the mystic gospel and the letter's concordance with Clement's program of Christian education.

---

9. Jeffery, *Secret Gospel of Mark Unveiled*. Jeffery's position is actually closer to the form of the baptismal thesis presented in Richardson's initial letter to Smith, which connects "secret" Mark to the rites of initiation into the church, than to Smith's form, which connects this text to a hypothetical second baptism practiced by an elite subgroup of gnostics within the Alexandrian church. See Smith, *Clement of Alexandria*, 168, 254, 283–84. Jeffery's evidence that the Alexandrian baptism liturgy and theology does not accord with the "secret" gospel would be much less relevant if this gospel pertains to a different kind of baptism that was practiced by a small sect within the church. As Judith L. Kovacs has documented, some Valentinians of Alexandria practiced second baptisms; see her "Concealment and Gnostic Exegesis," 429–30.

10. Brown, Review of *Secret Gospel of Mark Unveiled*, by Peter Jeffery.

11. Unless noted otherwise, quotations of the *Letter to Theodore* are as translated in Smith, *Clement of Alexandria*, 446–47, which I have slightly revised; block quotations from Clement's undisputed writings are by Roy Kotansky and myself; incidental quotations of Clement are by William Wilson, ANF 2; and Robert Pierce Casey (*The Excerpta ex Theodoto of Clement of Alexandria*) and are sometimes revised; quotations of Philo are by *Works of Philo Complete and Unabridged* (trans. C. D. Yonge); and quotations of Plato are from Harold North Fowler (from *Plato in Twelve Volumes*).

Before I examine the sanctuary metaphor, however, it would be helpful to bring together the existing research concerning the meaning of the lesser and great mysteries in Clement's corpus and situate these findings within the larger context of his conception of salvation.[12] The diagram on page [p. 283] presents a visual schematic of Clement's conception of the path to perfection within the church, a sequence of purifications and initiations that determine the soul's initial level in its postmortem ascent through seven heavens into "the Church far on high" (*Strom.* VI.14.108.1).

THE LESSER AND GREAT MYSTERIES IN PLATO AND CLEMENT

The Greek mystery religions promised initiates a better life in the hereafter and friendship with the divine. Plato co-opted these rewards for philosophy by describing the philosophical life as a mystery initiation that determines the soul's fate in the afterlife. His *Phaedo* describes how philosophy purifies the soul of everything material or bodily, allowing it upon death to separate completely from materiality and ascend to that which it is like (see esp. 67a–e, 69c, 81a). The purified soul rises to the realm of the gods (82b), or even higher (cf. 114c), to the forms, whereas the impure soul, "weighed down by [the earthly], is dragged back into the visible world," where it eventually reincarnates in a being whose character it resembles (81c–82a).[13] The myth of the chariot in Plato's *Phaedrus* borrows terms characteristic of the Eleusinian great mysteries to describe the experience of ascending beyond the stars to the back of the fixed sphere, where the forms of the immaterial cosmos are revealed like the sacred objects of the mysteries. In this way Plato associates the noetic world with the Telesterion, the sanctuary at Eleusis in which initiation in the great mysteries took place (247c–d, 250b–c). We will return to this passage when we examine Clement's use of the phrase "innermost sanctuary of the truth" at *Strom.* V.4.19.3.

Although Clement has a different understanding of the fate of impure souls,[14] he shares the general outlook that only the souls purified by

---

12. For my earlier discussions of the great mysteries, see Brown, *Mark's Other Gospel*, 128–31, 158–62; Brown, Review of *Secret Gospel of Mark Unveiled*, 3–14.

13. See White, *Myth and Metaphysics*, 117–25. Plato also has a conception of hell (Tartarus). See *Phaedo* 113a–114c.

14. See Daniélou, *History of Early Christian Doctrine*, 2:124. Citing Plato's description of Tartarus, Clement associates the judgment of unbelievers with "the rivers of fire

virtue and knowledge will ascend to the highest realms, and like Plato (*Symp.* 209e–210a; *Gorg.* 497c) Clement uses the metaphors of lesser and greater mysteries to describe this intellectual and spiritual process.[15]

In keeping with the Eleusinian lesser mysteries, which were mostly purificatory,[16] Clement's lesser mysteries involve "preliminary purifications and instruction" that prepare and qualify the believer for the great mysteries (*Strom.* IV.1.3.1–4). Their purpose, as reconceived by Plato, is to bring about a moral and intellectual transformation[17] that amounts to a progressive assimilation to God. "Initiates" purify themselves of the qualities that separate humans from angels, especially passions and sensual attachments that prevent them from seeing beyond appearances to the true essence of things. Hence Clement's lesser mysteries involve both higher ethics[18] and scientific knowledge (ἐπιστήμη) of the material cosmos or sensible (i.e., sense-perceptible) realm, which are grounded in the encyclical disciplines of Hellenic education: music, arithmetic, geometry, astronomy, dialectics (VI.10.80.1–4).[19] These give a basis for ethical behaviour (living in accord with nature) and intellectual comprehension, thereby preparing the aspiring gnostic for the great mysteries, which involve apprehending purely noetic and spiritual realities beyond the material cosmos, beginning with the noetic world of Platonic philosophy.

Thus the lesser mysteries concern scientific knowledge acquired through the senses, and the great mysteries involve supersensible realities apprehended by the mind/soul alone.[20] The transition between these two kinds of knowledge occurs through philosophy and the revealed knowledge of cosmogony, facilitated by a method of investigation Clement calls "the gnostic science of nature" (γνωστικῆς παραδόσεως φυσιολογία; IV.1.3.2). Through an intellectual process of abstraction, knowledge of the material cosmos is used "to discern the intelligible archetypes present in

and the depth of the earth" (*Strom.* V.14.91.2).

15. For Plato, see Farrell, "Plato's Use of Eleusinian Mystery Motifs"; for Clement, see, Riedweg, *Mysterienterminologie bei Plato, Philo und Klemens von Alexandrien*, 7–9, 21, 123–30, 159–61; or briefly, Wyrwa, *Die christliche Platonaneignung in den Stromateis des Clemens von Alexandrien*, 123–24.

16. Farrell, "Plato's Use of Eleusinian Mystery Motifs," 35, 116.

17. Ibid., 114.

18. Wagner, "Another Look at the Literary Problem," 251–60 (at 257).

19. Rizzerio, "L'accès à la transcendance divine," 160, 162–63. On Clement's views about the encyclical disciplines, see Sandnes, *Challenge of Homer*, 126–40.

20. For a discussion of the distinction between the lesser and great mysteries in Philo of Alexandria, see Wolfson, *Philo*, 1:47–48; Lilla, *Clement of Alexandria*, 190 n. 1.

sensible realities ... with a view to contemplating the Invisible out of the sensible."[21]

Clement's longest description of the lesser and great mysteries may suffice to illustrate some of the preceding observations:

> It is not then without reason that the mysteries of the Greeks commence with rites of purification (τὰ καθάρσια), as also the washing in water (τὸ λουτρόν) among the Barbarians (i.e., Jews and Christians). After these are the lesser mysteries (τὰ μικρὰ μυστήρια), which function to teach and prepare for what is to come after, then the great mysteries (τὰ δὲ μεγάλα), which concern the totality of things, in which nothing remains to be learned, but only to contemplate (ἐποπτεύειν) and comprehend both nature and things. We shall understand the mode of purification by confession, and that of contemplation (ἐποπτικόν) by analysis, advancing by analysis to the primary concept, beginning with the properties underlying it; abstracting from the body its physical properties, taking away the dimension of depth, then that of breadth, and then that of length. What remains is a point, a monad, so to speak, having position; if we take away position, we have the intellectual concept of unity. If, then, abstracting all that belongs to bodies and what are called incorporeal realities, we cast ourselves into the greatness of Christ, and from there advance by holiness into the abyss, we may somehow attain an intellectual conception of the Almighty, knowing not what he is, but what he is not. (*Strom.* V.11.70.7—71.3, trans. Wilson, revised by Brown)

As we can see from this passage, Clement's lesser and great mysteries accord with Plato's insofar as "they refer to a progressively more difficult and more refined apprehension of true reality."[22] But unlike Plato, knowledge of the forms is not the highest state of knowledge,[23] for, as Eric Osborn notes, "knowledge of the forms leads to vision (*epopteia*) of the first principle, so that all reality is seen in the light of the divine logos."[24] In order to move beyond the forms to arrive at Christ as the first principle, this science of nature,

---

21. Borella, *Guénonian Esoterism and Christian Mystery*, 255.

22. White, *Myth and Metaphysics*, 36.

23. See, e.g., Plato, *Phaedrus* 250c, where knowledge of a form is described in terms of *epopteia*, the pinnacle of the Eleusinian mysteries. Farrell, "Plato's Use of Eleusinian Mystery Motifs," 125–29.

24. Osborn, *Clement of Alexandria*, 212.

> must be supplemented by the divine revelation... In this sense, it should be said that Clement recognizes a double aspect to φυσιολογία. On the one hand he identifies it with a science of nature which can achieve the highest degree possible of knowledge of φύσις through reason. And on the other hand, he makes it correspond to a science of nature which was clarified by a revelation, and which thereby is able, in this way only, to arrive at the vision of divine realities. And it is at this time that it becomes ἐποπτεία.[25]

In the Eleusinian mysteries, *epopteia* denotes the highest point of the initiation, which climaxes in a vision of immense light. For Clement, *epopteia* denotes a direct and unmediated vision of God by the mind alone. This vision is a foretaste of the true repose, the direct ("face to face") contemplation of Christ as the face of God (*Exc.* 10.6; 12.1; cf. *Paed.* I.7.57.2; *Strom.* V.6.33.6—34.1) in the afterlife.

Thus the true gnostic moves beyond the realm of philosophy to "the domain of theology, *epopteia*, which," says Clement, "is what Plato deems to be the really great mysteries" and "Aristotle calls metaphysics" (*Strom.* I.28.176.2), eventually attaining visionary knowledge of divine realities. The whole process constitutes an ascent. As the initiate in the lesser mysteries learns the mysteries of the material cosmos, he or she metaphorically rises above the earth to contemplate higher and more divine truths. Clement alludes to this ascent throughout his writings (e.g., *Strom.* VI.10.80.3), but Philo of Alexandria describes it more fully and eloquently:

> And again, being raised up on wings, and so surveying and contemplating the air, and all the commotions to which it is subject, it [the human mind] is borne upwards to the higher firmament, and to the revolutions of the heavenly bodies. And also being itself involved in the revolutions of the planets and fixed stars according to the perfect laws of music, and being led on by love, which is the guide of wisdom, it proceeds onwards till, having surmounted all essence intelligible by the external senses, it comes to aspire to such as is perceptible only by the intellect: and perceiving in that, the original models and ideas of those things intelligible by the external senses which it saw here full of surpassing beauty, it becomes seized with a sort of sober intoxication like the zealots engaged in the Corybantian festivals, and yields to enthusiasm, becoming filled with another desire, and a more excellent longing, by which it is conducted

---

25. Rizzerio, "La notion de γνωστικὴ φυσιολογία," 321, my translation.

> onwards to the very summit of such things as are perceptible only to the intellect, till it appears to be reaching the great King himself. (*Opif.* 23.70–71)

As Charles L. Quarles has pointed out, the fairly similar description in Philo's *Spec.* 3.1–5 contains indications that the ascent is "purely figurative."[26] His language of a visionary ascent into the heavens is basically an extended metaphor for the life of the mind and the rapturous elation of being so engrossed in an idea that he forgets the troubling world around him. The same appears to be true for Clement. When he applies the imagery of heavenly ascent to living humans, his language is mainly literary and conventional. It describes progression in virtue and knowledge, and advancement within the church. However, his descriptions of the heavenly ascent of the soul after death can be highly mystical and unconventional (e.g., *Exc.* 27), and they describe realities that he believed the soul will experience after death and which the properly trained mind can already perceive before death. So there is a mystical and visionary aspect to the great mysteries, even though the imagery of ascent through the heavens is mainly conventional.

Although science, dialectic, and philosophy can figuratively raise the soul up to the noetic world, the even higher and more divine realities contemplated thereafter, which Philo describes as ecstatic visions, are more revelatory or apocalyptic in nature. Accordingly, initiation into the great mysteries also involves learning divine secrets, especially the unutterable "visions and revelations" that seers experience in the highest heaven (e.g., Paul in 2 Cor 12:1–4). Walter Wagner describes the great mysteries as "matters in the mind of God, heavenly hierarchies, the ascent of souls to the mansions, maleness and femaleness in God and the cosmos, and the consummation of all things in Logos."[27]

Unfortunately, these matters concern oral traditions that are the prerogative of the true gnostic, so Clement refrains from disclosing them in an overt way in his major works. Instead, he scatters bits and pieces of this gnosis throughout the *Stromateis* (I.1.18.1, 2.20.4; IV.2; VII.18.111.1–3), requiring his readers to prove their dedication to the truth by gathering together his disordered thoughts on gnostic subjects and figuring out how

---

26. Quarles, "Jesus as *Merkabah* Mystic," 10–11.

27. Wagner, *After the Apostles*, 181. See also Daniélou, *History of Early Christian Doctrine,* 2:453–55, who emphasizes the congruence of the gnostic tradition with Jewish apocalyptic and its "mysteries of the transcendent order" (454) such as angelology and the transformations in the nature of the ascending soul.

they fit together. His "patchwork" presentation of the gnostic truth is like a jigsaw puzzle for which the picture on the box is missing, half the pieces were prudently omitted (due to their graphic contents), and the other half were mixed in with pieces from other puzzles that depict complementary or competing pictures of the truth. It can take years to make sense of the most esoteric aspects of the *Stromateis*, and you are never sure you have properly figured something out.

CLEMENT'S COSMOLOGY AND CONCEPTION OF SALVATION

The mysteries are primarily related to the heavens and the soul's progression through them, both metaphorically, in terms of comprehending the universe, and literally, in terms of the soul's ascent in its spiritual body after death.[28] Accordingly, some brief comments about Clement's cosmology and conception of salvation are in order.

For Clement, the earth and the heavens as a whole constitute a single celestial temple, with each tier marking an increase in holiness, like the sequence of courts in an earthly temple (*Strom.* VI.14.114.1–4). The successive purifications of the Christian mysteries are what permit the soul's advancement through this temple, so that the level of initiation one attains within the church determines at death the initial level of one's heavenly abode. Thereafter the soul continues the process of perfection at the stage where it left off. A soul that, upon death, attains one of the lowest heavenly spheres is tormented and punished for sins committed after baptism (VI.14.109.3; VII.2.12.5). As in the lesser mysteries, the soul acquires virtue and purifies itself of all remaining passions and material attachments as it advances through higher heavens of the material cosmos (*Strom.* VI.14.109.1), with its spiritual body becoming progressively lighter and more brilliant (*Exc.* 27.1; *Strom.* IV.18.116.2—117.2). If I understand Clement correctly, perfection of the human condition is attained in the sixth heaven, and a well-earned repose occurs in the seventh, in keeping with God's creation of humans on the sixth day and his rest on the seventh (*Strom.* VI.16.141.3). The gnostic soul then leaves the material cosmos for the noetic world (VI.14.108.1), where it relinquishes its spiritual body (*Exc.* 27.1–2) and becomes an angel. It continues to ascend for six more stages, learning the great mysteries of the immaterial cosmos from within (*Ecl.* 57.5). The highest repose occurs thereafter.

28. On the spiritual body, see nn. 45 and 46.

Ancient Gospel or Modern Forgery?

Clement's cosmology owes a great deal to Philo's allegorical interpretation of the wilderness tabernacle as a symbolic embodiment of the universe (esp. *Mos.* 2.15.71—22.108).[29] Like the tabernacle, the celestial temple has two main sanctuaries. The earth and the lower seven heavens, or Hebdomad ("seven"), constitute the outer sanctuary or "holy place." The earth is represented by "the altar of incense, the symbol of the earth placed in the middle of this universe" (*Strom.* V.6.33.1). These heavens correspond to the planetary spheres (the moon, the sun, and the five known planets) and are symbolized by the seven lights on the branches of the menorah, which was housed at the south end of the holy place (34.8–9).[30] Above these heavens are the stars, which revolve in unison as one fixed sphere. They represent the terminus of the visible and material cosmos and form a boundary or veil between the two sanctuaries.

Beyond this veil lies the Ogdoad ("eight"),[31] the inner sanctuary or "holy of holies" of the celestial temple. This is the noetic world (*Strom.* V.6.35.5; VI.8.68.1), an ideational heaven and earth that existed before time and creation and formed the blueprint for the visible cosmos. Following Philo, Clement read the creation of this invisible and immaterial cosmos into Gen 1:2–5, where God first creates an earth that is "invisible and formless" (this is how Clement interprets "without form and void") and a light that exists apart from any material sources (God creates the sun and the stars on the fourth day). The noetic world contains all the forms of the living creatures, who were subsequently created in the material cosmos "according to their kinds"—a frequent expression in Gen 1:11–25 that Clement takes to mean "according to the intelligible patterns (τὰ νοητά)" (*Strom.* V.14.90.1, 93.4—94.2). Clement sometimes refers to "pneumatic" (or "spiritual") regions or realities above the noetic world (τὰ πνευματικά or τὰ πνευματικώτερα), within which he locates a hierarchy of

---

29. For discussion, see Van den Hoek, *Clement of Alexandria*, 116–47.

30. Because the moon and the sun appeared to move in fixed orbits that differ from the fixed movement of the stars, these two heavenly bodies were sometimes grouped with the five known planets but also recognized to be in their own category (e.g., *Strom.* V.6.38.3; VI.4.35.4). Clement explained that the sun is represented by the central stalk of the menorah, which casts light on the other planets "above and below it" (V.6.34.8–9); I assume that Clement concurred with his source, Philo, *Her.* 45.224, which arranged the spheres in this order (moving outward from the earth): the moon, Venus, Mercury, the sun, Mars, Jupiter, Saturn.

31. Clement expresses uncertainty in *Strom.* IV.25.159.2 about whether the fixed sphere is to be counted as part of the eighth sphere.

angels, archangels, and first-created angels (called *protoctists*), with Christ, the Logos, at the summit.[32]

THE GREAT MYSTERIES AND EXEGESIS

Clement supposed that Christ revealed the great mysteries to his disciples in private during his ministry (see the next paragraph) and after his resurrection (*Hypotyposeis* VII, cited in Eusebius, *Hist. eccl.* II.1.4). These teachings were subsequently transmitted orally and in secret from teacher to student (*Strom.* I.1.11.3; VI.7.61.1–3). While in the flesh, Christ concealed these mysteries from unworthy hearers by communicating on two levels: a literal level for *hoi polloi* and a figurative level for the worthy few. Hence his words recorded in the Gospels contain hidden significances (*Quis div.* 5.1–4; *Strom.* VI.15.124.6—125.2, 126.2–3, 127.3; cf. I.12.56.2), which Clement terms their "mystic" or "spiritual" meanings.[33] The same multivalence applies to the Old Testament and the other books of the New Testament, whose compositions Christ inspired before and after his incarnation.[34] Consequently, the unwritten gnostic tradition concerns truths about supersensible realities veiled in the scriptures, and the great mysteries are passed on and disclosed in the form of allegorical exegesis, an aspect of Clement's gnostic science that discloses the intelligible realities (the "mystic" meaning) behind the visible words.[35] This is how Clement would approach a "mystic" and "more spiritual" gospel (*Letter to Theodore* II.6, 12; I.21–22).

For proof that these metaphysical truths have been, and must remain, concealed from the unworthy, Clement occasionally turns to the Markan theme that Jesus spoke only in parables to the crowds but explained everything privately to his disciples (Mark 4:10–12, 34; e.g., *Strom.* I.12.56.2; VI.15.124.6—125.2; cf. *Exc.* 66). His proof that Christ himself believed that the great mysteries must be hidden from the masses includes Jesus'

---

32. I discuss the passages referring to the pneumatic realms later. Note also *Strom.* V.6.38.6, where Clement indicates that "the Lord" (meaning the Son) resides "above the noetic world." Philo, *QE* 2.68 similarly situates the Logos and the noetic world at the upper and lower extremities of the immaterial cosmos. On that passage, see Goodenough, *Introduction to Philo Judaeus*, 104–7; McIver, "'Cosmology' as a Key."

33. For examples, see Brown, *Mark's Other Gospel*, 131–34.

34. Christ/the Logos tends to take the place of the Holy Spirit in Clement's conception of scriptural inspiration.

35. Rizzerio, "Accès à la transcendance divine," 175. Cf. Philo, *Contempl.* 3.28–29, 10.78.

words, "To you it is given to know the mystery of the kingdom of the heavens" (*Strom.* V.12.80.6).[36] This saying, which conflates Mark 4:11 and Matt 13:11, shows that Clement understood the mystery of the kingdom of God as an alternative term for the great mysteries. That fact tells us how he would have interpreted the description of Jesus teaching the young man the mystery of the kingdom of God in the mystic gospel (*Secret Mark*). Rather than imagining a baptism, Clement would see this man receiving the unwritten gnostic tradition. That inference is quite natural given the phrase "for Jesus was teaching him" (ἐδίδασκε γὰρ αὐτὸν ὁ Ἰησοῦς), which, if not ignored or creatively rewritten, refers to an evening of private teaching.[37] The Christians in Clement's church who were permitted to hear this gospel would be doing the same thing, learning privately from a teacher the truths that Jesus concealed from the many by employing parables and other concealing tropes.

Thus the Christian great mysteries are inextricably related to the exegesis of scripture. A Jewish form of this idea was already more than a century old. Clement's Jewish predecessor Philo wrote: "For I myself, having been initiated in the great mysteries (μυηθεὶς τὰ μεγάλα μυστήρια) by Moses, the friend of God, nevertheless, when subsequently I beheld Jeremiah the prophet, and learnt that he was not only initiated (μύστης), but was also a competent hierophant (ἱεροφάντης), did not hesitate to become his pupil" (*Cher.* 14.49). Here particular books of the Bible (the five books of Moses and the book Jeremiah) have the special ability to metaphorically initiate a reader into the great mysteries. The *Letter to Theodore* similarly designates Mark's mystic gospel as a mystagogue, and the unwritten explanations ("the hierophantic teaching of the Lord") as the hierophant.

A brief explanation of how purely intellectual and pneumatic realities are revealed through allegorical exegesis appears in *Strom.* VI.11.86.1. Clement uses geometry, one of the disciplines studied in the lesser mysteries, to elucidate deeper meanings of certain design specifications presented in scripture. He explains that the tabernacle and Noah's ark were "built so as to be of the most rational proportions, divine in conception,

---

36. See Brown, Review of *Secret Gospel of Mark Unveiled*, 9–10.

37. Interpreters have been oddly reluctant to take the reference to teaching at face value despite the fact that similar instances of private teaching occur throughout the Gospel of Mark. Smith, for instance, rewrote the phrase so that it reads "for he gave him the mystery," thus allowing the mystery of the kingdom of God to be a rite rather than a subject (*Clement of Alexandria*, 183). Similarly, Stephen C. Carlson transformed the sentence into a sexual reference by reasoning that it must mean "Jesus taught him the mystery of the kingdom of God, for he spent that night with him" (*Gospel Hoax*, 66).

to accord with that gift of understanding which leads us from sensible to intelligible things, or rather from these particular objects to holy things and to the holy of holies."[38] The *Letter to Theodore*'s information that Mark "transferred to his former book the things suitable to those studies which make for progress toward gnosis" (I.20–21) would refer to passages of this sort, which are elucidated by knowledge gained through training in the encyclical disciplines that investigate the physical world (*Strom.* I.1.15.3).

ENTRY INTO THE INNERMOST SANCTUARY OF THE TRUTH

The preceding conclusions concerning the gnostic life setting of the mystic gospel are founded on the meaning of initiation into the great mysteries in Clement's *Stromateis* (I.28.176.1–2; IV.1.3.1; V.11.70.7—71.5; cf. I.1.15.3). That this is what the *Letter to Theodore* is referring to can now be confirmed through an examination of what its description of entering the innermost sanctuary of the truth would mean within a work attributed to Clement: "but to the stories already written he (Mark) added yet others and, moreover, brought in certain *logia* of which he knew the interpretation would, as a mystagogue, lead the hearers into the innermost sanctuary of the sevenfold veiled truth" (I.24–26, my translation). This figure clearly is a metaphor for how the interpretation of the longer gospel of Mark reveals its concealed truths, and that seems to be all that earlier commentators, including myself, have seen in it. But like "the great mysteries," this metaphor occurs in Clement's undisputed works, where it denotes the mystical experience of perceiving the immaterial cosmos and rising incrementally through it. In other words, to enter the innermost sanctuary is to begin experiencing the great mysteries of the immaterial cosmos. These are alternative ways of describing the same thing. Moreover, in Clement's elaborations of both of these metaphors, the one being initiated and metaphorically entering this sanctuary is described as having advanced well beyond the preliminary purification of baptism. These findings invalidate Jeffery's case that the mystic gospel does not fit within the history of Alexandrian Christianity.[39] More importantly, they direct us to

---

38. As quoted in Daniélou, *History of Early Christian Doctrine*, 2:247. Philo offers an explanation in *QE* 2.52.

39. Jeffery's research into the origins of Alexandria's baptism liturgy remains an important contribution; it is his framing of this research as evidence against this letter's authenticity that is invalid.

the one framework in which all of the *Letter to Theodore*'s statements about the nature, purpose, and use of the mystic gospel become fully intelligible.

The Hellenic and Jewish-Christian Backgrounds

The *Letter to Theodore*'s imagery of entering the innermost sanctuary is a mixed metaphor, combining Greek mystery initiation language with Jewish mystical reflection on the veils and sanctuaries of the Jerusalem temple. The metaphor of a mystagogue leading initiates evokes the practice at Eleusis, where persons who had already undergone the great mysteries served as sponsors for the first-time initiates and led them into the Telesterion, the temple in which the spectacle of the great mysteries occurred. The letter's reference to "the hierophantic teaching of the Lord" further elaborates this metaphor by alluding to the hierophant who makes the sacred symbols appear during this spectacle (I.23–24). And "the things not to be uttered" (τὰ ἀπόρρητα, I.22) correspond to the secrets revealed in the Greek mysteries themselves, the contents of which initiates were prohibited from divulging. The mystic Gospel of Mark does not contain these things because they are too secret and sacred to be written down (I.22). The author, therefore, is intentionally employing Eleusinian imagery of the highest grade of a secret initiation.

Whereas the image of the mystagogue draws upon the mystery religions, the notion of an ordinary person (someone who is not an authorized priest) entering the innermost sanctuary of a temple draws on Jewish and Christian sources, especially Philo and the Letter to the Hebrews. In real life, ordinary Jews were no more permitted to enter the holy of holies in Jerusalem than were the initiates in the Telesterion permitted to enter the innermost sanctuary of that temple (called the Anaktoron). The innermost shrine of a temple was normally the throne room of the god, and only cult-sanctioned housekeepers were permitted in these most holy areas. Hence the word *adytum*, which literally means "not to be entered." The author of Hebrews, however, used the image of entering the holy of holies as a metaphor for salvation, describing Christ as the high priest in the heavenly temple whose self-sacrifice has given Christians "confidence to enter the sanctuary by the blood of Jesus, by the new and living way which he opened for us through the curtain, that is, through his flesh," adding, "and since we have a great priest over the house of God, let us draw near with a true heart in full assurance of faith, with our hearts sprinkled clean from an evil conscience and our bodies washed with pure water" (10:19–22). Clement expanded on Hebrews' metaphor of Christians entering the inner shrine, using Philo's philosophical allegories about the wilderness tabernacle and the high priest as his main source. Three passages in the *Stromateis* and one in *Excerpta ex Theodoto* describe in detail who may enter the inner sanctuary and what penetrating the veil(s) entails.

Clement's Descriptions of Entering the Inner Sanctuary

STROMATEIS V.6

Let us begin with Clement's discussion in *Strom.* V.6 of the symbolism of the various objects within the sanctuaries of the wilderness tabernacle and the clothing of the high priest. As we have seen, Clement treats the tabernacle as a microcosm of the heavens and the earth. In keeping with the descriptions of the tabernacle in Exod 26–27, Clement differentiates between the outer courtyard and the two sanctuaries of the tabernacle proper. Concerning the holy place, he notes that some consider it "the middlemost point between heaven and earth," and others, "the symbol of the world of mind and of sense" (*Strom.* V.6.33.2). Annewies van den Hoek points out that Clement's own elaboration of these conceptions is concerned "less with cosmological position than with human position; people are related to that middle point as insiders and outsiders."[40] Furthest from divinity and truth are the ordinary Jews of the courtyard, who for Clement allegorically represent unbelievers (33.2–3). Closest to divinity and truth is the high priest, who alone may enter the holy of holies on one day of the year, the Day of Atonement (33.2; 34.5);[41] he represents both Christ (40.3) and the true gnostic (39.3–4). Inside the holy place,

---

40. Van den Hoek, *Philo in the Stromateis*, 124. Clement's anthropological focus produces some tension with his cosmological symbolism. From the latter perspective, the earth is included in the holy place, with the church in particular represented by the northern location of the table of the showbread, since "the most nourishing winds are those of the north" (*Strom.* V.6.35.3–4). This implies that unbelievers also reside within the holy place, an idea which Clement explicitly rejects through his anthropological interpretation, which places unbelievers in the courtyard (only priests, who represent believers, can enter the holy place). My diagram addresses this tension by using the outer courtyard to signify both the earth and the outsiders.

41. Clement refers to the high priest entering the holy of holies "on prescribed days," but it is more accurate to say that he enters "three or four times" on only one day of the year. For discussion, see Stökl Ben Ezra, *Impact of Yom Kippur on Early Christianity*, 30.

which is situated between the complete insiders and the complete outsiders, are the ordinary members of the church, whom Clement associates with the ordinary temple priests (35.3–4), who can approach the divine as near as the veil before the holy of holies but no closer.[42] This is a significant modification of the concept in Hebrews, where all Christians can enter the holy of holies through the veil of Christ's flesh.

The three groups of persons described in this allegory possess different levels of spiritual insight and knowledge. The complete outsiders perceive nothing of the divine. Clement describes them so:

> 33.3 So, then, the outer veil (κάλυμμα) is a barrier against popular disbelief, stretched out in front of the five pillars, shutting out those in the surrounding court. 4 Hence, mark you, most mystically are the five loaves broken at the hands of the Savior and multiplied for the benefit of the crowd of listeners. For large is the crowd devoting itself to objects perceptible to the senses as if the only objects in existence! 5 "Look round and see," says Plato, "that none of the uninitiated is listening. Now, such people are the ones who suppose that nothing exists except what they can hold tight with both hands, and actions and occurrences and all that is unseen are not accepted (by them) as part of what exists" (*Theaet.*155e). 6 Because such ones as these depend upon only the group of five senses, but the apprehension of God is inaccessible to the sense of hearing and to the kindred senses.

The complete insiders, on the other hand, see God and perceive the purely intellectual realities of the noetic world. Clement describes the moral and intellectual preparations that a gnostic undertakes in order to perceive these supersensible realities in the form of an exegesis of the high priest's preparations to enter the holy of holies on the Day of Atonement (Lev 16:3–4):

> 39.3 Now mark you, the "ruling" priest (ὁ ἀρχιερεύς), having undressed from his consecrated garment, ... washes himself and gets dressed in the other, so to speak, holy of holies garment, the one that goes with him into the innermost chambers (τὰ ἄδυτα), 39.4 representing, it seems to me, the Levite and gnostic as a "ruler" (ἄρχοντα) over the other priests—those priests washed in water and dressed in faith alone (μόνην) and expecting their own abode (μονήν)—he himself distinguishing the noetic things (τὰ νοητά) from those of sense perception, (and), according to a hierarchical progression, hastening past the other priests to the entrance to the

---

42. Cf. ibid., 239 n. 48.

noetic (world), to wash himself from the things here below—not in water, as he was previously cleansed on being enrolled in the tribe of Levi, but already by the Gnostic Word.

40.1 <Being> pure,[43] after having set right his whole heart, and having expanded measurably his administration to the highest degree beyond that of the priest, in short being sanctified both in word and life; having dressed in the array of glory; having received the ineffable inheritance of that spiritual and perfect man, "which eye has not seen and ear has not heard and which has not arisen in the heart of human beings" (1 Cor 2:9); having become son and friend, he is now satisfied with the insatiable contemplation "face to face" (1 Cor 13:12). There is nothing like obedience to the Word himself, who by means of the Scripture inspires fuller intelligence.

The first paragraph and part of the second (up to "having dressed in the array of glory") describe the gnostic's extensive preparations for entering the innermost sanctuary. Before he is worthy to enter, he must first surpass other Christians (priests) not only in virtue and understanding, but also in the extent of his service within the church (40.1). Clement expresses similar ideas in *Strom.* VII.1.3.1–5, where he compares the gnostic's duties in relation to other Christians with those of the deacons and elders, and in VII.10.56.2, where he speaks of the "very great preparation and previous training" requisite to receiving instruction in gnosis.

In Clement's mystery religion parlance, this stage of moral and intellectual purification that follows baptism constitutes the lesser mysteries and can be summed up metaphorically as a washing "from the things here below." Further, the words "himself distinguishing the noetic things from those of sense perception" refer to the gnostic's ability "to discern the intelligible archetypes present in sensible realities," which is acquired through the gnostic science of nature, the bridge between the lesser and great mysteries.[44] The remainder of the second paragraph describes the divine secrets, honours, and unmediated vision of God that the gnostic receives inside the *adyta*, which correspond to the great mysteries and the *epopteia* in Clement's mystery religion language.

As with Clement's description of the great mysteries in *Strom.* V.11, which I quoted earlier, the process of preparing to enter the innermost sanctuary is here specifically contrasted with the lesser purification of baptism. On the literal level, Clement is alluding to two priestly washings:

---

43. In Stählin's critical text, Wilamowitz added οὖν; we instead add ὤν.
44. Borella, *Guénonian Esoterism*, 255.

the ritual washing involved in any priest's enrolment (Exod 29:1, 4; Lev 8:6) and the washing required of the high priest before entering the holy of holies on the Day of Atonement (Lev 16:3–4). Since the other priests correspond allegorically to the ordinary Christians who lack gnosis, the former washing "in water" signifies the equally literal washing of Christian baptism. By contrast, the latter washing of the high priest "from the things here below" is "not in water, as he was previously cleansed." Unlike Christian baptism, this is a figurative washing, a thorough purification of the soul from earthly things preparatory to entering the noetic world and the eventual "insatiable contemplation 'face to face.'" That this process is completed by only a few is implicit in the high priest's status as "a ruler over the other priests" and is made explicit in *Strom.* V.6.35.5, which says that "the noetic world . . . is hidden and closed to the many." This passage comparing the gnostic to the high priest therefore further illuminates not only the mystical experience described by the *Letter to Theodore* as entering the innermost sanctuary of the truth (I.26) but also the contours of the process undergone by "those who were being perfected" (I.22). This is a lengthy process of moral and intellectual purification necessitated by the principle that only the holiest of the holy can enter God's presence.

Excerpta ex Theodoto 27

The experience of entering the holy of holies has both a present (before death) and a future (after death) dimension, inasmuch as the metaphorical ascent "to the entrance to the noetic (world)" that takes place through advancement in virtue and knowledge within the church reveals the same realities through which the soul will literally ascend after death. Clement tends to conflate the two ascents in his writings, but generally either the present or the future dimension comes to the fore. His allegory of the Day of Atonement rite in *Strom.* V.6 takes the perspective of the living gnostic. In *Exc.* 27, however, he interprets different elements of the same rite from the perspective of the postmortem journey of the soul:

> 1 The priest, when he enters within the second veil, lays aside the plate at the altar of incense. But he is wont to enter in silently, having the Name engraved on his heart, indicating the putting aside <of the body> of the, so to speak, golden plate which has become pure and light in weight through the purification of the soul,[45] on which (plate) is engraved the lustre of

45. Following the critical text of Sagnard, *Extraits de Théodote*, 112–18, which,

piety, by which lustre he was known to the Heavenly Powers and the Authorities as he was wearing the Name. 2 Now this body/metallic substance—the leaf that has become weightless—is laid aside within the second veil, in the noetic world (ἐν τῷ νοητῷ κόσμῳ), which is the second complete veil of the Universe, at the altar of incense, (meaning) at the side of the Ministering Angels of prayers carried aloft. 3 Now the soul, stripped by the power of him who has knowledge, as if it had become a body of the power, passes into the pneumatic (realms) (μεταβαίνει εἰς τὰ πνευματικά) and becomes now truly rational and high priestly, so that it might now be animated, so to speak, directly by the Logos, just as the archangels became the high priests of the angels, and the *protoctists* the high priests of the archangels. 4 Where is there still place for correction through scripture and learning for the soul that has become pure at a point where it is deemed worthy to see God "face to face" (1 Cor 13:12)? 5 But having transcended the angelic teaching (cf. *Ecl.* 57.5) and the Name that is taught in an engraved manner, (the soul) comes to the knowledge and direct apprehension of matters, no longer a bride, but already having been transformed into a Logos, and relaxes alongside the bridegroom together with the first-called and first-created (beings) (τῶν Πρωτοκλήτων καὶ Πρωτοκτίστων)—friends, on the one hand, through love, but sons, on the other hand, through the teaching and obedience, and brothers by commonality of birth. 6 Thus the (objective) of the program of training was to wear the (gold) plate and to study (it) towards gnosis; but the (objective) of the power (was) for the person to become a god-bearing (vessel), intensely activated by the Lord, even, as it were, becoming his body.

This otherworldly vision presupposes an otherwise unknown Day of Atonement practice whereby the high priest, upon entering the holy of holies, removes from his turban a golden plate that is inscribed with

---

concurring with a suggestion by Stählin, adds brackets to the phrase διὰ τὴν κάθαρσιν [τοῦ ὥσπερ σώματος] τῆς ψυχῆς [ἀπόθεσιν]. Lilla (*Clement*, 178) and Kovacs ("Concealment and Gnostic Exegesis," 435) reason that the body that Clement imagines the soul taking off must be a psychical element of the soul, noting that a material body could not enter the noetic realm. That may be true with respect to the material body, which in any event is lost upon death, but Clement does claim that all entities in the heavens possess some form of a non-material body (*Exc.* 10–16), and he argues "from the story of Lazarus and Dives" that "the soul (after death) is directly shown by its possession of bodily limbs to be a body" (14.4). In other words, I think he is referring in *Exc.* 27.1–2 to the σῶμα πνευματικόν (14.2) that the soul receives (or becomes) within the Hebdomad.

the tetragrammaton.[46] We find the same ideas here that we encountered in *Strom.* V.6, but with some differences: The second veil is the noetic world rather than the fixed sphere (unless the two are here equated); the laying aside of the body, symbolized by the golden plate instead of the high priest's regular robe (as in *Strom.* V.6.39.3, 40.3), occurs within the noetic world rather than at the entrance to it;[47] the altar of incense appears to be located not in front of the second veil, inside the holy place (as in *Strom.* V.6.33.1), but either within the veil itself or within the holy of holies, which would agree with the erroneous information in Heb 9:3–4; and the priest (i.e., the Christian) becomes truly high priestly (a gnostic) not before entering the noetic world (the holy of holies in *Strom.* V.6) but at the transition from the noetic world to the pneumatic realms (evidently the holy of holies represents only the pneumatic realms here, since the second veil represents the noetic world).

New ideas occur here as well, including the sexual and marital symbolism that Christian mystics used to describe the experience of union with Christ (cf. Eph 5:31–32), and the soul's transformation into "a body of the power" that is "animated ... directly by the Logos." Clement sometimes calls Christ the power of God (from 1 Cor 1:24),[48] so evidently he is picturing the soul becoming a body that is in some sense Christ's body and primarily controlled by Christ. This transformation in its nature constitutes a promotion in status, occurring "just as (καθάπερ) the archangels became the high priests of the angels, and the *protoctists* the high priests of the archangels." Most likely, Clement is here describing in a metaphysical way the gnostic soul's incorporation into the divine administration as an

---

46. See Clement's discussion of this plate at *Strom.* V.6.34.5, 38.6. The plate is described in, e.g., Exod 28:36; 29:6; 39:30. The theme of how "the bright impress of righteousness" manifests itself upon a purified spiritual body recurs in *Strom.* IV.18.116.2—117.2, where Clement suggests that this physical brightness functions as a "sacred symbol" that informs the celestial gatekeepers of the Hebdomad that the soul is free of passions and may proceed to a higher level.

47. We need to keep in mind that *Strom.* V.6 describes a mystic and mostly metaphorical ascent by a living human, so it might be more accurate to view the high priest's removal of his regular robe as representing detachment from the material world rather than the actual transition from the human state of existence to the angelic condition that is described in *Exc.* 27.1–3. The living gnostic is "equal to the angels" (*Strom.* VI.13.105.1; VII.10.57.4–5), but still human.

48. On this title, see Hägg, *Clement of Alexandria and the Beginnings of Christian Apophaticism*, 230–37.

angel.⁴⁹ The pneumatic realms are home to angelic beings, and the soul now becomes one, uniting with Christ, like a bride, in the process.

Eclogae propheticae 57.5 describes this transition in more detail as the beginning of an ages-long progression through the angelic ranks. In the first stage, which lasts a millennium, the perfected human is changed into the angelic nature and brought to perfection as an angel through instruction by the angels above it (μαθητεύονται ὑπὸ τῶν ἀγγέλων). In the second stage, the angelic instructors are promoted to the archangelic nature, and the souls that have become perfect angels take their place, instructing the new arrivals for a second millennium. Hence everyone moves up a step. The process repeats through the natures of the archangels and *protoctists*, for a total of six millennial stages. Upon the seventh stage, which *Exc.* 27.5 alludes to with the phrase "having transcended the angelic teaching," the soul retires (ἀναπαύσει) from all angelic service and attains "the first abode" (*Ecl.* 56.6–7), which "borders upon the Lord" (προσεχοῦς τοῦ κυρίου; *Strom.* VII.2.10.3). It now devotes itself "to the contemplation of God alone" (*Ecl.* 56.7), meaning Christ as the face of God, and becomes in a special sense a "son" and "friend" of God (*Strom.* VI.14.114.6; *Exc.* 27.5; cf. *Strom.* V.6.40.1).

These phases of angelic instruction in the divine realities of the Ogdoad are what Clement calls "the ineffable inheritance of that spiritual and perfect man, 'which eye has not seen and ear has not heard and which has not arisen in the heart of human beings'" (1 Cor 2:9). We encountered that description in *Strom.* V.6.40.1 and will encounter it again in VI.8.68.1. Principally concerned with the Son/Logos (*Paed.* II.12.129.4; *Exc.* 10.5–6), these teachings correspond to the distinctively Christian aspects of the great mysteries of Clement's school and culminate in their reward, *epopteia*, which is conceived as the consummate repose.

Although a few scholars attribute *Exc.* 27 to Clement's Valentinian source, its overall consonance with Clement's thought is clear.⁵⁰ What we are looking at is a fuller (less exoteric) description of the soul's ascent that focuses on the afterlife rather than progress made within the earthly church, and revolves around a different metaphor for the soul's separation from materiality. Both of Clement's meditations on the Day of Atone-

---

49. So van den Hoek, *Philo in the Stromateis*, 143 and n. 89.

50. For discussion of this passage, see Casey, *Excerpta ex Theodoto*, 121–26; Lilla, *Clement*, 173–81; Daniélou, *History of Early Christian Doctrine*, 2:452–53; van den Hoek, *Philo in the Stromateis*, 143; Kovacs, "Concealment and Gnostic Exegesis," 432–37; DeConick, "The True Mysteries," 260–61; Stökl Ben Ezra, *Yom Kippur*, 240–43; Osborn, *Clement*, 211; Ashwin-Siejkowski, *Clement of Alexandria*, 55–68.

Ancient Gospel or Modern Forgery?

ment ritual indicate that the human condition must be perfected (i.e., transcended as far as possible) prior to entering the innermost sanctuary, at which point everything material and sense-perceptible (including the human spiritual body, the "engraved" teaching of scripture, and the visible revelation of Christ's Incarnation—all represented by the golden plate) is left behind and the soul exists among purely noetic and pneumatic realities, becoming one with them.

Stromateis VI.8.68.1–3

The *Letter to Theodore* indicates that the *exposition* (ἐξήγησιν) of the mystic gospel leads the hearers into the innermost sanctuary of the sevenfold veiled truth. The reference to hearers (τοὺς ἀκροατάς) rather than readers implies that a teacher would expound the veiled meanings of this text to his students, which was the procedure that Clement and his own teachers used to transmit the unwritten gnostic tradition. In *Strom.* VI.8.68.1–3 Clement describes this practice as a progressive unveiling of the holy of holies:

> 1 <The wisdom> of truly perfect knowledge is involved beyond the cosmos in respect of noetic (realities)[51] (τὰ νοητά) and, beyond these, still more pneumatic (realities) (τὰ πνευματικώτερα), "which eye has not seen and ear has not heard, and which has not arisen in the heart of human beings" (1 Cor 2:9), until the Teacher explained to us plainly the word concerning these things, unveiling[52] the holy of holies (ἅγια ἁγίων) and, beyond these, according to a hierarchical progression, the (realities) still more sacred than these (τὰ ἁγιώτερα), to those most genuine and not spurious heirs of the Dominical adoption. 2 For now

---

51. Where the term "realities" appears in parentheses, the implied noun could alternatively be translated "realms." The metaphor of unveiling chambers suggests that Clement was thinking in terms of regions and their unique contents.

52. The genitive case of the participle ἀποκαλύψαντος is difficult to interpret. The parallelism with ἀναστρεφομένης in 68.1 suggests that the case is deliberate. But since the subject seems to be Jesus (τὸν διδάσκαλον), we adopt Lowth's suggested emendation ἀποκαλύψαντα instead. Except for the prefix, the *Letter to Theodore* combines the same verb (καλύπτω) with equivalent imagery of a sanctuary, so the translation "sevenfold veiled" is preferable to the less specific "covered." The veiling is temple imagery rather than clothing imagery, and involves no human, so Jeffery's perception of an allusion to the dance of the seven veils in Oscar Wilde's play *Salomé* (*Secret Gospel of Mark Unveiled*, 227–31) makes little sense, particularly in view of the fact that the Salome mentioned in the letter's second gospel quotation (III.16) is the disciple Salome (called a woman, γυνή, in 15:40), not the unnamed little girl (κοράσιον) who dances for Herod in Mark 6:22.

we dare to say (for herein is the gnostic faith) that he who is, in essence, a gnostic is knowledgeable in all things and is comprehending of all things, accustomed to a firm mental grasp of things, even in respect of what is (to us) perplexing. Of such a kind were James, Peter, John, Paul, and the rest of the apostles. 3 For prophecy is full of knowledge, as it were, having been given out by the Lord, and having been explained, again, through the Lord to the disciples. And lest any Gnosis does occur, for this reason it proves to be a unique feature of the reasoning soul trained for this cause: in order that through Gnosis it might lay claim to immortality.

In this passage Clement associates philosophical knowledge (noetic realities) and *epoptic* knowledge (more pneumatic realities) with teachings that Christ imparted to the apostles alone—the unwritten gnostic tradition (see also *Strom.* VI.7.61.3; I.1.11.3). Christ, as the pre-existent Logos, concealed these intellectual and divine matters in the scriptures (i.e., "prophecy" in v. 3) and is now revealing them to his disciples, explaining in a "plain" way "the word (of Scripture) concerning these things" (v. 2). Again, this is the same course of study that Clement means by initiation into the great mysteries. The *Letter to Theodore* refers to this revelatory teaching as "the hierophantic teaching of the Lord," and the mystic gospel depicts its transmission from Christ to his closest disciples in Mark 4 and in the description of Jesus teaching the young man the mystery of the kingdom of God.

The revelation of metaphysical truths concealed in the scriptures constitutes the "unveiling [of] the holy of holies." This is not, however, a onetime unveiling of all that pertains to the immaterial cosmos, but a sequential unveiling "according to a hierarchical progression" (κατ' ἐπανάβασιν). Clement's imagery of unveiling the holy of holies therefore implies a series of veils that divide the innermost sanctuary into a series of chambers. That idea was already implied in a previous passage we examined, *Strom.* V.6, where Clement describes the high priest putting on his special "holy of holies garment" but then says that this garment "goes with him into the innermost chambers (pl.: τὰ ἄδυτα)" (39.3).

Presumably, the chambers correspond to distinct regions within the Ogdoad. Through successive levels of teaching, Christ unveils "more sacred" aspects of divinity that exist, or at least become perceptible, within successively higher abodes. In relation to the soul's progression in the afterlife, these successive unveilings correspond to the six stages of progression through the three angelic ranks (*Ecl.* 57.5), which precede contemplation of Christ "face to face" in "the first abode," one level below Christ.

Clement's combination of the imagery of temple chambers with the unveiling of secrets concealed in the scriptures reminds us of another enigmatic passage, situated at the beginning of his tabernacle allegory. Introducing the subject of how "the prophets and the Law . . . almost the entire Scripture" conceals the truth in enigmas, he proffers:

> Now, connected with concealment is the special meaning of what is told among the Hebrews about the seven circuits around the old temple, and also the equipment on the [high priest's regular] robe, whose multicolored symbols allude to celestial phenomena, which indicates the agreement from heaven down to earth. (*Strom.* V.6.32.1–2)[53]

As van den Hoek points out, Clement used the term "circuits" (περιβόλων) in the singular to denote the courtyard around the tabernacle at 33.3.[54] Evidently Clement knew a Jewish tradition that an old form of the Jewish temple was surrounded by seven such courtyards, and thought that this tradition somehow illustrates how scripture conceals its truths. Clement does not directly divulge "the special meaning" of the seven circuits, but he hints at it by juxtaposing them with the ornamentation of the high priest's robe as described in Exodus 28. At this point he tells us that those ornaments "allude to celestial phenomena."[55] Later on in the same chapter he explains that "the five stones and two carbuncles" that adorn "the breast and the shoulders" of the high priest's robe represent, on the one hand, "the seven planets" and, on the other hand, "the various phases of salvation; some occupying the upper, some the lower parts of the entire saved body" (37.1–3). The two carbuncles (deep-red gemstones) specifically connote "Cronos and Selene," the gods associated with the highest

---

53. As translated in van den Hoek, *Philo in the Stromateis*, 118.

54. Van den Hoek, *Philo in the Stromateis*, 119.

55. The words διὰ ποικίλων τῶν πρὸς τὰ φαινόμενα συμβόλων could be translated "through various symbols related to visible things." However, the visible referents that Clement adduces with respect to the robe are all celestial. He does not have in mind the 360 bells suspended from the fringe of the robe, which symbolize the days of the year rather than visible things, or the ornamentation on the high priest's headdress, which is not part of the robe (*Strom.* V.6.37.1—39.1). The main emphasis is on the five stones (which are not actually in Exod 28) and two carbuncles on the robe itself that together represent the seven planets. The only other ornaments that might qualify are the stones on the ephod, which symbolize the zodiac as well as the sun and moon (38.2–4). However, Clement describes those stones separately as pertaining to the chest piece, so it is unclear whether he also has the fixed sphere in mind.

and lowest heavenly spheres of the Hebdomad (Saturn and the moon). In the cosmology of Clement's day, these seven "planets" were thought to orbit the earth in concentric circuits. They encompass the earth much like the seven circuits encompass the old temple. We may infer from this interesting correspondence that Clement perceives a connection between the seven circuits around the old temple, the planetary spheres, and the phases of salvation.

But how exactly do these seven temple circuits relate to the Hebdomad and the phases of salvation? As part of the old temple, these circuits would surround the two sanctuaries, including the holy place, which, as I noted earlier, is the sanctuary that Clement associates with the Hebdomad. In fact, they would comprise, and extend, the outer courtyard, which in Clement's tabernacle allegory symbolizes the place of unbelievers. So, conceived as "phases of salvation," these courtyards might seem peculiar. Surely Clement is not picturing seven phases of disbelief that precede conversion (admittance to the holy place) and the seven phases of salvation within the church. Nor would that supposition explain the implied connection between these circuits and the planetary spheres. However, these difficulties exist only when we construe the path of spiritual progression after the model of an *earthly* temple, where the movement toward the divine is from the periphery (the least holy precinct) inward. Clement's juxtaposition of the seven circuits with the planetary spheres suggests, rather, that he is picturing the old temple as a model of the celestial temple and therefore as an image of the universe. In the celestial temple, the movement toward the divine is reversed, going from the centre (the least holy precinct) to the periphery (the most holy). Viewed this way, the problem quickly disappears. The earth, at the centre of the universe, corresponds to the courtyard, the least holy precinct within the celestial temple;[56] the seven planetary spheres comprise the holy place of the celestial temple, whereas the fixed sphere and the noetic world correspond, respectively, to the inner veil and the holy of holies. But now the universe has seven clearly defined spheres above the noetic world in the part of the Ogdoad that Clement calls τὰ πνευματικά. Those spheres form another, immaterial Hebdomad, which accounts for Clement's association between the seven

---

56. Recall the difficulty posed by Clement's inconsistent association of the earth with both the outer courtyard and the holy place, which I described in n. 40. Clement's inability to include nonbelievers within the holy place requires an outer courtyard for outsiders, but from a strictly cosmological perspective, his symbolism implies that there is no outer courtyard in the celestial temple, for the whole material cosmos is represented by the holy place.

Ancient Gospel or Modern Forgery?

circuits and the seven planetary spheres. As phases of salvation they correspond to the seven stages of angelic existence.[57]

A rationale for this vision of the cosmos is not hard to find. Given the premise that the immaterial cosmos constitutes the archetypal blueprint for the material cosmos, Clement, as with Philo, likely pictured the region above the noetic world in terms of a Hebdomad and a fixed sphere.[58] Together, these two domains would constitute the immaterial heaven of the first day, as distinct from the immaterial earth, which corresponds to the noetic world. Christ, the Logos, would reside in the immaterial fixed sphere above the seven heavens of angels, each of which constitutes a chamber. These chambers are the *adyta* which Christ progressively unveils to the gnostic through his figurative interpretation of the scriptures.

For the purposes of understanding the *Letter to Theodore* it is not necessary to be this precise. It is sufficient to realize that *Strom.* VI.8.68.1–3 presents the notion of Christ's unveiling of progressively higher levels of divinity within the immaterial cosmos through allegorical explanations of the scriptures, an initiation into the great mysteries that corresponds to the gnostic soul's seven-stage progression through the Ogdoad in the afterlife. The letter evokes the same set of associations with its description of how the exposition of the mystic gospel's *logia* leads the hearers into the innermost sanctuary of the sevenfold veiled truth. This is the language of early Jewish and Christian mysticism, not a modern allusion to Oscar

---

57. My thinking on this subject has benefited from Andrew C. Itter's attempt to factor the seven circuits into his understanding of Clement's soteriological scheme. With reservations, Itter associates the seven circuits with the stages of Christian initiation from conversion through the first five stages of teaching presented in the *Stromateis* (*Esoteric Teaching in the Stromateis of Clement of Alexandria*, 39–47, 51–54). This understanding makes sense if we think of Clement's program of perfection after the model of an earthly temple and overlook (as I think we must) the conflicting anthropological elements of Clement's tabernacle allegory, which treat the courtyard as the place for unbelievers. If, however, we think of the temple as a model of the universe, Clement's soteriological scheme would begin at the outer veil (conversion), and the movement would continue upward past the noetic world represented by the holy of holies.

58. In *Decal.* 21.102–103 Philo proposed that the incorporeal heaven arose from the two most sacred numbers, the unit (monad) and the seven (hebdomad), with the former being the form for the fixed sphere of the material cosmos and the latter the form for the planetary spheres. I infer from his reasoning that Philo imagines archetypal counterparts to the Hebdomad and the fixed sphere within the immaterial cosmos, but it is difficult to be more specific. For discussion of this passage, see Arieti, *Philosophy in the Ancient World*, 303–5. For additional comments by Philo on the structure of the immaterial cosmos, see *Opif.* 7.29.

Wilde's play *Salomé* and its dance of the seven veils.[59] A comparable mystical tabernacle theology occurs in the Dead Sea Scrolls, especially the *Songs of the Sabbath Sacrifice*, which envisions the adept ascending through a series of seven temples/heavens in his approach to the divine throne and speaks of the "seven mysteries of knowledge in the wonderful mystery of the seven regions of the hol[y of holies.]" (4Q403 1 II, 27).[60]

STROMATEIS V.4.19.1—20.1

At this point it is clear that the contents of the great mysteries and of the metaphorical innermost sanctuary overlap so considerably that they are effectively one and the same thing: the immaterial cosmos. To be initiated into the great mysteries is to enter the innermost sanctuary and perceive its contents with the aid of allegorical exegesis of the scriptures. The *Letter to Theodore* brings these ideas together in one place, albeit very cryptically. The final passage that we will examine does the same thing:

> For this great crowd sanctions wisdom or justice not from truth but from whatever might please it, and it would be pleased not with different things but with things kindred to it. For as blind and deaf as the crowd is, having no understanding nor vision of a soul fond of seeing, a vision both unfazed and keen-sighted, which the Saviour alone instils, just like the uninitiated in the Mysteries or the unmusical in the choral dances, <being> not yet pure nor worthy of a sacred truth, but out of tune, disorderly, and *hylic*—it must "stand outside of the divine chorus" (*Phaedrus* 247a9-10). "For we discern spiritual matters by spiritual matters" (1 Cor 2:13). Therefore, mark you, by means of this manner of concealment, the Egyptians, by what is called by us *adyta*, on the one hand, and the Hebrews, by the veil, on the other hand, indicated in riddles the absolutely holy word—a word being truly divine and most necessary to us, stored away in the innermost sanctuary of the truth (τῷ ἀδύτῳ τῆς ἀληθείας), <by which means>, to the sacred alone, was it permitted to set foot therein; that is, to those laid up to God, circumcised from the desires of their passions, through love for the divine alone. "For it is not proper," as it seemed to Plato, "for (the) impure to come into contact with pure" (*Phaedo* 67b1-2). Therefore, prophecies

---

59. See n. 52.

60. As translated in García Martínez, ed., *Dead Sea Scrolls Translated*, 424. For discussion, see Wolfson, "Seven Mysteries of Knowledge"; Thomas, *"Mysteries" of Qumran*, 164-68.

and oracles are spoken through riddles, and the Mysteries are not shown just to anybody, willy-nilly, but only after certain purifications and prior instructions. (*Strom.* V.4.19.1—20.1)

This passage has four points of contact with the *Letter to Theodore*: the combination of mystery-initiation and inner sanctuary metaphors, the expression "the innermost sanctuary of the truth," the image of the truth being veiled, and Plato's notion that "it is not proper for (the) impure to come in contact with pure," which finds its counterpart in the saying "All things are pure to the pure" (Titus 1:15) quoted in the *Letter to Theodore* II.18–19. In both texts, sanctuary and veil are metaphors for divine truths concealed in scriptural symbolism, and the references to purity concern access to this truth. One must be pure in the sense of having consecrated one's life to God and purged oneself of worldly passions (= completion of the lesser mysteries) in order to approach this sanctuary and remove the concealing veil(s).

Although Clement mentions "the Mysteries" twice in the above passage, he only hints at their contents. His closing comment that "the Mysteries are not shown just to anybody, willy-nilly, but only after certain purifications and prior instructions" recalls his statement in *Strom.* IV.1.3.1–4, where he described "the lesser mysteries" as "preliminary purifications and explanations of the things needing to be passed on and communicated" prior to "the true gnostic science of nature" and "the great mysteries." It must be these latter mysteries that Clement is describing in the present passage—the great mysteries that follow the preliminary purifications and explanations that constitute the lesser mysteries.

A second, more illuminating indication appears in the phrase "stand outside the divine chorus" (ἔξω θείου χοροῦ ἵστασθαι). Clement plucked this phrase from Plato's myth of the chariot, which describes how souls experience true reality between incarnations (*Phaedrus* 246d–248c). Clement's implied reader should know what it means to stand inside this chorus, but the rest of us need to see the larger context. In the preceding sentence, Plato describes the "many blessed sights and many ways hither and thither within the heaven, along which the blessed gods go to and fro attending each to his own duties"; he then adds, "and whoever wishes, and is able, follows, for jealousy must stand outside the divine chorus" (φθόνος γὰρ ἔξω θείου χοροῦ ἵσταται, 247a5–10). Christoph Riedweg and Elizabeth Belfiore suggest that the divine chorus denotes the revolving cosmic dance of the stars, which Plato believed to be the gods.[61] The souls of humans can

---

61. Riedweg, *Mysterienterminologie*, 57, 58; Belfiore, "Dancing with the Gods," 205.

join in this dance if they are able. Following this statement Plato describes how, when the gods "go to a feast and a banquet, they proceed steeply upward to the top of the vault of heaven." The "chariots of the gods" make this journey with ease, but the chariots of human souls have difficulty because one of their two horses is apt to pull them downward (247b). Those that have nourished the wings of their souls through virtue (246e) and have become immortal through philosophy (248d–249c) eventually reach the top and pass outside the dome of heaven into "the region above the heaven," where, standing on the back of the fixed sphere, they gaze upon the forms (247a10–e7).

What, if anything, does this chorus have to do with the great mysteries? The answer appears in *Phaedrus* 250b–c, a passage which Clement quotes later in the same book, at *Strom.* V.14.138.2–3. Here Plato repeats the image of "the blessed chorus" while describing the vision of the forms as an initiation into "the most blessed of Mysteries." Anne Mary Farrell describes this passage as "the most explicit use of Eleusinian Mystery terminology in the *Phaedrus*." Her translation highlights the points at which the language might recall the great mysteries:

> Beauty it was ours to see (ἰδεῖν) in all its brightness (λαμπρόν) in those days when with the happy and blessed chorus (εὐδαίμονι χορῷ) we beheld with our own eyes that blessed vision (μακαρίαν ὄψιν)—we, following Zeus, and others after some other god. We saw and we were initiated (ἐτελοῦντο) into that which is rightly said to be the most blessed of Mysteries (τῶν τελετῶν . . . μακαριωτάτην). We celebrated the secret rites (ὠργιάζομεν) being complete and perfect (ὁλόκληροι) and without suffering the evils that awaited us in time to come. Complete and onefold and still and happy (εὐδαίμονα) also were the apparitions which were revealed to us (ἐποπτεύοντες) as initiates in pure light (αὐγῇ καθαρᾷ), being ourselves pure (καθαροί) and not entombed in this which we carry around with us and call a body, just like an oyster in its shell.[62]

We may infer from these two occurrences of the divine chorus metaphor in Plato's *Phaedrus* that those individuals who do stand within the divine chorus are the participants in the great mysteries of the immaterial cosmos, both the gods and the souls of philosophers who have succeeded

---

On Plato's view that the stars are gods, see Scott, *Origen and the Life of the Stars*, 17.

62. Farrell, "Plato's Use of Eleusinian Mystery Motifs," 93. See 93–96 for her explanation of the correspondences. See also Kerényi, *Eleusis*, 98–99; and esp. Schefer, "Rhetoric," 186–88.

in mastering the conflicting impulses of the soul. Whether or not the image of a procession to the top of the vault of heaven was meant to evoke the annual procession of the initiates along the Sacred Way from Athens to Eleusis,[63] it is clear that the realm above the heavens corresponds to the Telesterion, the sanctuary of the great mysteries. For Plato, the sacred objects revealed in these mysteries are the archetypes of reality—Beauty and the other forms, which he describes as "apparitions." It is Plato's likening of the noetic world to the Telesterion that reveals the intrinsic connection between the metaphorical great mysteries and the metaphorical sanctuary beyond the stars, which for Clement is the innermost sanctuary of the cosmic temple.

Clement's divine chorus, like Plato's, consists of those who have mastered their passions and thereby become ordered, musical, and non-*hylic*—what Plato calls "immortal." However, the composition of Clement's chorus is rather different: "So is he (the true gnostic) always pure for prayer. He also prays with angels, as being already of angelic rank (ἰσάγγελος), and he is never out of their holy keeping; and though he pray alone, he has the holy chorus standing with him (τὸν τῶν ἁγίων χορὸν συνιστάμενον ἔχει)" (*Strom.* VII.12.78.6). Where Plato imagines a chorus of Greek philosophers and the pagan gods, Clement pictures the fellowship of gnostics and angels. Yet "the Mysteries" they experience through prayer and contemplation are the same: the great mysteries of philosophy.

Since the *Letter to Theodore* employs the same set of interrelated metaphors (*adytum*, truth veiled in scripture, requisite purity, initiation in the great mysteries), it must presuppose the same idea that the truth unveiled through mystic exegesis is not for all and sundry but is restricted to those who have attained a level of perceptiveness, understanding, internal harmony, self-control, and purity that merits access to the inner sanctuary (cf. Philo, *Ebr.* 34.135–136). The author is not talking about neophytes but true gnostics.

CONCLUSIONS

The idea that the experience of entering the holy of holies is the prerogative of the gnostic is hard to miss in Clement's various discussions, as is the association of Christian baptism with a lower and more literal grade of initiation and purification. I find it very difficult to picture a hypothetical forger managing to discern and adapt Clement's multifaceted conception

---

63. So Riedweg, *Mysterienterminologie*, 58–60; Schefer, "Rhetoric," 187.

that the unveiling of scripture's mysteries through allegorical interpretation leads, as a mystagogue, to the visionary experience of noetic and more pneumatic realities without also noticing that this knowledge is reserved for the gnostic and concerns the most esoteric secrets of "the true philosophy," which Jesus imparted privately to his closest disciples. A gospel so described simply would not be read to neophytes, hence in connection with the rites of initiation into the church. Rather, it would be read to the Christians who have subsequently studied the encyclical disciplines, completely mastered their passions, and attained through the gnostic science of nature the ability to discern the purely intellectual and spiritual realities that exist beyond the sensible cosmos.

Everything that the *Letter to Theodore* says about the mystic gospel fits within this framework. It explains that Mark's Alexandrian gospel was expanded with "the things suitable to those studies which make for progress toward *gnosis*," which naturally implies an audience of aspiring gnostics (I.20–21; see the appendix on the meaning of "those who were being perfected"). Further, the letter tells us that the mystic gospel was "kept with utmost discretion, being read only to those who are being initiated into the great mysteries." This emphasis on how the audience of this text was carefully restricted to one group would be odd if the life setting were baptism, for in that case its audience would consist of everyone who was baptized into the church at Alexandria.[64] This sentence rather implies a select few, as we would expect if the audience consists of the gnostics, whom Clement frequently refers to as "the few" (see ὀλίγοις in, e.g., *Strom.* I.1.13.2, 3; IV.15.97.1; V.1.1.5, 7.6). The letter moreover describes this gospel as "mystic" and "more spiritual." Clement frequently uses the word "mystic" in reference to the hidden gnostic meanings disclosed through allegorical exegesis, and he uses the word "more spiritual" both in this sense and to denote the divine realities that exist above the noetic world (i.e., τὰ πνευματικώτερα in *Strom.* VI.8.68.1). And by referring to Jesus' "hierophantic teaching" and "the things not to be uttered," the letter adverts to a secret grade of teaching that parallels the secrets disclosed only to initiates in the great mysteries of Eleusis. Mark, we are told, was careful not to include these things in his mystic gospel. That fact would be too obvious to mention if this text dealt with the elementary teachings that precede baptism. But it would require comment if these unutterable secrets are disclosed through the proper (allegorical) exegesis of the mystic

---

64. Russo, "A Note on the Role of *Secret Mark*," 190, citing Jeffery, *Secret Gospel of Mark Unveiled*, 72.

gospel. Indeed, the author seems to be indicating that, although the "unspeakable teachings" (τὰς ἀρρήτους διδασκαλίας) of the Carpocratians are based on Carpocrates' interpretation of the mystic text, Mark is not to blame for this because he was careful not to include the true secret teachings in this text, only the passages that can reveal these secrets to properly prepared people. It is worth noting that the manuscript of the letter breaks off where Clement begins to expound the meaning of the gospel excerpts, which makes sense if that meaning discloses elements of the secret gnostic tradition. "All things are pure to the pure," but not all potential readers of this letter fit the bill. Most importantly, gnostic exegesis is the only setting that accords with the letter's use of the term "the great mysteries" and the metaphor of the innermost sanctuary to describe the realities disclosed by this gospel. Clement consistently uses these two conceptions to denote the noetic and more spiritual realities of the Ogdoad that are veiled in the scriptures, and he consistently stresses that these realities are the special prerogative of the true gnostic. Finally, the gospel pericope quoted in the letter depicts a disciple receiving *private* instruction in "the mystery of the kingdom of God." Clement interpreted this phrase as a synonym for the great mysteries and as proof that Christ believed that these mysteries pertaining to God ("the Unbegotten and his powers") must be concealed (*Strom.* V.12.80.3–8).

The letter is describing a text that was expounded allegorically (mystically) to the most advanced students as a means of transmitting the unwritten gnostic tradition. As the present paper illustrates, this practice is amply attested in Clement's undisputed writings. Its foundation in Alexandrian Judaism is visible in Philo's writings, especially his description of the Therapeutae, the senior members of which spent their days in the sanctuary of a special room being "initiated into the mysteries of the holy life" (τὰ τοῦ σεμνοῦ βίου μυστήρια τελοῦνται) by reading the Torah allegorically (*Contempl.* 25, 28, 30, 78). Incidentally, Philo tells us that these Jewish philosophers commonly dressed only in a linen sheet (ὀθόνη; 38), which is what the young man in the mystic gospel wears when Jesus teaches him the mystery of the kingdom of God (περιβεβλημένος σινδόνα ἐπὶ γυμνοῦ).[65] Hence, I can see no justification for treating this letter as a

---

65. See the excellent discussion of this group's clothing in Taylor, *Jewish Women Philosophers of First-Century Alexandria*, 287–302. Taylor notes that the choice of a linen sheet rather than a proper garment makes this attire both odd and distinctive, but in its simplicity the sheet makes sense as "ascetic attire" (288, 294). She further notes that a linen sheet would not necessarily be revealing and that the women wore it as well (295, 302).

work about some other practice, from some other era, written by someone else for reasons that nobody is quite sure about.⁶⁶

APPENDIX: THE LANGUAGE OF BEING PERFECTED

Although the theory of a baptismal life setting for the mystic gospel is untenable, it is worth considering one aspect of the letter that has seemed especially amenable to this interpretation, particularly since Peter Jeffery cited it in his symposium presentation as an unequivocal reference to baptism (p. 226). It is the statement that Mark created his "more spiritual Gospel for the use of those who were being perfected" (*Letter to Theodore* I.21–22). Is this language of being perfected specific to baptism? Or might it be compatible with a setting in gnostic exegesis?

Following Smith, Jeffery correctly noted that Clement describes perfection as a consequence of baptism. The same is true of illumination—hence, gnosis. In the *Paedagogus* Clement states in no uncertain terms that baptism imparts both of these qualities to the Christian: "Being baptized, we are illuminated; illuminated, we become sons; being made sons, we are made perfect (τελειούμεθα); being made perfect (τελειούμενοι), we are made immortal" (I.6.26.1). Clement also insists that both perfection and illumination are immediate consequences of baptism: "Straightway, on our regeneration, we attained that perfection (τὸ τέλειον) after which we aspired. For we were illuminated, which is to know God. He is not then imperfect who knows what is perfect" (25.1). Clement's postulate that the Christians of his church attain complete perfection and knowledge immediately upon baptism is the basis for his defence against a gnostic charge that ordinary Christians are mere children with inferior knowledge (25.1).

Clement's insistence that perfection results from baptism permitted Smith, and subsequently Jeffery, to read the letter's reference to "those who were being perfected" as denoting persons who are perfected through baptism. Yet Smith recognized other possible referents as well:

> Clement's notion of "perfection" is very hard to define and certainly makes possible the interpretation of "being perfected" as

66. I have already written a great deal about the letter's conformity with Clement's thought in *Mark's Other Gospel*, and in a subsequent study I demonstrated that the letter fits Clement's modus operandi in several unexpected ways that have seemed suspicious to non-experts. See Brown, "The *Letter to Theodore*." Jeff Jay concurrently demonstrated that the letter conforms to a previously unidentified genre of ancient letter that was used to rectify calamities produced by literary thefts like the one this letter describes. See "A New Look at the Epistolary Framework of the *Secret Gospel of Mark*."

> referring *either* to baptism *or* to some initiatory ceremony other than baptism *or* to a long process of perfection in gnosis. The last of these possibilities is clearly indicated by the discussion in *Paed.* I.6, following the passage quoted above. There Clement explains that the consequences [of baptism that] he has listed are present only potentially (28.3, "man has not yet received . . . the perfect gift") and that even Paul had to say "Not that I have already obtained this or am already perfect; but I press on to make it my own . . ." (Phil 3:12), to which Clement adds, "And yet (Paul) reckons himself perfect, because he has been emancipated from his former life, and strives after the better life, not as perfect in knowledge, but as aspiring after perfection" (*Paed.* I.6.52.2–3). Developing the thought of this passage, Clement conceives of "perfection" as a process which may affect only one or another aspect of a Christian's life . . . but when he writes of "perfection" without further specification he means perfection in gnosis (Völker, [*Der wahre Gnostiker,*] 301f).[67]

In other words, Clement thinks of the gifts of illumination, adoption, perfection, and immortality that the Holy Spirit imparts through baptism as fully complete yet—one might say—arriving unassembled, like home furnishings from IKEA. Everything you need is in these several "packages," but it might take you a lifetime or more to assemble them.

With respect to gnosis, Clement's understanding of the situation is apparent in his allegorical interpretation of Gen 22:3–4: "Abraham, when he came to the place which God told him of on the third day, looking up, saw the place afar off." Clement treats the third day as a reference to baptism ("the mystery of the seal"),[68] and interprets "the place" as the noetic world. Abraham can now perceive noetic realities, but only indistinctly, from afar. Likewise, baptized Christians can see noetic realities, but only "as through a glass." They must still metaphorically rise through the Hebdomad before they can see these things "face to face" (*Strom.* V.11.73.1—74.2).

In order to judge whether the letter's phrase "those who were being perfected" makes sense as referring to persons who are being perfected in

---

67. Smith, *Clement of Alexandria*, 33–34. In order to enhance the clarity without cluttering the text with brackets, I made the following silent revisions: I translated the Greek terms and quotations into English, used the conventional method for citing Clement, added the reference to Phil 3:12 and the words "to which Clement adds," and moved the parenthetical documentation for *Paed.* I.6.52.2–3 from the beginning to the end of the quotation.

68. See Le Boulluec, *Clément d'Alexandrie*, 251–52.

Scott G. Brown—Behind the Seven Veils, I

gnosis, we should consider how this phrase fits within the letter's two descriptions of Mark's literary activity (I.15–22), which are loosely parallel:

during Peter's stay in Rome, (Mark) wrote an account of the Lord's doings, ... selecting what he thought most useful for increasing the faith (πίστεως) of those who were being instructed (τῶν κατηχουμένων).	But when Peter died a martyr Mark came over to Alexandria, ... (and) transferred to his former book the things suitable to those studies which make for progress toward knowledge (γνῶσιν). (Thus) he composed a more spiritual Gospel for the use of those who were being perfected (τῶν τελειουμένων).

These descriptions of how Mark composed his Roman and Alexandrian gospels explain, in sequence, when, where, how, for what function, and for what audience they were written. Both gospels were tailored to the needs of particular stages of education that have different goals and different audiences. The one audience, referred to as "those who were being instructed," consists of persons whose faith might be increased through hearing the canonical gospel. Everyone agrees that these are the catechumens.[69] The other audience, referred to as "those who were being perfected," consists of persons whose knowledge might be increased by hearing the mystic gospel in the context of studies that increase gnosis. We know that the curricula of the lesser and the great mysteries served that function, so it is possible and entirely natural to equate "those who were being perfected" with the people who undertook such studies—the aspiring gnostics. That inference is reinforced by the fact that the sentence "(Thus) he composed a more spiritual Gospel for the use of those who were being perfected" appears to summarize the preceding information by restating in a different way what has already been expressed.

The idea that Christians become perfected in gnosis through particular disciplines and studies is basic to the *Stromateis*. The following remark is typical:

> Further, also, the philosophers regard the virtues as habits, dispositions, and sciences. And as knowledge (γνῶσις) is not born with men, but is acquired, and the acquiring of it in its elements demands application, and training, and progress; and then from incessant practice it passes into a habit; so, when perfected

---

69. On Clement's use of this term in reference to pre-baptismal instruction, see van den Hoek, "'Catechetical' School," 67–71.

(τελειωθεῖσα) in the mystic habit, it (*gnosis*) abides, being infallible through love. (VI.9.78.3–4)

The *Stromateis* is also where we find the dichotomy between faith and knowledge that appears in this part of the letter, as well as the imagery of the great mysteries and of entering the innermost sanctuary, so it makes sense to interpret the letter's idea of being perfected in light of how the *Stromateis* describes the perfection of gnosis. The audiences for these gospels are not two levels of catechumens but the simple faithful and the gnostics, which is the same distinction that we find, for example, in *Strom*. VI.14.111.3:

> As, then, to be simply saved is the result of medium actions, but to be saved tightly and becomingly is right action, so also all action of the gnostic (γνωστικοῦ) may be called tight action; that of the simple faithful (ἁπλῶς πιστοῦ), intermediate action, not yet perfected according to reason (μηδέπω κατὰ λόγον ἐπιτελουμένη), not yet made right according to knowledge (κατ᾽ ἐπίστασιν); but that of every heathen again is sinful. For it is not simply doing well, but doing actions with a certain aim, and acting according to reason, that the Scriptures exhibit as requisite.

We may reasonably interpret the term "being perfected" in the letter as referring to the long road to perfection that follows baptism, in keeping with the broad program of Clement's school, which van den Hoek aptly describes: "Clement depicts a gradual process that in its initial phase reaches faith through catechism and baptism. From there, through a continuous training, the faithful aim at a higher spiritual and virtuous realm, namely that of knowledge."[70]

---

70. Van den Hoek, "'Catechetical' School," 69. She notes (70) that the same program was followed by Origen (*Hom. Judic.* 5).

Path to Perfection	Universe	Church as Tabernacle	Celestial Hierarchy	Related Terms
Epopteia	Ogdoad / Pneumatic Realms / Noetic World	Holy of Holies	Christ as "Face of God" / Souls in First Abode / *Protoctists* (2 levels) / Archangels (2 levels) / Angels (2 levels)	Innermost Sanctuary / Logos, Monad, Light / Son, Friend, True Gnostic, High Priest / 8th/1st Day, Lord's Day / Immaterial Cosmos / YHWH, Golden Plate
Great Mysteries		Inner Veil		Fixed Sphere, Linen Robe, Veiled Truth
Gnostic Science of Nature (Philosophy, Cosmology)	Saturn / Jupiter / Mars	The Holy Place / Showbread	Messenger Angels / **Hebdomad** / Powers and Authorities	Gnostic Mystery of 7 & 8 / *Apatheia*, Godlikeness / Purification in Gnosis ("Not in Water") / Regular Robe / Mystic Stages
Lesser Mysteries (Encyclical Disciplines, Advanced Ethics)	Sun / Mercury / Venus			
Baptism				Clothed in Faith Alone
Catechism	Moon	Outer Veil	Disciplinary Angels	Church, Ordinary Christians/Priests
		Courtyard		Six days of Creation / Material Cosmos, Generation, Change
Conversion			Fallen Angels (Demons)	5 Senses / 4 Elements
Native Religion			Humans	Outsiders, Unbelief, Uninitiated, Impure, Discordant

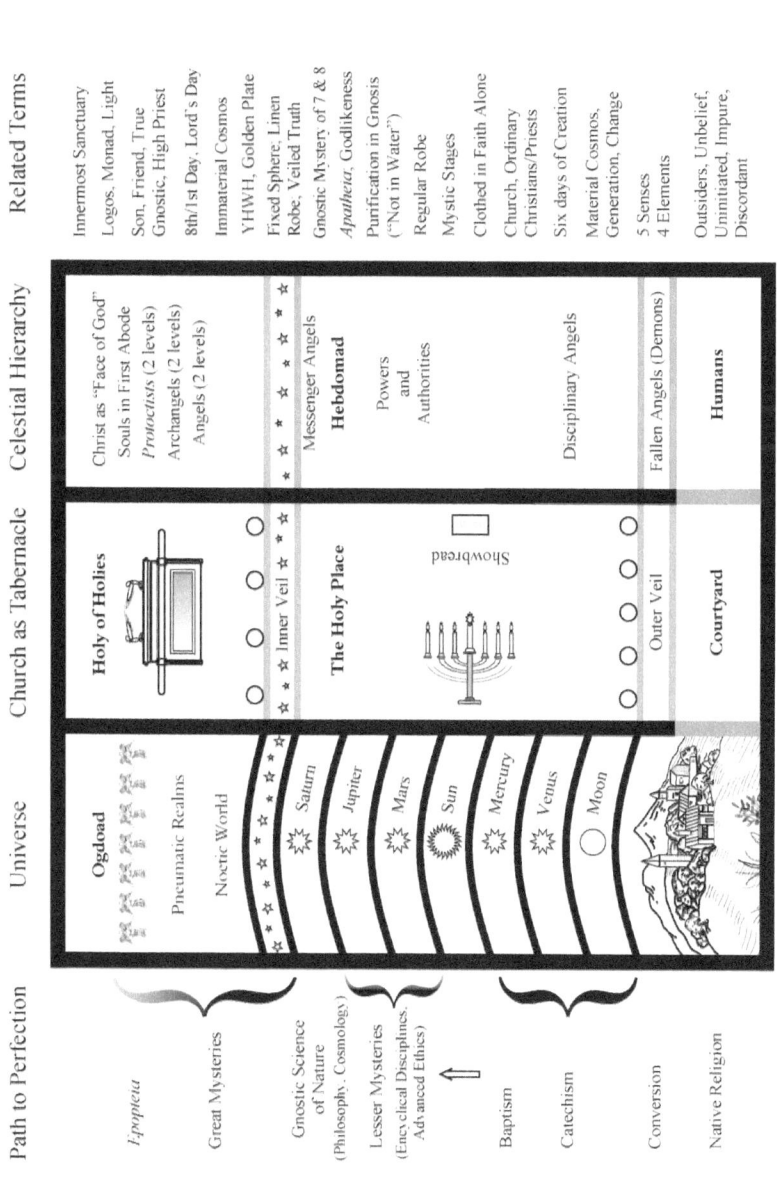

12

The *Secret Gospel of Mark* in Debate
A Scholarly Q and A

THE YORK CHRISTIAN APOCRYPHA Symposium on *Secret Mark* concluded with a Question and Answer session with four of the authors featured in this volume—two supporters of the text's authenticity: Scott Brown and Marvin Meyer, and two who consider it a forgery: Craig Evans and Peter Jeffery. After an introduction by Philip Harland, the panelists were asked five prepared questions and then the audience was invited to ask their own questions. For the sake of brevity, only a few of the audience questions are included here.

Q: *This is the first event in a series of symposia on apocryphal Christian literature. What do you see as the value of studying the Christian Apocrypha?*

Meyer: The fact of the matter is, if I could be somewhat anecdotal about this, I came to Claremont Graduate University to get my PhD and the program was a New Testament program—New Testament, early Christian Literature—and what I found rather quickly is that I more or less had my fill of a number of things in the New Testament. But in the face of all this new literature—the Berlin Gnostic Codex, The Nag Hammadi Library, all sorts of additional gospels sometimes called Gnostic

The Secret Gospel of Mark *in Debate*

gospels—this was a fertile kind of field for study. I've been studying those ever since with some attention also paid to the canonical gospels. I think the apocryphal texts are of immense significance. In fact, as a historian of early Christian literature, what I would encourage for all of us to think about is having a level playing field. That is, whatever one might think of the canon and the canonizing process, it is so enriching when we put all the texts together, including the so-called apocryphal texts, and not privilege any of the texts but try to understand that they are all texts that come out of the first centuries of the Christian movement. They all are texts that witness to the diversity of early Christianity and, as such, they all are valuable. That's why in my classes too, at Chapman—and I think the same applies to a number of us—when I do an introduction to the New Testament or an introduction to early Christian literature we deal not only with New Testament texts but we also deal with the most important of the so-called apocryphal texts— the *Gospel of Thomas*, the *Gospel of Mary*, the *Gospel of Judas* and, in fact, we also deal with the *Secret Gospel of Mark*. That allows us to have a really full and rich perspective on the variety of developments that took place within the life and the thought of the early church.

Evans: I second what Marvin said. I agree with him completely and this is rare [laughs].

Jeffery: For many centuries the usual Christian attitude was that the apocrypha don't matter because they're not in the Bible, they represent heretical points of view and so on. The orthodox faith was given to the apostles and developments since then were corruptions rather than improvements. But in the twentieth century many new texts were discovered that were lost for centuries. Plus, there's more appreciation among both orthodox Christians and everybody else for the fact that early Christianity was very diverse and there were also many quasi-Christian and non-Christian or whatever groups that were around at the same time, that were interacting with each other and influencing each other. In the apocrypha you can see, for instance, controversies that emerged—arguing about what kind of figure was Christ anyway (was he divine or human? was he more divine than human?), controversies about the authority of the apostles, the nature of the Christian community. What particularly interests me are controversies about how to do the rituals, what do the rituals mean, etc. One interesting observation that's been made is that, in the canonical gospels, Jesus' miracles tend to be acts of compassion that he does for people who are suffering, who are blind or lame or whatever. In many of the apocryphal texts Jesus' miracles are magic tricks to prove that he is God or to prove that Christians are right and the opponents of Christians are wrong. Why the shift is a very interesting question in itself. It shows a move toward more controversy and it shows a change in perception about who Jesus was and who God is—to the point that God is more interested in punishing the wrong than he is in curing the sick. Why did that happen? There are numerous issues like this that the apocrypha raise and it has indeed been enormously enriching to have access to many more texts, better knowledge of the languages, and just a greater willingness on everyone's part to recognize the diversity of the early Christian movement.

Q: *What brought you to working on* Secret Mark?

Brown: It was 1991, I believe, and I was taking a course on the resurrection narratives in the Gospels with Heinz Guenther. We all had to write an essay and my topic was the resurrection narrative in the Gospel of Mark. During that semester I noticed that there was what scholars call an *inclusio* in canonical Mark that involves the image of Jesus leading his disciples in the way to life through death. That is, in Mark 10:32–34, you have Jesus on the road going up to Jerusalem and his disciples are following him and they're afraid and amazed. And I noticed that, in the story of the empty tomb or open tomb, you've got the same motifs—you've got Jesus going before his disciples back to Galilee and you have the women afraid and amazed. So, I thought, this looks like an example of *inclusio*, which is a literary device used to bracket a section of the narrative so that the reader understands that what is in between is united in some way. I call this bracketed section of the narrative the Jerusalem section. This is what I was arguing in an essay when I just happened to read an issue of *The Fourth R*, which had a paper on *Secret Mark*; I'd never heard of it before, but I read it and I thought, "that's interesting." Right after 10:32–34 you now have another story that involves a resurrection or a raising at a tomb, and not only that: you've got both Jesus and an anonymous young man in the story as you do at the end of the gospel, and a linen sheet that plays a role. Here I'm arguing there's an *inclusio*, and in *Secret Mark* it's no longer an *inclusio*, it's a pair of frame stories. That is, it's a much more obvious instance of this narrative technique that I had been arguing existed in Mark's Gospel. I thought, "It's probably not a coincidence" and I just filed it away in the back of my head thinking maybe someday I'll look into it. And

The Secret Gospel of Mark *in Debate*

then "someday" came along when I had to decide what to do for a dissertation and I got pushed away from doing something on the Gospel of Matthew because the canonical texts had been done to death and I suggested *Secret Mark* and everybody thought that was a good idea. And so, I started reading the literature and in about a year of reading it I had a hypothesis. That's how I got started.

Evans: Well my experience was very similar to what you heard from Marvin Meyer. I was aware, of course, of some apocryphal writings related to Old Testament scripture, to New Testament, and so on. I went to Claremont, which was like a publishing factory and research beehive—very impressive. I have great memories and can compliment the faculty of the 1970s because, when I arrived, I was as green as could be and immediately it was, "OK now what are you going to be involved in?" And there was the Nag Hammadi seminar that was underway. Dieter Betz had his Corpus Hellenistica project underway. Burton Mack was interested in Jewish wisdom and had various things happening. And Bill Brownlee, one of the first scholars ever to see the Dead Sea Scrolls and recognize them for what they are, became my supervisor for my dissertation. Jim Sanders had just come over from Union and was an advocate of early Jewish literature, targums, Rabbinic literature, and so forth. And John Trever, of all things, moved into The Annex at the School of Theology Library, and he took me around and showed me his color photographs, each one framed column-by-column: the great Isaiah Scrolls with a little set of curtains in front of each frame. It was almost surreal. And so I realized I probably had a really similar experience to what Marvin described—you know what, there's a whole lot of other stuff out there and this is important for context. Just because something is outside of the canon, that doesn't mean it's blacklisted and therefore should not be studied, and therefore has no value and doesn't teach us anything. I agree with Marvin, it is a level playing field and the canon is interesting and it has its place for study and everything else, but when we're doing historically-oriented, contextually-oriented study we bear that in mind, but that doesn't control anything; and so we try to find the right generation, the right time when something was produced, and the right setting if at all possible in which it was prepared. And I think the one exhortation I would have for all of us who are interested in this field is: just because a document can't be dated to the first century, it doesn't lose value. It has value for whatever time and place it's a part of, and I throw that out as a little bit of an exhortation for my friend Marvin and for others that I think work a little too hard sometimes to take what I really think for good reasons are second-century writings and push them into the first. My point is that, if I argue that, "No, you can't put *Thomas* in the first-century," I'm not belittling *Thomas*, I'm not saying it loses value or necessarily can't possibly have anything in it that could reach back in one form or another to the historical Jesus. I'm just saying let's study these things inside the canon and outside the canon, and try to determine what they are, who wrote them, why, their intended audience, how they were understood, their function, their history of being handled and interpreted and perhaps edited and reshaped and so on, in whatever century that happens to be. The reward for doing that is a much more nuanced and contextualized understanding of Christian origins. Otherwise it's like putting on blinders and saying, "Look, I only want to read twenty-seven writings inside the New Testament. Anything else that's not in it, I ignore." From my point of view, that's very poor scholarship and is very uncritical.

Meyer: Let me just hang on for a moment to Craig's comment to show how we agree, but my take has a slightly different approach. Just as you mean no disrespect to *Thomas*, for instance, and having it in the first century, or the second century as you prefer it . . .

Evans: It's not a preference. I just don't want to slight our second-century Syrian friends [laughs].

Meyer: Well said, yes. In the same way I mean no disrespect to the Pastoral Epistles—First and Second Timothy and Titus—and other texts, possibly even the Gospel of John, in having them in the second century. What that creates is an interesting kind of continuity of texts. So it's not that we have a body of texts like the canonical texts that are all first-century; some may have to be pushed over the border into the second century. Nor should all apocryphal texts be situated in the second century and thereafter. There may be even a tendency to push them later into the second century and maybe bump them over the speed bump into the third century and so forth. We don't have to engage in that kind of approach. In fact, to be honest about it, when it comes to the first century and the second century nobody ever said (looking at their watches at the very end of what we now call the first century), "My God, I think it's about time for the second century to dawn." It wasn't that kind of a world. So I think we really agree about the need to look at all these texts and the excitement we feel at seeing all of these texts.

The Secret Gospel of Mark *in Debate*

Q: Secret Mark *is not the only text whose existence in antiquity is in doubt— the hypothetical sayings source Q comes to mind, which some scholars hesitate to acknowledge when discussing the historical Jesus and Christian origins. Given the uncertainty about the origins of* Secret Mark, *do you feel some trepidation in integrating the text into reconstructions of early Christian history?*

Jeffery: I would disagree that the text is part of early Christian history because I believe that it was written in the twentieth century. I do think it's a fascinating piece of twentieth-century literature; there's nothing else like it. It reveals a lot about those aspects of the twentieth century and communities of the twentieth century it emerges out of. I think the question you're asking . . . first of all no one wants to get caught being wrong. They're afraid to publish on something that might someday be discredited. Also, I think a lot of scholars of early Christianity think if this is not early Christian then it's a waste of time, they're not that interested. I would say they're wrong about that. And nobody lives forever, we all have pressures to advance in our field. We need to publish things that other people in our field recognize. This is a bit of a problem for me because in musicology, where my degree is, no one has ever heard of Morton Smith or *Secret Mark*. Nobody knows what to make of any of this stuff.

Meyer: My friends, we live in a world of ambiguity, and I think we know that, and in much of what we do the situation involves ambiguity as well. When it comes to dating, this is hardly a specific kind of science. We're always talking about possibilities for dating, possibilities for authorship. There are texts that have these and other kinds of ambiguities. You've mentioned Q, which is rather hotly debated. But I do believe the strongest arguments are on the side of the existence of Q, most likely in fact as a written text. But that doesn't mean that in this more-or-less ambiguous kind of world that we simply say, "Well, because we can't know for sure, we're simply going to have to push that aside." There are all kinds of ambiguities all the time when it comes to the texts that we study. Now, to be judicious about this I think it's very important to understand that there may be qualifications. That's why we have footnotes, to indicate qualifications, and there is a real need at times to make that qualification. If today has proven anything it has shown that there still are arguments on both sides when it comes to aspects of authenticity for *Secret Mark*. I didn't do any polling, I don't think any of us did, but I suspect that nobody changed his or her mind today. At least on the panel I do not think that we had any change of heart. I didn't sense any altar calls or conversion experiences or things like that and I wouldn't really expect that. In fact, I would have to say with the kind of ambiguity that we have in the argumentation about *Secret Mark*, it's likely this is going to remain uncertain for some time with people that are proponents of one side or the other. Now does that mean we should simply put it aside until some day in the sands of Egypt we find a piece of papyrus with a letter of Clement to Theodore, and here finally is the authentic papyrus text and so on? I don't think so. Perhaps I have a bit of a bias, because I do think that there is a good case that can be made for authenticity; so I do not hesitate to talk about it, but with qualifications—with the qualifications that indicate the degree of ambiguity. That's simply being honest and that simply is the thing, I think, we do all the time in the discipline when it comes to a number of kinds of ambiguity.

Brown: One thing that's always fascinated me, and Marvin's comments reminded me of it, is that so much scholarship in Christian origins deals with hypothetical texts. I'm a firm believer in Q and I believe that the scholars who try to reconstruct a certain type of Christianity based on Q are responsible scholars. I don't think there's anything wrong with what they're doing, but there are also scholars who come up with hypothetical texts that only they believe in, such as sources of the Gospel of John: the "sayings source," or the "signs source," and different reconstructions of their combination in a proto-gospel, and so on. With Q you've got a hypothetical text that we have no manuscript evidence for or any external attestation and it's quite acceptable in our guild to work with it and to build constructions of Christian origins on it. But now, with *Secret Mark* you actually have a text and a manuscript and people are quite upset that some people are actually factoring that evidence into their reconstructions of Christian origins. It just seems kind of hypocritical to me.

Q: *Is it difficult for scholars to admit defeat and embrace positions that are contrary to their own?*

Jeffery: Here's a thought experiment. You're at a major scholarly conference. You're standing in the lobby and behind you there are two people talking about you and they don't know that you're there. They're talking about something that you just published. The first person says, "Well, I think she's right, but such a plodding, boring way of being right. I could

The Secret Gospel of Mark in Debate

hardly even finish the thing it was so boring. But she's right." Or would you rather hear this: "I think she's wrong—but, man, brilliantly wrong! It's so interesting, and she knows so much. She connects things in such fascinating ways. Yeah, she's wrong, but what a great article!" Which would you rather hear? Most people would rather hear the second. The most important thing in our field is not being right but being brilliant. However, being proven wrong is one of the best indications that you're not brilliant. Therefore, most people don't want to be proven wrong. If you've published something arguing something is true, it's going to be very, very difficult to admit you spent all that time and effort on something that wasn't so. Yeah, it's very difficult for people to turn back on something they've said. In this very specific case Birger Pearson now says he once accepted *Secret Mark* as genuine and he now considers it a fake, partly because of my book. So some people will admit that they were wrong.

Evans: I would be added to that same list. As I said earlier today, I accepted Morton Smith's story the way he told it and I felt that, if some patristics scholars thought this could well be a genuine Clementine letter, that was good enough for me. I'm grateful now as I look back that I didn't invest more energy and write a book or something like that. And I'm a little sheepish because in 1994, in a book Jim Charlesworth and I co-edited, there was a chapter on various other gospels and we were reviewing them and assessing their value for historical Jesus research. And I actually wrote the part on *Secret Mark* that stated I thought it was a genuine find, but I just had reservations about dating the document any earlier than the second century. And maybe in one or two other places in passing I expressed the view that it was authentic. But I changed my mind. That happens. I never felt worried or intimidated or threatened or bothered or anything about *Secret Mark*, but I have changed my mind. With respect to Scott Brown's comment a moment ago, I don't think it's hypocritical for scholars [to work with Q but not *Secret Mark*]. Yes, of course, we have a text, you're right—Morton Smith found it in 1958 in Mar Saba, but that is really unusual. This isn't like the way all other texts are found. I don't see a big problem in inferring the existence of Q from two first-century documents, Matthew and Luke, which made use of Mark and have in common 270-some verses of material that they did not get out of Mark, and to infer from this some kind of common material. It's not hypocrisy to say I think there was a tradition—partly written, perhaps fully written, I'm

Ancient Gospel or Modern Forgery?

not sure about that—but some kind of a first-century tradition, even though I haven't found a Q text in a cave or a monastery. But the *Secret Mark* discovery is a horse of a different color. And there are other factors. I don't want to rehash them all, but I changed my mind, and it's a little awkward, and I agree with what Peter said a moment ago—who wants to lay it all on the line and then a few years later feel like eating crow and saying, "You know what? I got that wrong. I'm going to take a completely different view." That is a heavy psychological pressure.

Meyer: Maybe one caveat should be thrown out about Q because often it is said that there's no textual or manuscript evidence of this and it is indeed the case. We don't have one shred of papyrus that could be taken as part of the long-lost sayings gospel Q; but what we do have is the Synoptic Gospels. About changing one's mind or facing being wrong, I would hope that we don't change our minds too quickly. I would hope that we take strong positions with good evidence, and when we're faced with what is wonderful about the discipline—namely, other points of view—that we can be vigorous in our discussion. That's what today has been all about. We have good vigorous discussions, and if you have the good evidence, you shouldn't have to change your mind too quickly. I should be willing to argue for a point-of-view and be civil but firm in my convictions. But at the end of the day, we all are going to be mistaken about some things. We're all going to discover new things. We used to have a meeting at the Society of Biblical Literature annual gathering that was called, "How I Changed My Mind," and I think it added in parentheses "Or it Stayed the Same." Most people had some very creative things to say about what it means to change your mind. How, early on you looked at the evidence a certain way, but as time passed you decided that the evidence really was stronger on the other side and so you changed positions. There is nothing at all that is wrong with that and everything that is right about that. But I still do believe in sticking to one's position when it is a strong position and not giving up one's position willy-nilly but enjoying the fun of the debate until perhaps there is overwhelming evidence and one changes one's mind, I think that's the way to go.

Q: *Part of the resistance to this text is due to its somewhat homoerotic features (Jesus "spends the night" with a young man). Is this homoeroticism intended by the author? If not, could the text get a fairer hearing among more conservative scholars if this interpretation was dispensed with?*

The Secret Gospel of Mark *in Debate*

Jeffery: First of all, nobody in our culture can be totally impartial about Jesus. I think even people who have never been to church and have no intention of ever going to church still feel a certain weight of, "If I'm going to be the person who finally tells the world who Jesus really was, that is a really awesome responsibility." And not a lot of people are impartial about homosexuality or homoeroticism or whatever you want to call it. There are people who will say there is no homoeroticism in this text and those who see it are just seeing themselves in the text, or seeing others in the text, or seeing their nightmares in the text, or whatever it is. If this was being written up in *Newsweek* or something I'm sure they would present it as, "Was Jesus a homosexual? Radical scholars say maybe, conservative scholars say of course not." But that's really not the way the discussion is among us. In the final analysis the most we're ever going to have is a text that says Jesus was homosexual, a text which is not in the Bible. How bad can that be? I don't think it's that big a deal.

Meyer: Your comment reminded me of Albert Schweitzer who, in *The Quest of the Historical Jesus*, talks about all those who came before him and the various kinds of perspectives and biases that they had, and the way that they created Jesus in their own image, and so on and so forth. And he said, "He comes to us as a stranger." He's not a part of our world and he shouldn't be recreated as a historical person in our image. The historical Jesus was from a different world, spoke a different language, and was very different from us. And then Schweitzer would fiddle around with Jesus and the philosophy of Reverence for Life and at the end of his conversation he'd find he'd made Jesus into somebody who's a proponent like himself of Reverence for Life. And perhaps that is something that is a lesson for all of us here. That is, of course our point-of-view, of course our presuppositions, our perspectives will make a difference in what we have to say about the historical Jesus. I think of that in terms of the Jesus Seminar. There are some folks here, including myself, who have been members of the Jesus Seminar. And frankly, I've always appreciated the kind of wisdom of the Jesus that is emphasized—Jesus as a teacher of wisdom and so on. But there have been a few nervous times that we've looked at each other and we've said, "Okay now, if Jesus was this kind of wry guy who could throw out a good joke and a good one-liner and so forth, doesn't that make him into kind of a first-century university professor, kind of like us if he was secularized?" Perhaps we really have to be self-controlled about that as well. With all of this talk about homosexuality and homoeroticism in the text as if it is a steamy kind of text that is just reeking of sexuality and lust and so forth, frankly, I could care less if Jesus was straight or gay, but the fact of the matter is, there is very little here that would lead me to that conclusion. When I see some kind of description of a young man who is wearing linen and learns something about the mysteries of the evening, that sounds to me much more like the language of the mystery religions that often did not have anything to do with any kind of sexuality in terms of instructions of the evening.

Jeffery: But in Alexandria the mystery religions were full of sex.

Meyer: Yes, but look at the text, Peter. The fact of the matter is, there is nothing that is necessarily steaming with hot sexuality in this text. And I think that that particular element has been over-emphasized. Now to be sure, in some of the analysis of the text, in some of the language of Morton Smith, there is discussion of eroticism and so on—that is true. But I think if we were to take a look at the text and not impose that kind of emphasis we would see that sexuality is not a point or a strong point of the text, and we may have a rather different perspective of what is going on in that text.

Brown: My impression from reading the secondary literature is that some people see [the homoeroticism] very clearly and other people don't. When I started studying the text carefully in 1993, it never occurred to me there was something sexual going on. Nothing about the statement, "for he was teaching him the mystery of the kingdom of God," suggested to me sexuality. Now, the young man is wearing a linen sheet over his naked body and a lot of people say, "Well come on, that's overtly sexual, right?" But from my perspective you've got a young man wearing a linen sheet over his naked body in Mark 14 and he actually ends up running off naked; that never struck me as sexual in any respect. It just never occurred to me to think of the linen sheet on the young man in *Secret Mark* as being different. There is something about *Secret Mark* that encourages the imagination and I refer to it as "gap-laden narration." It's a literary technique; the story is told in such a way that you're given enough information to picture something happening but you're not told what. You're not told what the "mystery of the Kingdom of God" is, you're not told why the young man showed up wearing the linen sheet over his naked body, you're not told what Jesus commanded him to do prior to that. There are so many gaps that involve

The Secret Gospel of Mark *in Debate*

vital information that would tell us what exactly is going on here, and because those gaps are there we have to guess, we have to fill in the remainder of the story with our imaginations. So when you do that, a lot of your own interests naturally come into play. Carpocrates was one of the people who read this gap-laden story and saw something sexual. I think Clement read the same story and didn't. The possibility of reading it that way fired Carpocrates' imagination and he went off on his tangent. And today, when you look at what people write on the subject, they're often doing the same thing. Our debates over the sexual interpretation are a repeat of what's going on in the letter, which suggests to me that the letter depicts a real situation. It's very plausible when you consider how many unusual explanations there are of what's actually happening in this text: You've got some people saying it's a baptism, Morton Smith saying they're ascending up into the heavens with hypnosis, you've got the craziest idea—which is mine—that Jesus is teaching the young man the mystery of the kingdom of God, and you've got somebody on the internet saying Jesus is castrating him. You can see almost anything in a text like this.

Audience: *Are the more controversial works for which Morton Smith is known standing in the way of a fair discussion of* Secret Mark?

Meyer: When you survey the articles that Morton Smith wrote and his books, they are unusual. His perspectives are innovative. A lot of people didn't see his interpretations quite the same way that he saw them. His idea or theme of the Spirit in Christianity, for instance, he saw that in terms of the magical papyri and parchments. A number of us have seen encounters at SBL where somebody was talking about the Spirit and Morton would bring up the magical papyri because he talked about the possibility of doing a commentary on the New Testament on the basis of the magical papyri. What would the New Testament look like from that point-of-view? He thought that was a very creative and very exciting kind of approach, and it was an unusual kind of approach, not one that was taken up by many others or appreciated by many others. But I think that's part of the gift that he gave us—namely, that he did some innovative kinds of things, things that in fact are coming to light now in a new and fresh way as being worthy of more attention. It is that kind of approach that you're talking about that really is part of his gift, I think. And we can take a look at his books again—for instance, *Jesus the Magician*, a very odd book in a lot of ways but brilliant because he knew that literature very well and he put it together in terms of the historical Jesus in his own way. I know of very few people, even some devout students of the magical papyri, that would see it quite as he saw it in terms of his conclusions. There are gems in there and there's an approach that, frankly, is rather brilliant. Again, that's what we can learn from him. That's what we can carry on.

Audience: *How do you see the future of the scholarship on the* Secret Mark? *Should we continue to argue? Should we have more handwriting experts? Do we abandon* Secret Mark *or do we continue to analyze it? Can we work with what we have?*

Evans: Well, we have to prioritize as scholars. If *Secret Mark* was one of one or two items and that's all we had, we would all study it and keep debating. But we have a lot of other things to do, including unpublished texts, and scroll fragments that need to be reassembled and interpreted. I'm very concerned about all the unpublished papyri. We have sites that need to be excavated—only a small percentage of relevant sites have been excavated. Lots of texts have been found that are in storage bins waiting to be studied. The Genizah fragments, too, from Cairo. It's just a huge amount of work. There are two others here who are not skeptical of *Secret Mark* and believe it deserves to be studied. They invest their time and they're free to do that, of course, and who knows, down the road Marvin or Scott might come up with a brilliant aspect or insight that I hadn't thought of that might change my mind. Or maybe I find it rummaging around in bins of unpublished papyri. But in my mind, at this point, the warning flags are there; so, I'm going to move on and invest my time and energies in texts where there isn't this cloud hanging over them, where I know it's a first-century text for lots of reasons, and I just move on. But others have to speak for themselves and make up their own minds what they're going to do.

Meyer: And I think that really is the point. I don't think that as a guild we have to decide that we're taking this discussion and we're going to lock it up, and nobody talks about it again for awhile, or that we're all going to have to face it. I think it's up to us to decide as we look at the arguments—the arguments are out there. We've got a smorgasbord of arguments that we can deal with and we can draw conclusions. In fact, most of us have drawn conclusions about that.

Evans: We're reaching a consensus right now so listen carefully [laughs].

Meyer: Yes, and the fact of the matter is when it comes to the Gospel of Mark, on the one hand, from these two little paragraphs—the second being only a sentence—you might say there really isn't much at stake and that may be true. The Gospel of Mark, among all the gospels on that level playing field that we're talking about, is an interesting gospel. It always has been, at least in my mind, one of the most interesting of the gospels. I can put aside Matthew and Luke and John more readily than I put aside Mark for attention because of the issues in Mark, because of the questions with Mark. Whatever we can do to reach a better understanding of it is rather tantalizing; therefore, if I feel a good argument can be made for the authenticity of the *Secret Mark* fragments, I may be inclined or somebody else may be inclined to say, "Let's not forget about it entirely, recognizing the ambiguities to be sure, but lets move forward and see if it makes a difference." And in fact, in that very discussion of how possible fragments, fragments with ambiguities, may fit into a given text and may raise new kinds of issues of narration and interpretation, there may be more arguments that come out. I would say it's up to each one of us to decide what to do, but I hope there will be some that will not forget about this text.

Jeffery: Things we do not have: we do not have a fully developed statement by an expert in Greek handwriting as to the century or the part of the Greek world this script either actually does come from or falsely appears to come from. We do not have that. We do not have a robust discussion among Clement experts as to how this does or does not fit into the works of Clement. We do not have a good, serious study about Morton Smith's theory of magic. What exactly was his theory in all of its complexity? What are its sources? etc. And we could also use a good, serious, sympathetic biography of Morton Smith. Who was this man, and how was he shaped by the things he went through? While many of his friends, students, acquaintances, family are still alive, somebody who would earn their trust more easily than I would should go through and talk to them. I would very much like to see a sympathetic, well-documented biography and a study of his theory of magic.

Appendix I

Can the Academy Protect Itself from One of Its Own?
The Case of Secret Mark[1]

Stephen C. Carlson

FIFTY YEARS AGO, ONE of the most brilliant minds of the twentieth century, Morton Smith, returned from a manuscript hunting expedition to Mar Saba with photographs of a text no one had ever heard of before—a sensational, even scandalous *Secret Gospel of Mark* contained within an unknown letter in the name of Clement of Alexandria. Doubts about its attribution surfaced almost immediately,[2] and fifteen years later these doubts turned into questions of a modern forgery shortly after Smith published his authentication and interpretation of his text. Quentin Quesnell, troubled over the lack of physical examination of the actual document, argued that internal evidence alone cannot authenticate the text: "What

---

1. This paper was originally presented at the annual meeting of the Society of Biblical Literature in Boston, 24 November 2008. My deepest appreciation goes to Tony Burke for allowing this paper to be included among the York conference proceedings despite my inability to attend.

2. For example, the attribution to Mark was disputed by Pierson Parker at the 1960 annual meeting of the Society for Biblical Literature where Smith first publicized his findings, as reported by Knox, "Expert Disputes 'Secret Gospel,'" 7.

Appendix I

Smith is able to 'authenticate,' the 'mystifier' would have been able to imitate."[3] Because of these concerns, *Secret Mark* drifted into a state of scholarly limbo, until the summer of 2003 when the *Journal of Early Christian Studies* published an article about the stalemate over *Secret Mark* by Charles Hedrick.[4] In the article Hedrick rightly lamented the state of "benign neglect" over *Secret Mark* and called for a "full and impartial hearing" over the text.[5] Meanwhile, Bart Ehrman's book, *Lost Christianities*, was at the publisher's, and when it came out a few months later, its chapter exploring whether *Secret Mark* was a forgery served to rekindle interest in the controversy before a wider audience.[6]

Hedrick's call for greater scholarly interest in *Secret Mark* was heeded. Not only did it draw two responses in the same issue of *JECS* by Guy G. Stroumsa[7] and Bart Ehrman,[8] but it also independently inspired two monographs to be published on its authenticity, one in 2005 by me[9] and the other by Peter Jeffery in 2006.[10] Both of these books make the case that *Secret Mark* is a twentieth-century fake and implicate Smith himself in its creation, but they disagree as to the motive and as to whether *Secret Mark* is a "hoax" or "forgery," respectively.

Nevertheless, the renewed interest over *Secret Mark* had not been one-sided. Earlier in 2005, Scott Brown published an updated version of his dissertation on *Secret Mark*, arguing that Smith is not the forger and that the text was even composed by none other than the author of our canonical Mark.[11] The key to this defense of Smith was to question his competence. In particular, Brown argued that Smith lacked the expertise in Clement of Alexandria to have composed the letter: "The people who foster the romantic notion that Smith was capable of imitating the handwriting and the aged appearance of an eighteenth-century manuscript have not produced any supporting evidence, let alone demonstrated that Smith

---

3. Quesnell, "The Mar Saba Clementine," 56 n. 16.
4. Hedrick, "The Secret Gospel of Mark."
5. Ibid., 145.
6. Ehrman, *Lost Christianities*, 67–89.
7. Stroumsa, "Comments on Charles Hedrick's Article."
8. Ehrman, "Response to Charles Hedrick's Stalemate."
9. Carlson, *Gospel Hoax*, explicitly acknowledging that this article was a trigger for my interest in *Secret Mark* (xvii).
10. Jeffery, *Secret Gospel of Mark Unveiled*. Jeffery also acknowledged the role of the *JECS* articles in his own research (ix).
11. Brown, *Mark's Other Gospel*.

had developed any expertise in Clement prior to 1958."[12] Indeed, Brown has denied that Smith had much of an interest in Clement, claiming that "Smith published nothing on Clement prior to the 1970s and showed little interest in patristics in the period leading up to discovery."[13] If Brown's claims are correct, the case for Smith's composition of the text would be seriously flawed; however, a close inspection of Smith's writings published before the summer of 1958 shows these claims to be ill-founded. For example, Smith's interest in patristics is readily apparent from just reading the titles in his bibliography: Smith wrote twice on Isidore of Pelusium as well as once on the *Philosophumena* by Hippolytus of Rome.[14] As for Clement of Alexandria in particular, Smith published an article called "The Image of God" in March 1958 (just a few months before his fateful visit to Mar Saba) which cites Clement of Alexandria four times, one of them involving Clement of Alexandria's notion of secrecy.[15]

Just recently in 2008, new evidence has come to light showing that Smith's interest in Clement of Alexandria had been deeper than his published writings suggest. In particular, Guy Stroumsa has edited and published over a hundred private letters between Morton Smith and Gershom Scholem.[16] Despite Brown's claim that Smith's classical Greek was poor and that he had "little interest in patristics," Smith told Scholem in a letter dated August 17, 1948:

> Last February I came back to Harvard to work for the degree of Doctor Theology [sic], for which I am to make a special study of the New Testament and of Church history down to 400 and, for a thesis, probably produced [sic] under Jaeger's direction, an edition of one of the minor works of Gregory of Nyssa. For the past six months I have been working on the background—giving

---

12. Ibid., 73.

13. Ibid., 38.

14. See Carlson, *Gospel Hoax*, 75. Smith's articles include: "The Manuscript Tradition of Isidore of Pelusium"; "An Unpublished Life of St. Isidore of Pelusium"; and "The Description of the Essenes in Josephus and the Philosophumena."

15. Smith, "The Image of God," 507, reprinted in Smith, *Studies in the Cult of Yahweh*, 1:415. See also Carlson, *Gospel Hoax*, 9–10, 63–64, 71–72, and 75–76.

16. Stroumsa, ed., *Morton Smith and Gershom Scholem, Correspondence 1945–1982*. The exchange between Smith and Scholem is annotated with helpful information, some of which is contributed by Allan Pantuck. There are errors, however. For example, p. 9 n. 43 erroneously states that "Smith's father was H. J. Smith," but, according to census records, Henry Smith was Morton's grandfather, and Smith's father was named Rupert Smith.

Appendix I

> half my time to classical literature and half to the early Fathers, especially Clement of Alexandria.[17]

Indeed, Smith's interest in Clement of Alexandria may have gone back much earlier, to his time with Scholem in Jerusalem during World War II. In the preface to the first edition of his *Major Trends in Jewish Mysticism*, dated May 1941, Scholem thanked Smith, "a research student at the University," for reading the final manuscript.[18] Clement of Alexandria is mentioned in the notes three times, one of them associated with *Hagigah* 2.1.[19] This passage from the *Mishnah*, which states that teaching about forbidden sexual relations of Lev 18 should be limited,[20] would continue to fascinate Smith for years. In his ThD dissertation, *Tannaitic Parallels to the Gospels* (1951),[21] Smith associated this passage with "the mystery of the kingdom of God" in Mark 4:11. Later, in his "Image of God" article, Smith connected it with Clement's notions of secrecy (which, interestingly, Scholem did not). Finally, in the summer of 1958, Smith would return from Mar Saba with a never-before-seen letter ascribed to Clement of Alexandria talking about secrecy and quoting a secret gospel of Mark that links "the mystery of the kingdom of God" with a youth who spent the night with Jesus.

The other half of Smith's research time at Harvard involved classical literature, which belies Brown's other claim about Smith's Greek that "[t]hose most proficient in classical Greek tended to think that the letter surpassed his ability."[22] Those who knew Smith knew better. For example, Shaye J. D. Cohen wrote of Smith for his scholarly obituary: "Smith was a man who worked comfortably in Greek, Latin, and Hebrew, and had a good working knowledge of Syriac."[23]

Smith's correspondence also enlightens our understanding of Smith's expertise in paleography. After Smith passed his examinations at Harvard, he wrote to Scholem on January 6, 1950, that "I must begin work on a thesis, but the subject has not yet been decided, and as it will probably be the edition of some classical text, I shall have in any case to begin by

---

17. Letter 11 of 17 August 1948 (Stroumsa, *Correspondence*, 27–28).
18. Scholem, *Major Trends in Jewish Mysticism*, xxvii; see also Smith, *Secret Gospel*, 7.
19. Scholem, *Major Trends*, 355 n. 30, 367 n. 121, and 420 n. 57.
20. *The Mishnah*, trans. Danby, 212–13.
21. Smith, *Tannaitic Parallels to the Gospels*.
22. Brown, *Mark's Other Gospel*, 13.
23. Cohen, "In Memoriam Morton Smith," 279.

learning something about palaeography."²⁴ Thus, Smith had already begun to acquire expertise in paleography a full eight-and-half years before his second visit to Mar Saba from which he returned with photographs of *Secret Mark*. Moreover, Smith's mastery in early-modern Greek paleography is evident in the notes he published in 1956 from his manuscript-hunting expedition to Greece.²⁵

Moreover, obtaining the document itself, of which only photographs remain, was well within the capabilities of a twentieth-century book collector like Smith. It was written on a modern medium: on the blank pages of a popular seventeenth-century edition of the genuine epistles of Ignatius which can still be bought on the used book market for about $300.²⁶ Furthermore, the provenance of the writing cannot exclude a modern composition: there is no evidence that either the book or the handwritten supplement containing *Secret Mark* had been present at Mar Saba prior to Smith's visit. Indeed, neither one fits the literary interests of the monastery.²⁷

Accordingly, the case for the antiquity of *Secret Mark* cannot be made on Smith's supposed incompetence. The various technical details required to produce *Secret Mark* were well within his documented abilities, however daunting that may appear to the average scholar. Moreover, much about *Secret Mark* seems too good to be true for such a tiny text: it promises to contain two new gospel fragments, the only direct evidence of a letter from Clement, a new *testimonium* on the original of the Gospel of Mark, and additional material about an obscure second-century Christian sect, the Carpocratians. But this leaves us with Quesnell's conundrum: what can we do when the authenticator of a new text is also good enough to fabricate the text?

One approach is to do what Bruce Metzger did. He was able to identify Paul R. Coleman-Norton as the one who hoaxed the "Amusing *Agraphon*."²⁸ Coleman-Norton claimed that, when he was in Morocco during World War II, he came across a text, into which had been written a brief dialog between Jesus and a disciple. The disciple asked Jesus

---

24. Letter 23 of 6 January 1950 (Stroumsa, *Correspondence*, 42).

25. Smith, "Σύμμεικτα." As early as 1950, Smith had been planning to visit Greece to photograph Greek manuscripts; see Smith, letter 26 of 4 December 1950 (Stroumsa, *Correspondence*, 49–50).

26. Carlson, *Gospel Hoax*, 36, 45.

27. Ibid., 36–39.

28. Metzger, "Literary Forgeries and Canonical Pseudepigrapha"; and Metzger, *Reminiscences of an Octogenarian*, 136–39.

Appendix I

what would happen to people without teeth when they were cast in that place "where there will be weeping and gnashing of teeth." According to Coleman-Norton, Jesus retorted: "O thou of little faith . . . teeth will be provided."[29] Very funny, but how did Metzger show that it was a fake? Metzger knew that Coleman-Norton had been telling the denture joke for years before his purported discovery. People do not possess the contents of their supposed discovery before they discover it. The same can be said of *Secret Mark*. Its punch-line is the linkage between the "mystery of the kingdom of God" and a young man spending the night with Jesus, imbedded within a letter ascribed to Clement of Alexandria discussing secrecy. As disparate as these concepts may seem, all of them were linked in Smith's own writings, particularly in his dissertation and his "Image of God" article, before his purported discovery of *Secret Mark*.[30]

Even if we were not so lucky as we are in the cases of Paul Coleman-Norton and Morton Smith to show that they knew of their supposed discoveries ahead of time, it is still possible to detect a literary fake, but it takes time. All of us are creatures of our own time; neither the scholar nor the faker can escape the prejudices of the present. As Anthony Grafton in his survey of Western literary forgeries explained:

> If any law holds for all forgery, it is quite simply that any forger, however deft, imprints the pattern and texture of his own period's life, thought and language on the past he hopes to make seem real and vivid. But the very details he deploys, however deeply they impress his immediate public, will eventually make his trickery stand out in bold relief, when they are observed by later readers who will recognize the forger's period superimposed on the forgery's. Nothing becomes obsolete like a period vision of an older period.[31]

We are now fifty years from the time *Secret Mark* was unveiled upon the world. If *Secret Mark* is not a work of antiquity but a product of the mid-twentieth century, then it ought to exhibit features that most make sense for the time of its actual origin. Indeed, this is the case for *Secret Mark*, as numerous anachronisms that fit a mid-twentieth-century origin for the text have been identified: the excessive avoidance of *hapax legomena*,[32] the

---

29. Coleman-Norton, "An Amusing *Agraphon*," 443 n. 18.
30. Carlson, *Gospel Hoax*, 71–72.
31. Grafton, *Forgers and Critics*, 67.
32. Criddle, "On the Mar Saba Letter."

iodized salt metaphor,[33] the euphemism "spent the night with someone,"[34] the suggestion that Jesus was arrested in a public garden on a vice charge,[35] the outdated conception of Mark's compositional technique as splicing rather than intercalation,[36] the Anglican baptismal liturgy inherent in *Secret Mark*'s nocturnal initiation,[37] a homoerotic subculture,[38] and the mystery of the seven veils from Oscar Wilde's *Salome*.[39] To be sure, spotting some of these relies on extra-disciplinary expertise; for example, the liturgical anachronisms discerned by Peter Jeffery or the statistical anomaly in the *hapax legomena* detected by Andrew Criddle. Nevertheless, the main reason why so many of these anachronisms have now become apparent is that the mid-twentieth century is becoming more and more alien to us.

To be sure, Scott Brown has been attempting to answer these and other problems in Smith's text. For this paper, I have the space to focus on one of those attempts. Concerning my case that the connection between *Secret Mark* and the naked, fleeing youth of Mark 14:51–52 anachronistically reflects a mid-twentieth century legal situation, Brown responds as follows:

> [Carlson's] attempt to assign longer Mark to "a specific moment within a changing twentieth-century legal landscape that peaked in the 1950s" . . . is predicated on a patently false statement about what "*Secret Mark* easily conjures up to the twentieth-century reader." Among the hundreds of twentieth-century discussions of "secret" Mark that exist in print and on the internet, I have yet to come across the observation that LGM 1 implies that "Jesus was arrested for soliciting a homoerotic encounter in a public garden."[40]

Now, I cannot speak to the identity of the "hundreds of twentieth-century discussions . . . in print and on the internet" that Brown had researched, so I do not know if he happened to have overlooked the online article "Was Jesus Gay?" from 1999 which goes over Smith's *Secret Gospel* and, in connection with Mark 14:51–52, makes the following comment: "If a

33. Carlson, *Gospel Hoax*, 59–61.
34. Ibid., 66–68.
35. Ibid., 69–71.
36. Carlson, "Reply to Scott Brown."
37. Jeffery, *The Secret Gospel of Mark Unveiled*, 70.
38. Ibid., 225.
39. Ibid., 226–39.
40. Brown, "Factualizing the Folklore," 320.

modern man were caught in a park with a naked youth, he would have quite some explaining to do to the vice squad."[41] I do know, however, that Brown should have mentioned the evidence published in his own article in *JBL* that this observation about the fleeing naked youth of Mark 14:51 had already been made—by none other than Smith himself: "Smith could himself chuckle at the young man's naked flight, and in lectures would sometimes caption this pericope 'Cops Arrest Rabbi in Park with Naked Teenager.'"[42] As a result, I have to thank Brown for providing this wonderful piece of counter-evidence to his own claim that my statement is "patently false." I wish I had it for my book. Not only that but it also nicely exhibits Smith's sense of humor, further supporting the hoax motive for faking the text.

Because we are only able to see clearly these anachronisms with the passage of time, we should not be too hard on Smith's contemporaries for missing them. In fact, many were able to tell that something was wrong almost immediately and doubts have lingered ever since. In particular, Quentin Quesnell called the authenticity of *Secret Mark* into question just two years after Smith's publication in 1973 and demanded a physical examination of the original document.[43] This lack of physical examination continued to trouble scholars—for example, John Dominic Crossan, who wrote with some frustration: "*The authenticity of a text can only be established by the consensus of experts who have studied the original document under scientifically appropriate circumstances.* Twenty-five years after the original discovery this has not yet happened and that casts a cloud over the entire proceedings."[44] As a result, discussion of its authenticity was routine whenever *Secret Mark* was cited. Indeed, some scholars have refused to work with the text out of prudence even when it could help their case.[45] As such, the scholarly reception of *Secret Mark* resembles that of the Irenaeus fragments forged by Christoph Pfaff at the beginning of the eighteenth century. Like *Secret Mark*, doubts over the faked fragments broke out al-

---

41. Greene, "Was Jesus Gay?" The site is dated 1996–2011, but the comments on this page begin in 1999.

42. Brown, "Question of Motive," 360.

43. Quesnell, "Mar Saba Clementine." Smith answered Quesnell the following year: "On the Authenticity"; and Quesnell's rejoinder is "Reply to Morton Smith."

44. Crossan, *Four Other Gospels*, 68 (emphasis original).

45. For example, Haren, "The Naked Young Man," 531 n. 23: "The so-called Secret Gospel of Mark would portray Lazarus so dressed ... but its evidence does not seem worth adducing in view of the doubt that must be entertained ... about the authenticity of the letter of Clement in which it is communicated."

most immediately, and like *Secret Mark* it took decades for them to be conclusively attributed to their true author. Nevertheless, progress has been made, for it took almost four times longer to settle the controversy over the Pfaff fragments than it has for *Secret Mark*.[46]

The case of *Secret Mark* has engendered many mysteries, but it answers one puzzle well: can the academy protect itself from one of its own, even one of its most brilliant members? As the events of the past few years indicate, the answer is yes, the academy can protect itself because it has something on its side that the faker lacks: the passage of time. As time passes on, we are able to stand on our predecessors' shoulders and see the past better than even the sharpest minds of the previous generation.

---

46. See Harnack, *Die Pfaff'schen Irenäus-Fragmente*, summarized in Carlson, *Gospel Hoax*, 16.

Appendix 2

The *Letter to Theodore*

I ¹ἐκ τῶν ἐπιστολῶν τοῦ ἁγιωτάτου Κλήμεντος τοῦ στρωματέως· Θεοδώρῳ.

²καλῶς ἐποίησας ἐπιστομίσας τὰς ἀρρήτους διδασκαλίας τῶν Καρποκρατιανῶν.
³οὗτοι γὰρ οἱ προφητευθέντες "ἀστέρες πλανῆται," οἱ ἀπὸ τῆς στενῆς τῶν ἐντολῶν
⁴ὁδοῦ εἰς ἀπέρατον ἄβυσσον πλανώμενοι τῶν σαρκικῶν καὶ ἐνσωμάτων ἁμαρτιῶν.

⁵πεφυσιωμένοι γὰρ εἰς γνῶσιν, ὡς λέγουσιν, "τῶν βαθέων τοῦ Σατανᾶ," λανθάνουσιν εἰς

⁶"τὸν ζόφον τοῦ σκότους," τοῦ ψεύδους, ἑαυτοὺς ἀπορρίπτοντες· καὶ καυχώμενοι ⁷ἐλευθέρους εἶναι, δοῦλοι γεγόνασιν ἀνδραποδώδων ἐπιθυμιῶν. τούτοις οὖν ⁸ἀντιστατέον πάντῃ τε καὶ πάντως, εἰ γὰρ καί ει ἀληθὲς λέγοιεν οὐδ' οὕτω

⁹συμφωνοίη ἄν αὐτοῖς ὁ τῆς ἀληθείας ἐραστής. οὐδὲ γὰρ πάντα τἀληθῆ ἀλήθεια. οὐδὲ
¹⁰τὴν κατὰ τὰς ἀνθρωπίνας δόξας φαινομένην ἀλήθειαν προκριτέον τῆς

I ¹From the letters of the most holy Clement, the author of the *Stromateis*. To Theodore.

²You did well in silencing the unspeakable teachings of the Carpocratians.
³For these are the "wandering stars" [Jude 13] referred to in the prophecy, who wander from the
⁴narrow road of the commandments into a boundless abyss of the carnal and bodily sins.

⁵For, priding themselves in knowledge, as they say, "of the deep things of Satan" [Rev 2:24], they do not know that they are casting themselves away into
⁶"the nether world of the darkness" [Jude 13] of falsity, and, boasting ⁷that they are free, they have become slaves of servile desires. Such men ⁸are to be opposed in all ways and altogether. For, even if they should say something true, one who
⁹loves the truth should not, even so, agree with them. For not all true things are the truth, nor
¹⁰should that truth which merely seems true according to human opinions be preferred to the

The Letter to Theodore

¹¹ἀληθοῦς ἀληθείας τῆς κατὰ τὴν πίστιν. τῶν τοίνυν θρυλουμένων περὶ τοῦ θεοπνεύστου
¹²κατὰ Μᾶρκον εὐαγγελίου, τὰ μὲν ψεύδεται παντελῶς, τὰ δέ, εἰ καὶ ἀληθῆ τινα
¹³περιέχει, οὐδ' οὕτως ἀληθῶς παραδίδοται, συγκεκραμένα γὰρ τἀληθῆ
¹⁴τοῖς πλάσμασι παραχαράσσεται ὥστε—τοῦτο δὴ τὸ λεγόμενον—"καὶ τὸ
¹⁵ἅλας μωρανθῆναι." ὁ γοῦν Μᾶρκος, κατὰ τὴν τοῦ Πέτρου ἐν Ῥώμῃ διατριβήν,
¹⁶ἀνέγραψε τὰς πράξεις τοῦ Κυρίου, οὐ μέντοι πάσας ἐξαγγέλλων, οὐδὲ μὴν τὰς
¹⁷μυστικὰς ὑποσημαίνων ἀλλ' ἐκλεγόμενος ἃς χρησιμωτάτας ἐνόμισε πρὸς
¹⁸αὔξησιν τῆς τῶν κατηχουμένων πίστεως. τοῦ δὲ Πέτρου μαρτυρήσαντος, παρῆλθεν
¹⁹εἰς Ἀλεξάνδρειαν ὁ Μᾶρκος, κομίζων καὶ τὰ [τ] αὐτοῦ καὶ τὰ τοῦ Πέτρου
²⁰ὑπομνήματα ἐξ ὧν μεταφέρων εἰς τὸ πρῶτον αὐτοῦ βιβλίον τὰ τοῖς προκόπτουσι
²¹περὶ τὴν γνῶσιν κατάλληλα συνέταξε πνευματικώτερον
²²εὐαγγέλιον εἰς τὴν τῶν τελειουμένων χρῆσιν οὐδέπω ὅμως αὐτὰ τὰ ἀπόρρητα
²³ἐξωρχήσατο, οὐδὲ κατέγραψε τὴν ἱεροφαντικὴν διδασκαλίαν τοῦ
²⁴Κυρίου, ἀλλὰ ταῖς προγεγραμμέναις πράξεσιν ἐπιθεὶς καὶ ἄλλας, ἔτι
²⁵προσεπήγαγε λόγιά τινα ὧν ἠπίστατο τὴν ἐξήγησιν μυσταγωγήσειν τοὺς ἀκροατὰς
²⁶εἰς τὸ ἄδυτον τῆς ἑπτάκις κεκαλυμμένης ἀληθείας. οὕτως οὖν
²⁷προπαρεσκεύασεν, οὐ φθονερῶς οὐδ' ἀπροφυλάκτως, ὡς ἐγὼ οἶμαι. καὶ

¹¹true truth, that according to the faith. Now of the things they keep saying about the divinely inspired
¹²Gospel according to Mark, some are altogether falsifications, and others, even if they do contain some true
¹³elements, nevertheless are not reported truly. For the true things being mixed
¹⁴with inventions, are falsified, so that, as the saying goes, even the
¹⁵salt loses its savor [Matt 5:13/Luke 14:34]. As for Mark, then, during Peter's stay in Rome
¹⁶he wrote an account of the Lord's doings, not, however, declaring all of them, nor yet hinting at the
¹⁷secret ones, but selecting what he thought most useful for increasing the
¹⁸faith of those who were being instructed. But when Peter died a martyr, Mark came
¹⁹over to Alexandria, bringing both his own notes and those of Peter,
²⁰from which he transferred to his former book the things suitable to whatever makes for progress
²¹toward knowledge. Thus he composed a more spiritual
²²Gospel for the use of those who were being perfected. Nevertheless, he yet did not divulge the things not to be uttered,
²³nor did he write down the hierophantic teaching of
²⁴the Lord, but to the stories already written he added yet others and, moreover,
²⁵brought in certain sayings of which he knew the interpretation would, as a mystagogue, lead the hearers into the
²⁶innermost sanctuary of that truth hidden by seven veils. Thus, in sum,
²⁷he prepared matters, neither grudgingly nor incautiously, in my opinion, and,

309

Appendix 2

²⁸ἀποθήσκων κατέλιπε τὸ αὐτοῦ σύγγραμμα τῇ ἐκκλησίᾳ τῇ
II ¹ἐν Ἀλεξανδρείᾳ ὅπου εἰσέτι νῦν ἀσφαλῶς εὖ μάλα τηρεῖται, ἀναγινωσκόμενον
²πρὸς αὐτοὺς μόνους τοὺς μυουμένους τὰ μεγάλα μυστήρια. τῶν δὲ
³μιαρῶν δαιμόνων ὄλεθρον τῷ τῶν ἀνθρώπων γένει πάντοτε μηχανώντων, ὁ
⁴Καρποκράτης ὑπ' αὐτῶν διδαχθεὶς καὶ ἀπατηλοῖς τέχναις χρησάμενος,
⁵οὕτω πρεσβύτερόν τινα τῆς ἐν Ἀλεξανδρείᾳ ἐκκλησίας κατεδούλωσεν
⁶ὥστε παρ' αὐτοῦ ἐκόμισεν ἀπόγραφον τοῦ μυστικοῦ εὐαγγελίου, ὃ καὶ
⁷ἐξηγήσατο κατὰ τὴν βλάσφημον καὶ σαρκικὴν αὐτοῦ δόξαν, ἔτι
⁸δὲ καὶ ἐμίανε, ταῖς ἀρχράντοις καὶ ἁγίαις λέξεσιν ἀναμιγνὺς ἀναιδέστατα

⁹ψεύσματα. τοῦ δὲ κράματος τούτου ἐξαντλεῖται τὸ τῶν Καρποκρατιανῶν
¹⁰δόγμα. τούτοις οὖν, καθὼς καὶ προείρηκα, οὐδέποτε εἰκτέον,
¹¹οὐδὲ προτείνουσιν αὐτοῖς τὰ κατεψευσμένα συγχωρητέον τοῦ Μάρκου
¹²εἶναι τὸ μυστικὸν εὐαγγέλιον, ἀλλὰ καὶ μεθ' ὅρκου ἀρνητέον. "οὐ γὰρ ἅπασι πάντα
¹³ἀληθῆ λεκτέον." διὰ τοῦτο ἡ σοφία τοῦ Θεοῦ διὰ Σολομῶντος

¹⁴παραγγέλλει, "ἀποκρίνου τῷ μερῷ ἐκ τῆς μωρίας αὐτοῦ," πρὸς τοὺς τυφλοὺς τὸν
¹⁵νοῦν τὸ φῶς τῆς ἀληθείας δεῖν ἐπικρύπτεσθαι διάσκουσα, αὐτίκα

¹⁶φησί, "τοῦ δὲ μὴ ἔχοντος ἀρθήσεται," καὶ "ὁ μωρὸς ἐν σκότει πορευέσθω." ἡμεῖς

¹⁷δὲ "υἱοὶ φωτός" ἐσμεν, πεφωτισμένοι τῇ ἐξ ὕψους ἀνατολῇ τοῦ πνεύματος

²⁸dying, he left his composition to the church
II ¹in Alexandria, where it even yet is most carefully guarded, being read
²only to those who are being initiated into the great mysteries. But since the
³foul demons are always devising destruction for the race of men,
⁴Carpocrates, instructed by them and using deceitful arts, so enslaved
⁵a certain presbyter of the church in Alexandria
⁶that he got from him a copy of the secret Gospel, which he
⁷both interpreted according to his blasphemous and carnal doctrine and,
⁸moreover, polluted, mixing with the spotless and holy words utterly shameless

⁹lies. From this mixture is drawn off the teaching of the Carpocratians.
¹⁰To them, therefore, as I said above, one must never give way;
¹¹nor, when they put forward their falsifications, should one concede that the

¹²secret Gospel is by Mark, but should even deny it on oath. For, "Not all
¹³true things are to be said to all men" [Philo, QG IV,67]. For this reason the Wisdom of God, through Solomon,
¹⁴advises, "Answer the fool from his folly" [Prov 26:5], teaching that

¹⁵the light of the truth should be hidden from those who are mentally blind. Again
¹⁶it says, "From him who has not shall be taken away" [Matt 25:29/Luke 19:26], and, "Let the fool walk in darkness" [Eccl 2:14]. But we
¹⁷are "children of light" [1 Thess 5:5], having been illuminated by "the dayspring" of the spirit

The Letter to Theodore

[18] of the Lord "from on high," and "Where the Spirit of the Lord is," it says, "there is liberty" [2 Cor 3:17], for "All [19] things are pure to the pure" [Titus 1:15].

To you, therefore, I shall not hesitate to answer the questions you have asked, [20] refuting the falsifications by the very words of the Gospel. [21] For example, after, "And they were in the road going up to Jerusalem" [Mark 10:32], and what [22] follows, until "After three days he shall arise" [Mark 10:34], the secret Gospel brings the following material word for word:

[23] "And they come into Bethany. And a certain woman whose brother [24] had died was there. And, coming, she prostrated herself before Jesus and says to him, 'Son [25] of David, have mercy on me.' But the disciples rebuked her. And Jesus, being angered, [26] went off with her into the garden where the tomb was, and III [1] straightway a great cry was heard from the tomb. And going near Jesus [2] rolled away the stone from the door of the tomb. And straightway, going in where [3] the youth was, he stretched forth his hand and raised him, seizing [4] his hand. But the youth, looking upon him, loved him and [5] began to beseech him that he might be with him. And going out of [6] the tomb they came into the house of the youth, for he was rich. And after [7] six days Jesus told him what to do and in the evening the [8] youth comes to him, wearing a linen cloth over his naked body. And he [9] remained with him that night, for Jesus taught him [10] the mystery of the kingdom of God. And thence, arising,

Appendix 2

¹¹ἐπέστρεψεν εἰς τὸ πέραν τοῦ Ἰορδάνου." ἐπὶ μὲν τούτοις ἔπεται τὸ, "καὶ ¹²προσπορεύονται αὐτῷ Ἰάκωβος καὶ Ἰωάννης," καὶ πᾶσα ἡ ¹³περικοπή. τὸ δὲ "γυμνὸς γυμνῷ" καὶ τἄλλα περὶ ὧν ἔγραψας οὐχ

¹⁴εὑρίσκεται. μετὰ δὲ τὸ, "καὶ ἔρχεται εἰς Ἱεριχώ," ἐπάγει μόνον, "καὶ

¹⁵ἦσαν ἐκεῖ ἡ ἀδελφὴ τοῦ νεανίσκου ὃν ἠγάπα αὐτὸν ὁ Ἰησοῦς καὶ
¹⁶ἡ μήτηρ αὐτοῦ καὶ Σαλώμη, καὶ οὐκ ἀπεδέξατο αὐτὰς ὁ Ἰησοῦς."
¹⁷τὰ δὲ ἄλλα τὰ πολλὰ ἃ ἔγραψας ψεύσματα καὶ φαίνεται καὶ ἔστιν.

¹⁸ἡ μὲν οὖν ἀληθὴς καὶ κατὰ τὴν ἀληθῆ φιλοσοφίαν ἐξήγησις

¹¹he returned to the other side of the Jordan." After these words follows the text, "And ¹²James and John come to him" [Mark 10:35], and all that ¹³section. But "naked man with naked man," and the other things about which you wrote, are not

¹⁴found. And after the words, "And he comes into Jericho" [Mark 10:46], the secret Gospel adds only, "And

¹⁵the sister of the youth whom Jesus loved and his
¹⁶mother and Salome were there, and Jesus did not receive them."
¹⁷But the many other things about which you wrote both seem to be and are falsifications.

¹⁸Now the true explanation and that which accords with the true philosophy . . .

Bibliography

I. PRIMARY SOURCES

Aeschylus. *Agamemnon* in *Aeschyli septem quae supersunt tragoedias*. Edited by Denys Page. Oxford Classical Texts Series. 1972. Reprint, Oxford: Clarendon, 1975.
Aphrahat. *The Demonstrations of Aphrahat, the Persian Sage*. Translated by Adam Lehto. Gorgias Eastern Christian Studies 27. Piscataway, NJ: Gorgias, 2010.
Augustine. *De fide rerum invisibilium; Enchiridion ad Laurentium de fide et spe et caritate; De catechizandis rudibus; Sermo ad catechumenos de symbolo. Sermo de disciplina christiana; De utilitate ieiunii; Sermo de excidio urbis Romae; De haeresibus*. Edited by M. P. J. Van den Hout et al. CCSL 46. Turnhout: Brepols, 1969.
Berman, Samuel A., translator. *Midrash Tanhuma-Yelammedenu: An English Translation of Genesis and Exodus from the Printed Version of Tanhuma-Yelammedenu*. Hoboken, NJ: Ktav, 1996.
Braude, William G., translator. *The Midrash on Psalms*. New Haven: Yale University Press, 1959.
Buttmann, Philipp, editor. *Novum Testamentum Graece*. Leipzig: Teubner, 1860.
Butts, James R. "The Progymnasmata of Theon: A New Text with Translation and Commentary." Ph.D. diss., The Claremont Graduate School, 1986.
Cicero. *Ad C. Herennium de ratione dicendi (Rhetorica ad Herennium)*. Translated by Harry Caplan. LCL. Cambridge: Harvard University Press, 1977.
———. *De oratore*. 2 vols. Translated by E. W. Sutton. LCL. Cambridge: Harvard University Press, 1942.
Clement of Alexandria. *Christ the Educator*. Translated by Simon P. Wood. FC 23. New York: Fathers of the Church, 1954.
———. *The Excerpta ex Theodoto of Clement of Alexandria*. Translated by Robert Pierce Casey. London: Christophers, 1934.
———. *Exhortation to the Greeks, The Rich Man's Salvation, and the Fragment of an Address Entitled "To the Newly Baptized."* Translated by George William Butterworth. LCL. Cambridge: Harvard University Press, 1919.
———. *Extraits de Théodote*. 2nd ed. Translated by François Sagnard. SC 23. Paris: Cerf, 1970.

Bibliography

———. *Stromateis Books One to Three.* Translated by John Ferguson. FC 85. Washington, DC: Catholic University of America Press, 1991.

———. *Les Stromates: Stromate V.* 2 Vols. Translated by Alain Le Boulluec and Pierre Voulet. SC 278 and 279. Paris: Cerf, 2006–2009.

———. *Les Stromates: Stromate VII.* Translated by Alain Le Boulluec. SC 428. Paris: Cerf, 1997.

———. *Stromateis VII–VIII, Excerpta ex Theodoto, Eclogae propheticae, Quis dives salvetur, Fragmenta.* In *Clemens Alexandrinus*, vol. 3. 2nd ed. Edited by Otto Stählin, Ludwig Fruchtel, and Ursula Treu. GCS 17. Berlin: Akademie, 1970.

Coleman, Christopher B., editor and translator. *The Treatise of Lorenzo Valla on the Donation of Constantine: Text and Translation into English.* New York: Russell & Russell, 1922.

Danby, Herbert, translator. *The Mishnah.* Oxford: Oxford University Press, 1933.

Demosthenes. *Orations.* Vol. 3, *Against Meidas, Androtion, Aristocrates, Timocrates, Aristogeiton 1 and 2.* Translated by J. H. Vince. LCL. Cambridge: Harvard University Press, 1956.

Galen. *Galaudi Galeni Pergameni. Scripta Minora.* Edited by Ioannes Marquardt, Iwanus Mueller, and Georgius Helmreich. Leipzig: Teubner, 1884.

———. *Selected Works.* Translated by P. N. Singer. Oxford: Oxford University Press, 1997.

García Martínez, Florentino, editor. *The Dead Sea Scrolls Translated: The Qumran Texts in English.* 2nd ed. Leiden: Brill, 1996.

Holmes, Michael W., editor and translator. *The Apostolic Fathers.* 3rd ed. Grand Rapids: Baker, 2007.

Lucian. *Selected Dialogues.* Translated by Desmond Costa. Oxford: Oxford University Press, 2005.

Lysias. Translated by S. C. Todd. Oratory of Classical Greece 2. Austin: University of Texas Press, 2000.

Metzger, Marcel, translator. *Les Constitutions apostoliques.* 3 vols. SC 320, 329, and 336. Paris: Cerf, 1985–1987.

Neusner, Jacob, translator. *The Tosefta.* 6 vols. New York: Ktav, 1977–1986.

Pearson, Birger A., and Tim Vivian, editors and translators. *Two Coptic Homilies Attributed to St. Peter of Alexandria: On Riches; On the Epiphany.* Corpus dei manoscritti copti letterari. Rome: C.I.M., 1993.

Philo. *The Works of Philo Complete and Unabridged: New Updated Version.* Translated by C. D. Yonge. Peabody, MA: Hendrickson, 1993.

Plato. *Euthyphro; Apology; Crito; Phaedo; Phaedrus.* Translated by Harold North Fowler. LCL. Cambridge: Harvard University Press, 1960.

———. *Plato in Twelve Volumes.* 12 vols. Translated by Harold North Fowler, W. R. M. Lamb, Paul Shorey, and R. G. Bury. LCL. Cambridge: Harvard University Press, 1914–1930.

Pliny. *Letters.* 2 vols. Edited and translated by William Melmoth and W. M. L. Hutchinson. LCL. Cambridge: Harvard University Press, 1935.

Quintilian. *The Institutio Oratoria of Quintilian.* 4 vols. Translated by H. E. Butler. LCL. Cambridge: Harvard University Press, 1963.

Bibliography

II. SECONDARY WORKS

Accorinti, Domenico. Review of *Morton Smith and Gershom Scholem, Correspondence 1945–1982*, by Guy G. Stroumsa, ed. *Gnomon* 82 (2010) 261–71.

Adams, James Noel. *The Latin Sexual Vocabulary*. Baltimore: Johns Hopkins University Press, 1982.

Akenson, Donald Hamran. *Saint Saul: A Skeleton Key to the Historical Jesus*. Oxford: Oxford University Press, 2000.

———. *Surpassing Wonder: The Invention of the Bible and the Talmuds*. Chicago: University of Chicago Press, 1998.

Aland, B., K. Aland, J. Karavidopoulos, C. M. Martini, and B. M. Metzger, editors. *The Greek New Testament*. 4th ed. Stuttgart: Deutsche Bibelgesellschaft, 1993.

Aland, B. and K. Aland, editors. *Novum Testamentum Graece*. 27th ed. Stuttgart: Deutsche Bibelgesellschaft, 1993.

Anastasopoulou, Venetia. "Can a Document in Itself Reveal a Forgery?" Biblical Archaeology Review Scholar's Study (posted 22 July 2010). No pages. Online: http://www.bib-arch.org/scholars-study/secret-mark-handwriting-document-reveal-forgery.asp.

———. "Experts Report Handwriting Examination." Biblical Archaeology Review Scholar's Study (posted April 2010). Pages 1–39. Online: http://www.bib-arch.org/scholars-study/secret-mark-handwriting-analysis.asp.

Andreou, Georgia, Anargyros Karapetsas, and Ioannis Galantomos. "Modern Greek Language: Acquisition of Morphology and Syntax by Non-native Speakers." *The Reading Matrix* 8.1 (2008) 35–42.

Arieti, James A. *Philosophy in the Ancient World: An Introduction*. Lanham: Rowman & Littlefield, 2005.

Ascough, Richard S. "Translocal Relationships among Voluntary Associations and Early Christianity." *JECS* 5 (1997) 223–41.

Ashwin-Siejkowski, Piotr. *Clement of Alexandria: A Project of Christian Perfection*. London: T. & T. Clark, 2008.

Attridge, Harold W. *The Epistle to the Hebrews*. Hermeneia. Philadelphia: Fortress, 1989.

Baumgarten, Albert I. "Smith, Morton." In *The Eerdmans Dictionary of Early Judaism*, edited by John J. Collins and Daniel C. Harlow, 1235–37. Grand Rapids: Eerdmans, 2010.

Belfiore, Elizabeth. "Dancing with the Gods: The Myth of the Chariot in Plato's *Phaedrus*." *AJP* 127 (2006) 185–217.

Bell, H. Idris, and T. C. Skeat. *Fragments of an Unknown Gospel and Other Early Christian Papyri*. London: Trustees of the British Museum, 1935.

Benamozegh, Élie. *La kabbale et l'origine des dogmes chrétiens*. Lettres promises. Paris: In Press, 2011.

Bertalotto, Pierpaolo. *Il Gesù storico. Guida alla ricerca contemporanea*. Quality Paperbacks 299. Rome: Carocci, 2010.

Beskow, Per. *Strange Tales about Jesus: A Survey of Unfamiliar Gospels*. Philadelphia: Fortress, 1983.

Best, Ernest. "Uncanonical Mark." *JSNT* 4 (1979) 69–76. Reprinted in Best, *Disciples and Discipleship: Studies in the Gospel according to Mark*. Edinburgh: T. & T. Clark, 1986.

Bibliography

Betz, Hans Dieter. *The "Mithras Liturgy": Text, Translation, and Commentary.* Studien und Texte zu Antike und Christentum 18. Tübingen: Mohr/Siebeck, 2003.

Blum, Harold, editor. *Gershom Scholem.* Modern Critical Views. New York: Chelsea House, 1987.

Bockmuehl, Markus. "Syrian Memories of Peter: Ignatius, Justin and Serapion." In *The Image of the Judaeo-Christians in Ancient Jewish and Christian Literature,* edited by Peter J. Tomson and Doris Lambers-Petry, 124–46. Tübingen: Mohr/Siebeck, 2003.

Borella, Jean Borella. *Guénonian Esoterism and Christian Mystery.* Hillsdale, NY: Sophia Perennis, 2004.

Boustan, Ra'anan S. "The Study of Heikhalot Literature: Between Mystical Experience and Textual Artifact." *Currents in Biblical Research* 6 (2007) 130–60.

Braude, William G. *Jewish Proselyting in the First Five Centuries of the Common Era: The Age of the Tannaim and Amoraim.* Brown University Studies 6. Providence: Brown University, 1940.

Brent, Allen. *Hippolytus and the Roman Church in the Third Century: Communities in Tension before the Emergence of a Monarch-Bishop.* VCSup 31. Leiden: Brill, 1995.

———. *Ignatius of Antioch: A Martyr Bishop and the Origin of Episcopacy.* New York: Continuum, 2007.

Brodersen, Kai, and Jaś Elsner, editors. *Images and Texts on the "Artemidorus Papyrus": Working Papers on P.Artemid. (St. John's College Oxford, 2008).* Historia, Einzelschriften 214. Stuttgart: Steiner, 2009.

Brown, Raymond E. *The Gospel according to John.* AB 29–29A. Garden City, NY: Doubleday, 1966–1970.

Brown, Scott G. "Bethany beyond the Jordan: John 1:28 and the Longer Gospel of Mark." *RB* 100 (2003) 497–516.

———. "Factualizing the Folklore: Stephen Carlson's Case against Morton Smith." *HTR* 99 (2006) 291–327.

———. "The *Letter to Theodore*: Stephen Carlson's Case against Clement's Authorship." *JECS* 16 (2008) 535–72.

———. "The Longer Gospel of Mark and the Synoptic Problem." In *New Studies in the Synoptic Problem: Oxford Conference, April 2008: Essays in Honour of Christopher M. Tuckett,* edited by Paul Foster et al., 753–81. BETL 239. Leuven: Peeters, 2011.

———. *Mark's Other Gospel: Rethinking Morton Smith's Controversial Discovery.* ESCJ 15. Waterloo, ON: Wilfrid Laurier University Press, 2005.

———. "The More Spiritual Gospel: Markan Literary Techniques in the Longer Gospel of Mark." PhD diss., University of Toronto, 1999.

———. "My Thoughts on the Reports by Venetia Anastasopoulou." Biblical Archaeology Review Scholar's Study (posted 24 January 2011). No pages. Online: http://www.bib-arch.org/scholars-study/secret-mark-handwriting-response-brown.asp.

———. "Reply to Stephen Carlson." *ExpTim* 117 (2006) 144–49.

———. Review of *The Secret Gospel of Mark Unveiled: Imagined Rituals of Sex, Death, and Madness in a Biblical Forgery,* by Peter Jeffery. *RBL* (posted 15 September 2007). Pages 1–47. Online: http://www.bookreviews.org/pdf/5627_5944.pdf.

———. "The Question of Motive in the Case against Morton Smith." *JBL* 125 (2006) 351–83.

Brown, Scott G., and Allan J. Pantuck. "Stephen Carlson's Questionable Questioned Document Examination." *Salainan evankelista* (posted 14 April 2010). No pages.

Online: http://salainenevankelista.blogspot.com/2010/04/stephen-carlsons-questionable.html.
Browning, Robert. "Libanius." In *The Oxford Classical Dictionary*, edited by Simon Hornblower and Antony Spawforth, 853–54. 3rd ed. Oxford: Oxford University Press, 1999.
Brunelle, Richard L., and Robert W. Reed. *Forensic Examination of Ink and Paper.* Springfield, IL: Thomas, 1984
Brunelle, Richard L., and Kenneth R. Crawford. *Advances in the Forensic Analysis and Dating of Writing Ink*. Springfield, IL: Thomas, 2003.
Burchardt, Jacob. *The Civilization of the Renaissance in Italy*. 2 vols. Harper Torchbooks. New York: Harper, 1958.
Burgess, Matthew. "'Whatever Makes for Progress Towards Gnosis': Esoterism and Spiritual Advancement in the *Stromateis* and the *Letter to Theodore*." Confessions of a Bible Junkie (posted 16 June 2009). Pages 1–18. Online: http://matthewburgess.blogspot.com/2009/06/recent-research.html.
Burke, Tony. *De infantia Iesu euangelium Thomae graece*. CCSA 17. Turnhout: Brepols, 2010.
———. "Heresy Hunting in the New Millennium." *SR* 39 (2010) 405–20.
———. "Secret Mark at the 2008 SBL Meeting." Apocryphicity (posted 4 December 2008). No pages. Online: http://www.tonyburke.ca/apocryphicity/2008/12/04/secret-mark-at-the-2008-sbl-annual-meeting/.
Burkert, Walter. "Der geheime Reiz des Verborgenen: Antike Mysterienkulte." In *Secrecy and Concealment: Studies in the History of Mediterranean and Near Eastern Religions*, edited by Hans G. Kippenberg and Guy G. Stroumsa, 79–100. SHR 65. Leiden: Brill, 1995.
Byrne, Ryan, and Bernadette McNary-Zak, editors. *Resurrecting the Brother of Jesus: The James Ossuary Controversy and the Quest for Religious Relics*. Chapel Hill: University of North Carolina Press, 2009.
Calder, William M. III. "Morton Smith." In *Men in Their Books: Studies in the Modern History of Classical Scholarship*, edited by John P. Harris and R. Scott Smith, 229–31. 2nd ed. Zürich: Olm, 2002.
———. "Smith, Morton." In *Biographical Dictionary of North American Classicists*, edited by Ward W. Briggs Jr., 600–602. Westport, CT: Greenwood, 1994.
Cameron, Ron, editor. *The Other Gospels: Non-Canonical Gospel Texts*. Philadelphia: Westminster, 1982.
Campanini, Saverio. "A proposito di un carteggio recente: Saggio bibliografico." *Materia giudaica* 13 (2008) 397–405.
Camplani, Alberto. *Atanasio di Alessandria. Lettere festali—Anonimo: Indice delle Lettere festali*. Letture cristiane del primo millennio 34. Milan: Paoline, 2003.
———. *Le lettere festali di Atanasio di Alessandria: Studio storico-critico*. Corpus dei manoscritti copti letterari. Rome: Centro Italiano Microfiches, 1989.
———. "Sull'origine della Quaresima in Egitto." In *Acts of the Fifth International Congress of Coptic Studies, Washington, 12–15 August 1992*, edited by Tito Orlandi and David W. Johnson, 2:105–21. 2 vols. Rome: International Association for Coptic Studies and Centro Italiano Microfiches, 1993.
Canfora, Luciano. *La meravigliosa storia del falso Artemidoro*. La memoria 855. Palermo: Sellerio, 2011.
———. *The True History of the So-called Artemidorus Papyrus*. Bari: Pagina, 2007.

Bibliography

———. *Il viaggio di Artemidoro: Vita e avventure di un grande esploratore dell'antichità*. Milan: Rizzoli, 2010.

Carlson, Stephen C. "'Archaic Mark' (MS 2427) and the Finding of a Manuscript Fake." SBL Forum (posted August 2006). No pages. Online: http://sbl-site.org/Article.aspx?ArticleID=577.

———. *The Gospel Hoax: Morton Smith's Invention of Secret Mark*. Waco, TX: Baylor University Press, 2005.

———. "Kyle Smith's Critique of Gospel Hoax." Hypotyposeis (posted 23 December 2005). No pages. Online: http://hypotyposeis.org/weblog/2005/12/kyle-smiths-critique-of-gospel-hoax.html.

———. "Reply to Scott Brown." *ExpTim* 117 (2006) 185–88.

———. "Some Initial Reviews and a Second Opinion." Hypotyposeis (posted 26 November 2005). No pages. Online: http://www.hypotyposeis.org/weblog/2005/11/some-initial-reviews-and-second.html.

Casey, Maurice. *Jesus of Nazareth: An Independent Historian's Account of His Life and Teaching*. London: T. & T. Clark, 2010.

Chernow, Ron. *Washington: A Life*. New York: Penguin, 2010.

Chilton, Bruce. "Another Look at the James Ossuary." The Bible and Interpretation (posted April 2003). No pages. Online: http://www.bibleinterp.com/articles/Another_look.shtml.

———. "The Epitaph of Himerus at Woodstock." *Annandale* (Spring, 1989) 42–44.

———. "The Epitaph of Himerus from the Jewish Catacomb of the Appian Way." *JQR* 79 (1989) 93–100.

———. "'Gospel of Judas' Called an Authentic Fabrication." *New York Sun*, 7–9 April 2006, 1, 20

———. "'HEBR. 75' in the Bibliothèque Nationale." In *Targum and Scripture: Studies in Aramaic Translations and Interpretation in Memory of Ernest G. Clarke*, edited by Ernest G. Clarke and Paul V. M. Flesher, 141–48. Studies in the Aramaic Interpretation of Scripture 2. Leiden: Brill, 2002.

———. *Rabbi Jesus: An Intimate Biography*. New York: Doubleday, 2000.

———. Review of *The Gospel Hoax: Morton Smith's Invention of Secret Mark*, by Stephen Carlson. *The Review of Rabbinic Judaism* 10.1 (2007) 122–28.

———. "Scholars, Journalists and the Ossuary." The Bible and Interpretation (posted September 2003). No pages. Online: http://www.bibleinterp.com/articles/Chilton_Scholars.htm.

———. "Unmasking a False Gospel." *New York Sun*, 25 October 2006, 16. Online: http://www.nysun.com/arts/unmasking-a-false-gospel/42197/.

———. *The Way of Jesus: To Repair and Renew the World*. Nashville: Abingdon, 2010.

Chupungco, Anscar J. "A Definition of Liturgy." In *Handbook for Liturgical Studies*, edited by Anscar J. Chupungco, 1:3–10. 5 vols. Collegeville, MN: Liturgical, 1997.

———. *What, Then, Is Liturgy? Musings and Memoir*. Collegeville, MN: Liturgical, 2010.

Ciavolella, Massimo. "Eros/Ereos: Marsilio Ficino's Interpretation of Guido Cavalcanti's 'Donna Me Prega.'" In *Ficino and Renaissance Neoplatonism*, edited by Konrad Eisenbichler and Olga Zorzi Pugliese, 39–48. Toronto: Dovehouse, 1986.

Clahsen, Harald, and Claudia Felser. "How Native-like Is Non-native Language Processing?" *Trends in Cognitive Sciences* 10 (2006) 564–70.

Clark, Donald Lemen. *Rhetoric in Greco-Roman Education*. New York: Columbia University Press, 1957.

———. "Imitation: Theory and Practice in Roman Rhetoric." *QJS* 37 (1951) 11–22.

Clines, David J. A., editor. *The Dictionary of Classical Hebrew*. 8 vols. Sheffield: Sheffield Phoenix, 2007.

Cohen, Shaye J. D. "In Memoriam Morton Smith." In Morton Smith, *Studies in the Cult of Yahweh*. Vol. 2, *New Testament, Early Christianity, and Magic*, edited by Shaye J. D. Cohen, 279–86. Religions in the Graeco-Roman World 130.2. Leiden: Brill, 1996.

Coleman, Christopher B. *Constantine the Great and Christianity. Three Phases: The Historical, the Legendary, and the Spurious*. Studies in History, Economics, and Public Law 60. New York: Columbia University Press, 1914.

Coleman-Norton, Paul R. "An Amusing *Agraphon*." *CBQ* 12 (1950) 439–49.

Colish, Marcia L. *Ambrose's Patriarchs: Ethics for the Common Man*. South Bend, IN: University of Notre Dame Press, 2005.

Collins, Adela Yarbro. *Mark: A Commentary*. Hermeneia. Minneapolis: Fortress, 2007.

Condello, Federico. "'Artemidoro' 2006–2011: L'ultima vita, in breve." *Quaderni di storia* 74 (2011) 161–248.

Cosaert, Carl P. *The Text of the Gospels in Clement of Alexandria*. NTGF 9. Atlanta: Society of Biblical Literature, 2008.

Cosmopoulos, Michael B. *Greek Mysteries: The Archaeology and Ritual of Ancient Greek Secret Cults*. London: Routledge, 2003.

Coxe, Henry Octavius. *Report to Her Majesty's Government on the Greek Manuscripts Yet Remaining in Libraries of the Levant*. London: Eyre & Spottiswoode, 1858.

Cribiore, Raffaella. *Gymnastics of the Mind. Greek Education in Hellenistic and Roman Egypt*. Princeton: Princeton University Press, 2001.

———. *The School of Libanius in Late Antique Antioch*. Princeton: Princeton University Press, 2007.

Criddle, Andrew H. "On the Mar Saba Letter Attributed to Clement of Alexandria." *JECS* 3 (1995) 215–20.

———. "Secret Mark—Further Comments." Secret Mark Homepage (posted February 1999). No pages. Online: http://www-user.uni-bremen.de/~wie/Secret/Criddle-Feb99.html.

Crossan, John Dominic. *Four Other Gospels: Shadows on the Contours of Canon*. 1985. Reprinted, Eugene, OR: Wipf & Stock, 2008.

———. *The Historical Jesus: The Life of a Mediterranean Jewish Peasant*. San Francisco: HarperSanFrancisco, 1991.

Crowley, Aleister. *Mortadello, or The Angel of Venice: A Comedy*. London: Wieland, 1912.

Csapo, Eric. "Riding the Phallus for Dionysus: Iconology, Ritual, and Gender-Role De/Construction." *Phoenix* 51 (1997) 253–95.

Dalmais, Irénée-Henri. "'Raza' et sacrement." In *Rituels: Mélanges offerts au Père Gy, OP*, edited by Paul De Clerck and Eric Palazzo, 173-82. Paris: Cerf, 1990.

Daniélou, Jean. *A History of Early Christian Doctrine before the Council of Nicaea*. Vol. 2, *Gospel Message and Hellenistic Culture*. Edited and translated by John Austin Baker. Philadelphia: Westminster, 1973.

Davies, William David. "From Schweitzer to Scholem: Reflections on Sabbatai Svi." *JBL* 95 (1976) 529–58.

Bibliography

Davis, Tom. "The Practice of Handwriting Identification." *The Library: The Transactions of the Bibliographical Society* 8.3 (2007) 251–76.

Day, Juliette. *The Baptismal Liturgy of Jerusalem: Fourth- and Fifth-Century Evidence from Palestine, Syria and Egypt.* Aldershot, UK: Ashgate, 2007.

DeConick, April D., editor. *The Codex Judas Papers: Proceedings of the International Congress on the Tchacos Codex Held at Rice University, Houston, Texas, March 13–16, 2008.* NHMS 71. Leiden: Brill, 2009.

———. "The True Mysteries: Sacramentalism in the *Gospel of Philip*." *VC* 55 (2001) 225–61.

Dillard, Irving, editor. *The Spirit of Liberty: Papers and Addresses of Learned Hand.* New York: Vintage, 1959.

Doval, Alexis James. *Cyril of Jerusalem, Mystagogue: The Authorship of the Mystagogic Catecheses.* North American Patristic Society Patristic Monograph Series 17. Washington, DC: Catholic University of America Press, 2001.

Drijvers, Jan Willem. *Cyril of Jerusalem: Bishop and City.* VCSup 72. Leiden: Brill, 2004.

Dundes, Alan, and Carl R. Pagter. *Never Try to Teach a Pig to Sing: Still More Urban Folklore from the Paperwork Empire.* Detroit: Wayne State University Press, 1991.

Eckemann, Johann Peter. *Gespräche mit Goethe in den letzten Jahren seines Lebens.* 2 vols. Leipzig: Brockhaus, 1836.

Ehrman, Bart D. *Lost Christianities: The Battles for Scripture and the Faiths We Never Knew.* Oxford: Oxford University Press, 2003.

———. "Response to Charles Hedrick's Stalemate." *JECS* 11 (2003) 155–163.

Ellens, J. Harold. Review of *The Secret Gospel of Mark Unveiled: Imagined Rituals of Sex, Death, and Madness in a Biblical Forgery*, by Peter Jeffery. *RBL* (posted 1 June 2009). Pages 1–9. Online: http://www.bookreviews.org/pdf/5627_7785.pdf.

Elliott, J. K. *The Apocryphal New Testament: A Collection of Apocryphal Christian Literature in an English Translation.* 1993. Reprint, Oxford: Clarendon, 2009.

Ericsson, K. Anders et al., editors. *Cambridge Handbook on Expertise and Expert Performance.* Cambridge: Cambridge University Press, 2006.

Evans, Craig A. "The Apocryphal Jesus: Assessing the Possibilities and Problems." In *Exploring the Origins of the Bible: Canon Formation in Historical, Literary, and Theological Perspective*, edited by Caig A. Evans and Emmanuel Tov, 147–72. Acadia Studies in Bible and Theology. Grand Rapids: Baker, 2008.

———. *Fabricating Jesus: How Modern Scholars Distort the Gospels.* Downers Grove, IL: Inter-Varsity, 2006.

———. "The Gospel of Judas and the Other Gospels." In *The Gospel of Judas*, edited by Rodolphe Kasser, Marvin Meyer and Gregor Wurst (in collaboration with François Gaudard), 103–24. 2nd ed. Washington, DC: National Geographic Society, 2008.

———. "How Scholars Fabricate Jesus." In *Contending with Christianity's Critics: Answering New Atheists and Other Objectors*, edited by Paul Copan and William Lane Craig, 126–47. Nashville: B. & H. Academic, 2009.

———. "The Need for the 'Historical Jesus': A Response to Jacob Neusner's Review of Crossan and Meier." *BBR* 4 (1994) 127–34.

Evans, Craig A., and Emanuel Tov, editors. *Exploring the Origins of the Bible: Canon Formation in Historical, Literary, and Theological Perspective.* Acadia Studies in Bible and Theology. Grand Rapids: Baker Academic, 2008.

Eyer, Shawn. "The Strange Case of the Secret Gospel according to Mark: How Morton Smith's Discovery of a Lost Letter of Clement of Alexandria Scandalized Biblical

Scholarship." *Alexandria: The Journal for the Western Cosmological Traditions* 3 (1995) 103–29.
Fabry, Heinz-Josef. "סוד." In *Theological Dictionary of the Old Testament*. Edited by G. Johannes Botterweck and Helmer Ringgren et al., 10:171–78. Translated by Geoffrey W. Bromiley Grand Rapids: Eerdmans, 1999.
Farmer, William R. *The Last Twelve Verses of Mark*. SNTSMS 25. Cambridge: Cambridge University Press, 1974.
Farrell, Anne Mary. "Plato's Use of Eleusinian Mystery Motifs." PhD diss., University of Texas at Austin, 1999.
Farrer, James Anson. *Literary Forgeries*. London: Longmans, Green, 1907.
Feulner, Rüdiger. *Clemens von Alexandrien: Sein Leben, Werk und philosophisch-theologisches Denken*. Bamberger Theologische Studien 31. Frankfurt: Lang, 2006.
Field, Henry Martyn. *On the Desert: A Narrative of Travel from Egypt through the Wilderness of Sinai to Palestine*. London: Nelson, 1884.
Finn, Thomas M. *Early Christian Baptism and the Catechumenate: Italy, North Africa, and Egypt*. Message of the Fathers of the Church 6. Collegeville, MN: Liturgical, 1992.
Foerster, Hans. "The Celebration of the Baptism of Christ by the Basilideans and the Origin of Epiphany: Is the Seemingly Obvious Correct?" *Journal of Greco-Roman Christianity and Judaism* 5 (2008) 110–24.
Ford, David F., and Mike Higton, editors. *Jesus*. Oxford Readers. Oxford: Oxford University Press, 2002.
Foster, Paul. *The Gospel of Peter: Introduction, Critical Edition and Commentary*. Texts and Editions for New Testament Studies 4. Leiden: Brill, 2010.
———. Review of *Secret Gospel of Mark Unveiled: Imagined Rituals of Sex, Death, and Madness in a Biblical Forgery*, by Peter Jeffery. *ExpTim* 119 (2007) 50–51
———. "Secret Mark." In *The Non-Canonical Gospels*, edited by Paul Foster, 126–38. London: T. & T. Clark, 2008.
———. "Secret Mark: Its Discovery and the State of Research." *ExpTim* 117 (2005) 46–52.
France, Richard Thomas. *The Gospel of Mark: A Commentary on the Greek Text*. Grand Rapids: Eerdmans, 2002.
Franco, Emilia. *Falso d'autore. Simulazione di un processo creativo—Il Trono Ludovisi. Un'analisi comparata*. Historiae 63. Locri: Pancallo, 2009.
Frerichs, Ernest S. "Contemporary Ecclesiastical Approaches to Biblical Interpretation: Orthodoxy and Pseudorthodoxy." In *Christianity, Judaism and Other Greco-Roman Cults: Studies for Morton Smith at Sixty*, edited by Jacob Neusner, 2:217–27. 4 vols. SJLA 12. Leiden: Brill, 1975.
Frova, Antonio. "L'iscrizione di Ponzio Pilato a Cesarea." *Rendiconti dell'Istituto Lombardo* 95 (1961) 419–34.
Fuller, Reginald H. "Longer Mark: Forgery, Interpolation, or Old Tradition?" In *Longer Mark: Forgery, Interpolation, or Old Tradition? Protocol of the Eighteenth Colloquy: 7 December 1975*, edited by Wilhelm H. Wuellner, 1–11. Berkeley: Center for Hermeneutical Studies, 1976.
Geerard, Maurice. *Clavis Patrum Graecorum* 1: *Patres Antenicaeni*. CCCPG 1. Turnhout: Brepols, 1983.
Genesius, William. *Gesenius' Hebrew Grammar*. London: Bagsters, 1852.

Bibliography

Ginzburg, Carlo. *History, Rhetoric, and Proof.* The Menahem Stern Jerusalem Lectures. Hanover, NH: University Press of New England, 1999.

Golan, Oded. "The Authenticity of the James Ossuary and the Jehoash Tablet Inscriptions—Summary of Expert Trial Witnesses." Biblical Archaeology Review Scholar's Study (posted March 2011). Pages 1–27. Online: www.bib-arch.org/scholars-study/the-authenticity-of-the-james-ossuary.pdf.

Goldin, Judah. "Reflections on Translation and Midrash." *PAAJR* 41/42 (1973–1974) 87–104.

Goodenough, Erwin R. *An Introduction to Philo Judaeus.* 2nd ed. Oxford: Blackwell, 1962.

———. *Jewish Symbols in the Greco-Roman Period.* 13 vols. Bollingen Series 37. New York: Pantheon, 1953–1968.

Goodspeed, Edgar Johnson. *Strange New Gospels.* 1931. Reprinted as *Famous Biblical Hoaxes.* Grand Rapids: Baker, 1956.

Graffin, René, editor. *Patrologia Syriaca.* 2 vols. Paris: Firmin-Didot, 1894, 1907.

Grafton, Anthony. *Forgers and Critics. Creativity and Duplicity in Western Scholarship.* Princeton: Princeton University Press, 1990.

Greene, Roedy. "Was Jesus Gay?" (no date). No pages. Online: http://mindprod.com/religion/wasjesusgay.html.

Guetta, Alessandro. *Philosophy and Kabbalah: Elijah Benamozegh and the Reconciliation of Western Thought and Jewish Esotericism.* Translated by Helena Kahan. SUNY Series in Contemporary Jewish Thought. Albany: SUNY Press, 2009.

Haas, Christopher. *Alexandria in Late Antiquity: Topography and Social Conflict.* Ancient Society and History Series. Baltimore: Johns Hopkins University Press, 1997.

Hägg, Henny Fiskå. *Clement of Alexandria and the Beginnings of Christian Apophaticism.* Oxford: Oxford University Press, 2006.

Hall, F. W. *A Companion to Classical Texts.* 1913. Reprinted, Chicago: Argonaut, 1970.

Haren, Michael J. "The Naked Young Man: A Historian's Hypothesis on Mark 14,51–52." *Bib* 79 (1998) 525–31.

Hargis, Jeff. "New Fragmentary Lectionary in Bucharest." The Center for the Study of New Testament Manuscripts (posted 20 July 2010). No pages. Online: http://www.csntm.org/News/Archive/2010/7/20/NewFragmentaryLectionaryinBucharest.

Harmless, William. *Augustine and the Catechumenate.* Collegeville, MN: Liturgical, 1995.

Harnack, Adolf. *Die Pfaff'schen Irenäus-Fragmente als fälschungen Pfaffs.* TU n.f. 5.3. Leipzig: Hinrichs, 1900.

Harris, Robert. *Selling Hitler: The Story of the Hitler Diaries.* London: Faber & Faber, 1986. Reprinted, 1991.

Harris, William V. "A Bible Fantasy." *Times Literary Supplement* 5455, 19 October 2007, 23

Hedrick, Charles W. "An Amazing Discovery." *BAR* 35.6 (2009) 44–48, 86.

———. "Evaluating Morton Smith: Hoaxer Outed or Colleague Slandered?" *PRSt* 37.3 (2010) 1–12.

———. "The Secret Gospel of Mark: Stalemate in the Academy." *JECS* 11 (2003) 133–45.

———. "Survivors of the Crucifixion: Searching for Profiles in the Parables." In *Hermeneutik der Gleichnisse Jesu. Methodische Neuansätze zum Verstehen*

Bibliography

urchristlicher Parabeltexte, edited by Ruben Zimmermann and Gabi Kern, 165–80. WUNT 231.Tübingen: Mohr/Siebeck, 2008.
Hedrick, Charles W., and Paul A. Mirecki. *The Gospel of the Savior. A New Ancient Gospel*. Santa Rosa, CA: Polebridge, 1999.
Hedrick, Charles W., and Nikolaos Olympiou. "Secret Mark: New Photographs, New Witnesses." *The Fourth R* 13.5 (2000) 3–16.
Henderson, Jeffrey. *The Maculate Muse: Obscene Language in Attic Comedy*. 2nd ed. New York: Oxford University Press, 1991.
Henderson, Suzanne Watts. *Christology and Discipleship in the Gospel of Mark*. SNTSMS 64. Cambridge: Cambridge University Press, 2006.
Hill, Charles E. "What Papias Said about John (and Luke): A 'New' Papian Fragment." *JTS* 49 (1998) 582–629.
Hilton, Ordway. *Scientific Examination of Questioned Documents*. Chicago: Callaghan, 1956.
Hock, Ronald F. *The Infancy Gospels of James and Thomas with Introduction, Notes, and Original Text Featuring the NEW Scholars Version Translation*. Santa Rosa, CA: Polebridge, 1995.
———. "Writing in the Greco-Roman World." *SBL Forum* (posted May 2004). No pages. Online: http://sbl-site.org/Article.aspx?ArticleID=264.
Holl, Karl. *Fragmente vornicänischer Kirchenväter aus den Sacra Parallela*. TU 20.2. Leipzig: Hinrichs, 1899.
Hollinshead, Mary B. "'Adyton,' 'Opisthodomos,' and the Inner Room of the Greek Temple." *Hesperia* 68 (1999) 189–218.
Hunter, James Hogg. *The Mystery of Mar Saba*. New York: Evangelical Publishers, 1940.
Hurtado, Larry W. *The Earliest Christian Artifacts: Manuscripts and Christian Origins*. Grand Rapids: Eerdmans, 2006.
Idel, Moshe. *Ascensions on High in Jewish Mysticism: Pillars, Lines, Ladders*. Past Incorporated 2. Budapest: Central European University Press, 2005.
Irwin, John T. "Thomas Campion and the Musical Emblem." *Studies in English Literature, 1500–1900* 10.1 (1970) 121–41.
Itter, Andrew C. *Esoteric Teaching in the Stromateis of Clement of Alexandria*. VCSup 97. Leiden: Brill, 2009.
Jackson, Howard. "Why the Youth Shed His Cloak and Fled Naked: The Meaning and Purpose of Mark 14:51–52." *JBL* 116 (1997) 273–89.
Jakab, Attila. *Ecclesia Alexandrina: Évolution sociale et institutionnelle du christianisme alexandrin (IIe et IIIe siècles)*. Christianismes anciens 1. Bern: Lang, 2001.
———. "Une lettre 'perdue' de Clément d'Alexandrie? (Morton Smith et l'"Évangile secret' de Marc)." *Apocrypha* 10 (1999) 7–15.
Jay, Jeff. "A New Look at the Epistolary Framework of the *Secret Gospel of Mark*." *JECS* 16 (2008) 573–97.
Jeffery, Peter. "Monastic Reading and the Emerging Roman Chant Repertory." In *Western Plainchant in the First Millennium: Studies in the Medieval Liturgy and Its Music*, edited by Sean Gallagher et al., 45–103. Aldershot, UK: Ashgate, 2003.
———. "'The Mystical Chorus of the Truth Itself': Liturgy and Mystery in Clement of Alexandria." In *Inquiries into Eastern Christian Worship: Selected Papers of the Second International Congress of the Society of Oriental Liturgy, Rome, 17–21 September 2008*, edited by Bert Groen, Steven Hawkes-Teeples, and Stefanos Alexopoulos. 19–45. Eastern Christian Studies 12. Leuven: Peeters, 2012.

Bibliography

———. "Peter Jeffery: Additional Response to Handwriting Analysis." Biblical Archaeology Review Scholar's Study (posted 24 January 2011). No pages. Online: http://www.bib-arch.org/scholars-study/secret-mark-handwriting-response-jeffery-2.asp.

———. "Philo's Impact on Christian Psalmody." In *Psalms in Community: Jewish and Christian Textual, Liturgical, and Artistic Traditions*. Edited by Harold W. Attridge and Margot E. Fassler, 147–87. SBLSymS 25. Atlanta: Society of Biblical Literature, 2003.

———. "Response to Handwriting Analysis." Biblical Archaeology Review Scholar's Study (posted 19 April 2010). No pages. Online: http://www.bib-arch.org/scholars-study/secret-mark-handwriting-response-jeffery.asp.

———. "The Secret Gospel of Mark Revisited." Paper presented at the annual meeting of the Society of Biblical Literature, New Orleans, 21 November 2009 (available online at http://www.music.princeton.edu/~jeffery/Psybibssession.pdf).

———. *The Secret Gospel of Mark Unveiled: Imagined Rituals of Sex, Death, and Madness in a Biblical Forgery*. New Haven: Yale University Press, 2007.

———. "The Secret Gospel of Mark Unveiled: Reply to Scott G. Brown." Peter Jeffery's Home Page (posted 2008). Pages 1–21. Online: http://www.music.princeton.edu/~jeffery/replytobrown.pdf.

Jenkins, Philip. *Hidden Gospels: How the Search for Jesus Lost Its Way*. Oxford: Oxford University Press, 2001.

Jeremias, Joachim. *The Eucharistic Words of Jesus*. Translated by Norman Perrin. London: SCM, 1966. (Originally published as *Abendmahlsworte Jesu*. 3rd ed. Göttingen: Vandenhoeck & Ruprecht, 1960.)

Johnson, Maxwell E. Review of *The Secret Gospel of Mark Unveiled: Imagined Rituals of Sex, Death, and Madness in a Biblical Forgery*, by Peter Jeffery. Worship 82 (2008) 85–89.

Jones, Arnold. H. M. *Studies in Roman Government and Law*. Oxford: Blackwell, 1960.

Jónsson, Jakob. *Humour and Irony in the New Testament: Illuminated by Parallels in Talmud and Midrash*. 1965. Reprint, Leiden: Brill, 1985.

Kaestli, Jean-Daniel. "L'*Évangile de Thomas*: Que peuvent nous apprendre les 'paroles cachées de Jésus'?" In *Le mystère apocryphe: Introduction à une littérature méconnue*. Edited by Jean-Daniel Kaestli and Daniel Marguerat, 73–93. 2nd ed. EsBi 26. Geneva: Labor et Fides, 2007.

———. "L'*Évangile secret de Marc*. Une version longue de l'Évangile de Marc réservée aux chrétiens avancés dans l'Église d'Alexandrie? Fragment d'une lettre de Clément d'Alexandrie au sujet de l'*Évangile secret de Marc*." In *Le mystère apocryphe. Introduction à une littérature méconnue*, edited by Jean-Daniel Kaestli and Daniel Marguerat, 113–36. 2nd ed. EsBi 26. Geneva: Labor et Fides, 2007.

———. "L'utilisation de l'*Évangile de Thomas* dans la recherche actuelle sur les paroles de Jésus." In *Jésus de Nazareth: Nouvelles approches d'une énigme*, edited by Daniel Marguerat, Enrico Norelli, and Jean-Michel Poffet, 373–95. MoBi 38. Geneva: Labor et Fides, 1998.

Kasser, Rudolphe, Gregor Wurst, et al., *The Gospel of Judas: Critical Edition*. Washington, DC: National Geographic Society, 2007.

Kee, Howard Clark. *Miracle in the Early Christian World: A Study in Sociohistorical Method*. New Haven: Yale University Press, 1983.

Bibliography

Keener, Craig S. *The Historical Jesus of the Gospels: Jesus in Historical Context*. Grand Rapids: Eerdmans, 2009.
Kelly, Nicole E. Review of *The Secret Gospel of Mark Unveiled: Imagined Rituals of Sex, Death, and Madness in a Biblical Forgery*, by Peter Jeffery. *Magic, Ritual and Witchcraft* 4 (2009) 114–17.
Kerényi, Karl. *Eleusis: Archetypal Image of Mother and Daughter*. Translated by Ralph Manheim. Princeton: Princeton University Press, 1967.
Kermode, Frank. "The Quest for the Magical Jesus." *New York Review of Books* 25/16. 26 October 1978. Online at: http://www.nybooks.com/articles/archives/1978/oct/26/the-quest-for-the-magical-jesus/.
Kiernan, Kevin. "The Source of the Napier Fragment of Alfred's Boethius." *Digital Medievalist* 1.1 (posted Spring 2005). No pages. Online: http://www.digitalmedievalist.org/journal/1.1/kiernan/.
Klauck, Hans-Josef. *Die apokryphe Bibel: Ein anderer Zugang zum frühen Christentum*. Tria Corda 4. Tübingen: Mohr/Siebeck, 2008.
Kloppenborg, John S., and Stephen G. Wilson, editors. *Voluntary Associations in the Graeco-Roman World*. 1996. Reprint, London: Routledge, 2005.
Knox, Sanka. "Expert Disputes 'Secret Gospel': Theologian Says Style of Excerpts Does Not Show They Were by Mark." *New York Times*, 31 December 1960, 7.
———. "A New Gospel Ascribed to Mark: Copy of Greek Letter Says Saint Kept 'Mysteries' Out." *New York Times*. 30 December 1960, 1, 17.
Koester, Craig R. *Hebrews*. AB 36. New York: Doubleday, 2001.
Koester, Helmut. *Ancient Christian Gospels: Their History and Development*. Philadelphia: Trinity, 1990.
———. "History and Development of Mark's Gospel (From Mark to *Secret Mark* and 'Canonical' Mark)." In *Colloquy on New Testament Studies. A Time for Reappraisal and Fresh Approaches*, edited by Bruce C. Corley, 35–57. Macon, GA: Mercer University Press, 1983.
———. Review of *The Secret Gospel: The Discovery and Interpretation of the Secret Gospel according to Mark* and *Clement of Alexandria and a Secret Gospel of Mark*, by Morton Smith. *AHR* 80 (1975) 620–22.
———. "Was Morton Smith a Great Thespian and I a Complete Fool?" *BAR* 35.6 (2009) 54–58, 88–90.
Kolodner, Janet L. "From Natural Language Understanding to Case-Based Reasoning and Beyond: A Perspective on the Cognitive Model That Ties it All Together." In *Beliefs, Reasoning, and Decision Making: Psycho-Logic in Honor of Bob Abelson*, edited by Roger C. Schank and Ellen Langer, 55–110. Hillsdale, NJ: Earlbaum, 1994.
König, Gert. "Perspektive, Perspektivismus, perspektivisch." In *Historisches Wörterbuch der Philosophie*, edited by Joachim Ritter, Karlfried Gründer and Gottfried Gabriel, 7:363–75. 13 vols. Basel: Schwabe, 1971–2007.
Konstan, David. "The Invention of Fiction." In *Ancient Fiction and Early Christian Narrative*, edited by Ronald F. Hock, J. Bradley Chance, and Judith Perkins, 3–17. SBLSymS 6. Atlanta: Scholars, 1998.
Kovacs, Judith L. "Concealment and Gnostic Exegesis: Clement of Alexandria's Interpretation of the Tabernacle." In *Studia Patristica: Papers Presented at the Twelfth International Conference on Patristic Studies Held in Oxford, 1995*, edited by Elizabeth A. Livingstone, 414–37. StPatr 31. Leuven: Peeters, 1997.

Bibliography

Krashen, Stephen D. *Second Language Acquisition and Second Language Learning.* Oxford: Pergamon, 1981.
Krauss, Amanda, and Jess Miner. "From 'G' to 'PG-13': The Passion of Sostratos in Menander's *Dyskolos*." *Helios* 36 (2009) 99–116.
Kriegel, Maurice, editor. *Gershom Scholem.* Cahiers de l'Herne. Paris: L'Herne, 2009.
Lambeck, Peter. *Commentariorum de augusta bibliotheca caesarea vindobenensi.* 8 vols. Vienna: Typis M. Cosmerovii, 1665–1679.
Lampe, G. W. H. *A Patristic Greek Lexicon.* Oxford: Clarendon, 1961.
Lampe, Peter. *From Paul to Valentinus: Christians at Rome in the First Two Centuries.* Edited by Marshall D. Johnson. Translated by Michael Steinhauser. Minneapolis: Fortress, 2003.
Lane, William L. *The Gospel according to Mark: The English Text with Introduction, Exposition and Notes.* 1974. Reprinted, Grand Rapids: Eerdmans, 1993.
La Via, Stefano, "*Eros* and *Thanatos*: A Ficinian and Laurentian Reading of Verdelot's *Si lieta e grata morte*." *Early Music History* 21 (2002) 75–116.
Layton, Richard A. *Didymus the Blind and His Circle in Late-Antique Alexandria: Virtue and Narrative in Biblical Scholarship.* Urbana: University of Illinois Press, 2004.
Le Boulluec, Alain. *Alexandrie antique et chrétienne. Clément et Origène.* Edited by Carmelo G. Conticello. Collection des Études augustiniennes, Série Antiquité 178. Paris: Institut d'Études augustiniennes, 2006.
———. "'L'école' d'Alexandrie." In *Histoire du Christianisme.* Tome I, *Le nouveau people (des origines à 250),* edited by Luce Pietri, 531–78. Paris: Desclée, 2000.
———. "La lettre sur l'Évangile secret' de Marc et le *Quis dives salvetur?* de Clément d'Alexandrie." *Apocrypha* 7 (1996) 27–41.
———. *La notion d'hérésie dans la littérature grecque, IIe–IIIe siècles.* 2 vols. Paris: Études augustiniennes, 1985.
———. Review of *Mark's Other Gospel: Rethinking Morton Smith's Controversial Discovery,* by Scott G. Brown, and *The Gospel Hoax: Morton Smith's Invention of Secret Mark,* by Stephen C. Carlson. *Apocrypha* 19 (2008) 308–13.
Legrand, Émile. *Description des îles de l'Archipel par Christophe Buondelmonti, version grecque par un anonyme, publiée d'après le manuscrit du Sérail avec une traduction française et un commentaire.* Paris: Leroux, 1897.
Leonhardt, Jutta. *Jewish Worship in Philo of Alexandria.* Texts and Studies in Ancient Judaism 84. Tübingen: Mohr/Siebeck, 2001.
Levy, Jacob. *Wörterbuch über die Talmudim und Midraschim.* 4 vols. Darmstadt: Wissenschaftliche Buchgesellschaft, 1963.
Lilla, Salvatore R. C. *Clement of Alexandria: A Study in Christian Platonism and Gnosticism.* Oxford: Oxford University Press, 1971.
Llewellyn, Kathleen M. "Deadly Sex and Sexy Death in Early Modern French Literature." In *Sexuality in the Middle Ages and the Early Modern Age: New Approaches to a Fundamental Cultural-Historical and Literary-Anthropological Theme,* edited by Albrecht Classen, 811–35. Fundamentals of Medieval and Early Modern Culture 3. Berlin: de Gruyter, 2008.
Lowe, Kelly Fisher. *The Words and Music of Frank Zappa.* Praeger Singer-Songwriter Collection. Lincoln: University of Nebraska Press, 2007.
Lyell, *Patrick Ronaldson. The Sentence of Pontius Pilate, Being an Alleged Copy of the Formal Judgment against Jesus.* London: Grafton, 1922.

MacDonald, Dennis R. *The Homeric Epics and the Gospel of Mark*. New Haven: Yale University Press, 2000.
Mamet, David. *Theatre*. New York: Faber & Faber, 2010.
Marcus, Joel. *The Mystery of the Kingdom of God*. SBLDS 90. Atlanta: Scholars, 1986.
Martin, Annick. "À propos de la lettre attribuée à Clément d'Alexandrie sur l'Évangile secret de Marc." In *Colloque international "L'Évangile selon Thomas et les textes de Nag Hammadi" (Québec, 29-31 mai 2003)*. Edited by Louis Painchaud and Paul-Hubert Poirier, 277-300. Bibliothèque copte de Nag Hammadi, Section Études 8. Quebec, Leuven: Peeters, 2007.

———. *Athanase d'Alexandrie et l'Église d'Égypte au IVe siècle (328-373)*. Cahiers de l'École française de Rome 216. Rome: École française de Rome, 1996.

Mason, Steve. "*Philosophiai*: Graeco-Roman, Judean and Christian." In *Voluntary Associations in the Graeco-Roman World*. Edited by John S. Kloppenborg and Stephen G. Wilson, 31-58. 1996. Reprint, London: Routledge, 2005.
Mayeda, Goro. *Das Leben-Jesu-Fragment Papyrus Egerton 2 und seine Stellung in der urchristlichen Literaturgeschichte*. Bern: Paul Haupt, 1946.
McIver, Robert K. "'Cosmology' as a Key to the Thought-World of Philo of Alexandria." *AUSS* 26 (1988) 267-79.
McKeon, Richard. "Literary Criticism and the Concept of Imitation in Antiquity." *Modern Philology* 34 (1936) 1-35.
Meier, John P. *A Marginal Jew: Rethinking the Historical Jesus*. Vol. 2, *Mentor, Message, and Miracles*. ABRL. New York: Doubleday, 1994.
Metzger, Bruce M. "Literary Forgeries and Canonical Pseudepigrapha." *JBL* 91 (1972) 3-24. Reprinted in Metzger, *New Testament Studies: Philological, Versional, and Patristic*, 1-22. NTTS 10. Leiden: Brill, 1980.

———. *Reminiscences of an Octogenarian*. Peabody, MA: Hendrickson, 1997.

———. *A Textual Commentary on the Greek New Testament*. 2nd ed. Stuttgart: Deutsche Bibelgesellschaft, 2000.

Meyer, Marvin. "The Naked Youths in the Villa of the Mysteries, Canonical Mark, and *Secret Mark*." In *Secret Gospels: Essays on Thomas and the Secret Gospel of Mark*, 149-67. London: Continuum, 2003.

———. *Secret Gospels: Essays on Thomas and the Secret Gospel of Mark*. London: Continuum, 2003.

———. "Whom Did Jesus Love Most? Beloved Disciples in John and Other Gospels." In *The Legacy of John: Second Century Reception of the Fourth Gospel*. Edited by Tuomas Rasimus, 73-91. NovTSup 132. Leiden: Brill, 2009.

———. "The Youth in *Secret Mark* and the Beloved Disciple in John." In *Gospel Origins and Christian Beginnings: In Honor of James M. Robinson*. Edited by Jack T. Sanders, Charles W. Hedrick, and James E. Goehring, 94-105. Sonoma, CA: Polebridge, 1990.

———. "The Youth in the *Secret Gospel of Mark*." *Semeia* 49 (1990) 129-53.

Mitchell, Margaret M., Joseph G. Barabe, and Abigail B. Quandt, "Chicago's 'Archaic Mark' (ms 2427) II: Microscopic, Chemical and Codicological Analyses Confirm Modern Production." *NovT* 52 (2010) 101-33.
Mopsik, Charles. *Les grands textes de la cabale. Les rites qui font Dieu. Pratiques religieuses et efficacité théurgique dans la cabale des origines au milieu du XVIIIe siècle*. Les Dix Paroles. Lagrasse: Verdier, 1993.

Bibliography

Murgia, Charles E. "Secret Mark: Real or Fake?" In Reginald Fuller, *Longer Mark: Forgery, Interpolation, or Old Tradition? Protocol of the Eighteenth Colloquy: 7 December 1975,* edited by Wilhelm H. Wuellner, 35–40. Berkeley: Center for Hermeneutical Studies, 1976.

Murray, Robert. *Symbols of Church and Kingdom: A Study in Early Syriac Tradition.* Rev. ed. Piscataway, NJ: Gorgias, 2004.

Musurillo, Herbert. "Morton Smith's Secret Gospel." *Thought* 48 (1973) 327–31.

Nardi, Carlo. *Il battesimo in Clemente Alessandrino: Interpretazione di Eclogae propheticae 1–26.* Studia Ephemeridis "Augustinianum" 19. Rome: Institutum Patristicum "Augustinianum," 1984.

Neusner, Jacob. *Are There Really Tannaitic Parallels to the Gospels? A Refutation of Morton Smith.* SFSHJ 80. Atlanta: Scholars, 1993.

Noce, Carla. "Il Tema della nudità dell' anima." In *Origeniana Octava: Origen and the Alexandrian Tradition,* edited by L. Perrone et al., 1:679–86. 2 vols. Bibliotheca Ephemeridum Theologicarum Lovaniensium, 164A–B. Leuven: Peeters, 2003.

Nock, Arthur Darby. "Hellenistic Mysteries and Christian Sacraments." *Mnemosyne* 4th ser., 5 (1952) 177–213.

———. "Mysterion." *HSCP* 60 (1951) 201–4.

———. "Religious Symbols and Symbolism I." *Gnomon* 27 (1955) 558–72.

Norelli, Enrico. *Ascensio Isaiae: Commentarius.* CCSA 8. Turnhout: Brepols, 1995.

Osborn, Eric. *Clement of Alexandria.* Cambridge: Cambridge University Press, 2005.

———. "Clement of Alexandria: A Review of Research, 1958–1982." *SecCent* 3 (1983) 219–44.

Oulton, John Ernest Leonard, and Henry Chadwick, editors. *Alexandrian Christianity: Selected Translations of Clement and Origen.* Library of Christian Classics 2. Philadelphia: Westminster, 1954.

Owen, Alex. "The Sorcerer and His Apprentice: Aleister Crowley and the Magical Exploration of Edwardian Subjectivity." *Journal of British Studies* 36 (1997) 99–133. Reprinted in Owen, *The Place of Enchantment: British Occultism and the Culture of Modern,* 186–220 and 297–304. Chicago: University of Chicago Press, 2004.

Paananen, Timo S. "A Conspiracy of the Secret Evangelist: Recent Debate Concerning Clement of Alexandria's Letter to Theodore." Salainen evankelista (posted 3 June 2009). No pages. Online: http://salainenevankelista.blogspot.com/2009/06/masters-thesis-conspiracy-of-secret.html.

———. "A Short Interview with Quentin Quesnell." Salainen evankelista (posted 15 June 2011). No pages. Online: http://salainenevankelista.blogspot.com/2011/06/short-interview-with-quentin-quesnell.html.

———. "Toronto Conference in Review—A Summary" (posted 20 May 2011). No pages. Online: http://salainenevankelista.blogspot.com/2011/05/toronto-conference-in-review-summary.html.

Paananen, Timo S., and Roger Viklund. "Per Beskow and the Elusive MS: A Guest Post by Roger Viklund." Salainen evankelista (posted 21 November 2009). No pages. Online: http://salainenevankelista.blogspot.com/2009/11/per-beskow-and-elusive-ms-guest-post-by.html.

Pantuck, Allan J. "Response to Agamemnon Tselikas on Morton Smith and the Manuscripts from Cephalonia." Biblical Archaeology Review Scholar's Study (posted 19 August 2011). No pages. Online: http://www.bib-arch.org/scholars-study/secret-mark-handwriting-response-pantuck-2.asp.

———. "Solving the *Mysterion* of Morton Smith and the Secret Gospel of Mark." Biblical Archaeology Review Scholar's Study (posted 20 February 2011). No pages. Online: http://www.bib-arch.org/scholars-study/secret-mark-handwriting-response-pantuck.pdf.

Pantuck, Allan J., and Scott G. Brown. "Morton Smith as M. Madiotes: Stephen Carlson's Attribution of *Secret Mark* to a Bald Swindler." *JSHS* 6 (2008) 106–25.

Pearson, Birger A. "A Coptic Homily *On Riches* Attributed to St. Peter of Alexandria." In *Gnosticism and Christianity in Roman and Coptic Egypt*, 114–31. SAC. New York: T. & T. Clark, 2004.

———. "Earliest Christianity in Egypt: Some Observations." In *The Roots of Egyptian Christianity*. Edited by Birger A. Pearson and James E. Goehring, 132–59. SAC. Philadelphia: Fortress, 1986.

———. "The Secret Gospel of Mark: A 20th Century Forgery." *Interdisciplinary Journal of Research on Religion* 4 (2008). Article 6. Pages 1–14. Online: http://www.religjournal.com/articles/article_view.php?id=27.

Penfield, Wilder, and Lamar Roberts. *Speech and Brain Mechanisms*. Princeton: Princeton University Press, 1959.

Pietersma, Albert. "Bodmer Papyri." In *The Anchor Bible Dictionary*, edited by David Noel Freedman, 1:766–77. 6 vols. New York: Doubleday, 1992.

Pietruschka, Ute, and Alessandro Bausi. "Urbino, Giusto da." *Encyclopaedia Aethiopica* 4 (2010) 1043–45.

Pilch, John J. *Flights of the Soul: Visions, Heavenly Journeys, and Peak Experiences in the Biblical World*. Grand Rapids: Eerdmans, 2011.

Piovanelli, Pierluigi. "Une certaine 'Keckheit, Kühnheit und Grandiosität' ... La correspondance entre Morton Smith et Gershom Scholem (1945–1982): Notes critiques." *RHR* 228 (2011) 403–29.

———. "*L'Évangile Secret de Marc* trente-trois ans après, entre potentialités exégétiques et difficultés techniques." *RB* 114 (2007) 52–72, 237–54.

———. "'Un gros et beau poisson': *L'Évangile selon Thomas* dans la recherche (et la controverse) contemporaine(s)." *Adamantius* 15 (2009) 291–306.

———. "Pratiques rituelles ou exégèse scripturaire? Origines et nature de la mystique de la Merkavah." In *Mystique théorétique et théurgique dans la littérature juive d'époque hellénistique et romaine*. Edited by Simon C. Mimouni, Madeleine Scopello, and Arnaud Sérandour. Paris: Champion, forthcoming.

———. "Pre- and Post-canonical Passion Stories: Insights into the Development of Christian Discourse on the Death of Jesus." *Apocrypha* 14 (2003) 99–128

———. "Thomas in Edessa? Another Look at the Original Setting of the *Gospel of Thomas*." In *Myths, Martyrs, and Modernity: Studies in the History of Religions in Honour of Jan N. Bremmer*, edited by Jitse Dijkstra, Justin Kroesen and Yme Kuiper, 443–61. Numen Book Series 127. Leiden: Brill, 2010.

Potter, John, editor. *Clementis Alexandrini Opera quae exstant*. Oxford: George Mortlock, 1715.

Price, Robert M. "Second Thoughts on the Secret Gospel." *BBR* 14 (2004) 127–32.

Procter, Everett. *Christian Controversy in Alexandria: Clement's Polemic against the Basilideans and Valentinians*. American University Studies Series 7: Theology and Religion 172. New York: Lang, 1995.

Bibliography

Pryke, E. J. *Redactional Style in the Marcan Gospel: A Study of Syntax and Vocabulary as Guides to Redaction in Mark.* SNTSMS 33. Cambridge: Cambridge University Press, 1978.

Quarles, Charles L. "Jesus as *Merkabah* Mystic." *JSHJ* 3 (2005) 5–22.

Quesnell, Quentin. "The Mar Saba Clementine: A Question of Evidence." *CBQ* 37 (1975) 48–67.

———. "A Reply to Morton Smith." *CBQ* 38 (1976) 200–203.

Räisänen, Heikki. *The Rise of Christian Beliefs: The Thought World of Early Christians.* Minneapolis: Fortress, 2010.

Randall, Phyllis, and Ronald Butters. "*Hubba-Hubba*: Its Rise and Fall." *American Speech* 61.4 (1986) 363–65.

Rau, Eckhard. "Das Geheimnis des Reiches Gottes: Die esoterische Rezeption der Lehre Jesu im geheimen Markusevangelium." In *Jesus in apokryphen Evangelienüberlieferungen: Beiträge zu ausserkanonischen Jesusüberlieferungen aus verschiedenen Sprach- und Kulturtraditionen,* edited by Jörg Frey and Jens Schröter, 187–221. WUNT 1/254. Tübingen: Mohr/Siebeck, 2010.

———. "Weder gefälscht noch authentisch? Überlegungen zum Status des geheimen Markusevangeliums als Quelle des antiken Christentums." In *Jesus in apokryphen Evangelienüberlieferungen: Beiträge zu ausserkanonischen Jesusüberlieferungen aus verschiedenen Sprach- und Kulturtraditionen,* edited by Jörg Frey and Jens Schröter, 139–86. WUNT 1/254. Tübingen: Mohr/Siebeck, 2010.

Reynolds, L. D., and N. G. Wilson. *Scribes and Scholars: A Guide to the Transmission of Greek and Latin Literature.* 2nd ed. Oxford: Clarendon, 1974.

Richards, Jack C., and Willy A. Renandya, editors. *Methodology in Language Teaching: An Anthology of Current Practice.* Cambridge: Cambridge University Press, 2002.

Richardson, Cyril C. Review of *The Secret Gospel: The Discovery and Interpretation of the Secret Gospel according to Mark* and *Clement of Alexandria and a Secret Gospel of Mark,* by Morton Smith. *TS* 35 (1974) 571–77.

Richter, David H. "The Reader as Ironic Victim." *Novel: A Forum on Fiction* 14.2 (1981) 135–51.

Riedweg, Christoph. *Mysterienterminologie bei Plato, Philo und Klemens von Alexandrien.* Untersuchungen zur antiken Literatur und Geschichte 26. Berlin: de Gruyter, 1987.

Riordan, John Lancaster. "A Further Note on 'Hubba-Hubba.'" *American Speech* 22.4 (1947) 307–8.

Rizzerio, Laura. "L'accès à la transcendance divine selon Clément d'Alexandrie: dialectique platonicienne ou expérience de l''union chrétienne'?" *REAug* 44 (1998) 159–79.

———. *Clemente di Alessandria e la "φυσιολογία veramente gnostica": Saggio sulle origini e le implicazioni di un'epistemologia e di un'ontologia "cristiane."* Recherches de théologie ancienne et médiévale Supplementa 6. Leuven: Peeters, 1996.

———. "La notion de γνωστικὴ φυσιολογία chez Clément d'Alexandrie." In *Studia Patristica: Papers Presented at the Eleventh International Conference on Patristic Studies Held in Oxford, 1991.* Edited by Elizabeth A. Livingstone, 318–23. StPatr 26. Leuven: Peeters, 1993.

Rollston, Christopher A. "Non-Provenanced Epigraphs I: Pillaged Antiquities, Northwest Semitic Forgeries, and Protocols for Laboratory Tests." *Maarav* 10 (2003) 135–93.

Rousse-Lacordaire, Jérome. "Bulletin d'Histoire des Ésotérismes." *RSPT* 92 (2008) 849–50.
Royal Ontario Museum. "Royal Ontario Museum Statement: Oded Golan's arrest/ James Ossuary." Royal Ontario Museum (posted 23 July 2003). No pages. Online: http://www.rom.on.ca/news/releases/public.php?mediakey=vhggdo3048.
Ruina, David T. *Philo in Early Christian Literature: A Survey*. CRINT. Second Series 3. Minneapolis: Fortress, 1993.
Russell, Norman. *The Doctrine of Deification in the Greek Patristic Tradition*. Oxford Early Christian Studies. Oxford: Oxford University Press, 2004.
Russo, Nicholas V. "A Note on the Role of *Secret Mark* in the Search for the Origins of Lent." *Studia Liturgica* 37 (2007) 181–97.
Saenger, Paul. *Space between Words: The Origins of Silent Reading*. Stanford: Stanford University Press, 1997.
Sanders, E. P. *Jesus and Judaism*. Philadelphia: Fortress, 1985.
Sandnes, Karl Olav. *The Challenge of Homer: School, Pagan Poets and Early Christianity*. Library of New Testament Studies 400. London: T. & T. Clark, 2009.
Sandys, John Edwin. *A History of Classical Scholarship*. Vol. 2, *From the Revival of Learning to the End of the Eighteenth Century (in Italy, France, England, and the Netherlands)*. New York: Hafner, 1967.
Satterlee, Craig Alan. *Ambrose of Milan's Method of Mystagogical Preaching*. Collegeville, MN: Liturgical, 2002.
Schäfer, Peter. *The Origins of Jewish Mysticism*. Tübingen: Mohr/Siebeck, 2009.
Schefer, Christina. "Rhetoric as Part of an Initiation into the Mysteries: A New Interpretation of the Platonic *Phaedrus*." In *Plato as Author: The Rhetoric of Philosophy*. Edited by Ann N. Michelini, 175–96. Leiden: Brill, 2003.
Schenke, Hans-Martin. "The Mystery of the Gospel of Mark." *SecCent* 4 (1984) 65–82.
Schilderman, Hans. "Liturgical Studies from a Ritual Studies Perspective." In *Discourse in Ritual Studies*, edited by Hans Schilderman, 3–34. Empirical Studies in Theology 14. Leiden: Brill, 2007.
Schneider, Ulrich. *Theologie als christliche Philosophie: Zur Bedeutung der biblischen Botschaft im Denken des Clemens von Alexandria*. Arbeiten zur Kirchengeschichte 73. Berlin: de Gruyter, 1999.
Scholem, Gershom. *Alchemy and Kabbalah*. Translated by Klaus Hottmann. Putnam, CT: Spring, 2006.
———. *Kabbalah*. New York: Dorset, 1987.
———. *Major Trends in Jewish Mysticism*. 3rd ed. 1954. Reprint, New York: Schocken, 1995.
———. *The Messianic Idea in Judaism and Other Essays on Jewish Spirituality*. 1971. Reprint, New York: Schocken, 1995.
———. *On the Kabbalah and Its Symbolism*. Translated by Ralph Manheim. New York: Schocken, 1965.
———. *Sabbatai Tzevi: The Mystical Messiah, 1626–1676*. Translated by R. J. Zwi Werblowsky. Bollingen Series 93. Princeton: Princeton University Press, 1973.
Schwarz, Leo W. *Wolfson of Harvard: Portrait of a Scholar*. Philadelphia: Jewish Publication Society of America, 1978.
Scopello, Madeleine, editor. *The Gospel of Judas in Context: Proceedings of the First International Conference on the Gospel of Judas*. Paris, Sorbonne, October 27th–28th, 2006. NHMS 62. Leiden: Brill, 2008.

Bibliography

Scott, Alan. *Origen and the Life of the Stars: A History of an Idea.* Oxford: Clarendon, 1991.
Scroggs, Robin, and Kent I. Groff. "Baptism in Mark: Dying and Rising with Christ." *JBL* 92 (1973) 531–48.
Shanks, Hershel. "Annual Meetings Offer Intellectual Bazaar and Moments of High Drama." *BAR* 11.2 (1985) 16.
———. "First Person: Shakespeare, the Earl of Oxford and Morton Smith." *BAR* 36.6 (2010) 6–7, 66.
———. "Handwriting Experts Weigh in on 'Secret Mark,'" *BAR* 36.3 (2010) 18, 79.
———. "Morton Smith—Forger." *BAR* 35.6 (2009) 49–53, 86, 88.
———. "Restoring a Dead Scholar's Reputation." *BAR* 35.6 (2009) 59–61, 90–91.
Shepardson, Christine. "Controlling Contested Places: John Chrysostom's *Adversus Iudaeos* Homilies and the Spatial Politics of Religious Controversy." *JECS* 15 (2007) 483–516.
Shepherd, Massey H. "Response to Reginald H. Fuller." In *Longer Mark: Forgery, Interpolation, or Old Tradition? Protocol of the Eighteenth Colloquy: 7 December 1975*, edited by Wilhelm H. Wuellner, 46–52. Berkeley: Center for Hermeneutical Studies, 1976.
Slee, Michelle. *The Church in Antioch in the First Century C.E.: Communion and Conflict.* JSNTSup 244. London: Sheffield Academic, 2003.
Smith, Edward Reaugh. *The Temple Sleep of the Rich Young Ruler: How Lazarus Became the Evangelist John.* Great Barrington, MA: Steinerbooks, 2011.
Smith, J. Warren. *Christian Grace and Pagan Virtue: The Theological Foundation of Ambrose's Ethics.* Oxford Studies in Historical Theology. Oxford: Oxford University Press, 2011.
Smith, Jonathan Z. "The Garments of Shame." *HR* 5 (1966) 217–38.
Smith, Kyle. "'Mixed with Inventions': Salt and Metaphor in *Secret Mark*." The Secret Gospel of Mark Homepage (posted October 2005). Pages 1–20. Online: http://www-user.uni-bremen.de/~wie/Secret/SALT-PAPER.rtf.
Smith, Morton. "Aramaic Studies and the Study of the New Testament." *JBR* 26 (1958) 304–13.
———. *The Aretalogy Used by Mark: Proceedings of the Sixth Colloquy, 12 April 1973.* Edited by Wilhelm H. Wuellner. Berkeley: Center for Hermeneutical Studies in Hellenistic and Modern Culture, 1975.
———. "Ascent to the Heavens and the Beginning of Christianity." *ErJb* 50 (1981) 403–29.
———. *Clement of Alexandria and a Secret Gospel of Mark.* Cambridge: Harvard University Press, 1973.
———. "Clement of Alexandria and Secret Mark: The Score at the End of the First Decade." *HTR* 75 (1982) 449–61.
———. "Comments on Taylor's Commentary on Mark." *HTR* 48 (1955) 21–64.
———. "The Description of the Essenes in Josephus and the Philosophumena." *HUCA* 29 (1958) 273–313.
———. "Ἑλληνικὰ χειρόγραφα ἐν τῇ Μονῇ τοῦ ἁγίου Σάββα" ("Greek Manuscripts in the Monastery of St. Saba"). Translated by Archimandrite Constantine Michaelides. Νέα Σιών (*New Zion*) 52 (1960) 110–25, 245–56.
———. "Goodenough's Jewish Symbols in Retrospect." *JBL* 86 (1967) 53–68.
———. "Hebrew—Why Not Greek?" *Orthodox Observer* 24 (1958) 197–98.

———. *Hekhalot Rabbati*—רבתי היכלות: *The Greater Treatise Concerning the Palaces of Heaven*. 2nd ed. Corrected by Gershom Scholem. Transcribed and edited with notes by Don Karr. 2009. Pages 1–43. Online: http://www.digital-brilliance.com/contributed/Karr/HekRab/HekRab.pdf.

———. "Historical Method in the Study of Religion." *History and Theory* 8, Beiheft 8 (1968) 8–16.

———. "How Magic Was Changed by the Triumph of Christianity." In *Graeco-Arabica: Papers of the First International Congress on Greek and Arabic Studies*. Vol. 2, edited by V. Christides and M. Papthomopoulos, 51–58. Athens: Association for Greek and Arabic Studies, 1983.

———. "The Image of God: Notes on the Hellenization of Judaism, with Special Reference to Goodenough's Work on Jewish Symbols." *BJRL* 40 (1958) 473–512.

———. "In Quest of Jesus." *New York Review of Books* 25/20. 21 December 1978. Online at: http://www.nybooks.com/articles/archives/1978/dec/21/in-quest-of-jesus/.

———. *Jesus the Magician*. San Francisco: Harper & Row, 1978.

———. "The Jewish Elements in the Gospels." *JBR* 24 (1956) 90–96.

———. *Makbilot ben ha-Besorot le-sifrut ha-Tana'im* ("Parallels between the Gospels and the Literature of the Tannaim"). PhD diss., Hebrew University, Jerusalem, 1944.

———. "The Manuscript Tradition of Isidore of Pelusium." *HTR* 47 (1954) 205–10.

———. "Monasteries and their Manuscripts." *Archaeology* 13 (1960) 172–77.

———. "New Fragments of Scholia on Sophocle's *Ajax*." *GRBS* 3 (1960) 40–42.

———. "Observations on *Hekhalot Rabbati*." In *Biblical and Other Studies*. Edited by Alexander Altmann, 142–60. Studies and Texts 1. Cambridge: Harvard University Press, 1963.

———. "O'Keefe's *Social Theory of Magic*." *JQR* 74 (1984) 301–13.

———. "On the Authenticity of the Mar Saba Letter of Clement." *CBQ* 38 (1976) 196–99.

———. "The Origin and History of the Transfiguration Story." *USQR* 36 (1980) 39–44.

———. "Palestinian Judaism in the First Century." In *Israel: Its Role in Civilization*. Edited by Moshe Davis, 67–81. New York: Jewish Theological Seminary of America, 1956.

———. *Palestinian Parties and Politics That Shaped the Old Testament*. Lectures on the History of Religions 9. New York: Columbia University Press, 1971.

———. "Pauline Worship as Seen by Pagans." *HTR* 73 (1980) 241-49.

———. "Paul's Arguments as Evidence of the Christianity from which He Diverged." *HTR* 79 (1986) 254–60.

———. "The Present State of Old Testament Studies." *JBL* 88 (1969) 19–35.

———. "Prolegomena to a Discussion of Aretalogies, Divine Men, the Gospels and Jesus." *JBL* 90 (1971) 174–99.

———. "The Reason for the Persecution of Paul and the Obscurity of Acts." In *Studies in Mysticism and Religion Presented to Gershom G. Scholem*, edited by E. E. Urbach et al., 261–68. Jerusalem: Magnes, 1967.

———. Review of *The Midrash on Psalms*, by William G. Braude. *Religion in Life* 29 (1960) 161.

Bibliography

———. *The Secret Gospel: The Discovery and Interpretation of the Secret Gospel according to Mark.* New York: Harper & Row, 1973. Reprint, Clearlake, Calif.: Dawn Horse, 1982.

———. *Studies in the Cult of Yahweh.* 2 vols. Edited by Shaye J. D. Cohen. Religions in the Graeco-Roman World 130.1–2. Leiden: Brill, 1996.

———. "Σύμμεικτα: Notes on Collections of Manuscripts in Greece." Ἐπετηρὶς Ἑταιρείας Βυζανττιῶν Σπουδῶν [*Journal of the Society for Byzantine Studies*] 26 (1956) 380–93.

———. *Tannaitic Parallels to the Gospels.* JBLMS 6. 1951. Corrected reprint, Philadelphia: Society of Biblical Literature, 1968.

———. "Two Ascended to Heaven—Jesus and the Author of 4Q491." In *Jesus and the Dead Sea Scrolls*, edited by James H. Charlesworth, 290–301. ABRL. New York: Doubleday, 1992.

———. "Under the Sheet." *New York Review of Books* 26/1, 8 February 1979. Online: http://www.nybooks.com/articles/archives/1979/feb/08/under-the-sheet/.

———. "An Unpublished Life of St. Isidore of Pelusium." In Εὐχαριστήριον. Edited by Gerasimos Ioannou Konidaris, 429–38. Athens: [Apostolike Diakonia tes Ekklesias tes Hellados], 1958.

Solomon, Robert C. "Nietzsche ad hominem: Perspectivism, Personality, and Ressentiment." In *The Cambridge Companion to Nietzsche.* Edited by Bernd Magnus and Kathleen Higgins, 180–222. Cambridge: Cambridge University Press, 1996.

Sonnini, Charles Sigisbert. *Voyage en Grèce et en Turquie.* Paris: Buisson, 1799. English translation, *Travels in Greece and Turkey.* London: Longman & Rees, 1801.

Specter, Michael. "Tomb May Hold the Bones of Priest Who Judged Jesus." *New York Times*, 14 August 1992, 1, 2, 10.

Stählin, Otto, editor. *Clemens Alexandrinus.* Vol. 4, Register 1, *Zitatenregister, Testimonienregister, Initienregister für die Fragmente, Eigennamenregister.* GCS 39. Leipzig: Hinrichs, 1936. Re-edited by Ursula Treu. Berlin: Akademie, 1980.

Starks, Lisa S. "'Immortal Longings': The Erotics of Death in *Antony and Cleopatra*." In *Antony and Cleopatra: New Critical Essays.* Edited by Sara Munson Deats, 243–58. New York: Routledge, 2005.

Stephensen, Percy R. *The Legend of Aleister Crowley: Being a Study of the Documentary Evidence Relating to a Campaign of Personal Vilification Unparalleled in Literary History.* 2nd ed. Saint Paul, MN: Llewellyn, 1970.

Stökl Ben Ezra, Daniel. *The Impact of Yom Kippur on Early Christianity: The Day of Atonement from Second Temple Judaism to the Fifth Century.* WUNT 163. Tübingen: Mohr/Siebeck, 2003.

Strauss, David Friedrich. *The Life of Jesus Critically Examined.* Translated by George Eliot. 1860. Reprint, Lives of Jesus Series. Philadelphia: Fortress, 1973.

Strobel, Lee. *The Case for the Real Jesus: A Journalist Investigates Current Attacks on the Identity of Christ.* Downers Grove, IL: Inter-Varsity, 2006.

Stroumsa, Guy G., editor. "Comments on Charles Hedrick's Article: A Testimony." *JECS* 11 (2003) 147–53.

———, editor. *Morton Smith and Gershom Scholem, Correspondence 1945–1982.* Jerusalem Studies in Religion and Culture 9. Leiden: Brill, 2008.

Talley, Thomas. "Liturgical Time in the Ancient Church: The State of Research." *Studia Liturgica* 14 (1982) 34–51.

Taylor, Joan E. *Jewish Women Philosophers of First-Century Alexandria: Philo's "Therapeutae" Reconsidered.* Oxford: Oxford University Press, 2003.
Taylor, Vincent. *The Gospel according to St. Mark: The Greek Text with Introduction, Notes, and Indexes.* London: Macmillan, 1952.
Thomas, Samuel I. *The "Mysteries" of Qumran: Mystery, Secrecy, and Esotericism in the Dead Sea Scrolls.* SBLEJL 25. Atlanta: Society of Biblical Literature, 2009.
Thomassen, Einar, and Marvin Meyer. "Valentinian Exposition with Valentinian Liturgical Readings." In *The Nag Hammadi Scriptures: The International Edition*, edited by Marvin Meyer et al., 667–77. New York: Harper, 2007.
Thompson, Edward M. *An Introduction to Greek and Latin Palaeography.* Oxford: Clarendon, 1912.
Tigay, Jeffrey. Letter to the Editor. In "Queries and Comments." *BAR* 37.3 (2011) 10.
Trozzi, Nicola. *Lo Hatata Zar-a Yaiqob we-Walda Hiywat e P. Giusto da Urbino.* Chieti: Solfanelli, 1986.
Tselikas, Agamemnon. "Agamemnon Tselikas' Handwriting Analysis Report." Biblical Archaeology Review Scholar's Study (posted May 2011). No pages. Online: http://www.bib-arch.org/scholars-study/secret-mark-handwriting-agamemnon.asp.
———. "Response to Allan J. Pantuck." Biblical Archaeology Review Scholar's Study (posted 19 August 2011). No pages. Online: http://www.bib-arch.org/scholars-study/secret-mark-handwriting-response-tselikas.asp.
———. "Τὰ χειρόγραφα τῆς Μονῆς τῶν Θεμάτων στὴν Κεφαλονιά." Κεφαλληνιακὰ Χρονικὰ 4 (1982) 184–88.
van den Hoek. "The 'Catechetical' School of Early Christian Alexandria and Its Philonic Heritage." *HTR* 90 (1997) 59–87.
———. *Clement of Alexandria and His Use of Philo in the Stromateis: An Early Christian Reshaping of a Jewish Model.* VCSup 3. Leiden: Brill, 1988.
Viklund, Roger. "Reclaiming Clement's Letter to Theodoros—An Examination of Carlson's Handwriting Analysis." Jesus granskad (posted 7 February 2009). No pages. Online: http://www.jesusgranskad.se/theodore.htm.
———. "Tremors, or Just an Optical Illusion? A Further Evaluation of Carlson's Handwriting Analysis." Jesus granskad (posted 12 December 2009). No pages. Online: http://www.jesusgranskad.se/theodore2.htm.
Völker, Walther, editor. *Quellen zur Geschichte der Christlichen Gnosis.* Tübingen: Mohr/Siebeck, 1932.
Voss, Isaac. *Epistulae genuinae S. Ignatii Martyris.* Amsterdam: Blaeu, 1646.
Wagner, Walter H. *After the Apostles: Christianity in the Second Century.* Minneapolis: Fortress, 1994.
———. "Another Look at the Literary Problem in Clement of Alexandria's Major Writings." *Church History* 37 (1968) 251–60.
Wasserstrom, Steven M. *Religion after Religion: Gershom Scholem, Mircea Eliade, and Henry Corbin at Eranos.* Princeton: Princeton University Press, 1999.
Watson, Francis. "Beyond Reasonable Doubt: A Response to Allan J. Pantuck." Biblical Archaeology Review Scholar's Study (posted 2011). Pages 1–8. Online: http://www.bib-arch.org/scholars-study/secret-mark-handwriting-response-watson.asp.
———. "Beyond Suspicion: On the Authorship of the Mar Saba Letter and the Secret Gospel of Mark." *JTS* 61 (2010) 128–70.

Bibliography

Webb, Robert L. Review of *The Secret Gospel of Mark Unveiled: Imagined Rituals of Sex, Death, and Madness in a Biblical Forgery*, by Peter Jeffery. *JSHJ* 5 (2007) 216.

Weinberger, A. D. "Some Data and Conjectures on the History of 'Hubba-Hubba.'" *American Speech* 22.1 (1947) 34–39.

Weiss, Roberto. "The New Learning. Scholarship from Petrarch to Erasmus." In *The Age of the Renaissance*, edited by Denys Hay, 119–44. New York: McGraw-Hill, 1967.

———. *The Renaissance Discovery of Classical Antiquity*. New York: Humanities, 1969.

White, David A. *Myth and Metaphysics in Plato's Phaedo*. Selinsgrove, PA: Susquehanna University Press, 1989.

Witherington, Ben III. *Letters and Homilies for Jewish Christians: A Socio-Rhetorical Commentary on Hebrews, James and Jude*. Downers Grove, IL: InterVarsity, 2007.

Wolfson, Elliot. "The Seven Mysteries of Knowledge: Qumran E/Sotericism Recovered." In *The Idea of Biblical Interpretation: Essays in Honor of James L. Kugel*. Edited by Hindy Najman and Judith H. Newman, 177–213. JSJSup 83. Leiden: Brill, 2004.

Wolfson, Harry A. *Philo: Foundations of Religious Philosophy in Judaism, Christianity, and Islam*. 2 vols. Cambridge: Harvard University Press, 1948.

Wolters, Al. "Ficino and Plotinus' Treatise 'On Eros.'" In *Ficino and Renaissance Neoplatonism*, edited by Konrad Eisenbichler and Olga Zorzi Pugliese, 189–97. Toronto: Dovehouse, 1986.

Wrede, William. *Das Messiasgeheimnis in den Evangelien: Zugleich ein Beitrag zum Verständnis des Markusevangeliums*. Göttingen: Vandenhoeck & Ruprecht, 1901. English translation, *The Messianic Secret*. Translated by J. C. G. Grieg. Cambridge: James Clarke, 1971.

Wyrwa, Dietmar. *Die christliche Platonaneignung in den Stromateis des Clemens von Alexandrien*. Arbeiten zur Kirchengeschichte 53. Berlin: de Gruyter, 1983.

Yarnold, Edward. *The Awe-Inspiring Rites of Initiation: The Origins of the R[ite of] C[hristian] I[nitiation of] A[dults]*. 2nd ed. Collegeville, MN: Liturgical, 1994.

Ysebaert, Joseph. *Greek Baptismal Terminology: Its Origins and Early Development*. Graecitas Christianorum Primaeva 1. Nijmegen: Dekker & Van de Vegt, 1962.

Zacharias, Danny. "The Gospel Hoax." Deinde (posted 6 November 2005). No pages. Online: http://www.deinde.org/blog/deinde_archive_files/deinde%20archive%20 42.pdf.

Zeddies, Michael T. "A Critique of Watson." Synoptic Solutions (posted 18 April 2010). No pages. Online: http://synopticsolutions.blogspot.com/2010/04/critique-of-watson-part-1.html.

Index of Ancient Texts

HEBREW BIBLE/ OLD TESTAMENT

Genesis
	145
1:2–5	256
1:11–25	256
2:24	235
22:3–4	280
22:13	240
28:12	238

Exodus
	220
26–27	261
28	270
28:36	266
29:6	266
29:1	264
29:4	264
39:30	266

Leviticus
8:6	264
16:3–4	262, 264
18	302
18:6–30	83
18:22	83

Psalms
25:14	233

Proverbs
3:24	233
26:5	310

PSEUDEPIGRAPHA

Ascension of Isaiah
10–11	235

DEAD SEA SCROLLS

Songs of the Sabbath Sacrifice
1 II, 27	273

NEW TESTAMENT

Gospel of Matthew
	9, 49–50, 98, 108, 132, 154, 220, 225, 287, 291, 297
1:1	50
2:1	50
5:13	32, 309

Index of Ancient Texts

Gospel of Matthew (continued)

5:33–37	98
9:27	50
11:2–3	117
11:13	171
12:23	50
12:24	85, 115
13:11	258
14:12–13	117
15:22	50
19:13	50
20:30–31	50
21:9	50
21:15	50
25:1–13	234
25:29	310
25:30	79
27:61	50

Gospel of Mark

2:1—3:6	115
3:1–3	109
3:1	50
3:22	85, 115
4	269
4:1–2	49
4:10–12	119, 257
4:11	xvi, 82, 83, 86–87, 88, 105–12, 119, 231, 258, 302
4:33–34	112
4:34	59, 110, 257
5:6	50
5:11	50
5:18	238
5:35–43	47–48, 49, 51
6:1–31	116–17
6:22	268
7:15	236
8:22	50
8:27—9:1	111
8:33	155
8:38	111
9:2	239
9:9	111
10:1	58
10:10	59
10:13	50
10:17–22	152–53
10:21	236, 238
10:27	238
10:32–34	286
10:32	46, 58
10:34–35	58, 153
10:46	58, 152, 153
10:47–48	50
13:3	59
13:32	111
14	145, 154, 294
14:17	59
14:46–52	235
14:51–52	xvii, 9, 152, 305–6
14:51	153
15:19	50
15:40	268
16:1–8	149, 152, 154–56

Gospel of Luke

	9, 49, 108, 148, 154, 291, 297
1:4	223
6:6	50
8:32	50
10:31—13:29	41
11:15	85, 115
13:31–32	117
14:34	309
16:16	171
16:24	50
17:13	50
18:15	50
18:23	153, 238
18:38–39	50
19:2–6	238
19:26	310
24:29	33

Gospel of John

	29, 49–50, 83, 116, 118, 146, 153, 155, 210, 288, 290, 297
1:51	238
3:23	50

338

4:6	50
5:5	50
6:15–29	117
6:22	50
7:53—8:11	45
11	5, 86, 115, 165, 247
11:36	236
13:23	238
14:6	238
18:1	91
19:26	238
19:39	91
21:7	235
21:20	238

Acts

	148
18:25	223

1 Corinthians

1:24	266
2:1–7	82, 107
2:1–6	82, 106
2:6–7	82, 108, 232
2:6	119
2:7–8	235
2:7	232, 235
2:9	263, 267, 268
2:13	273
3:1–3	109
4:1–6	232
11	232
13:12	263, 265

2 Corinthians

12:1–4	254
12:2–4	240
3:17	311

Galatians

5:1	244
6:6	223

Ephesians

3:9	232
5:31–32	266
5:32	109, 234

Philippians

3:12	280

Colossians

2:2	109
2:15	235
2:18	234
3:1	234

1 Thessalonians

5:5	310

1 Timothy

	288

2 Timothy

	288

Titus

	288
1:15	274, 311

Hebrews

	260, 261, 262
6:1–5	218–19
9:3–4	266
10:20	238

1 John

	148

Revelation

	234, 238
2	308
5	218–19
7	218–19
7:9	154
15	218–19
19	218–19
19:7–9	234
21:2	234
21:9	234
21:17	234

RABBINIC WRITINGS

Hagigah

2.1–7	83
2.1	82–84, 106–7, 112, 119, 302
2.3	84

Hekhalot Rabbati

177–78, 180, 233

Targum Isaiah

70

EARLY CHRISTIAN WRITINGS

Acts of Pilate 73

Aphrahat
Demonstrations

| 4.5 | 238–39 |

Athanasius of Alexandria
Festal Letters

162

Clement of Alexandria
Eclogae propheticae

56.6–7	267
57.4	221
57.5	255, 265, 270

Excerpta ex Theodoto

10–16	265
10.5–6	267
10.6	253
12.1	253
14.2	265
14.4	265
27	254, 264–68
27.1–2	255, 265
27.1–3	266
27.5	267
66	257
76	220
77–80	220
85	220

Hypotyposeis

132, 226, 257

Protrepticus

1.2.4	134
2.11.1	241
2.13.1	237
2.21.1	240
2.22.3	237
2.22.5	240
2.22.7	240
2.26.1	240
2.34.3–5	237
2.34.5	240
7.74.3	240
10.94.2	221
12.120.1	221, 240

Index of Ancient Texts

12.123.2	221, 240

Paedagogus

I.1.1.4—2.1	221
I.1.1.1—2.1	228
I.1.3.3	221–22, 224
I.5.12.1—6.52.3	221, 223
I.5.18.4	221
I.5.20.1	221
I.6	162, 280
I.6.25.1—26.3	226
I.6.25.3—31.2	221
I.6.28.3	280
I.6.30.2	221, 230
I.6.31.2	230
I.6.36.3	221, 223
I.6.37.1	222
I.6.52.2–3	280
I.7.53.1—61.3	221
I.7.57.2	253
II.6.51.1	242
II.8.63.4	200
II.10.96.1	242
II.12.129.4	267
III.1.1.1—2.3	228
III.2.5.1–3	242
III.2.11.3	242
III.3.20.2	242
III.3.22.1	242
III.11.53.1—12.101.3	225
III.12.87.1–4	221–23
III.12.97.1—101.3	221–23

Quis dives salvetur

3.2	240
5.1–4	257
5.4	240
42.4	221

Stromateis

I.1.11.3	227, 257, 269
I.1.13–14	84, 112, 200
I.1.13.1–5	227
I.1.13.2	222, 240, 277
I.1.13.3	277
I.1.14.1	227
I.1.14.2	222, 240
I.1.14.4	227
I.1.15.1—16.3	228
I.1.15.1–3	222
I.1.15.3	259
I.1.18.1	254
I.2.20.4	254
I.2.21.2	222, 240
I.5.28.3	222
I.5.32.4	222
I.6.32.4	222
I.6.35.1	222
I.6.35.2	225
I.12.55.1-4	227
I.12.56.2	257
I.13.57.1-6	245
I.21.146.1	220
I.21.146.2	220
I.28.176.1-3	228
I.28.176.1-2	222, 229, 259
I.28.176.2	253
I.150.1	200
II.9.44.1-4	220
II.18.96.1-2	221
II.18.96.2	220
III.1.1.2–3	245
III.2–6	87
III.2	43
III.2.5.1—10.2	245
III.2.5	162
III.4.25.5	245
III.4.27.5	242
III.4.34.1—39.3	245
III.6.54.1	245
IV.1.1.1—3.4	222
IV.1.3.1–4	228, 251, 274
IV.1.3.1	222, 240, 259
IV.1.3.2	252
IV.2	254
IV.6.29.2	222
IV.6.29.3	222
IV.7.53.1	221–22
IV.8.56.1	240
IV.13.89.2–5	220
IV.15.97.1	277
IV.16.101.1	221, 225
IV.17.109.3	222
IV.18.116.2—117.2	255, 266
IV.18.117.1	242

Index of Ancient Texts

Stromateis (continued)

Reference	Page
IV.21.130.1	222, 229
IV.21.132.1	222, 229
IV.21.134.4	222
IV.25.159.2	256
IV.25.157.3—159.3	242
IV.25.162	240
IV.26.163.2	222
V.1.1.5	277
V.1.7.6	277
V.1.7.7–8	222, 229
V.1.7.8	240
V.1.10.2	240
V.4.19.1—20.1	273–76
V.4.19.3	241, 250
V.6	261–64, 266, 269
V.6.32.1-2	270
V.6.32.3—34.7	241
V.6.33.1	256, 266
V.6.33.2-3	261
V.6.33.6—34.1	253
V.6.34.5	261, 266
V.6.34.8—35.2	242
V.6.34.9—35.2	200
V.6.34.8-9	256
V.6.35.3-4	261
V.6.35.5	256, 264
V.6.37.1—38.1	242
V.6.37.1—39.1	270
V.6.38.3	256
V.6.38.6	257, 266
V.6.39.3-4	262
V.6.39.3	266
V.6.40.1	222, 241, 263, 267
V.6.40.3	262, 266
V.8.48.9	221–22, 226
V.9.57.3—10.64.3	227
V.9.58.1	240
V.9.60.2	222
V.10.60.2	228
V.10.64.4	222
V.10.65.3	227
V.10.66.2–5	221–22, 226, 229
V.11	263
V.11.7.1	248
V.11.70.7—71.1	228, 248
V.11.70.7—71.3	222, 252
V.11.70.7—71.5	259
V.11.73.1—74.2	280
V.11.73.2	220
V.11.73.4	240
V.12.79.1	240
V.12.80.3–8	278
V.12.80.6	119, 258
V.14.90.1	256
V.14.91.2	251
V.14.93.4—94.2	256
V.14.130.3	240
V.14.138.2–3	275
VI.1.1.3	221, 223, 226
VI.4.35.4	256
VI.4.37.1–3	242
VI.7.59.1—63.1	222
VI.7.60.2	221, 225
VI.7.61.1–3	257
VI.7.61.3	269
VI.8.65.1–5	221–22
VI.8.68.1–3	268–73
VI.8.68.1	256, 277
VI.9.78.3-4	281–82
VI.10.80.1-4	251
VI.10.80.3	253
VI.11.86.1	258
VI.12.102.2	222, 228
VI.13.105.1	266
VI.14.108.1	222, 250, 255
VI.14.109.1	255
VI.14.109.3	255
VI.14.111.3	221, 282
VI.14.114.1-4	255
VI.14.114.6	267
VI.15.122.1–4	221–22
VI.15.124.6—125.2	257
VI.15.126.2–3	257
VI.15.127.3	257
VI.15.129.4	228
VI.15.130.1	221, 223
VI.15.131.2–3	228
VI.16.137.4—145.7	242
VI.16.141.3	255
VI.16.141.4	222
VII.1.3.1–6	224
VII.1.3.1–5	263
VII.2.10.3	267
VII.2.12.5	255
VII.3.13.2	222

VII.3.17.2	240
VII.4.27.6	228
VII.7.49.3–4	225
VII.7.49.3	221
VII.9.53.2–3	245
VII.9.56.4	222
VII.9.57.2	222
VII.9.57.5	222, 242
VII.10	178
VII.10.55.2	222
VII.10.56.2	263
VII.10.57.1–5	221–22
VII.10.57.4–5	266
VII.10.57.5	242
VII.11.67.8	222
VII.12.78.6	276
VII.14.85.1–5	222
VII.16.95.4	221–22
VII.17	162
VII.17.106—108	227
VII.18.111.1–3	254

Dorotheus

Codex of Visions

	56

Egerton Gospel

	41–42

Epistle of Barnabas

	90, 97

Eusebius of Caesarea

Historia ecclesiastica

2.1.4	257
2.16	162
3.39.15	133
5.10–11	217
6.3.2	217
6.3.6	217
6.14.6	133
6.14.8–11	217
6.20	163

Gospel of Judas

	37, 62, 70, 158, 285

Gospel of Mary

	285

Gospel of Peter

	42, 148, 158

Gospel of Philip

67,29–30	218–19

Gospel of the Savior

	41–42

Gospel of Thomas

	158, 285, 288

Hippolytus of Rome

Refutatio omnium haeresium

7.20	87

Traditio apostolica

XXI.11	236

Ignatius of Antioch

To the Trallians

2.3	232–33
5.1	223

Infancy Gospel of James

	27–28

Infancy Gospel of Thomas

	27, 42

Index of Ancient Texts

Irenaeus

Adversus haereses

1.25	87
1.25.1–6	43
1.25.45	246
25.1–4	59
25.5	59

Justin Martyr

1 Apology

61.66–67	218–19

Letter to Theodore/Secret Gospel of Mark

I.2	88, 242
I.4	88
I.7	88
I.8–11	245
I.14	17
I.15–22	281
I.15–18	225
I.15	18
I.16–17	88
I.16	132
I.18–22	226
I.20–21	259, 277
I.21–22	228, 257, 279
I.22–26	240
I.22	24, 88, 228, 260, 264
I.23–24	88, 260
I.24–26	249, 259
I.25–26	24
I.26—II.1	242
I.26	241, 264
I.28—II.2	228
II.1–2	88, 248
II.1	205
II.2	228
II.5–7	88
II.6–10	151
II.6	88, 153, 257
II.12–13	88
II.12	257
II.18–19	274
II.23—III.6	49
II.23—III.11	46, 165
II.23	47
III.4	153
III.5	46
III.6–11	49
III.6–10	59
III.6–7	162
III.6	46
III.7	46
III.8–9	13
III.8	153
III.9–10	46
III.9	33
III.13–14	88
III.14–16	46, 49, 153
III.15	89
III.16	268
II.18–19	274

Origen

Homiliae in Judices

5	282

Shepherd of Hermas

90, 148, 220

Valentinian Exposition

22,1–39	218
40,1–29	218
40,30—41,38	218
42,1—43,19	218, 220
43,20–38	219
44,1–37	220

GRECO-ROMAN WRITINGS

Aeschylus

Agamemnon

1212	155

Index of Ancient Texts

Cicero

De oratore

I.xxxiv.154–55   54

Demosthenes

Oration 3   150–51

Oration 21   150

Dionysius Thrax

55

Euripides

Bacchae   240

Homer

Odyssey

10.552–60   149

Josephus

Antiquities

18.118   117

Libanius

Epistulae

125   57

Lucian

Quomodo Historia conscribenda sit   52

Peregrinus

11   232

Lysias

Oration 3

12   150–51
35   151

Mithras Liturgy   178, 234

Philo of Alexandria

De cherubim

14.49   258

De vita contemplativa

3.28–29   257
25   278
28   278
30   278
78   278

De decalogo

21.102–3   272

De ebrietate

34.135–36   276

Quis rerum divinarum heres sit

45.224   256

Index of Ancient Texts

De vita Mosis

| 2.15.71—22.108 | 256 |

De opificio mundi

| 7.29 | 272 |
| 23.70–71 | 253–54 |

Quaestiones et solutions in Exodum

| 2.52 | 259 |
| 2.68 | 257 |

Quaestiones et solutions in Genesin

| IV,67 | 88, 310 |

De specialibus legibus

| 3.1–5 | 254 |

Plato

Gorgias

| 497c | 251 |

Phaedo

67a–e	250
67b.1–2	273
69c	250
81a	250
81c–82a	250
82b	250
113a–114c	250

Phaedrus

243c	243
246d–248c	274
246e	275
247a10–e7	275
247a	273, 274
247b	275
247c–d	250
248d–249c	275
250b–c	250, 275
250c	252

Republic

| | 245 |

Symposium

| 209e–210a | 251 |

Theaetetus

| 155e | 262 |

Pliny the Younger

Epistulae

| VII.ix | 55 |

Polybius

Histories

| | 39 |

Sophocles

Ajax

| | 41 |

Pseudo-Cicero

Rhetorica ad Herennium

| I.ii.3 | 53 |
| 4.xx | 52 |

Quintilian

Institutio oratoria

| II.v.9 | 53 |
| II.v.10 | 53 |

II.vii.2–4	54	**Thucydides**	
X.v.4–8	54		
		History of the Peloponnesian War	
Tacitus			39
Annals		*Toledot Yeshu*	
15.44	96		173

Theon

Progymnasmata

55

Index of Modern Authors

Accorinti, Domenico, 160
Adams, James Noel, 243
Akenson, Donald Hamran, 7, 9, 14, 100
Aland, B., 92
Aland, K., 92
Anastasopoulou, Venetia, 18, 21, 34, 36, 92, 122–25, 137–38, 197–98
Andreou, Georgia, 186
Arieti, James A., 272
Ashwin-Siejkowski, Piotr, 230, 267
Attridge, Harold W., 219

Barabe, Joseph G., 92–93
Baumgarten, Albert I., 95
Bausi, Alessandro, 183
Belfiore, Elizabeth, 274
Bell, H. Idris, 41
Benamozegh, Élie, 176
Bertalotto, Pierpaolo, 181
Beskow, Per, 131–32, 181
Best, Ernest, 8, 20, 45–51, 98
Betz, Hans Dieter, 196, 234, 287
Blum, Harold, 176
Bockmuehl, Markus, 244
Borella, Jean Borella, 252, 263
Boustan, Ra'anan S., 177
Brent, Allen, 244
Brodersen, Kai, 183
Brown, Raymond E., 155
Brown, Scott G., xiv, xvi, xix–xx, 1, 5–8, 10–12, 15–18, 20–21, 24–25, 27–28, 30, 32–34, 46, 49, 57–58, 63, 76–77, 95, 107, 110, 116, 119, 123–25, 128, 132, 147, 159, 162, 169, 184, 196, 198, 203, 211, 215–16, 228–29, 235, 237, 244, 249, 250, 257, 258, 279, 284, 286, 290–91, 294, 300–302, 305–6
Browning, Robert, 56
Brunelle, Richard L., 213
Burchardt, Jacob, 39
Burgess, Matthew, 132
Burke, Tony, xiii–xv, 20, 27, 42, 157–58
Burkert, Walter, 237
Butters, Ronald, 236
Butts, James R., 55, 313
Byrne, Ryan, 71

Calder, William M. III, 95, 187, 207
Cameron, Ron, 58
Campanini, Saverio, 160
Camplani, Alberto, 162
Canfora, Luciano, 183
Carlson, Stephen C., xiv, xviii, xx, xxiii, 12–18, 21, 25–28, 31–33, 45, 73, 76–77, 80, 82, 84, 91–93, 95, 97–99, 107, 115, 121–25, 127–31, 137–38, 147, 159–60, 165–66, 168–69, 198–99, 206, 258, 300, 301, 303–5
Casey, Maurice, 191, 214, 249, 267, 313
Charlesworth, James H., 10
Chernow, Ron, 68
Chilton, Bruce, xv, 13, 20–22, 29, 70, 71–73, 181
Chupungco, Anscar J., 229
Ciavolella, Massimo, 243
Clahsen, Harald, 186

Index of Modern Authors

Clark, Donald Lemen, 52–55
Clines, David J. A., 233
Cohen, Shaye J. D., 10, 185, 302
Coleman, Christopher B., 38
Coleman-Norton, Paul R., xvi, 13, 21–22, 38, 78–81, 94–96, 99–104, 303–4
Colish, Marcia L., 226
Collins, Adela Yarbro, 10, 77
Condello, Federico, 183
Cosaert, Carl P., 225
Cosmopoulos, Michael B., 240
Coxe, Henry Octavius, 127
Crawford, Kenneth R., 213
Cribiore, Raffaella, 55–57
Criddle, Andrew H., 8, 11, 13, 45, 98, 239, 304–5
Crossan, John Dominic, 9, 74, 146–47, 152–53, 158, 306
Crowley, Aleister, vii, 23, 157, 159, 161, 163, 165, 167, 169, 171, 173, 175, 177, 179–81, 183, 230
Csapo, Eric, 237

Dalmais, Irénée-Henri, 239
Danby, Herbert, 83, 302
Daniélou, Jean, 250, 254, 259, 267
Dart, John, 10, 126
Davies, William David, 176
Davis, Tom, 124–25
Day, Juliette, 220
DeConick, April D., 158, 267
Dillard, Irving, 142
Doval, Alexis James, 218
Drijvers, Jan Willem, 226

Ellens, J. Harold, 77, 159
Elliott, J. K., 42
Elsner, Jaś, 183
Ericsson, K. Anders, 201
Evans, Craig A., xvi, xx, 8, 13, 21–22, 25–26, 28–29, 101–25, 127–34, 158, 198, 284–85, 287–88, 291, 296
Eyer, Shawn, 5, 9

Fabry, Heinz-Josef, 233
Farmer, William R., 58

Farrell, Anne Mary, 251–52, 275
Farrer, James Anson, 80
Felser, Claudia, 186
Feulner, Rüdiger, 224
Field, Henry Martyn, 127
Finn, Thomas M., 220
Foerster, Hans, 220
Ford, David F., 174
Foster, Paul, 5, 42, 77, 159, 213
France, Richard Thomas, 231
Franco, Emilia, 183
Frerichs, Ernest S., 167–68
Frova, Antonio, 96
Fuller, Reginald H., 44, 248

Galantomos, Ioannis, 186
García Martínez, Florentino, 273
Geerard, Maurice, 214
Genesius, William, 188
Ginzburg, Carlo, 38
Golan, Oded, 71–72
Goldin, Judah, 141, 184, 186, 208
Goodenough, Erwin R., 59, 85, 113–14, 168, 178, 194, 209, 257
Goodspeed, Edgar Johnson, 37, 80, 92
Graffin, René, 239
Grafton, Anthony, 51, 304
Greene, Roedy, 306
Groff, Kent I., 153–54
Guetta, Alessandro, 176

Haas, Christopher, 244
Hägg, Henny Fiskå, 266
Hall, F. W., 39
Haren, Michael J., 306
Hargis, Jeff, 41
Harmless, William, 218
Harnack, Adolf, 307
Harris, Robert, 93
Harris, William V., 77
Hedrick, Charles W., xiv–xv, 5, 9–12, 16, 18, 20, 24, 28, 30–32, 34, 41, 43, 53, 73, 76, 77, 97, 123, 131–32, 139, 141, 147, 160, 161, 163, 184, 300
Henderson, Jeffrey, 243
Henderson, Suzanne Watts, 231
Higton, Mike, 174

Index of Modern Authors

Hill, Charles E., 133
Hilton, Ordway, 93, 124
Hock, Ronald F., 27, 42, 52, 55
Holl, Karl, 163
Hollinshead, Mary B., 241
Hunter, James Hogg, 8, 11, 13, 17, 19, 21–22, 28, 81, 89–91, 102–5, 120–21, 159
Hurtado, Larry W., 13, 227

Idel, Moshe, 181
Irwin, John T., 243
Itter, Andrew C., 224, 241, 272

Jackson, Howard, 150
Jakab, Attila, 161–63
Jay, Jeff, 16, 35, 163, 199, 213, 279
Jeffery, Peter, xiv, xix–xx, 14–15, 18, 20, 23–26, 28, 31–34, 77, 92, 136, 147, 159, 178–79, 213, 215, 217, 219, 220, 224–27, 230, 233, 234, 237, 245, 249, 259, 268, 277, 279, 284–85, 289–90, 293–94, 297, 300, 305
Jenkins, Philip, 8, 100, 159
Jeremias, Joachim, 119
Johnson, Maxwell E., 77, 159
Jones, Arnold. H. M., 96
Jónsson, Jakob, 107

Kaestli, Jean-Daniel, 158
Karapetsas, Anargyros, 186
Karavidopoulos, J., 92
Kasser, Rudolphe, 70
Kee, Howard Clark, 214
Keener, Craig S., 105
Kelly, Nicole E., 159
Kerényi, Karl, 275
Kermode, Frank, 95
Kiernan, Kevin, 183
Klauck, Hans-Josef, 159
Kloppenborg, John S., 244
Knox, Sanka, 5, 299
Koester, Craig R., 219
Koester, Helmut, 9, 16, 18, 22, 45, 58, 74, 77–78, 100, 140, 146, 152, 172, 203, 211
Kolodner, Janet L., 215

König, Gert, 245
Konstan, David, 30
Kotansky, Roy, 196–97, 247, 249
Kovacs, Judith L, 249, 265, 267
Krashen, Stephen D, 185
Krauss, Amanda, 237
Kriegel, Maurice, 176

La Via, Stefano, 243
Lambeck, Peter, 27
Lampe, Geoffrey William Hugo, 223
Lampe, Peter, 244
Lane, William L., 58–59
Layton, Richard A., 244
Le Boulluec, Alain, 159, 161–63, 238, 280
Legrand, Émile, 40
Leonhardt, Jutta, 241
Levy, Jacob, 233
Lilla, Salvatore R. C., 251, 265, 267
Llewellyn, Kathleen M., 243
Lowe, Kelly Fisher, 237
Lyell, Patrick Ronaldson, 73

MacDonald, Dennis R., 149
Mamet, David, 215
Marcus, Joel, 231
Martin, Annick, 161–63
Martini, C. M., 92
Mason, Steve, 244
Mayeda, Goro, 41
McIver, Robert K., 257
McKeon, Richard, 52
McNary-Zak, Bernadette, 71
Meier, John P., 165, 214
Metzger, Bruce M., 44–45, 58, 78–80, 92, 94–96, 100, 102, 303–4
Metzger, Marcel, 244
Meyer, Marvin, xvii, xx, xxiii, 9, 22–25, 28, 52, 146, 148, 151, 153, 155, 219, 284, 287–89, 292–96
Migne, J.-P., 129, 130, 160, 161
Miner, Jess, 237
Mirecki, Paul A., 41
Mitchell, Margaret M., 92–93
Mopsik, Charles Mopsik, 171
Murgia, Charles E., 6, 16, 44, 98, 127, 132

Index of Modern Authors

Murray, Robert, 239
Musurillo, Herbert, 76

Nardi, Carlo, 223
Neusner, Jacob, 7-8, 15, 83
Noce, Carla, 237
Nock, Arthur Darby, 78, 85, 107, 114, 126, 141, 168, 181, 193-94, 200, 202, 231
Norelli, Enrico, 235

Olympiou, Nikolaos, xiv, 10-11, 43, 73, 76, 139
Osborn, Eric F., 214, 252, 267
Owen, Alex, 179

Paananen, Timo S., 14, 26, 131-32, 182, 184
Pagter, Carl R., 237
Pantuck, Allan J., xvi, xviii-xix, 1, 16-17, 19-21, 23, 26-28, 30, 32, 95-96, 105, 116, 123, 124, 128, 132, 147, 159, 167, 169, 202, 211, 301
Pearson, Birger A., 16, 18, 77, 147, 220, 225, 244, 291
Penfield, Wilder, 186
Pfaff, Christoph, 13, 306-7
Pietersma, Albert, 56
Pietruschka, Ute, 183
Piovanelli, Pierluigi, xviii, 5, 14, 23, 28-29, 77, 89, 96, 158, 159, 160, 175, 177, 181
Potter, John, 130
Price, Robert M., 8, 11, 159, 165
Procter, Everett, 230
Pryke, E. J., 46-48

Quandt, Abigail B., 92-93
Quarles, Charles L., 254
Quesnell, Quentin, 6-8, 10, 31, 76, 87, 107-8, 112, 131, 146, 159, 202, 206, 299-300, 303, 306

Räisänen, Heikki, 158
Randall, Phyllis, 236
Rau, Eckhard, 87, 99, 159
Renandya, Willy A., 186

Reynolds, L. D., 39-40
Richards, Jack C., 186
Richardson, Cyril C., 171, 210, 247-49
Richter, David H., 237
Riedweg, Christoph, 251, 274, 276
Riordan, John Lancaster, 236
Rizzerio, Laura, 228, 251, 253, 257
Roberts, Lamar, 186
Rollston, Christopher A., 94
Rousse-Lacordaire, Jérome, 215
Royal Ontario Museum, 71
Ruina, David T., 244
Russell, Norman, 243-44
Russo, Nicholas V., 277

Saenger, Paul, 227
Sanders, Ed Parish, 176, 181, 287
Sandnes, Karl Olav, 251
Sandys, John Edwin, 40
Satterlee, Craig Alan, 218
Schäfer, Peter, 177
Schefer, Christina, 275-76
Schenke, Hans-Martin, 5, 9, 146
Schilderman, Hans, 229
Schneider, Ulrich, 223
Scholem, Gershom, 11, 17, 22-23, 25, 140-41, 160, 166-80, 190-91, 194-95, 198, 200-201, 204, 209-10, 230, 245-46, 301-2
Schwarz, Leo W., 188
Schweitzer, Albert, 293
Scopello, Madeleine, 158
Scott, Alan, 275
Scroggs, Robin, 153-54
Shanks, Hershel, xvii, 7, 18-19, 22, 34-35, 77-78, 91-92, 99, 122, 137, 197
Shepardson, Christine, 244
Shepherd, Massey H., 90, 220, 248
Skeat, T. C., 41
Slee, Michelle, 244
Smith, Edward Reaugh, 12
Smith, J. Warren, 224, 226
Smith, Jonathan Z, 153
Smith, Kyle, 15-16, 33
Smith, Morton, xiii-xiv, xvi-xx, 1-2, 5-8, 10-11, 13-14, 17-29, 31-32, 34-37, 41, 45, 57, 59, 61-62,

64–66, 72–100, 102, 104–44, 146–48, 154, 157, 159–217, 219, 221, 223, 225, 227, 229–39, 241, 243–49, 258, 279–80, 289, 291, 294–95, 297, 299–306
Solomon, Robert C., 4, 245, 310
Sonnini, Charles Sigisbert, 80
Specter, Michael, 72
Stählin, Otto, 6, 98, 146, 178, 200, 207, 214, 263, 265
Starks, Lisa S., 243
Stephenson, Percy R., 179
Stökl Ben Ezra, Daniel, 261, 267
Strauss, David Friedrich, 165
Strobel, Lee, 122, 124
Stroumsa, Guy G., 10–11, 17, 31, 43, 73, 131, 140–41, 160, 163–77, 179, 181, 190–91, 194–95, 198, 201, 204, 209, 230, 246, 300–303

Talley, Thomas, 10–11, 136, 162
Taylor, Joan E., 278
Taylor, Vincent, 59, 83, 85, 107–9, 115–17, 145, 165, 200, 202
Thomas, Samuel I., 10, 27, 42, 136, 146, 158, 162, 243, 273, 285, 288
Thomassen, Einar, 219
Thompson, Edward M., 178, 198
Tigay, Jeffrey, 22, 141, 208
Tov, Emanuel, 122
Treu, Ursula, 163
Trozzi, Nicola, 183
Tselikas, Agamemnon, xvii, 18–21, 34–37, 43–44, 60–61, 63–66, 92, 124–25, 128, 130, 138–39, 142, 198, 206

van den Hoek, Annewies, 223, 228, 241, 256, 261, 267, 270, 281–82
Viklund, Roger, 17, 123, 131–32, 160
Vivian, Tim, 220
Völker, Walther, 59, 280
Voss, Isaac, xiv–xv, 2, 10–11, 21–23, 26–27, 43, 62–65, 73, 75, 97, 128–32, 161, 196, 206

Wagner, Walter H., 251, 254
Wasserstrom, Steven M., 170
Watson, Francis, 17–19, 28, 32, 77, 83, 86, 89–91, 94, 98, 100, 115–18, 120, 127, 132–34, 138, 159, 238
Webb, Robert L., 77
Weinberger, A. D., 236
Weiss, Roberto, 40
White, David A., 250, 252
Wilson, N. G., 39–40
Wilson, Stephen G., 69, 226, 244, 249, 252
Witherington, Ben III, 219
Wolfson, Elliot, 273
Wolfson, Harry A., 113, 187–95, 200–201, 251
Wolters, Al, 243
Wrede, William, 83–84
Wurst, Gregor, 70
Wyrwa, Dietmar, 251

Yarnold, Edward, 218
Ysebaert, Joseph, 223, 230

Zacharias, Danny, 122
Zeddies, Michael T., 19

Index of Subjects

Acts ch. 29, 80
amusing agraphon, 13, 21, 22, 78–81, 94–95, 100, 101–4, 303–4
Archaic Mark, 92–93
Aristarchos (Greek Orthodox Patriarchate librarian), 43, 60, 61
Artemidorus Papyrus, 183

baptism, 5, 12, 14, 15, 16, 24, 31, 89, 127, 136, 147, 153, 154, 159, 162, 211, 213, 218–21, 223–30, 231, 232–33, 235, 247–49, 255, 258, 259, 263–64, 277, 279–82, 295, 305
Basilides, 160, 220, 245
Bodmer Papyri, 56

Caiaphas ossuary, 72
Carpocratians (Carpocrates), 9, 28, 29, 43, 59, 74, 76, 87, 88, 89, 126, 162, 170, 171, 182, 209, 216, 230, 237, 242, 245–46, 278, 295, 303
Clement of Alexandria, on the ascent of the soul, 250, 253–44, 255, 264, 266–67; on baptism, 24, 221, 225, 228, 229, 279, 279–82; cosmology of, 255–57, 261–63, 269–73, 283; and Gnosticism, 229–30; and mysteries, 24, 217–30, 250–55, 257–59, 273–76; and the perfected person (gnostics), 24–25, 222, 224–30, 248, 249, 251, 253–61, 264, 267–69, 272, 274, 276, 277–78, 279–82

Dart, John (correspondence), 126
Donation of Constantine, 37–38, 51
Dourvas, Father Kallistos, 10–11, 43, 60, 73

Epitaph of Himerus, 72

forgeries (see Acts ch. 29, Archaic Mark, Donation of Constantine, Hitler Diaries, Irenaeus fragments, Second Book of Acts, Sentence of Pilate)
forgery hypotheses: double entendres, 13, 14, 28, 33, 136, 234–37, 243, 246, 249, 302, 305; "forger's tremor," 13, 17, 18, 26, 92, 122–24, 137, 147; Morton Salt Company, 12, 15, 16, 17, 26, 28, 32–33, 137, 147, 305; M. Madiotes, 13, 16–17, 26, 32, 147; and motives, 12, 15, 28, 137–38, 144, 166–69, 306; and Mystery of Mar Saba, 8, 11, 17–18, 19, 21, 22, 28, 80–81, 89–91, 102–5, 120–21, 159; and Oscar Wilde's Salomé, 32, 147, 230, 242, 268, 273, 305; and puns, 12, 17–18, 28, 138; "knowing the find before making the find," 21, 23, 25, 28, 82–89, 94–96, 100, 104–19, 125–27, 164–65, 199–203, 300–302, 304; too Clementine to be Clement, 8, 11, 13, 45, 98, 132, 239, 304–5; too Markan to be Mark, 8, 13, 20, 45–51, 98
Frank, Jacob, 170, 173, 176, 180

Index of Subjects

Goldin, Judah (correspondence), 208
Goodenough, Erwin (correspondence), 114, 209
Gospel of Mark, literary conventions, 12, 305; longer endings, 20, 44, 45, 58, 59; relationship to *Secret Mark*, 9, 12, 20-21, 44, 52, 57, 58-59, 74, 145-56, 215, 281, 297, 300
Gnosticism (Gnostics), 29, 70, 126, 178, 209, 217, 227, 230
Greek Orthodox Patriarchate Library, 2, 10-11, 34, 36, 42-43, 60-61, 63, 64, 73, 90, 131, 139, 143, 204

handwriting analysis, by Venetia Anastasopoulou, 18, 21, 34, 36, 92, 122, 124-25, 137, 197-98; by Julie C. Edison, 17, 26, 91, 92, 121-24, 137; by Agamemnon Tselikas, 18-19, 20, 21, 35-36, 60-66, 92, 122, 124-25, 137, 138, 142-43, 198
heavenly ascent, 5, 171-72, 177, 209, 215, 233-34, 235, 239, 250, 253-54, 255, 264, 266, 267
Hitler Diaries, 21, 93, 122

imitation in Christian literature, 20, 52-57
Irenaeus fragments, 13, 306-7

Jaeger, Werner (correspondence), 199, 207-8, 209, 217
James ossuary, 70-71
Jesus Seminar, 9, 293
John of Damascus, 130-31, 160, 163

Letter to Theodore (see also *Secret Mark*), *Biblical Archaeology Review* feature, 18, 77-78, 99; discovery of, 1-2, 75, 159, 299; epistolary conventions and, 16, 35, 163, 199, 213, 279-80; and liturgy, 77, 136, 147, 159, 162, 219, 229, 249, 305; photographs, 6, 10, 17, 26, 35, 42, 43, 73, 76, 97, 122-24, 129, 160, 206

Mar Saba Monastery, 1910 catalogue of, 21, 27, 63-64, 73, 97, 131; 1923 catalogue of, 63-64, 143; catalogue of old printed books, 63-64, 128-29, 143; Smith's catalogue of, 2, 13, 97, 128, 195, 199, 204; manuscript 22 of, 12-13, 17, 26
Meliton, Archimandrite, 10-11, 43
mystery of the kingdom of God, 5, 59, 82-89, 100, 105-12, 119, 127, 151, 172-73, 231-32, 234, 239, 242, 247, 258, 269, 278, 294, 295, 302, 304
mystery religions, 29, 151-52, 217, 223, 229, 233-34, 239, 250, 260-61, 294
Mystery of Mar Saba (see forgery hypotheses)

neaniskos, 9, 22-23, 145-56, 178

Papias of Hierapolis, 98, 132-34, 238

Richardson, Cyril (correspondence), 210, 248-49

Scholem, Gershom (correspondence), 11, 17, 23, 25, 140-41, 160, 190; letter **3**, 179, 230; **7**, 176; **8**, 164, 176; **9**, 164; **11**, 164, 201, 302; **16**, 168; **20**, 168; **23**, 198, 303; **24**, 168; **25**, 176; **26**, 194, 201; **28**, 191; **30**, 166; **31**, 164; **32**, 195; **36**, 166; **37**, 167; **38**, 167; **40**, 164, 181; **42**, 164, 168, 181; **45**, 164; **52**, 167, 168; **53**, 167, 168; **55**, 164, 204; **59**, 164; **61**, 164; **63**, 169; **65**, 170; **66**, 170; **68**, 170, 177; **70**, 173; **71**, 170; **72**, 171, 209; **73**, 171; **76**, 171; **77**, 209; **81**, 170; **84**, 169; **86**, 164; **91**, 169; **94**, 169, 172; **95**, 172; **96**, 172, 173; **97**, 172, 174; **104**, 172, 175; **108**, 172; **111**, 172
Second Book of Acts, 80
Secret Mark (see also *Letter to Theodore*), homoeroticism in (see

also forgery hypotheses, double entendres), 7, 10, 11, 13, 14–15, 25, 32, 76, 81, 147, 172, 179, 215, 292–95, 305; Johannine traits in, 82, 85–87, 89, 90–91, 105, 115–16, 118–19, 165

Sentence of Pilate, 73

Smith, Morton, correspondence (see Dart, Goldin, Goodenough, Jaeger, Richardson, and Scholem); interest in Aleister Crowley, 23, 179–80, 230; interpretation of the *Gospel of Mark*, 116–18, 202–3; interpretation *of Secret Mark*, 5, 11–12, 29, 83–84, 127, 146, 215, 248, 300; and libertine Jesus, 5, 7, 23, 114–15, 169–75, 209–10, 236, 238–39, 244–45, 248; and magic, 5, 174, 178, 217, 230–34, 297; and manuscript research, 19, 35, 61, 63, 64, 65–66, 120, 138, 142, 194; personal character of, 15, 22, 32, 139–42, 147, 249; scholarly abilities of, 15, 20, 23, 24, 27, 32, 148, 184–211, 214–15, 232–37, 246, 295, 302–3; works collected in the Archives of The Jewish Theological Seminary Library, 16, 23, 98, 123, 128, 197, 198, 202, 204, 205, 207

Society of Biblical Literature, Annual Meetings: 1960, 5, 75, 172, 203, 207–8, 210, 247, 299; 1984, 7; 2008, 15, 19–20, 32, 77, 95, 147, 299

Stählin, Otto (Clement of Alexandria concordance), 6, 98, 146, 207, 214

streaker (see *neaniskos*)

Therapeutae, 224, 278

Tzevi, Sabbatai, 23, 170, 173, 175–78, 180, 245–46

union (physical and/or spiritual), 5, 28, 84–85, 88, 95, 112–15, 127, 235, 266

Valentinus, 162, 220, 224, 229, 249, 267

Voss Ignatius book, 2, 10, 21, 22, 23, 27, 42, 43, 62–65, 73–74, 97–99, 127–32, 139, 143–44, 161, 197, 206, 213, 303

Wolfson, Harry A. (correspondence), 187–95

www.ingramcontent.com/pod-product-compliance
Lightning Source LLC
Chambersburg PA
CBHW022227010526
44113CB00033B/527